
VOLUME XXV/4

EU Legal Acts
Challenges and Transformations

The Collected Courses of the Academy of European Law
Edited by Professor Nehal Bhuta, Professor Marise Cremona, and Professor Claire Kilpatrick
Assistant Editor: Anny Bremner

Each year the Academy of European Law in Florence, Italy, invites a group of outstanding lecturers to teach at its summer courses on Human Rights law and the European Union.
A 'general course' is given in each of the two fields by a distinguished scholar or practitioner, who examines the field as a whole through a particular thematic, conceptual, or philosophical lens, or looks at a theme in the context of the overall body of law.
In addition, a series of 'specialized courses' brings together a group of highly qualified scholars to explore and analyse a specific theme in relation to Human Rights law and EU law.
The Academy's mission, to produce scholarly analyses which are at the cutting edge of the two fields, is achieved through publication of this series, the Collected Courses of the Academy of European Law.

EU Legal Acts

Challenges and Transformations

Edited by
MARISE CREMONA AND CLAIRE KILPATRICK

OXFORD
UNIVERSITY PRESS

OXFORD
UNIVERSITY PRESS

Great Clarendon Street, Oxford, OX2 6DP,
United Kingdom

Oxford University Press is a department of the University of Oxford.
It furthers the University's objective of excellence in research, scholarship,
and education by publishing worldwide. Oxford is a registered trade mark of
Oxford University Press in the UK and in certain other countries

First Edition published in 2018

Published in the United States of America by Oxford University Press
198 Madison Avenue, New York, NY 10016, United States of America

British Library Cataloguing in Publication Data
Data available

Library of Congress Control Number: 2017953028

ISBN 978–0–19–881746–8

Contents

Table of Cases

n = footnote.

CJEU CASES (IN NUMBER ORDER)

GENERAL COURT CASES (IN NUMBER ORDER)

NATIONAL CASES

Belgium

Table of Legislation

n = footnote.

Directives (in chronological order)

Regulations (in chronological order)

Resolutions (in chronological order)

Decisions (in chronological order)

Declarations, Guidelines and other non-binding instruments

Non-passed legislation

INTERNATIONAL CONVENTIONS

BILATERAL/TRILATERAL AGREEMENTS

Notes on Contributors

Marise Cremona is Emeritus Professor of European Law in the Law Department of the European University Institute, Florence, and a former Co-Director of the Academy of European Law. Before joining the EUI she held the Chair of European Commercial Law at the Centre for Commercial Law Studies, Queen Mary University of London. Marise's research interests are in the external relations law of the European Union; she is particularly interested in the constitutional basis for EU external relations law and the legal and institutional dimensions of the EU's foreign policy.

Deirdre Curtin is Professor of European Law at the European University Institute in Florence, where she holds a Joint Chair of the Law Department and the Robert Schuman Centre of Advanced Studies. She is also Director of the Centre for Judicial Cooperation. Previously, she directed the Amsterdam Centre for European Law and Governance, which she founded in 2009, and was research leader of several research projects embracing both law and political science. Deirdre has authored and co-authored a number of scientific monographs published with leading international publishers, including *Executive Power of the European Union* (2009) and *The Real World of EU Accountability: What Deficit?* (2010, with Paul 't Hart and Mark Bovens), and publishes regularly in leading law and political science journals. In 2009 she was awarded the Spinoza Prize by the NWO (Dutch Scientific Organization) and has been an elected member of the Dutch Academy of Science since 2003.

Sir Alan Dashwood was Professor of European Law at the University of Cambridge from 1995 to 2009 and is now Professor Emeritus. He is a Fellow, now Emeritus, of Sidney Sussex College. In January 2012 he became a part-time Professor of Law at City University. He is also a Barrister in Henderson Chambers, a Bencher of the Inner Temple and took Silk in 2010. Before election to his Chair at Cambridge, he was a Director in the Legal Service of the Council of the EU from 1987 to the end of 1994. He was the founding editor of *European Law Review* and was one of the joint editors of the *Common Market Law Review* until December 2008. He is a co-author of *Wyatt and Dashwood's European Union Law*, the sixth edition of which appeared in 2011, and contributes frequently to legal periodicals. He was appointed CBE in 2004 and KCMG in 2013 for services to the development of European Law.

Mark Dawson is Professor of European Law and Governance at the Hertie School of Governance, Berlin. His research focuses on the relationship between law and policy-making in the EU, particularly economic governance and human rights protection. His most recent book, published in 2017, is *The Governance of EU Fundamental Rights*. He was previously an Assistant Professor at Maastricht University, where he remains a scholar within the Maastricht Centre for European Law. He is currently the Principal Investigator of LEVIATHAN, a research project exploring the legal and political accountability structure of EU economic governance. LEVIATHAN is supported by a Starting Grant of the European Research Council.

Bruno De Witte is Professor of European Union Law at Maastricht University, The Netherlands, and co-Director of the Maastricht Centre for European Law. He is also a part-time Professor of Law at the European University Institute, Florence. Previously, from 2000 to 2010, Bruno was Professor of European Union Law at the European University Institute, Florence, and co-Director of the Academy of European Law there.

Claire Kilpatrick is Professor of International and European Labour and Social Law at the European University Institute, Florence, and Co-Director of the Academy of European Law. Before coming to the EUI in 2011 she taught at the London School of Economics and prior to that at Cambridge University. Claire's interests lie mainly in the law and policy construction of Social Europe, especially the EU's roles. A focus of her recent work has been on EMU and Social Europe, with a particular focus on sovereign debt loan arrangements and legal challenges to those arrangements from those within debtor EU states.

Päivi Leino is Professor of International and European Law at the University of East Finland Law School, an Academy of Finland Research Fellow, and a Visiting Fellow at the European University Institute Law Department. She has previously worked as a legal adviser for the Finnish government and participated in various legislative negotiations in the EU, including the Lisbon Treaty, the EU Fundamental Rights Agency, the Single Resolution Mechanism and Fund, and the reform of Regulation 1049/2001 on public access to documents. She specializes in EU institutional and constitutional law and frequently appears before the committees of the Finnish and European Parliament. She currently leads a research project (2015–2020) on the relationship between law and politics in EU law-making, funded by the Academy of Finland.

Thibault Martinelli is a PhD researcher at the European University Institute, Florence. He was previously a trainee at the Legal Service of the European Commission after completing an LL.M at the Harvard Law School and a Master in Law at the University of Liège, Belgium.

Aukje A.H. van Hoek is Professor of Private International Law and Civil Procedure at the University of Amsterdam. Before being appointed in Amsterdam, she worked at the Center for the Enforcement of European Law of the University of Utrecht and at Tilburg University. While working in Tilburg she was awarded a Jean Monnet Chair in transnational social justice and European integration. Aukje is a recognized expert on issues of transnational employment, both as regards individual employment contracts and collective aspects of labour law. She was a member of the Dutch standing advisory committee on private international law and is an honorary justice in the Court of Appeals of 's-Hertogenbosch where she sits on employment cases.

Introduction

Marise Cremona and Claire Kilpatrick

At the heart of the integration project of the European Union (EU) and fundamental to its distinctiveness is a complex network of legal tools, of rules, principles, and practices. The ability of the EU's legal structure to adapt, creating new tools and finding new uses for existing ones, is striking. It is also somewhat surprising given the nature of the EU as an organization whose powers are confined to those granted by the Treaties, and given that the legal instruments at the Union's disposal appear essentially the same as they were when the Treaty of Rome came into force 60 years ago (regulations, directives, decisions, and international agreements). The adaptability of the EU's legal toolbox and its responsiveness to a changing political landscape is demonstrated in the development of new rule-making processes and in the working together of new and traditional sources of legal norms. It has enabled the EU to respond (more or less successfully) to changing conceptions of regulation, to the growing importance of international rule-making, to its own expansion into significant new fields of policy, including monetary policy and economic governance, and to the seismic shocks of the euro crisis. At the same time it poses challenges for the EU's legal order, alterations to institutional balance, and the roles of the different institutional actors and challenges to the rule of law.

In this collection of essays, which were first presented at the Academy of European Law in Florence in 2014, we bring together a series of contributions which explore the changing landscape of the EU's legal acts, and the boundaries between legal acts and acts and processes which may create norms but which do not create 'law' in the traditional sense.[1] Two different ways of looking at this picture have emerged. The first is to focus on the transformations in, and challenges to, the EU's 'classic' or traditional legal acts, in particular since the reconfiguration of the categories of legal act and the procedures for their adoption by the Lisbon Treaty. What are these legal acts and who can adopt them? How do the hierarchies and typologies of legal acts reflect the realities of practice? To what extent do changing practices alter the decision-making and institutional checks and balances? How transparent can law-making be and what is the role of politics in EU law-making?

The second perspective is to focus on those acts found at—or beyond—the margin of the classic EU legal acts, including acts of the Member States such as *inter se*

[1] The contributions reflect the legal position as of the beginning of 2016.

treaties, self-regulation, and collective agreements, so-called soft law and decision-making outside the normal legislative procedures. The emergence of these processes, which may have originally appeared marginal but which are increasingly central to EU governance structures, raises some fundamental questions about their relationship with legal rules and the relationship between rules, principles, and practices. How are these relationships changing and how robust are the EU's constitutional structures in managing these shifts?

In Chapter 1, Deirdre Curtin outlines the debates regarding the development of a hierarchy of legal acts and the outcome of the negotiations leading up to the Constitutional Treaty and the Treaty of Lisbon. As she comments, although the typology of acts as regulations, directives, decisions, and recommendations does not seem to have altered since the early years of the European Economic Community (EEC), and although the Lisbon Treaty did away with the different types of act created by the former third pillar (such as framework decisions), this apparent simplicity and continuity hides considerable complexity, such as the fact that the term 'decision' covers acts with three distinct types of legal effect,[2] and the many different types of 'unlisted' act, such as interinstitutional agreements, guidelines, conclusions, action plans, and strategies.

There is another way in which this apparent simplicity hides complexity: the relation of substance to procedure. Acts are defined as 'legislative'—or not—according to the procedure by which they are adopted. This is simple on its face but lacks any substantive content: there is no attempt to require that acts which carry certain types of effect (e.g. acts which are of general application) should be subject to a legislative procedure, and the distinction between legislative and non-legislative acts can appear arbitrary. The normality of the ordinary legislative procedure is complicated by practices that have grown up to facilitate decision-making but which may undermine accountability and transparency (such as the trilogue meetings discussed in Chapter 2[3]). The special legislative procedure excludes the European Parliament from full participation while retaining the limited possibilities for judicial review which is a characteristic of legislative acts; and other types of act which are not adopted according to the ordinary legislative procedure nevertheless have effects similar to legislative acts in substantive terms.

In Chapter 2, Päivi Leino continues the examination of the relation between formal rules and practice (both informal and formalized) within legislative procedures and their implication for the political dimension of EU decision-making. In particular, she considers choice of legal basis, the balance to be struck (and by whom?) between transparency and effectiveness, and rights of participation. As she says, '[d]iscretion and flexibility have a key function in the EU legislative process'. Choice of legal basis not only concerns the outer boundaries of EU competence (the need to

[2] A decision with an addressee (Member State or individual), a decision without an addressee such as a decision concluding an international agreement, and a decision adopted within the context of the Common Foreign and Security Policy (CFSP). Indeed, the CFSP decision itself represents two distinct types of act, the 'common position' and 'joint action' of the pre-Lisbon TEU, the former concerned with policy orientation and the latter with operational action.

[3] Trilogues are meetings between the Council of Europe, the European Parliament, and the European Commission intended to speed up the legislative process.

demonstrate that the EU has a competence to act) but also the relative balance of power between the institutions and the obligation they are under to act within the limits of their powers (Article 13(2) of the Treaty on European Union (TEU)). Hence the frequency with which legal basis becomes a battleground, 'political debates conducted in legal language' as Leino puts it. The Court of Justice has repeatedly insisted that choice of legal basis must be based on 'objective factors' that are amenable to judicial review (in particular the act's 'aim and content'), but it is abundantly clear both that political considerations play an important part in such choices and that, as long as the act contains the necessary 'triggers' for the legal basis chosen, the Court is unlikely to try to second-guess the institutional choice. The flexibility of the Treaty rules allow considerable room for institutional negotiation and compromise, operating within legal parameters which give, as Leino points out, considerable influence to the institutions' legal services. The Council legal service's unhappiness, documented in Chapter 2, with the operation of transparency as regards its own legal advice is linked to the perceived need to conceal both legal uncertainties and institutional disagreement. Where the institutions agree there is room for flexibility; when there is institutional disagreement the limits of discretion (such as whether the power of initiative given to the European Commission gives it the right to withdraw a legislative proposal even at the eleventh hour if it is unhappy with the outcome of Council and European Parliament negotiation) are tested.[4] Leino argues that both informal practices and an emphasis on efficiency over transparency and participation tend to favour actors in already powerful positions; rules, as lawyers often point out, may play an important role in protecting the interests of weaker parties.

From this initial focus on the issues and practices that complicate seemingly *standard* exercises of EU legislative and executive power to create legal acts, the analysis shifts to what we might term *non-standard* exercises of EU power to create non-standard EU legal acts. The examples chosen in the volume to illustrate and examine different facets of this phenomenon focus on the broad and expanding field of EU social and economic governance. For better and for worse, this area has provided perhaps the richest terrain in EU law for non-standard acts to date and accordingly can serve as a reference point for understanding similar or emergent developments in other substantive fields of EU law.

Starting at the sharpest and most novel end of the non-standard EU spectrum, in Chapter 3 Claire Kilpatrick examines the institutional actions and acts produced in the context of the EU sovereign debt crisis. While much legal analysis of the EU sovereign debt crisis has concerned its various constitutional dimensions, this chapter highlights how turning our focus instead to legal sources and ECB institutional mandates uncovers distinctive and important problems in rule of law compatibility of EU actions in the sovereign debt crisis. It suggests how diagnoses and policy choices at EU level in the wake of the 2007–2008 financial crisis laid the ground for unconventional actions and acts to take root. By identifying a number of these acts and actions as *abnormal* rather than merely non-standard or atypical, attention is

[4] Case C-409/13, *Council v. Commission*, judgment of 14 April 2015 (ECLI:EU:C:2015:217).

drawn to the features of these acts and actions that trouble the law/non-law boundary. Significantly, they trouble it not because they are soft law, but rather because they act as law without fulfilling the requirements or desiderata of binding acts adopted by public authorities. This includes obviously problematic features such as secret sources and institutional actions. It also opens for consideration the cumulative and not easily visible institutional power conferred by the interaction of a series of different levers possessed by the European Central Bank (ECB) to require states to enter into sovereign debt programmes while also setting down and monitoring the conditions in sovereign debt programmes. The role of the ECB in the provision of Emergency Liquidity Assistance is the linchpin of the analysis.

Rather than focusing on such exceptional manifestations of non-standard sources, in Chapter 4 Mark Dawson considers how the broader overhaul of EU economic governance in the euro crisis sits in relation to the academic debates on EU new governance which were a prominent new reading of EU sources in the early 2000s. The Open Method of Co-ordination (OMC) developed after the Treaty of Maastricht in areas such as economic, employment, and social inclusion governance, and premised on revisable and differentiated soft-law guidelines to deliver law and policy change at domestic level, was seen as providing a new direction for the EU, decentring traditional legal acts and the Court of Justice. Yet, as Dawson illustrates, the claims for OMC as the standard-bearer for this new era of EU new governance turned out to be overstated as, on the one hand, OMCs did not achieve their goals while, on the other, traditional legal mechanisms demonstrated their continuing strength and relevance. Against this backdrop, Dawson asks how best to characterize the swathe of new sources introduced from 2010 onwards to deal with the euro-area crisis, in particular the legislative six and two packs of 2011 and 2013 and the Fiscal Compact Treaty of 2010. He develops a reading by which much of this new body of norms, aimed at centralizing control of macroeconomic policy, is closely related to the new governance mode of revisable regulation and proceduralization of policy-making. At the same time, in so doing, he argues that the lessons of new governance in socio-economic governance have not been learnt, as it is unlikely to fulfil its assigned task of driving convergence in distributive policy areas. That is to say, Dawson's analysis takes the dramatic changes to a central focus of EU new governance studies—EU macroeconomic governance, which is a form of EU governance distinctive from the classic command and control model associated with legal acts—and considers what remains of its central features. In so doing, he problematizes and deepens our understanding in the EU order of the interrelated roles that 'legal acts' and 'non-legal acts' can play by looking, for instance, at what gives norms authority, exploring the differences between decisions and rules, and stressing the role of law in underpinning EU processes of multilevel deliberation.

In Chapter 5 Aukje van Hoek examines a rather different non-standard way of creating EU legal acts: by recourse to the EU-level social partners whose agreements can be transformed into EU social law by Council decisions.[5] One can identify this

[5] Articles 154 TFEU and 155 TFEU are the key provisions.

as non-standard in at least three different ways: the Treaty provisions granting this role to the social partners were themselves largely drafted by the social partners themselves; the right of legislative initiative is taken out of the hands of the Commission, which is obliged to see first if the social partners can come to an agreement in the range of areas covered by this special process; and it substitutes the democratic legitimacy of the standard EU co-legislature of Council and Parliament (and post-Lisbon the national parliaments via the subsidiarity mechanism) with that of the representatives of labour and employers. Van Hoek examines how this law-making role of the EU social partners meshes both with their other roles and with the standard EU legislative architecture. One particular feature—the need for a Commission proposal to Council to convert a social partner agreement into EU law—has recently opened up the question of how the Commission's discretion to make that proposal to Council is best framed and understood. It is established practice that the Commission should check whether the EU social partners are representative, whether the social partner agreement falls within the relevant EU competences, and its appropriateness. A choice by the Commission to exercise intense review brings the process closer to the classic EU law-making process but weakens the autonomy and recognition of the social partners as law-makers. The decision by the Commission in 2012 not to propose for Council decision a social partner agreement of 2010 concerning health and safety in the hairdressing sector, as part of its commitment to reduce red tape in the REFIT package, has provoked a debate on this central issue. By providing a detailed sense of the operation of this non-standard area of EU law-making, Chapter 5 also invites new reflections on the standard EU law-making process.

As we move further away from the legal acts envisaged in the Treaties and adopted by the institutions, we turn, in Chapter 6 by Bruno De Witte and Thibault Martinelli, to legal acts which they identify as 'quasi-instruments of EU law'—treaties concluded by the Member States between themselves which have a close link to EU law. We are not therefore concerned with treaties which the Member States may conclude within their own sphere of competence (such as double tax treaties) and which must simply conform to the Member States' EU obligations; these quasi-instruments of EU law fulfil a function similar to EU secondary law. This category of inter-Member State treaties occupies an intermediate place between the EU's founding Treaties (which form the EU's primary law) and EU secondary law. It is a practice with a long history, even referred to in the EEC Treaty (Article 220 EEC[6]) and later in the Maastricht Treaty (Article K.3 TEU), and it has recently become more common. They may in themselves be instruments of flexibility, allowing the Member States to supplement or complement EU law, or allowing for differentiated integration if a group of Member States wish to use an *inter se* treaty to move ahead to a new level of integration or into a new field of action. De Witte and Martinelli trace the evolution

[6] For an example of a treaty concluded under the auspices of Article 220 EEC, see the 1968 Brussels Convention on jurisdiction and enforcement of judgments (Convention 90/C 189/02 on Jurisdiction and the Enforcement of Judgment in Civil and Commercial Matters, OJ 1990 C 189/2), which later became an EU regulation.

and map the different kinds of *inter se* treaties of this type, and the somewhat uneasy relationship they have with both EU law as a whole and the role of the EU's institutions in particular. Is it permissible for Member States to decide to act outside the Treaty decision-making framework in a case where the EU possesses the necessary competence and an EU legal act could have been used? Indeed, as De Witte and Martinelli point out, the 'complementary' *inter se* agreements (those concluded by all Member States) have fallen into disuse, partly because of their normative defects: while keeping the Member States centre stage, this in itself created difficulties in achieving full ratification, coping with the accession of new Member States, and getting agreement on the interpretative jurisdiction of the Court of Justice, which is necessary to avoid the risk of divergent interpretations in national courts. The 'classic' legal acts have the merit of a tried and tested procedural structure and known legal effects; they are an 'off-the-shelf' solution which has its own advantage. These *inter se* agreements nevertheless played a role in spearheading the development of EU law into new fields, such as private international law, which have now become fully integrated into the EU system. Partial *inter se* agreements, such as the Schengen Convention,[7] have also played this pioneering role, although in the form of differentiated integration. More recently, they have been used as a tool in the context of the euro crisis and to establish a Unified Patent Court. These cases have varied rationales and it is perhaps not possible to identify a general reason for the turn towards *inter se* treaties; it does not seem to be part of a general move towards intergovernmentalism, but rather a reaction to the exigencies (whether political or financial) of particular situations. In any event, each of these cases has provoked debate and in some cases litigation, over their compatibility with EU law.

One of the most 'classic' of EU legal acts is the decision by which the EU signs or concludes an international agreement, although in the early years of the EEC, before it was accepted that a decision need not have an addressee, this act often took the form of a regulation. The Lisbon Treaty brought together in one expanded provision almost all the procedural rules governing the negotiation and conclusion of international agreements by the EU, even agreements in the field of the CFSP.[8] As Alan Dashwood says in Chapter 7, '[t]he special constitutional significance of Article 218 TFEU lies in the fact that international agreements provide one of the sources of the EU's positive law'. The years since the Lisbon Treaty entered into force have seen an impressive amount of litigation, largely interinstitutional, testing the re-calibration of powers in the revised institutional framework for external relations. There have been cases on: the extent to which the Council may, through a consultative committee, guide the Commission's negotiating strategy; the limits to the Commission's power to conclude agreements; EU representation in bodies established by international agreements; the link between substantive and procedural

[7] Convention implementing the Schengen Agreement of 14 June 1985 between the Governments of the States of the Benelux Economic Union, the Federal Republic of Germany and the French Republic on the gradual abolition of checks at their common borders, OJ 2000 L 239/19.

[8] Article 207 TFEU contains some 'special provisions' which operate alongside Article 218 for the negotiation and conclusion of trade agreements, and monetary or foreign exchange agreements are governed by Article 219 TFEU.

legal basis; and the role of the European Parliament and its right to be informed on the negotiation of a treaty. Through these cases, as well as through practice guided by the interinstitutional agreement between the European Commission and the European Parliament,[9] we are beginning to see the emergence of an understanding of the distinctive roles of the institutions outlined in Articles 13–18 TEU. The Commission's representative role, for example (Article 17(1) TEU) and the requirement that the institutions should 'practice mutual sincere cooperation' (Article 13(2) TEU) guide the Court in establishing the degree of Commission autonomy in international negotiations. This recourse to the provisions in the TEU setting out the primary responsibilities and functions of the institutions as a lens through which to interpret the specific procedural rules of Article 218 of the Treaty on the Functioning of the European Union (TFEU), demonstrates the impact of the Lisbon Treaty's revised constitutional structure.

If the conclusion of treaties is a classic form of legal act, the process of negotiating international agreements may also display more experimental features, or the 'procedural imagination' referred to by Leino. The chapters by Dawson and van Hoek have shown, in very different contexts, ways in which the Member States can be integrated into non-standard decision-making. The need to find effective ways to bring together the EU and its Member States within a unified framework that nevertheless respects the autonomy and competences of both is a perennial challenge in the field of external relations. Despite the exclusive nature of some external competences, the Member States have not, of course, lost their sovereign status and continue to operate alongside the EU. Indeed, they may sometimes need to represent the EU where the international framework (a treaty or international organization) does not provide for participation by an organization such as the EU. Article 218 TFEU has proved quite flexible enough to accommodate such cases even where the EU is not a party to the agreement in question.[10] It has also been able to accommodate (within limits) the 'mixed agreement', whereby an agreement is concluded by both the EU and the Member States. Despite being a central feature of EU external practice the mixed agreement is invisible in the EU Treaties; it is not mentioned at all in Article 218 TFEU. On the EU side, it would seem, the treaty should be concluded as if the EU were acting alone. And yet, of course, in practice both the EU and Member States are careful to coordinate their negotiating positions, and are required to do so by the general duty of cooperation (Article 4(3) TEU). And, especially in the case of bilateral agreements, they will ensure that the EU does not formally conclude the agreement until it has been ratified by all the Member States. One way of giving expression to this coordination might be to adopt a joint decision, by the Council on behalf of the EU and by the representatives of the governments of the Member States, on the signature of mixed agreements. But these so-called

[9] Framework Agreement on Relations between the European Parliament and the European Commission OJ 2010 L 304/47, paras 23–29 and Annex III.

[10] Opinion 1/13, *Opinion pursuant to Article 218(11) TFEU*, 14 October 2014 (ECLI:EU:C:2014:2303); Case C-399/12, *Germany v. Council (OIV)*, judgment of 7 October 2014 (ECLI:EU:C:2014:2258).

'hybrid' decisions are not expressly sanctioned in the Treaties and have now been declared contrary to Article 218 TFEU by the Court of Justice.[11] Here of course the act was a formal decision, and necessarily so since we are talking about signing an international agreement, and there was less room for flexibility; in less formal contexts the Commission is able to put forward a joint statement on behalf of 'the EU and its Member States'. This signals attention to the institutional and constitutional constraints which shape in legally enforceable ways the forms in which EU acts are adopted but also to the sites of EU action where such constraints are less evident or remain nebulous. The broad but not entirely unconstrained freedom for some or less typically all Member States to 'go outside the Treaties' is one good example explored by De Witte and Martinelli. Whether judicial review can be brought against the Commission for its failure to respond to the request of the social partners to propose one of their agreements to the Council for adoption as a decision is another example evidenced in the chapter by van Hoek. EU sovereign debt crisis management, discussed by Kilpatrick, has created a large new set of norms in which the EU institutions are central actors but where their legal and EU nature remain troublesome and unclear despite repeated requests for clarification before the Court of Justice over the last decade.[12] Other examples, such as the recent denial of the EU status of the agreement which is commonly known as the 'EU–Turkey' agreement,[13] suggest this is a new phenomenon in the area of 'EU legal acts' whose roots and consequences it is important for EU legal scholars to explore.

Overall, this volume aims to provide a sense of the richness and variety of EU legal acts, the range of ways in which acts linked to or associated with the EU can cross the boundaries between EU and non-EU norms and between law and non-law, and the challenges that this poses to EU constitutional structures and traditional forms of accountability.

[11] Case C-28/12, *Commission v. Council*, judgment of 28 April 2015 (ECLI:EU:C:2015:282).

[12] See the recent *Ledra Advertising* case (Case C-8/15 P *Ledra Advertising Ltd and Others v. European Commission and European Central Bank (ECB)*, judgment of 20 September 2016 (ECLI:EU:C:2016:701)) where the Court in its Grand Chamber formation accepted for the first time that an action for damages could lie against the Commission for its signature of a Memorandum of Understanding on behalf of the European Stability Mechanism, but that the conditions for such an action were not met.

[13] Cases T-192/16, T-193/16, and T-257/16, *NF, NG, and NM v. European Council*, Orders of 28 February 2017.

1

Legal Acts and the Challenges of Democratic Accountability

Deirdre Curtin

1. Introduction

Enhancing the democratic legitimacy of the European Union (EU) was a key objective of the reforms which eventually led to the adoption of the Lisbon Treaty.[1] Closely tied to democratic legitimacy is accountability, which was also an aim of the Treaty reformers.[2] One of the main strategies for achieving greater accountability was strengthening the role of the European Parliament (EP) in legislative and executive rule-making.[3] Parliamentary accountability (also with respect to national parliaments) was viewed as a key way of enhancing the democratic legitimacy of the EU. But do the rules that were agreed in the end actually guarantee a high level of accountability in the form of strong parliamentary involvement in the decision-making process? Is the post-Lisbon practice of the institutions in line with the rules laid down in the Lisbon Treaty? These are the key issues addressed in this chapter. In answering the latter question, the impact of the euro crisis on the powers of EU institutions must also be considered.[4]

The Lisbon Treaty established three main categories of legal acts: legislative, delegated, and implementing. Yet there is a fourth category—non-legislative acts directly based on the Treaties—which was part of the ill-fated Constitutional Treaty, but did not make its way explicitly into the Lisbon Treaty. With regard to accountability in

[1] Laeken Declaration on the Future of the European Union adopted by the European Council on 15 December 2001, 4–5; Final Report of Working Group IX on Simplification, CONV 424/02, 29 November 2002, 2.

[2] Dougan, 'The Treaty of Lisbon 2007: Winning Minds, Not Hearts', 45 *Common Market Law Review* (2008) 617, at 620.

[3] See, e.g. Bast, 'New Categories of Acts after the Lisbon Reform: Dynamics of Parliamentarization in EU law', 49 *Common Market Law Review* (2012) 885; Kohler, 'European Governance and the European Parliament: From Talking Shop to Legislative Powerhouse', 52 *Journal of Common Market Studies* (2014) 600; Christiansen and Dobbels, 'Delegated Powers and Inter-Institutional Relations in the EU after Lisbon: A Normative Assessment', 36 *West European Politics* (2013) 1159.

[4] See, e.g. Schwarzer, 'The Euro Area Crises, Shifting Power Relations and Institutional Change in the European Union', 3 *Global Policy* (2012) 28, at 31–33. See also more specifically in this volume, the chapter by Mark Dawson on new modes of governance in the EU after the euro crisis and the chapter by Claire Kilpatrick on abnormal legal sources in the EU sovereign debt crisis.

legislative and executive rule-making, the following questions may be identified in relation to each of the four categories of acts: 1) Do the Council of the European Union ('the Council'), the EP, and the European Commission keep each other in check when enacting *legislative acts*? What about the accountability of the European Council in the context of its increased role in legislative rule-making? 2) Are the EP and the Council able to effectively control the Commission when it enacts *delegated acts*? 3) Do the new comitology rules, put in place under the ordinary legislative procedure, enable the EU Member States to really hold the Commission accountable when it adopts *implementing acts*? Who is to guarantee the Council's accountability when *it* exercises implementing powers? 4) Finally, what about accountability when it comes to the adoption of *non-legislative acts directly based on the Treaties* by the Council, the Commission, the European Council, and the European Central Bank (ECB)? These questions will be explored in this chapter. However, prior to addressing them, a short overview of the Lisbon reforms to the legal acts of the Union is provided.

2. Background: The Lisbon Reforms to Legal Acts

The Lisbon Treaty brought about major changes to the system of legal acts of the Union. One aim of the reforms was to introduce a hierarchy between legislative and executive acts. Another aim was to narrow down the number of legal instruments, creating a clearer and more consistent typology of acts. Both of these changes served the overarching objective of achieving a clearer separation of powers and greater accountability and democratic legitimacy in the Union.

A. Hierarchy

Proposals for the establishment of a hierarchy of norms in the Union legal order date as far back as the 1984 draft Treaty on the European Union (TEU).[5] Those proposals resulted in Declaration No. 16 which was annexed to this Treaty and provided that the 1996 Intergovernmental Conference (IGC) would examine the possibility of establishing a hierarchy between various categories of acts.[6] The reports[7] of the Reflection Group preparing the 1996 IGC highlight the tensions that have characterized the debate on hierarchy of norms in the EU ever since. The reports indicate the division between two opposing camps. Those in favour of hierarchy proposed a ranking of acts based on their source of origin—constitutional, legislative, and implementing acts—as well as a clear division between the legislative and the executive functions of the Community institutions. The main argument of those who opposed this hierarchical system was that it was 'based on the idea of separation of

[5] Bieber and Salomé, 'Hierarchy of Norms in European Law', 33 *Common Market Law Review* (1996) 907, at 921. This section draws on Curtin and Manucharyan, 'Legal Acts and Hierarchy of Norms in EU Law', in A. Arnull and D. Chalmers (eds), *The Oxford Handbook of EU Law* (2015), 103.

[6] Bieber and Salomé, *supra* note 5, at 922, 907.

[7] Progress Report from the Chairman of the Reflection Group on the 1996 Intergovernmental Conference, SN 509/1/95 of 1 September 1995; Final Report of the Reflection Group of 5 December 1995.

powers within a State, since this approach would transform the Council into a second legislative chamber and the Commission into the European executive'.[8] This second group favoured maintaining the existing system of acts: regulations, directives, decisions, and recommendations. The final outcome was somewhere in between these two opposing positions.

The current hierarchy of norms in the EU legal order is primarily the product of the work done by the Convention on the Future of Europe (hereinafter the 'Convention') between 2002 and 2003. Within the Convention, Working Group IX focused on the simplification of the Union's instruments and procedures and the ranking of norms. The Working Group's definition of simplification was one of making the EU legal order more comprehensible to the citizens of the Union and providing 'a guarantee that acts with the same legal/political force have the same foundation in terms of democratic legitimacy'.[9] With regard to the question of how to simplify the Union legal instruments, the Working Group consulted three experts: Michel Petite, Director-General of the Commission Legal Service; Koen Lenaerts, at the time, a judge at the Court of First Instance; and Jean-Claude Piris, Legal Adviser and Director-General of the Council Legal Service. The final report of the Working Group was very much in line with the recommendations of Koen Lenaerts.[10] In accordance with his suggestions,[11] the Group proposed a hierarchy of acts based on adoption procedures rather than the identity of the authors of the acts; the classification of legislative acts as those which contain the essential elements of an area or, as Lenaerts termed it, 'basic policy choices'; and, finally, the division of executive acts into two categories—delegated and implementing.[12] The outcome was the creation of three levels of hierarchy: legislative, delegated, and implementing acts.[13]

What the Lisbon Treaty's section on legal acts does not explicitly mention is the category of non-legislative acts *directly based on the Treaties*. Both the Constitutional Treaty (CT) and the Draft Constitutional Treaty (DCT) *did* include a fourth category—that of 'non-legislative acts'—placed between the provisions on legislative and delegated acts. The latter category should not be confused with delegated and implementing acts based on secondary measures. Non-legislative acts, within the meaning of Article I-35 CT[14] (and Article 34 DCT), are binding legal acts adopted by the European Council, the Council, the Commission, or the ECB directly on the basis of the Constitution (under the current legal order, this would be on the basis of the Treaty). This unlisted category of acts certainly represents a major gap in the current hierarchy of EU legal acts.

[8] Final Report of the Reflection Group, *ibid.*, Second Part, point 126.

[9] Final Report of Working Group IX on Simplification, CONV 424/02, 29 November 2002, 2.

[10] C. Bergström, *Comitology: Delegation of Powers in the European Union and the Committee System* (2005), at 339–340.

[11] K. Lenaerts, 'How to Simplify the Instruments of the Union', Working Group IX Working Document 07, 6 November 2002, at 2–3, 5.

[12] Bergström, *supra* note 10, at 339–340.

[13] Final Report of Working Group IX on Simplification, *supra* note 9, at 9.

[14] Note that only the third paragraph of Article I-35 has made it into the Lisbon Treaty in the form of Article 292 TFEU.

Although this contribution is primarily concerned with legislative, delegated, and implementing acts (along with non-legislative acts directly based on the Treaties), the *complete* hierarchy in the Union legal order in descending order is as follows: the constituent Treaties and the Charter of Fundamental Rights of the European Union; general principles of law; legislative acts; delegated acts; and implementing acts.[15]

B. Typology

Article 249 EC listed the legal acts of the Community in the pre-Lisbon legal order. Its successor in the Lisbon Treaty is Article 288 Treaty on the Functioning of the European Union (TFEU).[16] A comparison between the two shows that the *substance* of the new provision on legal instruments of the Union is not much different from that of its predecessor. The definitions of regulations and directives, recommendations and opinions are exactly the same in both articles. The only substantial change is in relation to decisions.[17] In the pre-Lisbon legal regime, a second type of decision (in addition to the one listed in Article 249 EC) was created. This was the *sui generis* decision—without an addressee—also known by its German name '*Beschluss*'.[18] It was used for 'detailed institutional arrangements in the internal operation of the European Union, such as in laying down rules of procedure or setting up new committees or new administrative bodies... the adoption of the budget... as well as the multi-annual action programmes adopted in all kinds of policy areas'.[19] Article 288 TFEU now takes into account the existence of this second type of decisions: by referring to 'a decision which specifies those to whom it is addressed' it makes clear that there are also decisions which do not have specific addressees. Thus, the new legal definition of a decision actually includes two different instruments, which, while sharing the same name, perform quite different functions.[20] According to De Witte, there are two problems with this arrangement: the fact that the distinction between this new type of addressee-less decision and a regulation is not quite clear and the fact that it is uncertain whether this decision is the same as the one used in the context of the Common Foreign and Security Policy (CFSP).[21] Were the latter presumption to be true, we would have acts with three different functions covered by the umbrella term 'decision'.

The *number* of instruments, as listed under Articles 249 EC and 288 TFEU, has also remained the same. The issue, however, lies not in the instruments listed in these articles, but the ones which are utilized by the Union institutions in practice—without

[15] P. Craig and G. de Búrca, *EU Law: Text, Cases and Materials* (5th edn, 2011), at 103.

[16] This section draws on Curtin and Manucharyan, *supra* note 5.

[17] Best, 'Legislative Procedures After Lisbon: Fewer, Simpler, Clearer?' 15 *Maastricht Journal of European and Comparative Law* (2008) 85, at 87.

[18] *Ibid.*

[19] De Witte, 'Legal Instruments and Law-Making in the Lisbon Treaty', in S. Griller and J. Ziller (eds), *The Lisbon Treaty: EU Constitutionalism without a Constitutional Treaty?* (2008) 79, at 82.

[20] *Ibid.*, at 95.

[21] *Ibid.*, at 96. He argues that this is probably not the case because decisions within the meaning of Article 288 TFEU can have direct effect in the national systems—something that would not be desirable in the area of CFSP from the perspective of the Treaty drafters (*Ibid.*, at 90).

being expressly acknowledged in the provisions on legal acts. The *sui generis* decision is one such act, which has now (somewhat problematically) found its way into Article 288 TFEU, yet the wide range of unlisted acts has been an issue since the pre-Lisbon times, as illustrated in the following statement by the Convention Praesidium:

> A range of more than 30 different types of act is the outcome of the addition to the initial catalogue in Article 249 of the TEC (decision, regulation, directive, recommendation and opinion) of a whole series of other instruments (guidelines, framework programme, implementing decision, etc.) to be found elsewhere in the Treaties. Yet more (decision as a general rule, declarations, resolutions, conclusions, etc.) have been added in practice.
>
> The pillar structure has also contributed to the proliferation of instruments by introducing types of act specific to foreign policy (common strategy, common position, joint action, etc.) and to cooperation in criminal matters (decision, framework decision, etc.).[22]

Although this description applied to the system under Article 249 EC, a closer look at the text of the Lisbon Treaty reveals that the issue of unlisted acts persists. While the legal instruments of the former third pillar (now the Area of Freedom, Security, and Justice) have been abolished and replaced by 'mainstream' legal instruments (regulations, directives, and decisions), the same did not happen in relation to the former second pillar, that is, the area of CFSP today. The 'decision' within the meaning of Article 288 TFEU is (most likely) not the same instrument as the one used in the context of CFSP. Moreover, the CFSP decision is an umbrella term, which covers a wide range of instruments applied in that area under the pre-Lisbon legal regime. In that sense, 'the terminological simplification is somewhat deceptive'.[23]

Finally, regulations, directives, and decisions may take the form of legislative, delegated, and implementing acts.[24] It follows that there are nine *basic* categories of binding legal acts (although the Treaty acknowledges other forms of binding acts, such as interinstitutional agreements under Article 296 TFEU, international agreements under Article 216 TFEU,[25] and specific forms of acts, such as those for budget matters under Article 313 TFEU).[26]

3. Legislative Acts and Accountability

With the extension of codecision to many new fields of EU activity, the Council and the EP are the main legislators of the Union—placed on a more equal footing. However, the important role of the Commission and the increasing role of the European Council in legislative initiative also needs to be emphasized. As Craig observes, '[i]n the EU, legislative power has been divided between the Council,

[22] Mandate of Working Group IX on the simplification of legislative procedures and instruments, CONV 271/02, 6.

[23] De Witte, *supra* note 19, at 90.

[24] Craig and de Búrca, *supra* note 15, at 104.

[25] See the chapter by Alan Dashwood in this volume for a discussion on the conclusion and implementation of international agreements in the EU.

[26] Hofmann, 'Legislation, Delegation and Implementation under the Treaty of Lisbon: Typology Meets Reality', 15 *European Law Journal* (2009) 482, at 486. See also the chapter by Aukje A.H. van Hoek in this volume on collective labour agreements as a source of law in the EU.

European Parliament, and Commission, with the European Council playing a significant role in shaping the overall legislative agenda'.[27] Accordingly, we need to assess the accountability of these institutions in legislative rule-making.

A. *De Jure* Accountability

Under Article 289 TFEU, legislative acts are defined as 'legal acts adopted by legislative procedure'. This is a formal definition, which disregards the content of the act. The legislative procedures in question are the ordinary legislative procedure (OLP) and the special legislative procedure (SLP).[28] Although it may not be clear from the wording of Article 289(2) TFEU, a close examination of the relevant provisions of the Treaty shows that in the majority of cases, the SLP stands for decision-making *by the Council* (rather than by the EP), which requires only *consultation* (as opposed to the consent) of the EP.[29]

This is problematic from the perspective of political accountability as the controls over the Council, when it legislates on its own, are very limited. Two key accountability mechanisms can be identified in this regard. One is the requirement for the Council to meet in public when it deliberates and votes on a draft legislative act.[30] The other is that, pursuant to Article 2, Protocol 1 on the Role of National Parliaments in the European Union, all draft legislative acts must be forwarded to national parliaments. However, the Council's security rules and its extensive use of unclassified ('limited') documents prevent the public and often national parliaments from having timely access to ongoing legislative discussions.[31] Even if national parliaments receive this information from their own national governments they are constrained by these 'internal' rules (enforced by their governments) to keep it secret.[32] Even if EU 'limited' documents are received by the national parliament from its own government, the national parliament is required to keep them out of the public domain. Genuinely *public* debate is very rarely possible although there is a trend emerging for more plenary debates in parliaments in advance of important decision-making.[33]

That an act adopted without strong parliamentary involvement is considered a 'legislative act' is an anomaly of the EU system and would be unthinkable at the national level.[34] Not only are the acts adopted according to the SLP shielded from genuine parliamentary scrutiny, they also cannot be directly challenged under the post-Lisbon reformed rules of Article 263(4) TFEU. According to the ruling of the

[27] P. Craig, *The Lisbon Treaty, Revised Edition: Law, Politics, and Treaty Reform* (2013), at 72.

[28] See the chapter by Päivi Leino in this volume for a discussion on the formal rules and the informal practices in the making of legal acts.

[29] Türk, 'Lawmaking after Lisbon', in A. Biondi, P. Eeckhout, and S. Ripley (eds), *EU Law after Lisbon* (2012) 62, at 69.

[30] Article 16(8) TEU.

[31] See Curtin, 'Overseeing Secrets in the EU. A Democratic Perspective', 52 *Journal of Common Market Studies* (2014) 684.

[32] *Ibid.*

[33] Curtin, 'Challenging Executive Dominance in European Democracy', 77 *The Modern Law Review* (2014) 1.

[34] See Türk, *supra* note 29, at 69–70, 73.

Court of Justice in *Inuit*, legislative acts are *not* regulatory acts within the meaning of Article 263(4) TFEU.[35] This is certainly problematic from the point of view of accountability.

Another issue is that there are numerous provisions in the Lisbon Treaty that include a decision-making procedure very similar to the SLP yet without an explicit reference to it. Due to the wording of Article 289 TFEU (the phrase 'in the specific cases provided in the Treaties') these cases cannot be viewed as instances of SLP; therefore, acts enacted under these provisions are not legislative acts, even if substantively they may very well be.[36] Instead, they belong to the category of non-legislative acts directly based on the Treaties.[37] Accordingly, measures such as the ones under Article 103 TFEU (competition) and the ones under Article 109 TFEU (state aid) are not legislative acts under the current legal regime.[38] It must be noted that Regulation 1/2003[39] was adopted based on Article 83 EC, which is now Article 103 TFEU. As Dougan rightly observes: 'Is a measure such as Regulation 1/2003 on competition enforcement really any less "legislative" in nature – in terms of the procedure for its adoption, or its substantive content – than many of the "legislative acts" which would be adopted elsewhere under the Treaties?'[40] The fact that acts of general application, such as the ones adopted under Articles 103 and 109 TFEU, are classified as non-legislative even though their adoption procedure is very similar to the SLP with EP consultation means that the Council is free from the accountability standards which apply to it during the adoption of legislative acts—such as open public deliberation[41] or scrutiny by national parliaments.[42]

Regarding the accountability of the Commission, the Lisbon Treaty states that it is 'responsible' to the European Parliament.[43] Further details on this political responsibility are provided in the framework agreement on relations between the EP and the Commission, adopted in 2010.[44] Point 9 of the agreement provides: 'The Commission guarantees that it will apply the basic principle of equal treatment for Parliament and the Council, especially as regards access to meetings and the provision of contributions or other information, in particular on legislative and budgetary matters.' According to Point 11 of that agreement, 'the President of the Commission will have a regular dialogue with the President of Parliament on key horizontal issues and major legislative proposals. This dialogue should also include

[35] Case C-583/11 P, *Inuit Tapiriit Kanatami and Others v. Parliament and Council* [2011], ECLI:EU:C:2013:625, at para. 61.

[36] Craig, *supra* note 27, at 257–258.

[37] See further on this phenomenon, Section 6 later in this chapter.

[38] Dougan, *supra* note 2, at 647.

[39] Council Regulation 1/2003 of 16 December 2002 on the implementation of the rules on competition laid down in Articles 81 and 82 of the Treaty, OJ 2003 L 1/1.

[40] *Ibid.* [41] Article 16(8) TEU.

[42] Article 2, Protocol 1 on the Role of National Parliaments in the European Union. These acts can, however, be challenged under the looser standing rules of Article 263(4) TFEU.

[43] Article 17(8) TEU. See Corbett, 'The Evolving Roles of the European Parliament and of National Parliaments', in A. Biondi, P. Eeckhout, and S. Ripley (eds), *EU Law after Lisbon* (2012) 248, at 251.

[44] Framework Agreement on relations between the European Parliament and the European Commission, OJ 2010 L 304/47.

invitations to the President of Parliament to attend meetings of the College of Commissioners.' Point 37 provides: 'The Commission undertakes to carefully examine amendments to its legislative proposals adopted by Parliament, with a view to taking them into account in any amended proposal.' Lastly, Point 40 states: 'For special legislative procedures on which Parliament is to be consulted, including other procedures such as that laid down in Article 148 TFEU, the Commission . . . shall take measures to better involve Parliament in such a way as to take Parliament's views into account as far as possible, in particular to ensure that Parliament has the necessary time to consider the Commission's proposal'. These provisions certainly create greater accountability of the Commission to the EP in relation to the adoption of legislative acts. However, as will be seen later, the informal practices of the institutions, namely increasing reliance on 'trilogue' negotiations, diminish the effect of these formal rules and agreements, by placing the Commission and the Council in a more favourable position compared to the EP and not leaving much room for true dialogue and debate on important legislative files.

Another recent development has contributed to increased accountability of the Commission to the EP, which may also have implications in legislative matters. The Lisbon Treaty provides that the EP 'shall elect the President of the Commission'.[45] The Treaty further specifies that the European Council proposes a candidate for President of the Commission 'taking into account the elections to the European Parliament'.[46] The EP successfully utilized this somewhat vaguely formulated provision to its utmost advantage in the 2014 European elections.[47] As a result, Jean-Claude Juncker, the nominee of the political group which got the highest number of votes in the EP elections, was appointed as Commission President.[48] In addition to this newly 'seized' power of electing the Commission President, the EP approves the College of Commissioners nominated by the Commission President and the European Council.[49] Last but not least, it has always enjoyed the power to censure the Commission (as a whole).[50] Under the terms of the Framework Agreement between the EP and the Commission, the EP also has a greater say in censuring individual Commissioners.[51]

As mentioned earlier, the European Council has increasingly interfered in the legislative sphere. This has been the case especially since the beginning of the euro crisis. Instead of limiting itself to shaping the overall legislative agenda, it has

45 Article 14(1) TEU.

46 Article 17(7) TEU.

47 See Editorial Comments, 'After the European Elections: Parliamentary Games and Gambles', 51 *Common Market Law Review* (2014) 1047, at 1047–1052; Hobolt, 'A Vote for the President? The Role of Spitzenkandidaten in the 2014 European Parliament Elections', 21 *Journal of European Public Policy* (2014) 1528, especially at 1532–1533.

48 For a discussion on the negative effects of politicizing the Commission, see Dougan, *supra* note 2, at 693–695.

49 Article 17(7) TEU.

50 Article 17(8) TEU and Article 234 TFEU. Although it is difficult to apply in practice: See Peers, 'The EU's Political Institutions', in C. Barnard and S. Peers (eds), *European Union Law* (2014) 36, at 44–45.

51 EP-Commission Framework Agreement, *supra* note 44, para. 5. No individual Commissioner has been fired to date: See, Peers, *supra* note 50, at 45.

provided *detailed instructions* to the Commission for the enactment of legislative measures.[52] The Parliament's concern over the European Council's involvement in legislative rule-making is evident from its strongly worded resolution, where it stresses 'that any further initiative... must imperatively be established in accordance with the Community method' and calls upon the European Council to 'stop instructing the Commission on the form and/or content of any further legislative initiative', emphasizing in this respect that '[the European Council] does not have any Treaty-based prerogative of legislative initiative'.[53] Despite this development, there are very few ways in which the European Council can be held accountable on the European level. The Treaties provide that the European Council President must present a report to the EP after each European Council meeting.[54] In addition to the presentation of a report, the President engages in other regular contact with the EP, such as meeting the leaders of the political groups following each European Council meeting.[55] Needless to say, these basic information provision practices do not amount to real accountability to the EP.[56]

B. *De Facto* Accountability

With the extension of codecision under the Lisbon Treaty, the practice of trilogues was also extended.[57] As many codecision files are now negotiated in trilogue meetings, this makes the effect of the Lisbon reforms rather questionable. Trilogues are informal meetings that are held between the EU's two legislative institutions (Parliament and Council) and the Commission in order to facilitate the search for agreement on draft legislation.[58] The underlying objective is to allow a limited number of legislators to work out the broad contours for a formal agreement, and thereby speed up the legislative process as a whole.[59] Therefore, while trilogues can be held at any stage of the legislative process, they are most often employed at the outset.

[52] Bocquillon and Dobbels, 'An Elephant on the 13th Floor of the *Berlaymont*? European Council and Commission Relations in Legislative Agenda Setting', 21 *Journal of European Public Policy* (2014) 20, at 22–23.

[53] EP resolution of 12 June 2013 on strengthening European democracy in the future EMU (2013/2672 (RSP)), point 3.

[54] Article 15(6)(d) TEU.

[55] Corbett, *supra* note 43, at 253.

[56] See further, De Waele and Broeksteeg, 'The Semi-Permanent European Council Presidency: Some Reflections on the Law and Early Practice', 49 *Common Market Law Review* (2012) 1039, at 1066–1067; Bovens and Curtin, 'An Unholy Trinity of EU Presidents? Political Accountability of EU Executive Power', in D. Chalmers, C. Joerges, and M. Jachtenfuchs (eds), *The End of Eurocrat's Dream* (2016) 190.

[57] De Ruiter and Neuhold, 'Why Is Fast Track the Way to Go? Justifications for Early Agreement in the Co-Decision Procedure and Their Effects', 18 *European Law Journal* (2012) 536, at 536–537; Huber and Shackleton, 'Codecision: A Practitioner's View from Inside the Parliament', 20 *Journal of European Public Policy* (2013) 1040, at 1047. See also the chapter by Päivi Leino in this volume.

[58] This paragraph draws on Curtin and Hillebrandt, 'Transparency in the EU: Constitutional Overtones, Institutional Dynamics, and the Escape Hatch of Secrecy', in S. Blockmans and A. Lazowski (eds), *Research Handbook on EU Institutional Law* (2016), 190.

[59] Häge and Kaeding, 'Reconsidering the European Parliament's Legislative Influence: Formal vs. Informal Procedures', 29 *Journal of European Integration* (2007) 341, at 342.

In a trilogue a delegation of three Parliament representatives negotiate with three Council representatives, with the Commission acting as a facilitator.[60] These representatives can be described as coming from the decision-making elites: from the Parliament's side, they typically include one or several 'rapporteurs' on a specific political dossier, while the Council generally delegates trilogue negotiations to a senior member of the acting Presidency. This certainly pays off in terms of the smooth passage of legislation. Figures published by the seventh European Parliament (2009–2014) show that 85 per cent of legislative acts were passed at first reading with another 13 per cent passed at second reading. These figures fit in a longer-term trend towards the ever-faster adoption of legislation.[61] However, it also comes at a price in terms of transparency, which is protected by only a rather tentative provision in the applicable interinstitutional agreement. Article 9 of this document states that '[i]n order to enhance transparency, trilogues taking place within the European Parliament and Council shall be announced, where practicable'.[62] However, the meetings themselves remain protected by professional confidentiality, which places the 'relais actors' involved in a strong negotiating position both within the trilogue meeting and vis-à-vis their 'backbench'.[63] The trilogues thus risk 'short-circuiting' the formal legislative process, as relevant information is not discussed publicly.[64]

The fact that closed door negotiations take place and agreements are reached on the content of legislation at a very early stage of the legislative process means that the 'independence' of the input of the EP as opposed to the Council may be queried. It seems that the values of parliament (open public deliberation) are being dominated in practice by the values of the executive (efficient negotiations and results) and that the EP has gone along with this informal method of having an interinstitutional dialogue. It is difficult to see either institutional separation here or genuine dialogue that would fit within a thicker understanding of accountability.

Thus, trilogues have a significant impact on the accountability of the Council, the Commission, and the EP in legislative rule-making. According to some estimates trilogues take place on 76 per cent of Commission proposals under the ordinary legislative procedure.[65] As Chalmers put it: 'The biggest challenge to democratic legitimacy posed by the trilogue is their sidelining of checks and balances and lack of formality and transparency. Formal procedures do no more than rubber stamp prior agreements.'[66]

[60] R. Schütze, *An Introduction to European Law* (2012), at 42.

[61] European Parliament, Conciliation and Codecision: statistics. See http://www.europarl.europa.eu/code/about/statistics_en.htm (last visited 25 September 2017).

[62] Joint Declaration on practical arrangements for the codecision procedure (2007/C145/5), 30 June 2007, OJ 2007 C 145/5, Article 9.

[63] Häge and Kaeding, *supra* note 59, at 346. For an example of how '*relais* actors' may wield such influence in practice, see Bjurulf and Elgström, 'Negotiating Transparency: The Role of Institutions', 42 *Journal of Common Market Studies* (2004) 249, at 264.

[64] Huber and Shackleton, *supra* note 57; de Leeuw, 'Openness in the Legislative Process in the European Union', 32 *European Law Review* (2007) 295, at 315. See also Case OI/8/2015/FOR opened by the European Ombudsman on 26 May 2015 on Disclosure, by the European Parliament, Council of the EU and European Commission, of documents relating to trilogues and transparency of trilogues in general.

[65] R. Kardasheva, 'Legislative Package Deals in EU Decision-Making 1999–2007' (2009) (PhD thesis on file at London School of Economics and Political Science, London), at 25.

[66] D. Chalmers, G. Davies, and G. Monti, *European Union Law* (3rd edn, 2014), at 123.

According to this view, the Commission is 'a big winner' of trilogues, as it not only drafts the legislative proposal but also forms one part of the institutional triangle that adopts it.[67] The Council is also a major beneficiary as some studies indicate that the outcomes of trilogues are usually closer to the Council's positions and preferences than to those of the EP.[68] Accordingly, the EP's participation in trilogues not only leads to less accountability to the European public, as public debates and discussions on a given measure become largely a formality, but it also means that the Parliament is in a less advantageous position compared to the other two institutional players. For all these reasons, reliance on trilogue negotiations in the legislative process is highly controversial.

4. Delegated Acts and Accountability

Under the Lisbon Treaty, the Council and the EP are formally in charge of controlling delegated rule-making by the Commission. Placing delegated acts under the joint control of the legislators, as opposed to comitology committees, was *inter alia* meant to enhance the transparency and accountability of the process. Yet it is questionable whether the EP and the Council are able to effectively exercise their *ex ante* and *ex post* checks over the Commission. Moreover, the important role of expert groups in delegated rule-making is problematic due to their lack of transparency and some evidence suggesting that the Council is trying to influence the preparation of delegated acts through these groups. These issues are discussed in detail in the following sections.

A. Treaty Provisions versus Institutional Practice

As is evident from the wording of Article 290(1) TFEU, the Commission has the sole prerogative of enacting delegated acts. This was not the case prior to the Lisbon Treaty, as the Council could adopt acts of quasi-legislative nature. The reform of that system is due to the European Convention's objective of creating a clearer separation between the legislative and executive powers of the Union institutions—with the EP and the Council exercising (primarily) legislative functions and the Commission exercising executive functions.[69] This section explores the ability of the EP and the Council to effectively hold the Commission accountable in delegated rule-making. In this regard, a major change was brought about by the Lisbon Treaty: delegated acts, unlike quasi-legislative acts in the pre-Lisbon era, are *not* controlled by comitology committees. Instead, the Commission is subject to *ex ante* and *ex post* controls jointly exercised by the EP and the Council. Regarding the *ex ante* control mechanism, Article 290(1) TFEU provides that '[t]he objectives, content, scope and duration of the delegation of power shall be explicitly defined in the legislative acts'. As to the *ex post* controls, Article 290(2) TFEU states:

[67] *Ibid.*

[68] *Ibid.* See also Costello and Thomson, 'The Distribution of Power among EU Institutions: Who Wins under Codecision and Why?', 20 *Journal of European Public Policy* (2013) 1025.

[69] Bergström, *supra* note 10, at 345.

Legislative acts shall explicitly lay down the conditions to which the delegation is subject; these conditions may be as follows: (a) the European Parliament or the Council may decide to revoke the delegation; (b) the delegated act may enter into force only if no objection has been expressed by the European Parliament or the Council within a period set by the legislative act.

The effectiveness of the *ex ante* and *ex post* controls compared to the pre-Lisbon comitology controls for delegated legislation is a debatable question.[70] Commentators raise doubts with regard to both the efficiency and the democratic accountability of the current mechanism.[71] For instance, according to Craig, the comitology system 'allowed for regularized, general and detailed input into the content of [delegated] norms by Member State representatives, with increasing control exercised by the EP, more especially since the 2006 reforms'.[72] In contrast, the *ex ante* controls provided in Article 290 TFEU may be difficult to exercise, in practice because the Council and the European Parliament 'will often have neither the knowledge, nor the time to delineate precise parameters for the exercise of delegated regulatory choices in the legislative act'.[73] Regarding the *ex post* controls, it is argued that the EP's (and the Council's) power to revoke delegation is 'a nuclear option' which will not often be used in practice, while the power to object to individual acts will require the screening of a huge number of delegated acts—a task for which the EP is not well equipped.[74]

A related issue is that the EP and the Council will have to rely on information from expert groups instead of comitology committees in order to exercise the controls contained in Article 290 TFEU.[75] However, unlike comitology committees, expert groups are not subject to any transparency and accountability standards, and very little is known about their number, composition, and meetings.[76] The Common Understanding between the Commission, the EP, and the Council, which outlines the practical arrangements for the delegated acts procedure, only refers to the expert groups in passing, simply stating that '[t]he Commission . . . will . . . carry out appropriate and transparent consultations well in advance, including at expert level'.[77] Another interinstitutional document, the EP-Commission Framework Agreement, does state that:

The Commission will provide *full information and documentation* on its meetings with national experts within the framework of its work on the preparation and implementation of Union legislation, including soft law and delegated acts. *If so requested by Parliament,* the Commission may also invite Parliament's experts to attend those meetings.[78]

[70] See further Curtin and Manucharyan, *supra* note 5.

[71] Craig, 'The Role of the European Parliament under the Lisbon Treaty', in S. Griller and J. Ziller (eds), *The Lisbon Treaty: EU Constitutionalism without a Constitutional Treaty?* (2008) 109, at 115–119; Christiansen and Dobbels, *supra* note 3, at 1173; Peers and Costa, 'Accountability for Delegated and Implementing Acts after the Treaty of Lisbon', 18 *European Law Journal* (2012) 427, at 454–455.

[72] Craig, *supra* note 71, 115.

[73] Craig, *The Lisbon Treaty*, *supra* note 27, 267.

[74] Christiansen and Dobbels, *supra* note 3, at 1173.

[75] Peers and Costa, *supra* note 71, 453.

[76] *Ibid.*, at 454–455.

[77] Common Understanding: Delegated Acts, Council doc. 8753/11, 10 April 2011, point 4.

[78] EP-Commission Framework Agreement, *supra* note 44, para. 15 (emphasis added). Details are provided in Annex I of the agreement.

The fact that EP experts may attend expert group meetings is indeed a move in the right direction in terms of accountability. However, a report by the EP points to a number of problems in this regard, such as the need for the Commission to simplify the procedure which the EP representatives must go through in order to attend each meeting; and the need for the Commission to notify the EP of the calendar of expert group meetings in a more timely manner.[79] In addition, the EP points out the need to make a clear distinction between expert group and comitology committee meetings.[80] The reason for this is that the same experts that prepare delegated acts may also participate in comitology committees.[81] Since the EP is precluded from taking part in the work of the latter, it wants to make sure that the preparation of delegated acts is not discussed at comitology meetings.[82] Some research also suggests that the Council as an institution (not to just Member State representatives outside its institutional framework) is trying to influence the preparation of delegated acts through expert groups.[83] Lastly, a recent letter sent by the European Ombudsman to the Commission, as a part of her own-initiative inquiry on the composition of expert groups, highlights additional problems related to the membership and transparency of these bodies.[84] All these issues make the effectiveness of democratic controls over the Commission under the new delegated acts procedure highly questionable.

5. Implementing Acts and Accountability

In relation to implementing acts, in theory, both the Council and the EP are *not* to be involved in controlling the Commission as after the Lisbon reforms, this is the prerogative of the Member States—outside the institutional framework of the Council. Yet it seems that due to channels of communication, the Council does in fact control the Commission while the EP is unable to do the same. Furthermore, the new comitology regulation may render the control over the Commission less effective than in the past. These issues are further detailed in the next section.

A. Controlling the Commission—The New Comitology Regulation

Article 291 TFEU on implementing acts emphasizes that Member States are primarily in charge of implementation. However, when 'uniform conditions for implementing legally binding Union acts are needed' the Commission or the

[79] European Parliament, 'One Hundred Steps Forward: The European Parliament and the Upgrading of European Democracy since the Lisbon Treaty', Report prepared by the Cabinet of the Secretary-General of the EP, April 2014, at 96.

[80] *Ibid.* [81] *Ibid.*, at 95. [82] *Ibid.*, at 96.

[83] Christiansen and Dobbels, *supra* note 3, at 1169; Christiansen and Dobbels, 'Comitology and Delegated Acts after Lisbon: How the European Parliament Lost the Implementation Game', 16 *European Integration Online Papers* (2012), at 17.

[84] Letter to the European Commission requesting an opinion in the European Ombudsman's own-initiative inquiry OI/6/2014/NF concerning the composition of Commission expert groups, available at http://www.ombudsman.europa.eu/en/cases/correspondence.faces/en/58861/html.bookmark (last visited 18 January 2017).

Council—the latter in 'duly justified cases' and in the cases provided for in Articles 24 and 26 TEU—may exercise implementing powers. The formulation in Article 291 TFEU that implementing acts can be made pursuant to 'legally binding Union acts' means that these acts can be based both on a legislative and on a delegated act. This suggests that the Commission may be able to sub-delegate implementing powers to itself through delegated rule-making, without much democratic oversight.[85]

In exercising its implementing powers, the Commission is formally accountable to the Member States which exercise control over it based on Regulation 182/2011[86]—the revised comitology regulation, adopted by the Council and the EP according to the ordinary legislative procedure. This is a major change from the pre-Lisbon state of affairs, where *the Council* was in charge of controlling the Commission under rules which it adopted, with EP *consultation*. However, research shows that although the new comitology rules were adopted according to the ordinary legislative procedure, in practice the EP was sidelined, and the negotiations were primarily dominated by the Council and the Commission.[87]

Regulation 182/2011 entered into force on 1 March 2011. Unlike the previous comitology regime, it entails only two procedures—the advisory and the examination procedures. Where no agreement is reached in the context of the examination procedure, the draft implementing act may be forwarded to an appeal committee, which is chaired by the Commission under the current comitology rules. In line with the objective of separation between executive and legislative powers of the EU institutions (pursued by the Treaty reformers), the new regulation does not entail any *formal* involvement of the Council or the EP in comitology procedures. However, some scholars argued that despite the new rules, the Council might still be indirectly involved in comitology through 'channels of communication' between Member State representatives in the Council and those in comitology committees.[88] This presumption is supported by recent research, which suggests that the appeal committee of comitology may still be very much dominated by the 'Council in disguise'. According to Christiansen and Dobbels:

> In four out of the five first meetings [of the appeal committee] after the entry into force of regulation 182/2011, a majority of member states were represented by their Deputy Permanent Representative (DPR), almost mirroring a meeting of Coreper I... It thus seems that even though the Council has been formally removed from the new procedure, the appeal committee mirrors its role, and is in fact the Council in disguise – the only difference being that meetings are presided over and organised by the Commission, and that a majority of member states are represented at DPR, instead of ministerial level.[89]

[85] Hofmann, *supra* note 26, at 502.

[86] Regulation 182/2011 laying down the rules and general principles concerning mechanisms for control by Member States of the Commission's exercise of implementing powers, OJ L 2011 55/13.

[87] Christiansen and Dobbels, *supra* note 3, at 1166. See also Christiansen and Dobbels, *supra* note 83.

[88] Craig, 'Delegated Acts, Implementing Acts and the New Comitology Regulation', 36 *European Law Review* (2011) 671, at 686.

[89] Christiansen and Dobbels, *supra* note 3, 1168.

Thus, it appears that the Council has found its way back into comitology. At the same time, the EP has no means of influencing the Commission in a manner similar to the Council. Since the Commission was able to secure the presidency of the appeal committee (after difficult negotiations with the Council and with the backing of the EP), this gives it considerable influence in the comitology procedures.[90] Therefore, when it comes to controls under the new comitology regulation, and particularly in the appeal committee, it is mainly a game between the Commission and the Council, from which the EP is left out.

The new regulation does oblige the Commission to make the following available to both the Council *and the EP*: the agendas of committee meetings; the draft implementing acts on which the committees are asked to deliver an opinion; and the final draft implementing acts following delivery of the opinion of the committees (this is done at the same time as the transmission of these documents to committee members).[91] Moreover, both the EP and the Council enjoy a right of scrutiny: in cases when the basic act is adopted according to the OLP, the EP or the Council may object to a draft implementing act if in their view it 'exceeds the implementing powers provided for in the basic act'.[92] In that case the Commission will review the act and inform the two institutions whether it will maintain, amend, or withdraw the draft implementing act.[93] Since the reference is specifically to acts adopted under the OLP, this implies that the right of scrutiny does not apply when the basic act is made according to an SLP or when an implementing act is based on a delegated act.[94] In addition, in a 2014 resolution on the delegated and implementing powers of the Commission, the Parliament stated that 'the time between the transmission of final draft implementing acts and their adoption by the Commission is often too short, thereby not allowing for adequate oversight by Parliament'; therefore, it urged the Commission to 'fully respect the Parliament's right to scrutinise final draft implementing acts within a period of one month in accordance with the 2008 agreement between Parliament and Commission on comitology procedures'.[95] Thus, here too the EP is in a weak position, as, in practice, the Commission is not giving it enough time to exercise its right of scrutiny effectively.

B. Controlling the Council?

As stated earlier, according to Article 291 TFEU, the Council may exercise implementing powers in 'duly justified cases' and in the cases provided for in Articles 24 and 26 TEU. Thus, while it may no longer enact what are now termed 'delegated

[90] Molino and Sellez, 'The Implementation of the Lisbon Treaty through the Reform of the "Comitology System": Self-Empowerment of the European Commission?', in M. Chang and J. Monar (eds), *The European Commission in the Post-Lisbon Era of Crises: Between Political Leadership and Policy Management* (2013) 87.

[91] Article 10(4) Regulation 182/2011, *supra* note 86.

[92] Article 11 Regulation 182/2011, *supra* note 86.

[93] *Ibid.*

[94] Craig, *supra* note 88, 683–684.

[95] EP Resolution of 25 February 2014 on follow up on the delegation of legislative powers and control by Member States of the Commission's exercise of implementing powers (2012/2323(INI)), point 14.

acts', it has retained the power to adopt implementing acts. This is problematic considering the Convention's aim of creating a clear separation between the legislative and executive powers of the Union institutions[96] and from the point of view of accountability as, unlike the Commission's implementing powers, which are subject to the comitology regulation, those of the Council are not governed by a clear accountability framework.

The Council's exercise of implementing powers 'in duly justified cases' is particularly questionable from the point of view of accountability, as this vague formulation leaves much room for arbitrary exercise of power. Based on Article 291(2) TFEU, the Council also exercises implementing powers under Articles 24 and 26 TEU. Under Article 24(1) TEU, the Council (along with the European Council) defines and implements the CFSP. Article 26(2) TEU provides that 'the Council shall frame the common foreign and security policy and take the decisions necessary for defining and implementing it on the basis of the general guidelines and strategic lines defined by the European Council'. When it comes to the implementation of CFSP, the EP is involved to a certain extent, either by providing consent, being consulted, or being informed.[97] Article 36 TEU, second subparagraph, also provides that '[t]he European Parliament may address questions or make recommendations to the Council or the High Representative. Twice a year it shall hold a debate on progress in implementing the common foreign and security policy, including the common security and defence policy'. The EP also uses its budgetary powers as a means of gaining leverage in CFSP matters.[98] Nevertheless, it is still the case that the Council is not truly accountable to the EP in this area.[99] Also noteworthy is the fact that the EU Courts have very limited jurisdiction in CFSP.[100] Accordingly, the low level of accountability to the EP cannot be mitigated through full legal accountability.

6. Accountability and Non-legislative Acts Based on the Treaties

This section highlights the accountability of the Council, the Commission, the European Council, and the ECB in the adoption of binding legal acts directly on the basis of the Lisbon Treaty.[101]

The Council has a policy-making role in numerous areas such as the conclusion of international agreements,[102] competition,[103] state aid,[104] Area of Freedom, Security

[96] See Lenaerts and Desomer, 'Towards a Hierarchy of Legal Acts in the European Union? Simplification of Legal Instruments and Procedures', 11 *European Law Journal* (2005) 744, at 756.

[97] See, in general, Articles 205–222 TFEU on EU external action. See, more specifically, Articles 207, 209, 212, 214, and 218 TFEU. For a discussion of the EP's role in the conclusion of international agreements, see Section 4(D) of the chapter by Alan Dashwood in this volume.

[98] P. Eeckhout, *EU External Relations Law* (2011), at 497. See also, Kohler, *supra* note 3, at 608, on the role of interinstitutional agreements in strengthening the role of the EP in CFSP.

[99] Eeckhout, *supra* note 98.

[100] Article 24(1) TEU, second paragraph, and Article 275 TFEU.

[101] For a discussion on non-legislative acts directly based on the Treaties, see, e.g. Dougan, *supra* note 2, at 644–648; De Witte, *supra* note 19, at 100–102.

[102] Article 218(6) TFEU. [103] Article 103(1) TFEU. [104] Article 109 TFEU.

and Justice (AFSJ),[105] and CFSP.[106] In these areas it adopts non-legislative acts directly based on the Lisbon Treaty. When adopting these acts, the Council is not required to deliberate in public or to send the draft act to the national parliaments. A seemingly comprehensive summary of these types of acts adopted by the Council on the basis of the TFEU is provided by Best.[107] He identified 18 different procedures (a total of 25 different TFEU legal bases) of this kind.[108] It must be noted that while some of these procedures used by the Council require EP consent, most of them do not.[109] Moreover, many of these non-legislative acts are very similar to legislative acts adopted by the Council on the basis of SLP, which require EP consultation.[110] Thus, the distinction between the latter variant of legislative acts and this version of non-legislative acts is highly arbitrary, and often simply based on the inclusion or exclusion of the term 'special legislative procedure' in a given Treaty provision.[111] What aggravates this issue is the fact that the substance of the act often has nothing to do with its classification as either legislative or non-legislative. Some legislative acts adopted according to the SLP are administrative in nature,[112] while some non-legislative acts (e.g. the measures under Articles 103 and 109 TFEU discussed in Section 2) are acts of general application and legislative in substance.[113]

The Commission adopts non-legislative acts based on the Treaty in the areas of competition and state aid.[114] In this area, the Commission enjoys a great deal of discretion.[115] While political accountability may not be the best way to oversee this discretion, stronger review by an independent adjudicator would be welcomed by many commentators.[116]

Under the Treaty of Lisbon, the European Council exercises a wide range of non-legislative functions.[117] It decides on certain constitutional matters, the most important of which is its role in the Treaty revision process under Article 48 TEU. It also serves an important function in enlargement (as it specifies the conditions of

[105] Articles 70, 74 TFEU. [106] Articles 24(1) and 26(2) TEU.

[107] Best, *supra* note 17, at 93–95. He states that these procedures are 'quite apart from the specific procedures for CFSP and CSDP under the TEU'.

[108] Cf. Stancanelli, who identified a total of 76 legal bases in the Constitutional Treaty for non-legislative acts of the Council. See Stancanelli, 'Le système décisionnel de l'Union', in G. Amato, H. Bribosia, and B. De Witte (eds), *Genèse et destinée de la Constitution européenne/Genesis and Destiny of the European Constitution* (2007) 485, at 532–534.

[109] See Best, *supra* note 17, at 94–95. [110] Türk, *supra* note 29, at 71.

[111] See Dougan, *supra* note 2, at 646–648; Craig, *supra* note 27, at 257.

[112] De Witte, *supra* note 19, at 92. [113] Dougan, *supra* note 2, at 647.

[114] Articles 105(3), 106(3), and 108(4) TFEU. Article 105(3) provides that the Commission 'may adopt regulations relating to the categories of agreement in respect of which the Council has adopted a regulation or a directive pursuant to Article 103(2)(b)'; Article 106(3) states: 'The Commission shall ensure the application of the provisions of this Article and shall, where necessary, address appropriate directives or decisions to Member States'; Article 108(4) provides: 'The Commission may adopt regulations relating to the categories of State aid that the Council has, pursuant to Article 109, determined may be exempted from the procedure provided for by paragraph 3 of this Article.'

[115] Wils, 'Discretion and Prioritisation in Public Antitrust Enforcement, in Particular EU Antitrust Enforcement', 34 *World Competition* (2011) 353.

[116] Wilsher, 'Achieving Better Decision-making in Competition Enforcement Cases: A Public Law Perspective on the Role of the Executive and the Courts', 30 *World Competition* (2007) 263, at 269–271.

[117] Stancanelli, *supra* note 108, identified 17 legal bases *in the Constitutional Treaty* for non-legislative acts of the European Council.

eligibility for EU membership under Article 49 TEU) and secession of a Member State from the Union (under Article 50 TEU). Moreover, it decides on a number of key institutional matters such as the composition of the EP and the Commission; the appointment and dismissal of the High Representative; the configurations and the presidency of the Council; and the selection of the President and the Board of the ECB.[118] Another highly important area where it adopts non-legislative acts is CFSP. As Dougan rightly observes: 'One of the most important categories of non-legislative acts adopted directly under the Treaties is measures of the European Council and the Council in the field of the CFSP (where the use of legislative instruments is precluded, and unanimity remains the general rule)'.[119] It is very well known that the EP has a very limited role in CFSP.[120] Therefore, at present, it does not have the power to scrutinize the European Council's or the Council's decision-making in this area. The President of the European Council is also largely unaccountable to the EP, as the latter has no sanctioning powers over the former.[121] Thus, the European Council's non-legislative decision-making is not subject to any formal accountability measures other than the requirement to inform the EP after each one of its meetings.

The ECB is also authorized to adopt various forms of non-legislative acts: regulations, decisions, recommendations, and opinions.[122] It is clear that '[t]he institutions and bodies of the Community – with the notable exception of the Court of Justice – do not have the power to approve, suspend, annul or defer decisions of the ECB, nor are the institutions entitled to vote during the meetings of the Executive Board and the Governing Council'.[123] Given this high degree of institutional independence, the ECB accountability to the EP seems rather thin.

The ECB's accountability to the EP is governed by Article 284(3) TFEU (ex-Article 113(3) TEC) which provides that the ECB will send the EP an annual report on its activities and on the monetary policy of both the previous and current year.[124] Moreover, the President of the ECB is to present this report to the EP which then may hold a general debate on it. In addition, the President of the ECB and the other members of the Executive Board may, at the request of the EP or on their own initiative, be heard by the competent committees of the EP. While Article 113(3) TEC only mandated the presentation of the annual report to the EP, Rule 113 of the EP Rules of Procedure[125] created the additional requirement of the ECB President appearing before the ECON committee at least four times a year.[126] These

[118] Respectively Articles 14(2) TEU, 17 TEU, 18(1) TEU, 236(a) and (b) TFEU, and 283(2) TFEU.

[119] Dougan, *supra* note 2, at 645.

[120] See 'The EU's Common Foreign and Security Policy: The Quest for Democracy' Special issue of the *Journal of European Public Policy*, Volume 18, Issue 8 (2011).

[121] De Waele and Broeksteeg, *supra* note 56, at 1066–7. See also Bovens and Curtin, *supra* note 56.

[122] Article 132(1) TFEU.

[123] Opinion of AG Jacobs in Case C-11/00, *Commission v. ECB* (known as the '*OLAF case*'), [2003] ECR I-07147 (ECLI:EU:C:2002:556), at para. 152.

[124] This part draws on Bovens and Curtin, *supra* note 56.

[125] Rules of Procedure of the European Parliament, 7th Parliamentary Term, March 2014 version, available at http://www.europarl.europa.eu/sides/getDoc.do?pubRef=-//EP//NONSGML+RULES-EP+20140310+0+DOC+PDF+V0//EN&language=EN (last visited 25 September 2017).

[126] Fasone, 'European Economic Governance and Parliamentary Representation. What Place for the European Parliament?', 20 *European Law Journal* (2014) 164, at 175.

appearances of the ECB President before the EP—in plenary and in the ECON committee—is what became known as the Monetary Dialogue.[127] Finally, according to Rule 118 of the EP Rules of Procedure, any Member of the European Parliament may also put a question to the ECB for a written answer.

Accountability to the EP within the framework of the ECB's newly acquired supervisory tasks is governed by Article 20 SSM Regulation[128] and the Interinstitutional Agreement signed by the ECB and the EP.[129] The requirements of accountability with regard to the supervisory role of the ECB are more demanding than those in relation to its monetary policy function. Thus, under Article 20, SSM Regulation, the Chair of the Supervisory Board is not only required to present an annual report to the EP in plenary, reply to questions from MEPs, and appear before the ECON committee upon request, but she must also divulge sensitive information—although in 'confidential oral discussions behind closed doors'—and cooperate with EP investigations.

Views diverge on the question of whether the EP is able to hold the ECB accountable through monetary dialogues,[130] and only time will tell whether the supervisory hearings in the context of the ECB's powers of banking supervision will prove to be an effective accountability mechanism.

7. Concluding Remarks

Increasing parliamentary accountability was a key objective of the Lisbon Treaty reformers in their endeavours to enhance the democratic legitimacy of the EU. Yet as the discussion in this chapter reveals, the final product of the reforms—the Lisbon Treaty—leaves much room for improvement with respect to accountability in the new system of legal acts. Moreover, the silver lining of this analysis is the wide discrepancy between the formal rules and the informal practices of the institutions post-Lisbon which give rise to further accountability concerns.

[127] *Ibid.*

[128] Council Regulation 1024/2013 of 15 October 2013 conferring specific tasks on the ECB concerning policies relating to the prudential supervision of credit institutions, OJ 2013 L 287/63.

[129] Interinstitutional Agreement between the European Parliament and the European Central Bank on the practical modalities of the exercise of democratic accountability and oversight over the exercise of the tasks conferred on the ECB within the framework of the Single Supervisory Mechanism, OJ 2013 L 320/1.

[130] On the EP–ECB monetary dialogue, see Eijffinger and Mujagic, 'An Assessment of the Effectiveness of the Monetary Dialogue on the ECB's Accountability and Transparency: A Qualitative Approach', 39 *Intereconomics* (2004) 190; Amtenbrink and van Duin, 'The European Central Bank Before the European Parliament: Theory and Practice after Ten Years of Monetary Dialogue', 34 *European Law Review* (2009) 561; Claeys, Hallerberg, and Tschekassin, 'European Central Bank Accountability: How The Monetary Dialogue Could Evolve' (2014) Bruegel Policy Contribution, Issue 2014/04. See also the critical views on Monetary Dialogue 2009–2014 expressed by various scholars in their briefings for the ECON Committee meeting of 3 March 2014: http://www.europarl.europa.eu/committees/en/econ/monetary-dialogue.html?tab=2014 (last visited 25 September 2017).

A. Reforming Legislative and Executive Rule-making

With regard to legislative acts, two types of acts were identified as particularly problematic from the perspective of accountability: those adopted by the Council under the consultation variety of the SLP and those adopted by the Council directly on the basis of the Treaty, yet virtually indistinguishable from legislative acts both in terms of their adoption procedure and their content. In each of these cases the democratic checks over the Council are inadequate, to say the least. Future Treaty reform would be required in order to address this issue. Moreover, the fact that the extension of codecision to many more areas of EU activity was accompanied by increased reliance on trilogue negotiations constitutes a major accountability deficit since, as was discussed earlier, this mode of rule-making advantages the Council and the Commission at the expense of the EP and open dialogue and deliberation. Given the prevalence of trilogues in the post-Lisbon era, more could be done by all three institutions in order to increase the transparency of these negotiations, for example, through greater public access to the relevant documents and more open deliberation.[131] As to the informal involvement of the European Council in legislative rule-making (particularly since the beginning of the euro crisis), this development must necessarily be accompanied by greater accountability of the European Council to the EP.

Regarding delegated acts, the EP's limited resources for effectively exercising controls over delegated rule-making by the Commission has been highlighted. This is a major concern which the Parliament needs to address promptly. Another important area, which urgently requires attention, is expert groups. Considering their crucial role in delegated rule-making, these groups should be subject to the same transparency standards as comitology committees.[132] At the very least, the Commission's online register of expert groups, which has been in place since 2005, should be complete and up to date.[133] In addition, the Commission should follow up on the recommendations of the European Ombudsman regarding the transparency of expert groups.[134] Lastly, the Council must refrain from trying to influence the preparation of delegated acts through these groups.

The gap between formal rules and informal practices is also evident in the making of implementing acts. As stated earlier, although the new comitology regulation was adopted under the ordinary legislative procedure, in practice, the EP's input into the making of these rules was very limited. While the Commission has increased its powers under the new regulation (e.g. presiding over the appeal committee) and the Council is *de facto* influencing the work of comitology committees, the EP is struggling even to exercise its rights of scrutiny over the Commission. This renders the

[131] See further, Huber and Shackleton, *supra* note 57, at 1052–1053. Specifically with regard to changes (that should be) undertaken by the EP, see Reh, 'Is Informal Politics Undemocratic? Trilogues, Early Agreements and the Selection Model of Representation', 21 *Journal of European Public Policy* (2014) 822. See also the chapter by Päivi Leino in this volume for a discussion on access to EP, Commission, and Council documents in legislative rule-making.

[132] Peers and Costa, *supra* note 71, at 454–455.

[133] The register is available at http://ec.europa.eu/transparency/regexpert/ (last visited 25 September 2017).

[134] See *supra* note 84.

new comitology regime far from optimal in terms of democratic accountability. The lack of adequate controls over the Council's implementing powers further contribute to this problem.

Finally, with regard to non-legislative acts directly based on the Treaties, the Council's adoption of these acts is especially disconcerting as many of them are virtually indistinguishable from legislative acts both in terms of their adoption procedure and content. Resolving this issue would require Treaty reform.

B. Constitutionalizing Executive Rule-making Procedures

Values such as publicity and participation could be crucial normative standards to be included in the further design of administrative procedures in the EU. This goes beyond current reform efforts[135] and existing suggestions to expand these to executive rule-making procedures.[136] It would apply horizontally across all the institutions irrespective of their powers and functions. Special rules may apply in specific contexts (e.g. deliberations among the judges or ECB deliberations). Procedures and the application of 'meta norms' can have a decisive impact on substantive outcomes. Procedures channel the flow of information that decision-making requires and reduces information asymmetries between separate institutions and actors.[137] They are techniques that allow for the balancing and articulation of interests that lie at the core of the administrative function, and can concretize constitutional rights.[138] In the words of Stewart, the administrative procedure is a 'surrogate of political process'.[139] Proceduralization may enhance the rationality of decision-making and the equality of access. First significant steps are now being taken in systematizing, at least to some extent, the more visibly changing rules of the game.[140] Those first steps include the drafting of a proposal for a regulation on the administrative procedure law of the EU by the JURI committee of the European Parliament.[141] The preparatory stages of decision-making, from the moment of its being put on the agenda to the moment of its formal adoption, are precisely the stages that are newly influenced by core constitutional principles. This may now be made visible and operationalized—even if the road ahead is long and full of uncertainty. It shows that even in the absence of formal Treaty reform processes, progress can be made both in law and in practice.

[135] EP Resolution of 15 January 2013 with recommendations to the Commission on a Law of Administrative Procedure of the European Union (2012/2024), (2012/2024(INL)), available at http://www.europarl.europa.eu/sides/getDoc.do?type=TA&reference=P7-TA-2013-0004&language=EN (last visited 18 January 2017).

[136] Curtin, Hofmann, and Mendes, 'Constitutionalising EU Executive Rule-Making Procedures: A Research Agenda', 19 *European Law Journal* (2013) 1.

[137] McCubbins *et al.*, 'Administrative Procedures as Instruments of Political Control', 3 *Journal of Law, Economics, and Organization* (1987) 243, at 246 and 255 (referring to the US context).

[138] Curtin, Hofmann, and Mendes, *supra* note 136, at 3.

[139] Stewart, 'The Reformation of American Administrative Law', 88 *Harvard Law Review* (1975) 1669.

[140] Curtin, Hofmann, and Mendes, *supra* note 136, at 3.

[141] This draft builds on the work done within ReNEUAL—the Research Network on EU Administrative Law and its Model Rules 2014 which was designed to identify best practices in different specific policies of the EU, http://www.reneual.eu (last visited 25 September 2017).

2

The Politics of Efficient Compromise in the Adoption of EU Legal Acts

*Päivi Leino**

1. A Legal Framework for Political Deliberation

The EU Treaties create a legal framework within which the EU Commission, the European Parliament, and the Council interact with the purpose of adopting EU legislation.[1] In this chapter, I explore what legal rules affect EU legislative decision-making and how legal arguments, concepts, and tools affect political discourse and the exercise of power. My interest relates to the EU law-making process, and what factors and players influence decision-making. I focus on the interplay between formal and informal rules of legislative decision-making in the context of the ordinary legislative procedure.[2] I argue that the current framework for the adoption of legal acts builds on flexibility, which relies on agreement among the institutions. The EU institutions and Member State governments justify the current framework with the need to guarantee efficient law-making. The legal rules regulating law-making in the EU set some limits to institutional imagination. The arrangements benefit particular players in the process and come at a high cost for the implementation of rights of participation.

I mirror these questions in particular against the core provisions on democratic principles included in the Treaty on the European Union (TEU). The principle of representative democracy is respected through the participation of the European Parliament, representing the citizens directly at EU level, and through the governments forming the European Council and the Council that are democratically accountable either to their national parliaments or to their citizens. Even participatory

* Thanks to all the participants in the Academy of European Law and the October 'Authors' Workshop' for discussions, and Dr Anna Hyvärinen and Dr Samuli Miettinen for a number of useful comments on an earlier draft. The manuscript was largely completed soon after the October 2014 workshop, but I have been able to add some references to developments in early 2015.

[1] Even other institutions and bodies participate in the EU legislative procedures. The focus of the current contribution is, however, on the three main EU institutions: the European Parliament, the Commission, and the Council.

[2] Under Article 289 TFEU, in addition to the ordinary legislative procedure, which is regulated under Article 294 TFEU, legal acts may also be adopted in special legislative procedures.

democracy enjoys a pivotal role in the new Treaty framework. In order to guarantee the right of 'every citizen' to 'participate in the democratic life of the Union', the Treaty establishes that '[d]ecisions shall be taken as openly and as closely as possible to the citizen' and that both citizens and representatives should be given opportunities to 'make known and publicly exchange their views in all areas of Union action'.[3] These principles are of particular importance in the legislative context. The Treaties place the institutions under an obligation to maintain an open, transparent, and regular dialogue with representative associations and civil society. The rights related to, and limits of, participation also come to the fore when discussing the role of the thousands of lobbyists targeting European institutions in order to influence legislation during various stages of the legislative procedure.

From a constitutional point of view, the role of law in European integration has been elaborated in the jurisprudence of the Court of Justice, including its ruling in *Les Verts*. This case introduced the slogan referring to the Union as 'a Community based on the rule of law'.[4] The maxim was justified with how the law and the EU Founding Treaties subject EU measures to constitutional review. For EU lawyers, the rule of law principle is usually approached in terms of legal basis and division of competence. They concern questions relating to the EU competence to act and what types of measures it can take. The choice of legal basis has various implications both for the various stages of the legislative procedure, but ultimately also for its substantive outcome. The European Court of Justice (CJEU) tends to stress that the choice of legal basis for an EU measure must rest on objective factors that are amenable to judicial review.[5] The questions relating to legal basis and competence are routinely treated as a domain reserved for lawyers, as if it is somehow separate from policy-making.

'Law' is linked to the legitimacy of the EU. It appeals to those wishing to limit power politics, integrationist ambitions, and institutional discretion. Law thus has a 'powerfully symbolic dimension, an important aspect of which entails the invocation of a claim to legitimacy'.[6] These considerations are reflected in the second part of this study focusing on the formal and informal rules of the EU legislative procedure, and link with questions of participation, accountability, and democratic decision-making. The legal basis thus also serves a guarantee function, ultimately intended to protect

[3] See Article 10 TEU.

[4] Case C-294/83, *Les Verts v. Parliament*, [1986] ECR 01339 (ECLI:EU:C:1986:166), at para. 23. The case concerned whether the European Parliament could act as a respondent in annulment proceedings initiated by Les Verts—Parti écologiste, a French association. The Court affirmed this, with reference to how '[i]t must first be emphasized in this regard that the European Economic Community is a Community based on the rule of law, inasmuch as neither its Member States nor its institutions can avoid a review of the question whether the measures adopted by them are in conformity with the basic constitutional charter, the Treaty' (para. 23). The Court then moved on to explain the complete system of legal remedies and procedures permitting the Court of Justice to review the legality of measures adopted by the institutions.

[5] See, e.g. Case C-411/06, *Commission v. Parliament and Council*, [2009] ECR I-07585 (ECLI:EU:C:2009:518), at para. 45.

[6] De Búrca, 'Rethinking Law in Neofunctionalist Theory', 12 *Journal of European Public Policy* (2005) 310, at 319–320.

individuals from *ultra vires* acts by the EU institutions.[7] However, a discrepancy exists 'between the formal allocation of powers provided in the Treaties and the actual legal practice', which has so far been little studied.[8] Keeping in mind the very general formulation of many of the EU objectives in the Treaties, the implementation of these objectives and thus also EU competence to act cannot take place without the attribution of a significant degree of discretionary powers.[9]

Discretion and flexibility have a key function in the EU legislative process. The Treaties establish only its main building blocks. Analysing the EU decision-making process and its dynamics has remained the domain of political scientists. Their studies remain largely unknown to lawyers, and seem fundamentally detached from the legal considerations relating to EU decision-making.[10] Lawyers tend to focus on formal institutional decision-making rules reflected in the Treaty, which establish the main procedural stages. These studies often seem remote from the daily practice of decision-making. Political decision-making processes are multidimensional and transcend the formal procedures regulated by the Treaties. Law-making in the EU builds to a large extent on practice and interinstitutional agreements. These more informal arrangements are linked to the way in which 'the EU institutions make conscious decisions about whether to be bound in their interactions by informal institutional rules or follow the normal constitutional paths prescribed by the treaty'.[11]

In fact, as Kleine has demonstrated, the EU governments and institutions 'have adopted a number of practices that seem to *contradict* the formal rules' very purpose... In short, a plethora of informal practices, nowhere mentioned in the treaties, operate parallel to the formal rules and yet differ from them substantially.' She calls these practices 'informal governance'.[12] The indeterminacy of the formal rules, complemented by the existence of informal rules, also makes it difficult to measure the relative power of the Commission, European Parliament, and the Council in the legislative process.[13] The interinstitutional relationships are affected by a great number of factors reaching beyond the formal rules of the (ordinary) legislative procedure.

My interest relates to the relationship between 'law' and 'politics' in the adoption of legislative acts. I combine studies of EU decision-making with legal arguments relating to competence, in particular CJEU jurisprudence concerning the legal limits of institutional action within the framework of the legislative procedure.

[7] Barents, 'The Internal Market Unlimited: Some Observations on the Legal Basis of Community Legislation', 30 *Common Market Law Review* (1993) 85, at 92.

[8] Azoulai, 'Introduction' in L. Azoulai (ed.), *The Question of Competence in the European Union* (2014) 1, at 3.

[9] See, e.g. Barents, *supra* note 7, at 89.

[10] See, however, Anna Hyvärinen's doctoral thesis, Suomen mahdollisuudet vaikuttaa Euroopan unionin lainsäädäntömenettelyyn ('How can Finland exert influence in EU law-making?') (May 2015) defended at the University of Turku, which elegantly combines methods of law and political science in examining EU decision-making, available at http://urn.fi/URN:ISBN:978-951-29-6122-1 (last visited 16 January 2017).

[11] Häge and Kaeding, 'Reconsidering the European Parliament's Legislative Influence: Formal vs. Informal Procedures', 29(3) *European Integration* (2007) 341.

[12] M. Kleine, *Informal Governance in the European Union. How Governments Make International Organizations Work* (2013), at 3 (emphasis in original).

[13] Thomson and Hosli, 'Who Has Power in the EU? The Commission, Council and Parliament in Legislative Decision-making', 44(2) *JCMS* (2006) 391, at 393.

While there is very little case law on the different stages of the legislative procedure, the Court jurisprudence relating to competence litigation offers interesting avenues for examining institutional politics. An interdisciplinary approach that combines legal and political studies seems justified by the way in which law and politics rely heavily on each other in the process of integration:

> Integration is fundamentally a political process: whether to engage in it, its pace, shape, success and failure are largely determined by political actors and political will. But the law has a vital role to play in the process. It defines many of the political actors and the framework within which they operate, controlling and limiting their actions and relations and determining, at least partially, the effects and effectiveness of their acts. At the same time it performs a role in ordering social life, translating the highly visible political acts into more mundane daily applications and, through this implication, it determines the implications of the political decisions.[14]

Law and politics constantly interact also in the context of EU law-making. Jean-Paul Jacqué, with years of insight into the politics of EU law-making, describes how:

> Law is a natural instrument of the political debate, since states prefer to oppose a measure through legal arguments that give an objective appearance to their political preferences rather than openly displaying a political position that is purely based on national interests.[15]

In the following, I will first examine the interplay between the formal and informal rules relating to the choice of legal basis for a legal act. I will focus in particular on the relationship between the claimed objectivity of these choices and their institutional implications, and examine the informal rules flowing from the formal rules established in the Court's jurisprudence. I will then turn to the formal and informal rules relating to the stages of the legislative procedure, examining in particular interinstitutional power relations and participation in the process, and how these choices are affected by legal rules.

2. The Politics of Legal Basis in the EU Legislative Process

A. The Choice of Legal Basis is a Constitutional Matter

The fundamental consideration in every EU legislative procedure relates to the choice of legal basis: being a Union based on conferred powers, the EU cannot act without an appropriate one. The key position of the choice of legal basis in the EU legislative process rests on two fundamental premises flowing from the Court of Justice's jurisprudence: that the choice of legal basis is a constitutional matter, and that it should rest on objective factors amenable to judicial review.

[14] M. Cappelletti, M. Seccombe, and J. Weiler, *Integration Through Law* (1986), Book 1, Volume 1, Chapter 2, at 4.

[15] Jacqué, 'The Role of Legal Services in the Elaboration of European Legislation' in A. Vauchez and B. De Witte (eds), *Lawyering Europe. European Law as a Transnational Social Field* (2013) 43, at 43.

Various Treaty provisions concern the principle of conferral or allocation of powers, and thus the fundamental question of whether the EU is competent to act, albeit on a general level.[16]

> Under the principle of conferral, the Union shall act only within the limits of the competences conferred upon it by the Member States in the Treaties to attain the objectives set out therein. Competences not conferred upon the Union in the Treaties remain with the Member States.[17]

The duty to indicate a legal basis is linked in the Court jurisprudence specifically to the principle of the allocation of powers:

> The choice of the appropriate legal basis has constitutional significance. Since the Community has conferred powers only, it must tie the Protocol to a Treaty provision which empowers it to approve such a measure. To proceed on an incorrect legal basis is therefore liable to invalidate the act . . .[18]

According to the Court, the principle of conferred powers also requires that the Treaty basis must be determined before the Union acts, and appear in the measure taken.[19] The Court has specified that the Union acts 'ordinarily on the basis of specific powers which . . . are not necessarily the express consequence of specific provisions of the Treaty but may also be implied from them'.[20] Mere practice cannot derogate from rules laid down in the Treaty.[21] The indication of a legal basis is linked to the essential procedural requirement of stating reasons,[22] and an explicit reference forms an indispensable part of such requirements in particular 'where, in its absence, the parties concerned and the Court are left uncertain as to the precise legal basis'.[23] Therefore,

[16] See, e.g. Article 3(6) TEU, Article 4(1) TEU, and Article 5 TEU.

[17] Article 5(2) TEU.

[18] Opinion 2/00, *Opinion pursuant to Article 300 EC*, [2001] ECR I-09713 (ECLI:EU:C:2001:664), at para. 5.

[19] Case C-291/98, *Sarrió v. Commission*, [2000] ECR I-09991 (ECLI:EU:C:2000:631), at para. 73, relating to a Commission decision on fines on undertakings; Case C-378/00, *Commission v. Parliament and Council*, [2003] ECR I-00937 (ECLI:EU:C:2003:42), at para. 66, in which the Court concluded that a declaration adopted by the Council alone cannot in any event serve as a statement of reasons for a regulation adopted jointly by the Parliament and the Council.

[20] Opinion 2/94, *Opinion pursuant to Article 228 of the EC Treaty*, [1996] ECR I-01759 (ECLI:EU:C:1996:140), at paras 23–25.

[21] Case C-68/86, *United Kingdom v. Council*, [1988] ECR 00855 (ECLI:EU:C:1988:85), at para. 24; Case C-271/94, *Parliament v. Council*, [1996] ECR I-01689 (ECLI:EU:C:1996:133), at para. 24. The relevant legal basis is determined separately in each case, since 'it is not possible to determine the legal basis for a measure in the light of the legal basis used for the adoption of other Community measures which might, in certain cases, display similar characteristics'. See C-155/07, *Parliament v. Council*, [2008] ECR I-08103 (ECLI:EU:C:2008:605), at para. 74.

[22] See C-291/98, *supra* note 19, at para. 73.

[23] See Case C-45/86, *Commission v. Council*, [1987] ECR 01493 (ECLI:EU:C:1987:163), which concerned an application by the Commission that the Court declare two Council Regulations applying generalized tariff preferences void due to the absence of a precise legal basis, which is in itself contrary to Article 190 of the EEC Treaty, and resulted in recourse being had to a procedure entailing a unanimous vote rather than the procedure applicable under Article 113 of the Treaty, which in the Commission's view is the only correct legal basis.

as the Court has repeatedly held, Community legislation must be clear and its application foreseeable for all interested parties. As a result of that requirement for legal certainty, the binding nature of any act intended to have legal effects must be derived from a provision of Community law which prescribes the legal form to be taken by that act and which must be expressly indicated therein as its legal basis.[24]

The role of law in the process of political integration is thus not only to empower or compel political actors to pursue certain ends by using particular means, but also relates to functioning as a constraining force, limiting the actions or policies of these actors.[25]

B. The Choice of Legal Basis is Based on Objective Factors

Second, according to settled case law, the choice of the legal basis for an EU measure must rest on objective factors amenable to judicial review, including in particular the aim and the content of the measure.[26] Usually one legal basis is enough. Even when a measure pursues a twofold purpose or has a twofold component, one should aim at identifying one of them as the main or predominant purpose or component, and choose a single legal basis accordingly.[27] It is only if this proves impossible, and an institution's power is genuinely based on two provisions of the Treaty, that it is bound to adopt the relevant measures on the basis of the two relevant provisions,[28] presuming that they are procedurally complementary.

However, recourse to dual legal basis is not possible when the procedures are incompatible with each other, as was the case in the classic matter concerning *Titanium dioxide*. In that case, one of the possible legal bases required the use of the old cooperation procedure, while the other required the Council to act unanimously after merely consulting the European Parliament. The Court referred to the 'very purpose of the cooperation procedure, which is to increase the involvement of the European Parliament in the legislative process of the Community' and that this would be jeopardized if their two legal bases were combined, divesting the 'cooperation procedure of its very substance':

Under the cooperation procedure, the Council acts by a qualified majority where it intends accepting the amendments to its common position proposed by the Parliament and included by the Commission in its re-examined proposal, whereas it must secure unanimity if it intends taking a decision after its common position has been rejected by the Parliament or if it intends modifying the Commission's re-examined proposal. That essential element of the cooperation procedure would be undermined if... the Council were required, in any event, to act unanimously.[29]

[24] Case C-325/91, *France v. Commission*, [1993] ECR I-03283 (ECLI:EU:C:1993:245), at para. 26.

[25] De Búrca, *supra* note 6, at 319–320.

[26] See Case C-411/06, *supra* note 5, at para. 45, Case C-178/03, *Commission v. Parliament and Council*, [2006] ECR I-00107 (ECLI:EU:C:2006:4), at para. 41, and Case C-155/07, *supra* note 21, at para. 34.

[27] Case C-411/06, *supra* note 5, at para. 46; Case C-490/10, *Parliament v. Council*, judgment of 6 September 2012 (ECLI:EU:C:2012:525), at para. 45.

[28] Case C-165/87, *Commission v. Council*, [1988] ECR 5545 (ECLI:EU:C:1988:458), at para. 11.

[29] See Case C-300/89, *Commission v. Council (Titanium dioxide)*, [1991] ECR I-02867 (ECLI:EU:C:1991:244), at paras 17–21.

The Court then referred to the role of the European Parliament, stressing that its participation in the legislative procedures 'reflects a fundamental democratic principle that the peoples should take part in the exercise of power through the intermediary of a representative assembly'. Subsequently, it is necessary to determine which of the two provisions was the single appropriate legal basis for the adoption of the act.[30]

The legal bases in the Treaty not only specify, in more or less general terms, what can be done on their basis, but also how—following what procedure—this is to be done.[31] The legal basis of an act is selected based on the principle objective or 'centre of gravity', that is, what in the view of the institution concerned constitutes the principal objective of the measure in question.[32] Therefore, the method of selecting the legal basis already 'offers a considerable flexibility for subjecting the choice of a legal basis to the political preferences of the institution concerned', which is at odds with the guarantee function of a legal basis.[33] Consequently, while the Court's jurisprudence consistently highlights the objectivity of the choices relating to legal basis, it largely relates to and reflects the political, substantive, and procedural implications of these choices. The Council argued this specifically in the *Council v. Sophie in't Veld* case:

> According to the Council, since the legal basis of an EU act determines the decision-making procedure that applies, it necessarily affects the balance of powers between the institutions as well. Disputes concerning the applicable legal basis therefore remain, by their very nature, of very great political significance and are potentially highly contentious.[34]

Since the legal basis determines the position of each of the institutions and the Member States in the legislative process, it is 'inevitable that the interpretation of these provisions by each of the actors involved is influenced by their political interests'.[35]

The *CITES* ruling[36] usefully explores the various fundamental implications of the choice of legal basis, including for the distribution of competence between the EU and the Member States and for the roles played by the EU institutions in the legislative procedure. The case concerned a Council decision establishing a

[30] These questions have been more recently explored in the case concerning loans to the European Investment Bank, which involved the choice between ex-Articles 179 (codecision) and 181 EC (consultation of the Parliament by the Council, which acted by qualified majority) and their compatibility. Unlike in the *Titanium dioxide* case, the use of a dual legal basis did not encroach upon the Parliament's rights, since the use of codecision would involve greater participation by the Parliament. The Court relied on an examination of the complementary aims and relationship of the two legal bases and confirmed the compatibility of the two procedures, establishing that the contested decision should have been founded, exceptionally, on the dual legal basis of Articles 179 EC and 181a EC. See Case C-155/07, *supra* note 21. According to the Court, '[s]uch an approach is still valid, after the entry into force of the Treaty of Lisbon, in the context of the ordinary legislative procedure'. Case C-130/10, *Parliament v. Council*, judgment of 19 July 2012 (ECLI:EU:C:2012:472), at para. 46.

[31] Cf. Article 16 TFEU and Article 8 of the Charter for Fundamental Rights. While both concern the protection of personal data, only the former establishes a legal basis for the adoption of rules concerning the matter. The fact that the Charter cannot be used as a basis for competence to act is also specifically confirmed by Article 51(2) of the Charter.

[32] Barents, *supra* note 7, at 101. [33] *Ibid.*, at 102.

[34] Case C-350/12 P, *Council v. Sophie in't Veld*, judgment of 3 July 2014 (ECLI:EU:C:2014:2039), at para. 29.

[35] Barents, *supra* note 7, at 89.

[36] Case C-370/07, *Commission v. Council*, [2009] ECR I-08917 (ECLI:EU:C:2009:590).

Community position with regard to certain proposals submitted at a party conference under the Convention on International Trade in Endangered Species of Wild Fauna and Flora (CITES), which the Commission had proposed to be adopted under ex-Articles 175(1) EC[37] and 133 EC,[38] together with the second subparagraph of ex-Article 300(2) EC,[39] with reference to the regulation of trade in species and the conservation of those species being of equal importance. The legal basis was contested also within the Council, which subsequently adopted the contested decision without indicating a legal basis. The Council argued that the decision at hand was of a *sui generis* nature and had no effects on the legal rights and obligations of third parties outside the institutions and Member States. In any case, in its view the absence of a reference was a purely formal defect. The Court repeated its earlier case law relating to the principle of the allocation of powers, and how the choice of legal basis is of constitutional importance. It then moved to explain the implications of this choice. The prerogatives of the institutions concerned by the procedure were likely to affect the powers of the Parliament and the voting procedure within the Council. Furthermore, it was likely to determine the division of powers between the Union and the Member States. While common commercial policy falls under exclusive competence,[40] environmental policy is an area of shared competence,[41] which also affects the role of the Commission. Therefore, the failure to indicate a legal basis was capable to 'give rise to confusion as to the nature of the Union powers'.[42]

The CITES ruling illustrates how sometimes the choice of legal basis settles the nature of competence that the Union exercises,[43] and what effect Union action has on future Member State choices. Moreover, the choice of legal basis may also have consequences for the discretion of the legislature in selecting the applicable legislative

[37] Article 175(1) EC: 'The Council, acting in accordance with the procedure referred to in Article 251 and after consulting the Economic and Social Committee and the Committee of the Regions, shall decide what action is to be taken by the Community in order to achieve the objectives referred to in Article 174.'

[38] Article 133 EC established that the Commission was to submit proposals to the Council for implementing the common commercial policy. If agreements with third states or international organizations needed to be negotiated, the Commission was to make recommendations to the Council, which would authorize the Commission to open the necessary negotiations and conduct the negotiations in consultation with a special committee appointed by the Council. Council would act by a qualified majority.

[39] 'By way of derogation from the rules laid down in paragraph 3, the same procedures shall apply for a decision to suspend the application of an agreement, and for the purpose of establishing the positions to be adopted on behalf of the Community in a body set up by an agreement, when that body is called upon to adopt decisions having legal effects, with the exception of decisions supplementing or amending the institutional framework of the agreement.'

[40] In the area of exclusive competence, 'only the Union may legislate and adopt legally binding acts'. See also Case C-804/79, *Commission v. United Kingdom*, [1981] ECR 01045 (ECLI:EU:C:1981:93).

[41] Under shared competence both 'the Union and the Member States may legislate and adopt legally binding acts in that area. The Member States shall exercise their competence to the extent that the Union has not exercised its competence'.

[42] Case C-370/07, *supra* note 36, at paras 48–49 of the ruling.

[43] See, e.g. Article 168 TFEU on public health: while public health in general falls under supportive competence, para. 4 establishes a legal basis that falls under shared competence.

instrument,[44] the extent to which the measure can be used to harmonize national legislation,[45] or the way in which harmonization can be done.[46] In addition, the choice of legal basis affects the right of initiative, which usually is with the Commission, but can under some legal bases be reserved to a group of Member States, the CJEU, or the European Central Bank (ECB).[47] The legal basis may bring in the European Council through the operation of the emergency breaks applicable in some policy areas and result in a swift move to enhanced cooperation.[48]

In addition, the choice of legal basis may also affect the geographical scope of application of the instrument. This has been topical for horizontal international agreements with some provisions falling under justice and home affairs.[49] The Court has recently addressed the relevance of the Protocols regulating the status of the UK, Ireland, and Denmark for the choice of legal basis and established that these Protocols

> are not capable of having any effect whatsoever on the question of the correct legal basis for the adoption of the contested decisions. Indeed, it is the legal basis for a measure... which determines the protocols to be applied, and not vice versa.[50]

While this certainly reiterates the formal rule, informally it would be understandable if attempts were made to avoid the complexities relating to the use of certain legal bases necessitating the application of Member State opt-outs. There are also legislative techniques that can be invoked to revisit some of the Treaty-based limitations. The Treaties include no specific powers for the establishment of a banking union, which is largely set up on the basis of internal market legal bases. Its scope of application is limited from the general scope of implementation of internal market legislation (EU-28) to reflect participation in the euro area.[51]

[44] See, e.g. Article 207(2) TFEU, which refers to the use of regulations defining the framework for implementing the common commercial policy, or Article 82(2) TFEU, which establishes that directives can be used to facilitate mutual recognition of judgments and judicial decisions and police and judicial cooperation in criminal matters having a cross-border dimension.

[45] On this, see Article 82(2) TFEU, which refers to the adoption of 'minimum rules [which] shall not prevent Member States from maintaining or introducing a higher level of protection for individuals'. See also Article 168(5) TFEU, which specifically excludes 'any harmonisation of the laws and regulations of the Member States'.

[46] On the interpretation of Article 114 TFEU in this respect, see Case C-270/12, *United Kingdom v. Parliament and Council* (ESMA), judgment of 22 January 2014 (ECLI:EU:C:2014:18), at para. 102 *et seq.*

[47] See Article 289(4) TFEU, Article 76 TFEU (Member States), (CJEU) Article 281 TFEU, and Article 129(4) of the Statute of the ECB.

[48] See, e.g. Article 86(1) TFEU.

[49] See, e.g. the Partnership and Cooperation Agreement between the European Union and its Member States, of the one part, and the Republic of Iraq, of the other part, OJ 2012 L 204/20.

[50] Case C-137/12, *Commission v. Council*, judgment of 22 October 2013 (ECLI:EU:C:2013:675), at paras 73–74. These Protocols were not of any relevance, since they do not relate to common commercial policy.

[51] See, e.g. Regulation (EU) 806/2014, OJ 2014 L 225/1, establishing uniform rules and a uniform procedure for the resolution of credit institutions and certain investment firms in the framework of a Single Resolution Mechanism and a Single Resolution Fund, adopted under Article 114 TFEU, which 'establishes uniform rules and a uniform procedure for the resolution of the entities referred to in Article 2 that are established in the participating Member States'. Participating Member States for the purposes of the said Regulation are defined under Council Regulation 1024/2013, OJ 2013 L 287/63, conferring specific tasks on the ECB concerning policies relating to the prudential supervision of credit institutions, adopted under Article 127(6) TFEU, as Member States whose currency is the euro or a Member State whose currency is not the euro but which has established a close cooperation with the ECB.

The Court has justified the need to maintain the objectivity of the choices relating to legal basis with reference to the need to maintain institutional balance.[52] The prerogatives of institutions:

> are one of the elements in the institutional balance created by the Treaties. The Treaties set up a system for distributing powers among the different Community institutions, assigning to each institution its own role in the institutional structure of the Community and the accomplishment of the tasks entrusted to the Community. Observance of the institutional balance means that each of the institutions must exercise its powers with due regard for the powers of the other institutions.[53]

Political scientists have mainly understood the principle as referring to the relative power positions of the EU institutions in respect to one another. From a legal point of view the principle links with the limits of the powers allocated to each EU institution and rules of decision-making under the Treaty.[54] While the principle also links with the idea of separation of powers:

> it does this in a normatively unclear way, and by supplanting a separation of powers model, it in practice can help deflect criticism of the institutions if they act outside the obvious core of their authority, perhaps this being most significantly so in relation to the lawmaking, constitution-building role the ECJ has tended to play.[55]

In its jurisprudence, the Court has demonstrated a specific concern for the prerogatives of the European Parliament,[56] which has also been reflected in the discussion on incompatible legal bases quoted earlier.[57]

Since the legal basis defines the institutional roles and the nature and delimitation of competence between the Union and its Member States,[58] this choice also affects the outcome of the legislative process in fundamental ways. Legal debates concerning these choices have a natural tendency to turn into political debates conducted in legal language. There is a great deal of case law relating to the choice of legal basis demonstrating its top relevance for institutional politics. While these debates are

[52] See, e.g. Jacqué, 'The Principle of Institutional Balance', 41(2) *Common Market Law Review* (2004) 383; O'Dwyer, 'La dynamique historique des relations interinstitutionnelles. Le point de vue d'un praticien sur l'évolution de la procédure de codécision', 2 *Revue du Droit de l'Union européenne* 2010, 487.

[53] Case C-70/88, *Parliament v. Council*, [1991] ECR I-04529 (ECLI:EU:C:1991:373), at paras 21–22.

[54] Smulders and Eisele, 'Reflections on the Institutional Balance, the Community Method and the Interplay between Jurisdictions after Lisbon', 31(1) *Yearbook of European Law* (2012) 112, at 114–115. See also Article 13(2) TEU.

[55] Conway, 'Recovering a Separation of Powers in the European Union', 17(3) *European Law Journal* (2011) 304, at 321.

[56] On the Parliament's right to intervene in proceedings, see Case C-138/79, *Roquette Frères v. Council*, [1980] ECR 03333 (ECLI:EU:C:1980:249), at para. 20; on the EP's right to be consulted, see Case C-408/95, *Eurotunnel*, [1997] ECR I-06315 (ECLI:EU:C:1997:532), at paras 45–46. In the latter, the Court confirmed that under the consultation procedure, the Parliament needs to be 'consulted again whenever the text finally adopted, taken as a whole, differs in essence from the text on which the Parliament has already been consulted, except in cases in which the amendments substantially correspond to the wishes of the Parliament itself' (para. 46). On the Parliament's right to bring an action of annulment, see Case C-302/87, *Parliament v. Council*, [1988] ECR 05615 (ECLI:EU:C:1988:461).

[57] Case C-155/07, *supra* note 21, at para. 78.

[58] For a discussion of these effects, see, e.g. the *CITES* case, C-370/07, *supra* note 36.

usually dressed in objective terms, they often relate to institutional power. Cullen and Charlesworth have demonstrated how both the European Parliament and the Member States:

> appear to have embraced legal basis litigation as a potentially useful tool in advancing wider political aims designed to expand, or to confirm, their own powers. As such, legal basis challenges form part of a political strategy to maximize power and influence over the legislative programme of the EC.[59]

Member State litigation is often driven by a 'nostalgia for the veto', and is based on legal arguments relating to the need to build on unanimity and respect subsidiarity. However, such litigation has in practice often led to reduced Member State sovereignty over internal policies. Instead of a purely legal exercise, the main function of litigation may relate to the communication of concerns through the court process.[60] This is particularly so when litigation functions as a way of communicating with other parties to the legislative process.[61] While it is evident that the Court is also 'capable of being influenced by the political debates presented to it',[62] it is not straightforward to what extent its rulings reflect institutional or Member State positions in such debates.[63]

The Parliament's prerogatives include participation in the drafting of legislative measures when the Treaty so provides.[64] This is a right that the Parliament itself interprets expansively and justifies with reference to being the only institution at EU level that is directly elected by the citizens. For the Parliament, legal basis litigation constitutes part of an 'institutional strategy with both overt and covert

[59] Cullen and Charlesworth, 'Diplomacy by Other Means: The Use of Legal Basis Litigation as a Political Strategy by the European Parliament and Member States', 36 *Common Market Law Review* (1999) 1243, at 1243.

[60] *Ibid.*, at 1268.

[61] *Ibid.*, at 1269. There are some recent examples in the area of enhanced cooperation relating to the EU patent regime. Member States have brought annulment proceedings while the legislative process has been ongoing to stress the importance of their arguments and to demonstrate their willingness to continue the discussion in Court unless their concerns are not sufficiently taken into account. Joined Cases C-274/11 and C-295/11, *Spain and Italy v. Council*, judgment of 16 April 2013 (ECLI:EU:C:2013:240). The Court dismissed the actions. In relation to the financial transaction tax, the UK requested the Court to annul the council decision authorizing enhanced cooperation in the area of financial transaction tax even if negotiations on the file are still ongoing and the result remains unclear. In its application, the UK fully acknowledged that its action constituted a precautionary measure, which could be considered to be premature. See Case C-209/13, *United Kingdom v. Council*, judgment of 30 April 2014 (ECLI:EU:C:2014:283). While the Court was not convinced by the arguments raised, the proceedings created an additional channel for the UK to raise its concerns.

[62] Cullen and Charlesworth, *supra* note 59, at 1270.

[63] There are several cases that would offer interesting avenues for further analysis of, in particular, the effect of Member State positions on the Court. For example, in Case C-176/03, *Commission v. Council* (environmental crimes), [2005] ECR I-07879 (ECLI:EU:C:2005:542), the European Parliament supported the Commission while 11 Member States intervened in support of the Council; in Case C-440/05, *Commission v. Council* (ship-source pollution), [2007] ECR I-09097 (ECLI:EU:C:2007:625), the Parliament again supported the Commission while 19 Member States intervened in support of the Council; and in Opinion 2/13, *Opinion pursuant to Article 218(11) TFUE*, 18 December 2014 (ECLI:EU:C:2014:2454), apart from the three main institutions, 24 Member States submitted observations to the Court. In all of these cases, Member State positions proved unpersuasive.

[64] Case C-70/88, *supra* note 53, at para. 28.

elements',[65] and it frequently brings cases to protect publicly its institutional prerogatives with reference to how the key motive behind the Council and/or Commission actions is to prevent the Parliament exercising its prerogative. This is not always convincing.[66] A recent example is the *Kadi* case, which concerned the choice of legal basis for freezing of funds and economic resources when implementing Security Council Resolution 1390(2002), and which elegantly illustrates the latter point.[67] The institutional debate within the EU concerned in particular the choice between two legal bases. The Parliament advocated Article 75 Treaty on the Functioning of the European Union (TFEU), which provides for the ordinary legislative procedure.[68] The Council and the Commission argued for Article 215(1) TFEU, which only requires the Council to inform the Parliament. The Parliament stressed the general scheme and spirit of the Treaties and the fact that the contested regulation was linked to the protection of individuals and groups. In its view, the EU could, post-Lisbon, only adopt measures concerning fundamental rights either under the ordinary legislative procedure or with the Parliament's consent. The Council contested these arguments with reference to how the Parliament's proposition in fact amounted to procedures determining the choice of legal basis, rather than the other way around.

The Court noted that the procedures under the two possible legal bases were incompatible: thus it was not possible to cumulate the two provisions in order for them to serve as a twofold legal basis. After an examination of the ambit of Article 215 TFEU and the purpose and tenor of the contested decision, the Court confirmed that the Article did indeed constitute the appropriate legal basis for the measures in question, which were directed to addressees implicated in acts of terrorism and who affect fundamentally the EU's external activity. The Court then moved to consider the implications of this choice for the Parliament's prerogatives, establishing that while the choice had consequences for the Parliament's position, this fact could not determine the choice of legal basis. While the Court accepted that the participation of the Parliament reflects the principle of democracy at Union level, the difference in the degree of Parliament's involvement under the two Articles 'is the result of the choice made by the framers of the Treaty of Lisbon conferring a more limited role on the Parliament with regard to the Union's action under the CFSP'.[69] Subsequently, the Court rejected this plea as unfounded and dismissed the action.

The amount of case law demonstrates that the choice of legal basis is far from being an objective, neutral, or non-political exercise. In practice, if there is agreement between the institutions, the act will stand. Interinstitutional compromises

[65] Cullen and Charlesworth, *supra* note 59, at 1257.

[66] For the argument in general, see *ibid.*, at 1257.

[67] Case C-130/10, *supra* note 30. In greater detail, see Leino, 'In Principle the Full Review – What Justice for Mr Kadi?' in R. Liivoja and J. Petman (eds), *International Law-making: Essays in Honour of Jan Klabbers* (2013) 225.

[68] See Article 75 TFEU, which falls under the Treaty Title on the area of freedom, security, and justice, to which the UK, Irish, and Danish exceptions apply under Protocols 21 and 22.

[69] Case C-130/10, *supra* note 30, at para. 82.

play a key function in legislative decision-making. This also applies to legal debates, where compromises represent 'an important pattern of praxis regulating the crystallization of a legal argument'.[70] A legal proposal then becomes 'less about saying the right thing and more about reflecting a temporary equilibrium, which is bound to change again'.[71]

C. Between Formal Rules and Informal Practices

The formal rules concerning the choice of legal basis are complemented by a number of practices informed by the politics of competence. In practice, the Commission is likely to lean towards the use of a legal basis that enables qualified majority voting in the Council, which strengthens its own position, since the Council can only amend the Commission proposal by unanimity (Article 293 TFEU). The Parliament naturally argues for legal bases that support its own position, and the Council defends its own institutional role,[72] the rights of Member States, and the use of special legislative procedures. Since this simultaneously buttresses its own role, one could envisage the Commission making choices in favour of Treaty Articles enabling the exercise of exclusive or shared competence at the expense of those relating to supportive action.[73] More recently, many old directives have been replaced by regulations. Therefore, the objective nature of these choices is often quite relative.

Various choices can be maintained in the European Court of Justice by invoking the right legislative techniques. The politics of competence and legal basis result in the practice of using the preambles of acts to justify the choices made by the legislature, defining the main and predominant objectives of the act.[74] The Court has accepted this, and it relies, often heavily, on the thinking of the legislature. Its case law has enabled the legislature to overrule the choices of the Commission, if thoroughly explained in the preamble, which logically guides interpretation in the wished direction. While some references to the Commission proposal and attached background documents are occasionally made in the Court rulings, the main emphasis of interpretation is on the choices made by the legislature in identifying the appropriate means for promoting the objectives it is aiming to achieve and establishing what is

[70] Sideri, 'The European Commission and the Law-Making Process: Compromise as a Category of Praxis', 1(2) *International Journal of Law in Context* (2005) 155, at 156.

[71] *Ibid.*, at 174. [72] See, e.g. Case C-130/10, *supra* note 30.

[73] Supportive competence limits the Union to carrying out 'actions to support, coordinate or supplement the actions of the Member States, without thereby superseding their competence in these areas'. See, e.g. Decision 1082/2013/EU on serious cross-border threats to health and repealing Decision 2119/98/EC, OJ 2013 L 293/1, which is based on Article 168(5) TFEU.

[74] Case C-411/06, *supra* note 5, in which the Commission disagreed with the justifications of the European Parliament and the Council. The Court accepted the arguments of the latter, see especially paras 51–54. 'By contrast, and as observed by the Parliament and the Council, the preamble to the contested regulation does not make any reference to the pursuit of objectives falling within the common commercial policy' (para. 54). See also Case C-217/04, *United Kingdom v. Parliament and Council (ENISA)*, [2006] ECR I-03771 (ECLI:EU:C:2006:279), at paras 48–53 and 63.

necessary in a particular situation.[75] The recent *ESMA* ruling offers an example of this method. Following a number of quotations from the preamble indicating the intentions of the EU legislature, the Court concludes:

It follows that the purpose of the powers provided for in Article 28 of Regulation No 236/2012 is in fact to improve the conditions for the establishment and functioning of the internal market in the financial field. It is apparent from all the foregoing considerations that Article 28 of Regulation No 236/2012 satisfies all the requirements laid down in Article 114 TFEU. The latter provision therefore constitutes an appropriate legal basis for the adoption of Article 28.[76]

This technique of interpretation of course stresses both the flexibility of the legislature in choosing the legal basis—if there is agreement on it between the European Parliament and (and within) the Council—and adjusting the legal act accordingly. The same applies to discretion concerning alternative measures. The ruling concerning the working time directive elegantly illustrates this point:

the Council must be allowed a wide discretion in an area which, as here, involves the legislature in making social policy choices and requires it to carry out complex assessments. Judicial review of the exercise of that discretion must therefore be limited to examining whether it has been vitiated by manifest error or misuse of powers, or whether the institution concerned has manifestly exceeded the limits of its discretion.[77]

Since the Court primarily resorts to interpretative techniques, it has set the threshold for annulling acts relatively high:

A measure is vitiated by misuse of powers only if it appears, on the basis of objective, relevant and consistent evidence to have been taken solely, or at the very least chiefly, for ends other than those for which the power in question was conferred or with the aim of evading a procedure specifically prescribed by the Treaty for dealing with the circumstances of the case.[78]

As regards the application of procedural rules the Court has firmly established that decision-making rules do not fall under Member States' or institutional discretion, but that such rules are established by the Treaties alone.[79] However, there still is some degree for procedural imagination—in cases where the institutions agree on the need to use it. The introduction of 'reverse qualified majority voting' under the procedures relating to economic governance is one example of such imagination.[80]

[75] See, e.g. Case C-58/08, *Vodafone and Others*, [2010] ECR I-04999 (ECLI:EU:C:2010:321), at paras 38–46, where following numerous references to the Preamble of Regulation 717/2007, the Court concludes that '[s]uch a situation justified the Community legislature's seeking to protect the proper functioning of the internal market, as stated in paragraph 38 of this judgment. It follows from the foregoing that the object of Regulation No 717/2007 is indeed to improve the conditions for the functioning of the internal market and that it could be adopted on the basis of Article 95 EC' (paras 47–48 of the ruling).

[76] Case C-270/12, *supra* note 46, at paras 116–117.

[77] Case C-84/94, *United Kingdom v. Council* (working time directive), [1996] ECR I-05755 (ECLI:EU:C:1996:431), at para. 58.

[78] Joined Cases C-274/11 and C-295/11, *supra* note 61, at para. 33.

[79] See, e.g. Case C-540/13, *Parliament v. Council*, judgment of 16 April 2015 (ECLI:EU:C:2015:224), at para. 32.

[80] For a discussion, see Leino and Salminen, 'Going "Belt and Braces"—Domestic Effects of Euro-crisis Law', *EUI Working Papers LAW* 2015/15; Palmsdorfer, 'The Reverse Majority Voting under the "Six Pack": A Bad Turn for the Union?', 20(2) *European Law Journal* (2014) 186.

Since all the relevant institutions agreed on the need to streamline decision-making, the compatibility of the procedures with the Treaties has never been addressed by the Court. Another example of procedural imagination relates to the EU Fundamental Rights Agency. The three institutions disagreed on whether the Regulation establishing the Agency was to be set up on the basis of a combination of legal bases presuming codecision[81] or ex-Article 308 EC building on unanimity in the Council and consultation of the Parliament. The legislative procedure that was informally agreed on built on quasi-codecision with informal trialogues, during which a shared position between the three institutions was found, and which the Parliament then formally approved in the consultation procedure. The innovative interpretation of EU competence and the applicable procedure was never addressed by the Court, since the three institutions agreed on the arrangement enabling the Agency to be set up.[82] Thus the legislature ultimately has a great deal of discretion. It is evident that the increasing use of the ordinary legislative procedure means that most parts of files are closed in first reading during the informal trialogue procedure. Noting this trend, it would seem that the use of special legislative procedures, especially, with a lower level of participation for the Parliament, results in debates between institutions and package deals.[83]

These examples illustrate further the function of the law in the political process: it structures the parameters within which courts, legislators, executives, administrators, and other social actors operate.[84] Within these parameters, law leaves leeway for political choices. The formal rules ultimately avail the legislature with a great deal of discretion. They are often indeterminate, and therefore definite or objective choices might be difficult to make. Instead, solutions build on compromises concerning both the interpretation of the rules and the substance of the legislative file. Together, they form a package deal. The rules of informal governance leave ample room for interpretation. During the legislative procedure, this task is largely handled by the members of legal services appointed by the institutions and Member State governments' and legal advisers.

[81] See the draft European Parliament legislative resolution on the proposal for a Council regulation on establishing a European Union Agency for Fundamental Rights, available in the legislative observatory at: http://www.europarl.europa.eu/sides/getDoc.do?type=REPORT&mode=XML&reference=A6-2006-306&language=EN (last visited 16 January 2017).

[82] See Council Regulation 168/2007 of 15 February 2007 establishing a European Union Agency for Fundamental Rights, OJ 2007 L 53/1. In the preamble, the choice of legal basis is described as follows: 'The contribution made by the Agency to ensuring full respect of fundamental rights in the framework of Community law is likely to help achieve the Community's objectives. With regard to the adoption of this Regulation, the Treaty does not provide for powers other than those set out in Article 308.'

[83] See, e.g. the package deal consisting of Council Regulation 1024/2013, *supra* note 51, conferring specific tasks on the European Central Bank concerning policies relating to the prudential supervision of credit institution and Regulation 1022/2013 of the European Parliament and of the Council of 22 October 2013 amending Regulation (EU) 1093/2010 establishing a European Supervisory Authority (European Banking Authority) as regards the conferral of specific tasks on the European Central Bank pursuant to Council Regulation 1024/2013, OJ 2013 L 287/5, which the European Parliament voted upon as a package even though the first is based on Article 127(6) TFEU presuming the use of a special legislative procedure, and the latter is based on Article 114 TFEU and the ordinary legislative procedure.

[84] De Búrca, *supra* note 6, at 310, 319–320.

The role of the institutions' legal services remains little studied in settling the limits of the 'legally possible'. They exercise significant institutional powers.[85] The Council Legal Service, which forms a part of the Council Secretariat, is the most powerful of the legal services. The Council Rules of Procedure define its role in relation to the quality of legislative drafting,[86] but its tasks are in fact multiple, and relate to checking the legality of measures, respect for the procedural rules, and include a potential power to suggest amendments and strike a political balance.[87] While the Commission Legal Service might be secondary during the legislative procedure, it affects decision-making longer, starting from the stage of internal preparation to following the implementation of an act and possible infringement proceedings. Jean-Paul Jacqué has described the task of legal advisers as follows:

> The basic mission of a lawyer is to check that legislation complies with EU law. However, the tasks of a lawyer may extend well beyond this, provided he or she has the trust of the political authorities or, in the case of the Council, that of the delegations of the Member States.[88]

While this role presumes capacity to 'resist any pressures coming from those holding the political power', it also turns the lawyer into 'the actor within the legislative theatre'. Consequently, 'it is difficult for a Member State to take a position that is at odds with the position of the Council's legal service', especially if the Commission legal service shares its opinion.[89] However:

> the aim is not to lay obstacles on the path of the legislator but to find solutions that respect its wishes while sheltering any decisions that have been taken from the risk of litigation. In this case, creativity is a fundamental skill.[90]

Jacqué describes the way in which matters are discussed and negotiated informally between the legal services:

> Before raising a legal issue, it is deemed courteous to warn the interested parties so as to test one's position with them and allow them to prepare their arguments in the event that they disagree. Such bilateral contacts often provide an opportunity to search for a compromise.[91]

While it is 'the lawyer's job is to decompose the legal arguments to show that this is not a legal debate but a political issue that must be dealt with by the political authorities', the lawyers' function also risks 'shifting political responsibility, supposedly in favour of a given legal expertise'.[92]

When a compromise acceptable to all parties cannot be identified within a reasonable time, or there is no interest in looking for one, debates result in interinstitutional litigation.[93] Annulment proceedings can be brought within a strict two-month

[85] On this, see Leino, 'Transparency, Participation and EU Institutional Practice: An Inquiry into the Limits of the "Widest Possible"', 3 *EUI Law Working Paper* (2014), available at http://cadmus.eui.eu/handle/1814/30580 (last visited 16 January 2017).

[86] Article 22, Council Decision 2009/237 adopting the Council's Rules of Procedure, OJ 2009 L 325/35.

[87] These roles are further elaborated in Jacqué, *supra* note 15.

[88] *Ibid.*, at 49. [89] *Ibid.*, at 47, 49. [90] *Ibid.*, at 46. [91] *Ibid.*

[92] *Ibid.*, at 50.

[93] See Cullen and Charlesworth, *supra* note 59; Lenaerts, 'How the ECJ Thinks: A Study on Judicial Legitimacy', 36 *Fordham International Law Journal* (2013) 1302.

deadline. The threshold for defending institutional prerogatives in court is low and the cost aspect—which might often act as a deterrent—is not an obstacle. This is based on an interinstitutional 'gentleman's agreement' that the institutions and Member States cover their own costs. Litigation is a mundane part of EU institutional practice and thus almost an everyday occurrence in EU institutional politics. Its effects are seldom dramatic.[94] In practice, the effects of annulled instruments are often maintained. The Treaty stipulates that '[i]f the action is well founded, the Court of Justice of the European Union shall declare the act concerned to be void' (Article 264 TFEU). The institutions are required to take the necessary measures to comply with the judgment (Article 266 TFEU). The Court may also state on the effects of the ruling. It is common for the parties to request it to maintain the effects of the contested legal act until a new act has been adopted and to rule on the effect of, for example, payments made or commitments entered into on the basis of the act, in the case where it is annulled,[95] with reference to the requirements of legal certainty and legitimate expectations. The Court also frequently does this, which further lowers the threshold for bringing annulment actions. Partial annulment of an act is, in principle, also possible.[96]

The vagueness of formal rules emphasizes the role of the Court in determining what ultimately count as proper choices. In his recent strategic analysis of 'How the CJEU thinks', Koen Lenaerts, Vice-President of the CJEU, argues that the Court is 'constantly seeking to strike the balance imposed by the rule of law among the different interests at stake in a multilayered system of governance',[97] but stresses the need of drawing the borderline between law and politics, which coincides with the contours of the Court's own legitimacy. Contested acts of secondary law cannot be

[94] But there are also more dramatic results of interinstitutional litigation. For example, in the EU–US PNR Agreement case the Court annulled both the Council Decision concluding the EU–US Agreement on the processing and transfer of PNR data by air carriers to the US Department of Homeland Security and the relating Commission Decision on the adequate protection of personal data. This ruling took effect 90 days from the date of notification. This entailed in practice a need to re-open negotiations on the Agreement with the US authorities with a significant risk of disruptions in the air traffic between the EU and US had the new Agreement not been concluded on time. See Joined Cases C-317/04 and C-318/04, *Parliament v. Council and Commission*, [2006] ECR I-04721 (ECLI:EU:C:2006:346).

[95] The Court tends to justify maintaining the legal effects of annulled acts for a reasonable period until a new act is adopted with reference to grounds for legal certainty. See, e.g. Case C-166/07, *Parliament v. Council* (Community financial contributions to the International Fund for Ireland), [2009] ECR I-07135 (ECLI:EU:C:2009:499), at para. 70, where the Court established that 'annulment of the contested regulation without maintenance of its effects could have adverse consequences, particularly with regard to financial contributions made for actions and projects planned and in the course of implementation, and would be liable to give rise to uncertainties damaging to present and future financing operations of the Fund'. See also Case C-155/07, *supra* note 21 (Community guarantee to the European Investment Bank against losses under loans and loan guarantees for projects outside the Community), at paras 86–89, in which the Court concluded that '[i]t is common ground that annulling that decision without maintaining its effects would be liable to have adverse consequences for the EIB's credit rating and would lead to damaging uncertainties for current and future EIB financing operations'.

[96] Case C-376/98, *Germany v. Parliament and Council (Tobacco advertising)*, [2000] ECR I-08419 (ECLI:EU:C:2000:544), at paras 115–118. In this case, however, the Court decided to annul the directive in its entirety.

[97] Lenaerts, *supra* note 93, at 1304.

rewritten by the Court, but it 'must avoid inter-institutional conflicts which could arise if the contested act is annulled'. According to established case law, the wording of secondary EU legislation must be interpreted, in so far as possible, in a manner consistent with the provisions of the Treaties. This follows from the general principle of interpretation that a provision must be interpreted, as far as possible, in such a way as not to affect its validity.[98] Therefore the CJEU often has recourse to 'reconciliatory interpretation', entailing that EU law is interpreted in line with primary EU law as far as it is not *contra legem*. Lenaerts also stresses the importance of compromises within the CJEU itself, where consensus building requires bringing on board as many opinions as possible and is simultaneously limited to solving the legal questions that are necessary to solve the case at hand.

The insights offered by Judge Lenaerts demonstrate how legal basis choices and litigation not only concern institutional politics by the institutions involved in the legislative process (the Commission, the European Parliament, the Council, and the Member States) but also involve choices and compromises within the Court. In practice, the rules relating to the objectivity of these choices have produced a great number of informal practices within the framework of formal rules, which stress institutional discretion and rely on compromises for their existence and application. Even though subjective choices follow as a logical consequence of the game, the credibility of legal basis argumentation presumes that too apparently subjective choices are not often made,[99] and that the institutional choices made are usually subject to scrutiny by the CJEU.

3. Politics of Compromise and Participation in the Ordinary Legislative Procedure

A. A Framework of Informal Rules

According to Article 294 TFEU, the ordinary legislative procedure offers four opportunities for finding agreement on the substance of the legislative act. The different stages of the procedure—known as first, second, and third reading, with a stage of conciliation between the last two—aim at approaching the positions of the Council and the Parliament, which are formulated in the beginning, during first reading. The procedure ends at the stage when agreement is found. In practice the great majority of files are closed at first reading (83 per cent),[100] which means that the use of the later stages of the procedure is becoming an exception. Most of the rules regulating the ordinary legislative procedure are based on informal practice, in particular a joint declaration on practical arrangements for the procedure.[101] The key solutions in that joint declaration also form the basis of the envisaged

[98] Case C-540/13, *supra* note 79. [99] Lenaerts, *supra* note 93, at 1245.

[100] Agreement can also be found at early second reading (EP) (8%), during second reading (Council) (7%), and Conciliation and third reading (2%), but these stages are turning into an exception. The figures are from the European Parliament website.

[101] Joint declaration on practical arrangements for the codecision procedure (2007/C 145/02), OJ 2007 C 145/5.

Interinstitutional Agreement on Better Regulation. The overall objective of the joint declaration and the institutional arrangements it introduces is clear: to 'ensure the maximum efficiency of the legislative procedure' and to adopt acts at an early stage of the legislative procedure. Efficiency largely relates to the use of trialogues, which are informal tripartite meetings between the three key institutions, but which are unknown to the Treaties.

The Treaty includes some provisions relating to interinstitutional relations in the context of law-making. Of particular importance is Article 293 TFEU, which regulates the relationship between the Council and the Commission. Its first paragraph establishes that when the Council acts on a Commission proposal, it may, as the main rule, amend that proposal only by acting unanimously,[102] except in conciliation and third reading. In practice, this means that the Council decides unanimously on those amendments proposed by the European Parliament that the Commission has opposed in its opinion. Therefore, as long as the Commission agrees to amending its proposal, no matter how substantively, the Council can formally decide by qualified majority. Therefore, 'making amendments' in practice refers to making amendments that the Commission does not agree with, keeping in mind that decision-making in the Council usually takes place with consensus anyway. At the same time, the Commission's role as the neutral broker in the legislative procedure is weakening as the Council and the Parliament are finding new ways to make political deals. The informal rules entail that, usually, the Commission considers the positions of the Council and the Parliament expressed during the trialogues, and bases its final position on this deal. Article 293(2) TFEU establishes that '[a]s long as the Council has not acted, the Commission may alter its proposal at any time during the procedures leading to the adoption of a Union act'. The Commission's right of initiative and the right to withdraw its proposals will be discussed further later.

The obvious direction in interinstitutional relations relates to the empowerment of the European Parliament in legislative matters in particular. While the Council has retained its key functions and roles, the institutional balance has shifted to the Commission's disadvantage. Jacqué offered a simple explanation to this as long ago as 2004. The Commission's authority in relation to the Council is dependent on its capacity to express the general interest in an independent way. To the extent that the Commission is in the hands of the Parliament, it loses its credibility vis-à-vis the Council, which instead negotiates directly with the Parliament rather than with a Commission which simply acts as the Parliament's spokesman.[103] Since 2004, the close linkages between the Commission and the European Parliament have been further strengthened, as reflected in their interinstitutional framework agreement

[102] The Court has interpreted the provision in Eurotunnel, in which it confirmed that the Council could amend the Commission proposal unanimously (which was the applicable decision-making procedure under the relevant legal basis anyway) and that the amendments made by the Council remained within the scope of the relevant directive as defined in the original Commission proposal. Thus, 'the Council did not exceed its power to make amendments under Article 149 of the Treaty'. Case C-408/95, *supra* note 56, at paras 37–39.

[103] Jacqué, *supra* note 52, at 390.

and the 'special partnership', which it aims to develop.[104] At the same time, the formal agenda-setting power of the Commission and the Parliament 'varies directly with the realistic possibility of majority voting in the Council, not merely its legal authorization'.[105] Therefore, while formal procedural rules have a considerable impact on the power of the institutional actors,[106] power relations are not merely the result of formal institutions.[107]

The interacting and intertwined legal and political dimensions of decision-making bring forward many fundamental questions relating to power. In the following, I will examine the procedural rules relating to the ordinary legislative procedure contained in the Treaties and the kind of informal arrangements that have resulted in practice. I will first discuss the roles of the three key institutions—the Commission, the European Parliament, and the Council—in the procedure, followed by an examination of the role of trialogues in settling legislative deals. When the rules are flexible, and their implementation is subject to analysis, then the actor in the position of settling the relevant interpretation enjoys significant powers. During the legislative procedure, this role is held by the legal advisers, whose role is briefly discussed. The overall theme of the following section relates to the way in which participation is realized during the EU legislative procedure, and how the enforcement of rights of participation is taken into account in the design of legislative frameworks.

B. Commission Proposal

The Treaty establishes that 'Union legislative acts may only be adopted on the basis of a Commission proposal, except where the Treaties provide otherwise' (Article 17(2) TEU).[108] Very few Commission proposals are in practice entirely killed during the legislative process. The right of initiative is a significant power especially in relation to those questions that can only be regulated by the Union. If the Commission does not provide a legislative proposal, then there will be no legal act.[109]

The Treaty does not stipulate in any great detail how a legislative proposal is prepared. The drafting and impact assessment stage of legislative proposals visualizes an interplay between legal questions framing the possible options, their political desirability, and technical data evaluating needs and the uncertain impact of the envisaged measures. In practice, in terms of political power, the Commission monopoly

[104] Framework Agreement of relations between the European Parliament and the European Commission, OJ 2010 L 304/47.

[105] Golub, 'In the Shadow of the Vote? Decision Making in the European Community', 53(4) *International Organization* (1999) 733, at 759.

[106] Thomson and Hosli, *supra* note 13, at 414.

[107] *Ibid.*, at 415.

[108] Even the adoption of other than legal acts may require a Commission proposal, see, e.g. Case C-27/04, *Commission v. Council* (Stability and Growth Pact), [2004] ECR I-06649 (ECLI:EU:C:2004:436), at paras 91–92.

[109] See Case C-804/79, *supra* note 40 relating to the use of exclusive competence. The legal basis provided in Article 298 TFEU for the adoption of rules on good administration applicable to the EU institutions is an example of such a case. Since the Commission is reluctant to regulate the exercise of its own administrative powers in a legally binding manner, it continues to 'consider' its proposal, thus effectively vetoing the act from entering the legislative procedure.

on setting the legislative agenda is relative—in most cases the Commission is acting on requests from national leaders, who are the true agenda setters.[110] The Commission adopts initiatives that are compromises with national governments.[111] Together with considerations relating to possible legal bases discussed earlier, such discussions constitute political imperatives and constraints that affect how the Commission formulates its proposals.[112] In practice, Commission proposals conclude bilateral talks between the Commission, Member States, various expert positions, and lobbies, which strengthens consensus-oriented decision-making. Initiatives are only made public following such consultations. The Commission has been criticized for often presenting its proposals to the public as a subtle compromise, which embodies the 'common interest', and justifying them with reference to how 'there is no other choice'.[113] The quality of its proposals has been debated in the context of the various better-regulation initiatives tabled during recent years.

The rejected alternatives are seldom made publicly known. The drafting stage can be technical, but it can also be political and highly influential. The procedure of impact assessments, for example, plays a significant role in assessing options. The Commission Impact Assessment Board, working under the authority of the Commission President, has the task of ensuring quality control by examining and issuing opinions on all draft impact assessments accompanying draft Commission proposals. The Board acts independently of Commission departments, and is constituted by high-level Commission officials appointed in a personal capacity. A positive opinion by the Board is needed before a proposal can be adopted by the Commission. The meetings of the Board are not public, but its reports and opinions are, once the Commission proposal has been adopted.[114] However, since the Board opinions concern drafts, these may have subsequently changed considerably. So far there is little legal research on the role of impact assessments and the functioning of the Board and its influence.[115]

The lack of research is related to how the elaboration of initiatives and the choices made early in the legislative process remain largely confidential. Even if the Commission consults interest and expert groups, the focus is on the possibilities for the Commission to gain input.[116] Most emphasis on increasing transparency during this phase of decision-making has been placed on half-hearted attempts to watch the

[110] Kleine, *supra* note 12, at 2.

[111] Novak, 'Is there a tension between transparency and efficiency in decisions? The case of the Council of the European Union', 33 *EUI Working Papers MWP* (2011), 3.

[112] Barents, *supra* note 7, at 91.

[113] Magnette, 'European Governance and Civic Participation: Can the European Union be Politicised?', *Jean Monnet Working Paper* No. 6/01, at 7.

[114] The mandate of the Impact Assessment Board is available at http://ec.europa.eu/smart-regulation/impact/iab/docs/iab_mandate_annex_sec_2006_1457_3.pdf (last visited 17 January 2017).

[115] See most notably A.C.M. Meuwese, *Impact Assessment in EU Lawmaking* (2008). The new Interinstitutional Agreement on Better Regulation stipulates that the Boards are to be replaced by Commission's Regulatory Scrutiny Boards.

[116] See the old Commission Communication, 'Towards a reinforced culture of consultation and dialogue. General principles and minimum standards for consultation of interested parties by the Commission', COM(2002) 704 final.

lobbyists[117] with the Commission as one of their main targets. Little discussion has so far taken place concerning access to documents produced by the Commission during the preparatory stages of the legislative procedure, and there is limited case law on this question.[118] So far, the Commission's institutional strategy has been to cut its losses and make available individual documents if its negative replies to applications for them are appealed to the Court. In this way, unlike the Council, the Commission has largely managed to avoid rulings that would have broad implications outside the context of the individual request. The question that can be raised is whether the possibilities for representatives of particular interest groups to access and influence Commission deliberations might in fact be greater than those of citizens. Whether this is true is challenging to evaluate, in particular since much of the evidence is not in the public domain.

How far in time does the Commission monopoly over initiative stretch? This is the relevant question when considering the conditions under which the Commission may subsequently withdraw its proposal. A withdrawal is less problematic if all parties to the procedure agree that the proposal is stuck or obsolete. This happens relatively seldom.[119] But if the matter at stake is more related to interinstitutional disagreement between the Commission, on the one hand, and the European Parliament and the Council, on the other, concerning the substantive choices made in the act, this might be a more acute problem. There is a pending case concerning a matter in which the Commission withdrew its proposal for a regulation laying down general provisions for macrofinancial assistance to third countries.[120] The Commission did this after a large number of trialogues, on the same day as the Council and the European Parliament were to close their deal. The Council asserted that there is no Treaty provision conferring on the Commission a general prerogative

[117] Agreement between the European Parliament and the European Commission on the establishment of a transparency register for organizations and self-employed individuals engaged in EU policy-making and policy implementation, OJ 2011 L 191/29; EU Transparency Register website available at http://ec.europa.eu/transparencyregister/info/homePage.do?locale=en (last visited 17 January 2017).

[118] See, however, the case brought by the Nickel Institute concerning a Commission refusal to grant access to certain 'internal documents, in particular to opinions of the Commission's Legal Service, drawn up in the context of two consecutive procedures which resulted in the classification of, inter alia, certain nickel carbonate compounds in Annex I to Council Directive 67/548/EEC'. After the Nickel Institute lodged its appeal, the Commission decided to hand out the requested document. The Court subsequently ordered that the dispute had become devoid of purpose and that there was therefore no longer any need to adjudicate on the matter. See Case T-180/10, *Nickel Institute v. Commission*, Order of 6 September 2012, not yet reported (ECLI:EU:T:2012:408). Regarding the early stages of legislative procedures, see Case T-402/12, *Schlyter v. Commission*, judgment of 16 April 2015 (ECLI:EU:T:2015:209), which concerned an application for the Commission opinion and observations issued in response to notification 2011/673/f relating to the content and submission conditions of annual declarations of nanoparticle substances, made by the French Republic under Directive 98/34/EC. The General Court annulled the Commission refusal to grant access.

[119] For a list of proposals withdrawn by the Commission in 2014, see COM(2014) 910 final, Annex 2 to the Commission Work Programme 2015. A New Start. However, some files are more political than others. The negotiations on the reform of Regulation 1049/2001 have been pending since the Commission presented its first proposal to amend the Regulation in 2008, COM(2008) 229 final. There has subsequently been another proposal to update the Regulation to the Treaty of Lisbon legal framework, but the legislative process is in a stalemate. Yet the 2008 proposal has not been withdrawn.

[120] Case C-409/13, *Council v. Commission*, judgment of 14 April 2015 (ECLI:EU:C:2015:217).

to withdraw a proposal. The power of withdrawal should not be a matter for the Commission's discretion and cannot be used in an abusive manner. In the view of the Council, withdrawing a proposal at such a late stage of a legislative process would constitute a form of veto, turning the Commission into a co-legislator. It would go far beyond the right of initiative and deprive of practical effect the Council's right to amend a proposal under Article 293(1).

The Court dismissed the action in April 2015. It established that the Commission's prerogatives under the ordinary legislative procedure reach beyond the mere submission of a proposal and then promoting contacts between the Parliament and the Council, seeking to reconcile their positions. However, the Treaties do not confer a right of veto on the Commission in the conduct of the legislative process. In practice, this means that a possible withdrawal needs to be 'supported by cogent evidence or arguments' (para. 76). The Court accepted that the amendments agreed by the Parliament and the Council were of a kind that the Commission could legitimately interpret as depriving the proposal of its *raison d'être*.

There are two particular points of interest in this judgment that I wish to raise. First, the Court noted that the decision of the Commission Vice-President informing the Parliament and the Council of the withdrawal of the proposal is silent on its grounds. However, the Court referred to the working party meetings and trialogue meetings in which the Commission had threatened the other institutions with possible withdrawal. For the Court, this was sufficient, since the grounds had been orally brought sufficiently to the attention of the two other institutions. However, keeping in mind the limited publicity regime of the relevant meetings, it seems that there is no requirement for the Commission to justify its withdrawal in a manner that would be publicly accessible. This can hardly be a satisfactory solution. Second, as regards the late timing of withdrawal, the Court referred to the late lack of consensus between the co-legislators concerning the possible retaining of the ordinary legislative procedure for the adoption of decisions: 'the Commission cannot be reproached for not having already mentioned at that time the possibility that the proposal for a framework regulation would be withdrawn' (para. 100). This stresses the role of agreement between the co-legislators. In all, the ruling emphasizes how the Commission's Treaty-based power of initiative is subject to political realities. The discretion it uses in exercising this right falls largely beyond public scrutiny.

C. European Parliament

The Treaties establish the European Parliament's legislative, budgetary, political control, and consultation functions. They also include provisions on the number of its Members (MEPs), the way in which its composition is decided, and how its Members and President are elected (Article 14 TEU). In addition, the Treaties lay down the Parliament's basic decision-making rules (Article 231 TFEU). For the Court, the effective participation of the Parliament in the adoption of legal acts is of the essence:

Effective participation of the Parliament in the Community's legislative process, in accordance with the procedures laid down by the Treaty, represents an essential factor in the institutional balance intended by the Treaty.[121]

The Treaties remain silent concerning the way in which the Parliament organizes its legislative work in committees and political groups. These matters are primarily regulated through the Parliament's Rules of Procedure.[122] In practice, coordinators of political groups divide legislative and other files among the groups, which allocate them further among the MEPs for the purpose of nominating rapporteurs with main responsibility for the dossier, and shadow rapporteurs, the rapporteurs appointed by the other political groups, for individual files. The responsible committee drafts a report based on the work of the main rapporteur, who is supported by the Committee secretariat and the group's policy advisers. The stage when reports are drafted is also a significant phase of lobbying. The degree to which a report represents the individual work of the rapporteur thus varies a great deal, depending, for example, on his/her personal interest in the file and the level of technical expertise that is needed to grasp its core elements. It is questionable whether parliamentarians have sufficient expertise for the adoption of EU legislation, which is often very technical. After all, the majority of MEPs are generalists who lack technical policy expertise:[123]

Modern decision-making is complex, technical and knowledge-demanding. Elected representatives are not experts in all fields (even if the sectoral division of EP committees has fostered many quite specialised MEPs), but are politicians with general (rather than specialist) knowledge.[124]

This gives decision-making in the Parliament—unlike in the Commission or the Council—a political character. Reports are first discussed and voted upon in the Committees. In particular the responsible Committee is central in first reading deals. The Committee reports are voted by the plenary, where amendments are made by political groups, which stresses their importance at the plenary stage. Political groups also prepare detailed voting lists for their members. The plenary first votes on amendments and then on the final report as a whole.

Informal negotiations also have a key function in the Parliament's legislative law-making. Such negotiations empower particular actors and groups within the Parliament, including party group coordinators and rapporteurs, at the expense of others. The format of informal decision-making also presents 'incentives to individual members or party groups that have a private interest in specific issues to renegade and engage in these negotiations if they have the opportunity to do so'.[125] Thus, the representativeness gained through the increased influence of the EP is at least partly

[121] Case C-408/95, *supra* note 56, at para. 45.

[122] European Parliament Rules of Procedure (7th parliamentary term—July 2013) in particular Rules 37, 38a, 39, 53–59; see also *Codecision and Conciliation. A Guide to How the Parliament co-legislates under the Treaty of Lisbon*, December 2014. Available at http://www.europarl.europa.eu/code/information/guide_en.pdf (last visited 17 January 2017).

[123] Thomson and Hosli, *supra* note 13, at 415.

[124] A.-E. Stie, *Democratic Decision-making in the EU. Technocracy in Disguise?* (2013), at 176.

[125] Häge and Kaeding, *supra* note 11, at 358.

lost because of the biased distribution of influence within the EP. The Parliament has generally wished to profile itself as the most pro-transparency EU institution, and its plenary and committee sessions are open for the public. During most of the major stages of the legislative process, Parliamentary documents are made public automatically. However, the informal modes of functioning in practice entail lower levels of transparency. This is true in particular for shadow meetings, meetings in political groups, and interinstitutional discussions, which are not accessible by the public. The informal modes of functioning and their lack of transparency thus have effects on the Parliament's input legitimacy, which is derived not only from the fact that it is directly elected by citizens, but also from the openness of its proceedings.[126]

D. Council

Article 16 TEU lays down the main parameters of the Council's functioning: the Council consists of a 'representative of each Member State at ministerial level', meets in different configurations, and acts 'by a qualified majority except where the Treaties provide otherwise'. The Treaty also lays down the formal rules on defining qualified majority. A Committee of Permanent Representatives of the Governments of the Member States (Coreper) is given the responsibility for preparing the work of the Council (Article 240 TFEU). The Treaty stipulates that the Council is to 'meet in public when it deliberates and votes on a draft legislative act'. In addition, the Treaty establishes that the Presidency of Council configurations is held by each Member State in turn on the basis of equal rotation.

The Treaty rules only touch upon the surface of how the Council operates. A key question for analysing the legislative work of the Council is what actually counts as 'the Council' and how its position is formulated.[127] Even though negotiation strategies and coalition formation in the Council have been analysed by political scientists, its decision-making structures have been subject to relatively little study.[128] Since negotiations in the Council are highly secretive, there is limited knowledge of factors determining bargaining power.[129] The basic principle in planning the work of the Council is simple. Deals are closed at the lowest possible level. As a result, the Council largely operates at lower decision-making levels.[130] Most legislative files are closed at expert level in the Council among Member State civil servants. First-hand access to expert knowledge is a comparative advantage that Council decision-making

[126] *Ibid.*

[127] Guide to the ordinary legislative procedure by the Council Secretariat, November 2011, available at http://www.consilium.europa.eu/uedocs/cms_data/librairie/PDF/QC3212175ENrevGPO2012.pdf (last visited 17 January 2017); Council Rules of Procedure, *supra* note 86.

[128] F.M. Häge, *Bureaucrats as Law-makers: Committee Decision-making in the EU Council of Ministers* (2013), at 14–15.

[129] For a review of current literature on bargaining success, see Bailer, 'What Factors Determine Bargaining Power and Success in EU Negotiations?', 17(5) *Journal of European Public Policy* (2010) 743.

[130] A list of Council preparatory bodies can be found in the Council Note 5312/14, available at http://register.consilium.europa.eu/doc/srv?l=EN&f=ST%205312%202014%20INIT (last visited 17 January 2017). On this, see Häge, *supra* note 128; Lewis, 'Strategic Bargaining, Norms and Deliberation', in D. Naurin and H. Wallace (eds), *Unveiling the Council of the European Union. Games Governments Play in Brussels* (2008/2010) 165, at 167.

has in relation to the European Parliament.[131] Coreper is the forum where both national interests and a more general interest are balanced. During the negotiation process, the Presidency acts as a broker within the Council and as its representative in interinstitutional negotiations. The Council Chairs thus 'fulfil agenda-management, brokerage and representation functions that make it more likely for EU negotiations to succeed, and possess privileged informational and procedural resources that make it possible to steer negotiations toward the agreements they most prefer'.[132]

In this work, the Presidency is assisted by the Council Secretariat, which plays a 'key behind-the-scenes facilitating leadership role, oiling the wheels of compromise, ensuring that more "integrative" agreements are reached in the Council than would otherwise have been the case'.[133] The Secretariat is a bureaucratic and strategic actor.[134] While the Secretariat officials might not have strong interests in substantive policies, they promote what in their view counts as 'workable' solutions based upon 'professional norms and prior experience'.[135] In the political process, the Secretariat, including the legal service, plays a clear role in the political process as the 'honest broker':

> when governments want a deal but are prevented from translating their broad preferences into an actual contractual agreement due to high transaction costs, they have incentives to delegate many leadership functions such as drafting texts and formulating compromises to the Council Secretariat, as it possesses a unique combination of comparative informational advantages, such as process expertise and drafting skills, and enjoys an unmatched level of trust among governments.[136]

The Council is the institution where the reality of law-making differs the most from the picture one gets by studying the Treaties. Negotiation strategies in the Council include arguing, problem-solving, framing, bargaining, coalition-building, networking, lobbying, and regional coordination.[137] Silence, in practice, indicates that you approve the proposal on the table. Especially at the working group level, being active and arguing well counts more than actual size or number of votes.[138] Individual questions or matters of principle are taken to Coreper if they cannot be decided at lower levels and there is a possibility of reaching agreement. The Presidency will place the file on the Coreper agenda when it wishes to move in the direction of other institutions in a more structuralized setting, but there is no formal rule on how and when this is done. If a first reading deal is aimed at, then the European Parliament position, once available, is in practice studied in parallel with internal Council deliberations. The timing of Coreper discussions 'depends very much on the Presidency's assessment of the political situation for one file or another, so it cannot

131 Thomson and Hosli, *supra* note 13, at 415.

132 Tallberg, 'The Power of the Chair: Formal Leadership by the Council Presidency', in Naurin and Wallace (eds), *supra* note 130, at 187.

133 Beach, 'The Facilitator of Efficient Negotiations in the Council: The Impact of the Council Secretariat', in Naurin and Wallace, *supra* note 130, at 220.

134 *Ibid.*, at 226. 135 *Ibid.*, at 225. 136 Beach, *supra* note 133, at 220.

137 Panke, 'Small States in EU Negotiations: Political Dwarfs or Power-Brokers?', 46(2) *Cooperation and Conflict* (2011) 123.

138 *Ibid.*, at 135.

be organized in a systematic way'.[139] In principle, the Presidency needs a mandate from the Council in order to open negotiations with the other institutions. However, in practice it is possible to have informal talks with the Parliament if deemed necessary:

> The only time when it is an absolute legal necessity for the Presidency to have a mandate from COREPER is when they sign the letter to Parliament at the end of the first reading saying, 'If you were to vote amendments along those lines the Council would be ready to approve them'.[140]

Only the politically most delicate issues are decided at ministerial level. Following this, the relevant question (also relevant to Commission decision-making) concerns the relationship between 'governance by experts' and 'governance by democracy'. As Stie has noted, in the Council, the working groups, the Secretariat and Coreper contribute to efficient law-making by solving problems, producing technical expertise and finding early agreement between a heterogeneous set of Member State positions. In this way, the experts not only run the 'daily show', but also influence the way in which matters are formulated and discussed at political level.[141] This has consequences for democracy: experts may become too powerful and outmanoeuvre the 'elected generalists' in the Council, where 'the ministers play second violin to working group, Secretariat and Coreper officials in the important opinion- and will-formation process prior to formal decision-taking'.[142]

From the Presidency's point of view, placing a matter on the ministerial agenda indicates failure to reach agreement.[143] To avoid this, extra time is regularly spent searching for a consensus-based outcome even after a qualified majority has formed. The informal Council decision-making rules stipulate that it is considered inappropriate for a majority to push an isolated delegation to a vote or to use their veto.[144] In practice, as Kleine has demonstrated:

> The EU legislative process is governed by a norm of discretion, which prescribes that governments facing unmanageable domestic pressure ought to be accommodated. The norm of discretion manifests itself in collective informal governance practices at every step of the EU's legislative procedure. However, the norm's precise boundaries are vague; they are also prone to abuse when it is difficult to verify that legitimate demands are being made for the use of informal governance. This means that the actual use of informal governance is fraught with difficulties, since the governments are bound to disagree about its necessity.[145]

The decisive factor in designing decision-making is how the Presidency understands the state of the legislative file and the prospects of finding agreement. The Presidency is in the best position to evaluate this, since it has access to most information con-

[139] Mr Hubert Legal, Council Legal Service, quoted in the House of Lords Report with Evidence. 'Codecision and national parliamentary scrutiny', HL Paper 125 (2009), at 53, available at http://www.statewatch.org/news/2009/jul/eu-hol-codecision-nat-scrutiny.pdf (last visited 17 January 2017).

[140] *Ibid.*, at 52.

[141] For a similar finding in a national context, see Hyvärinen and Raunio, 'Who Decides What EU Issues Ministers Talk About? Explaining Governmental EU Policy Co-Ordination in Finland', 52(5) *JCMS* (2014) 1019.

[142] Stie, *supra* note 124, at 177.

[143] Lewis, *supra* note 130, at 167.

[144] *Ibid.*, at 170.

[145] Kleine, *supra* note 12, at 123.

cerning Member States and institutional positions. The Presidency seldom calls for a vote. Instead, it states orally that there is a qualified majority in favour of a given measure, and if nobody objects, the proposition is sent to the ministers for formal adoption.[146]

For this reason, the formal Treaty rules on voting and forming a qualified majority are of a lesser practical relevance when in practice consensus is usually sought irrespective of the formal voting rule.[147] While lawyers tend to focus their energy on speculating on the number of votes that each Member State possesses in the Council, their exact allocation in fact settles very little in terms of bargaining power:

> small member states are not per se any less active than bigger states, as a high level of expertise can compensate for limited financial, economic and staff capacities. Smaller states are neither per se political dwarfs nor power-brokers. Size is what they make of it. Small states can compensate for size-related difficulties through institutionalized learning and through the possession of expertise.[148]

Still, it is a fundamental analytical premise in political science that 'the formal possibility of calling a majority vote on a matter, rather than recourse to the actual vote itself, determines strategic actor behavior and decision-making outcomes'.[149]

The Treaties include some provisions referring to the participation and role of national parliaments in EU matters, in particular through the subsidiarity control mechanism.[150] The main part of their functions is, however, based on provisions of national constitutions and relates to how each Member State formulates the positions for the purpose of decision-making in the Council. Therefore, the way in which Member State position-building and the participation of national parliaments is arranged during the EU legislative process is a matter left to national constitutions to settle.[151] Arrangements vary so greatly that it is almost impossible to draw any general conclusions from them, ranging from next to no participation to actually establishing the national position, with full rights of access to documents produced at every stage of EU decision-making. The main challenge for many national parliaments relates to gaining access to the information relating to EU matters that would be needed in order to hold the government accountable. Some parliaments are in practice largely dependent on information that is in the public domain without any privileged channel to information through their own government.

How much of the discussion within the Council is public knowledge? Not too much. In principle, Articles 16(8) TEU and 15(2) TEU stipulate the publicity of the Council's meeting when deliberating and voting on draft legislative act. In practice, the Council has interpreted these provisions strictly as referring to the stage of

[146] Novak, *supra* note 111, at 4. [147] Lewis, *supra* note 130, at 170.

[148] Panke, *supra* note 137, at 137.

[149] For further references, see Golub, *supra* note 105, at 733.

[150] See P. Kiiver, *The Early Warning System for the Principle of Subsidiarity: Constitutional Theory and Empirical Reality* (2013).

[151] For a thorough analysis of the role of national parliaments in EU decision-making pre-Lisbon, see P. Kiiver, *The National Parliaments in the European Union: A Critical View on EU Constitution-building* (2006).

Council deliberation or voting in the composition of ministers.[152] This raises the rather fundamental question of the relevance of the stage of decision-making for the application of legislative transparency. If it was indeed limited to only those documents that are issued days before a formal Council meeting where a legislative file is to be deliberated or approved, often without any discussion, then access to documents relating to a legislative file would in practice be limited to one document generated at the point in time when the file is to be closed. All the documents produced during the time when the majority of questions are settled at lower levels and between the institutions would be excluded from the scope of access.

Council practice has gained obvious criticism from the European Parliament, which is dependent on the Presidency and the possible direct contacts of MEPs with Member State governments for its flow of information, and has its own interinstitutional interest in gaining access to Council deliberations as early as possible:

> there are several worrying Council and Commission practices in place which de facto hide the real content of Member States' positions in the Council/Commission preparatory bodies such as: – the growing number of working documents which are not timely cited in the institution's register (for example, the Council Meeting Documents (MD or SD) which are diffused only afterwards); – the fact of systematically hiding the names of Member States in the outcome of proceedings (when available) that makes it impossible to understand what kind of majority/minority is taking shape in the Council/Commission committees.[153]

The need for efficient decision-making has also been used by the Council to justify a refusal to hand out documents identifying the positions of Member States.[154] The general Council practice has been to grant access to such documents, but deleting the relevant Member State symbols first[155] as 'the only legally defendable option' that guarantees 'a right balance between transparency and the protection of the Council's deliberations'.[156] The question has direct linkages with the Member States' national arrangements as well. Positions becoming public during the EU process is painful if these positions are not publicly available in the national arena, or if the flow of information between the government and the national parliament is limited.

Access to Member State positions came to the fore when Access Info Europe, a European non-governmental organization (NGO) specializing in freedom of information, requested access to certain information from the Council Secretariat to the Council Working Party on Information, consisting of Member States' civil servants, concerning the reform of Regulation 1049/2001 on public access to documents.

[152] See, e.g. Council Confirmatory application No. 05/c/01/12 of 20 March 2012.

[153] Committee on Civil Liberties, Justice and Home Affairs, Working document (1) on the Annual Report on public access to documents (Rule 104(7) of the Council Rules of Procedure) for 2009–2010, Rapporteur: Heidi Hautala, PE456.867v01-00.

[154] The Council practice has been that when Member States participate in the work of the Council and its committees and bodies, they form a part of the latter, and thus the positions expressed and recorded in this context form a part of Council documents. See Council Note 6203/02, Public access to documents—Issues of principle, 1 March 2002.

[155] Council Outcome of Proceedings 10425/03, Item 3b of the agenda: Requests for access to documents concerning draft legislative acts, 13 June 2003.

[156] Council Note 6203/02, *supra* note 154.

The Council handed out the document but blanked out the Member State symbols, which made it possible to know what had been said but not who had said it. Access Info won its case in the General Court,[157] but the Council appealed and had its claims defeated for a second time by the CJEU.[158] The central question was whether public access to Member State positions distracts the effectiveness of decision-making and if yes, which one should take priority: effectiveness or openness in decision-making. In the Council's view, the General Court's reading had attached 'undue and excessive weight to the transparency of the decision-making process, without taking any account of the needs associated with the effectiveness of that process', and disregarded the balanced approach laid down both in primary law and secondary law between the two objectives. The Council, supported by several Member State governments, argued that 'its legislative process is very fluid and requires a high level of flexibility on the part of Member States so that they can modify their initial position, thus maximising the chances of reaching an agreement'. This presumes ensuring a 'negotiating space' enabling Member States maximum room for manoeuvre in the discussions and thereby preserving the effectiveness of the legislative process: 'That room for manoeuvre would be reduced if the identity of the delegations were disclosed too early in the procedure, in that it would have the effect of triggering pressure from public opinion' (para. 24). In the Council's view, identifying the delegations was not necessary for ensuring a democratic debate.

The CJEU rejected these arguments with reference to the aim of ensuring public access to the entire content of Council documents, including Member State positions. The CJEU also rejected the Council's arguments relating to the particularly sensitive nature of the document and that the exception relating to 'space to think' had been interpreted too narrowly. According to the CJEU, the application of exceptions to access presumes such a high standard of proof to establish a level of harm that in practice it becomes impossible to invoke that provision.[159] The Council had also claimed that the unauthorized publication of Member State positions had resulted in an 'impasse over the legislative dossier', since the Member States wishing to restrict access risked being shown in a bad light. As a result, the level of detail in the reports for the legislative file had been lowered. In other words, demands for transparency and participation from the civil society in the discussions concerning the EU's future transparency regime had, in fact, resulted in less transparency.[160] The Court argued that the Council had not demonstrated the accuracy of this premise. The General Court's conclusion had been correctly:

> based, rather, on the finding that the various proposals for amendment or re-drafting made by the four Member State delegations which are described in the requested document are part of the normal legislative process, from which it follows that the requested documents could

[157] Case T-233/09, *Access Info Europe v. Council*, [2011] ECR II-01073 (ECLI:EU:T:2011:105).
[158] Case C-280/11 P, *Council v. Access Info Europe*, judgment of 17 October 2013 (ECLI:EU:C:2013:671).
[159] *Ibid.*, at para. 40.
[160] See also Thompsen, 'Public Access to Documents. The Council's Transparency Policy and Practice from Maastricht to Lisbon', paper presented at the Conference on *Transparency and Access to the Records and Archives of the EU Institutions*, 25 January 2013, 13. On file with author.

not be regarded as sensitive – not solely by reference to the criterion concerning the involvement of a fundamental interest of the European Union or of the Member States, but by reference to any criterion whatsoever.[161]

It is difficult to think of a more straightforward way of interpreting the principle in the context of a legislative procedure. But the Council's response has not been impressive, since it continues to have enormous difficulties living up to this standard.[162]

The Council Legal Service, backed up by the Commission Legal Service, has strongly argued for an interpretation according to which during ongoing legislative procedures there should not be any general right for the public to access documents, including in particular their own legal opinions.[163] These questions are also of relevance when discussing the considerable influence of legal advisers in the legislative process. Access to its legal service opinions relating to pending legislative procedures has been discussed in case law.[164] In the view of the CJEU, many of the excuses relied on by the Council to justify its refusal to grant access 'were in no way substantiated by detailed arguments' and thus, the Court could see 'no real risk that is reasonably foreseeable and not purely hypothetical of that interest being undermined'.[165] Regarding the Council's concerns about public pressure on its legal service, the Court established that:

if the members of that legal service were subjected to improper pressure to that end, it would be that pressure, and not the possibility of the disclosure of legal opinions, which would compromise that institution's interest in receiving frank, objective and comprehensive advice and it would clearly be incumbent on the Council to take the necessary measures to put a stop to it.[166]

Following this, the Court established 'in principle, an obligation to disclose the opinions of the Council's legal service relating to a legislative process'.[167]

Ideally, a Court ruling entails that uncertainties are settled and that implementation becomes easier. But this has not been the case here. For the Council (and to a lesser extent for the Commission) the *Turco* ruling has proved immensely difficult to live with.[168] The mindset of the Council (legal service) is nicely illustrated in an appeal brought by ClientEarth, an NGO working to protect the environment

[161] Case C-280/11 P, *supra* note 158, at para. 63.

[162] See Leino, *supra* note 85.

[163] Legal, *supra* note 139.

[164] Joined Cases C-39/05 P, C-52/05 P, *Sweden and Turco v. Council*, [2008] ECR I-04723 (ECLI:EU:C:2008:374).

[165] *Ibid.*, at para. 63.

[166] *Ibid.*, at para. 64. See, however, also Joined Cases C-514/07 P, C-528/07 P and C-532/07 P, *Sweden and Others v. API and Commission*, [2010] ECR I-8533 (ECLI:EU:C:2010:541), at para. 93, where the CJEU is worried about the effect that disclosure of Court pleadings, 'exposing judicial activities to external pressure, albeit only in the perception of the public, and would disturb the serenity of the proceedings'. See Leino, 'Just A Little Sunshine in the Rain: The 2010 Case Law of the European Court of Justice on Access to Documents', 48(4) *Common Market Law Review* (2011) 1215.

[167] Joined Cases C-39/05 P, C-52/05 P, *supra* note 164, at para. 69. However, it remained possible to refuse to disclose a specific legal opinion, given in the context of a legislative process, but being of a particularly sensitive nature or having a particularly wide scope that goes beyond the context of the legislative process in question.

[168] Leino, *supra* note 85.

through advocacy, litigation, and research, before the General Court following the Council's refusal to grant—ironically enough—more than an extremely limited partial access to a legal service opinion relating to the reform of Regulation 1049/2001 on public access to documents.[169] In its reply, the Council argued that as to its contents, the legal advice given was 'particularly sensitive in nature':

> Were it to be released to the public and thus to the European Parliament, the Legal Service's analysis of the European Parliament's amendments – intended to solely facilitate internal discussions within the Council on the legal matters referred to above – is likely to prompt divergences with the European Parliament and could negatively impact on the upcoming negotiations.[170]

We are thus to understand that disclosure of documents to the public—in this case to a well-known NGO representing civil society—cannot take place if the institutions are of a different opinion on a matter. One would think that differences of opinion are a rather natural part, even a precondition, of functioning democracy.

The horror scenario informing Council position-building would seem to consist of the possibility that an institution might ultimately approve legislation that its own legal service might have found unconstitutional as far as the EU Treaties are concerned; a fact that should not in its view be public knowledge. This is an argument that the Court specifically rejected in the *Turco* case quoted earlier:

> an overriding public interest is constituted by the fact that disclosure of documents containing the advice of an institution's legal service on legal questions arising when legislative initiatives are being debated increases the transparency and openness of the legislative process and strengthens the democratic right of European citizens to scrutinize the information which has formed the basis of a legislative act . . .[171]

Therefore, should not even such an institutional choice and its justification be publicly available, especially considering that the consequences of these appeals are not necessarily that dramatic, and can usually be limited quite effectively by the Court? In fact, whether a matter is known by the wider public seldom has consequences for whether a matter ends up before the Court or not. Annulment claims originate primarily from the Member States or the other EU institutions. The Member States and the Commission not only have access to the Council opinions anyway, but also employ their own reserve of EU lawyers capable of producing similar analyses. The latter point also applies to the Parliament. One might also think that if and when serious doubts exist about the constitutionality of an EU act, it would be extremely positive if the Court indeed looked into the matter and settled it.

What is perhaps the most striking feature of this case law is the argumentation that the Council uses. It sticks to its guns to the last minute, defending a right of institutions and Member States to conduct the vast part of EU legislative work in secrecy. This should be politically embarrassing and cause problems in a Union

[169] For the Council's reply to ClientEarth, see Council 'IA' Item Note 12068/10, Public access to documents—Confirmatory application No. 15/c/01/10, 20 July 2010, available at http://register.consilium.europa.eu/pdf/en/10/st12/st12068.en10.pdf (last visited 17 January 2017).

[170] *Ibid.*, at para. 8 of the reply.

[171] Joined Cases C-39/05 P, C-52/05 P, *supra* note 164, at paras 66–67.

persistently struggling with legitimacy related challenges. While many of the exceptions seeking to limit access to information have a valid legal basis and a proper scope of application, they are also open to abuse to the detriment of access to information, provoking claims on how the Council is a legislative body more closed than the Congress of the People's Republic of China.[172] If the Council had its way, the Lisbon amendments aiming to improve openness and citizen access would in practice result in very little. Council decision-making builds largely on informal rules aiming at increasing efficiency through flexibility, while emphasizing the search for consensus. These rules stress the role of the Presidency and the need to produce decisions that every Council member can live with. At the same time, these rules weaken the possibilities of participation and openness at the EU level. This should be a matter of some concern, especially since 'efficient decision-making' at EU level simultaneously weakens the possibilities of guaranteeing democratic debates at national level.

E. Trialogues

Informal decision-making is at its peak during the trialogues, since the Treaties make no reference to this forum. In first reading deals trialogues function as the forum for interinstitutional agreement, and trialogues are increasingly taking over as the main forum for making legislative deals between the three institutions.[173] In the joint declaration quoted earlier, the three institutions argue that the trialogue 'system has demonstrated its vitality and flexibility in increasing significantly the possibilities for agreement at first and second reading stages'. The key to their success is flexibility. According to the declaration, trialogues 'may be held at all stages of the procedure and at different levels of representation, depending on the nature of the expected discussion'.[174] Informal contacts between the institutions also take place outside the trialogue format: discussions are held concerning institutional positions and how they could be aligned during all stages of the procedure.[175] The use of informal formats is not in any way restricted to technical, urgent, or uncontested files.[176] Questions relating to the existence of EU competence frequently appear on trialogue agendas as a part of the wider package deal, and are thus in no way beyond political deliberations in the trialogue.[177] Trialogues are an incredibly efficient format for accommodating institutional positions, and have led to a great majority of deals being closed early in the legislative procedure. First reading solutions are often

[172] See S. Hix, *What's Wrong with the European Union and How to Fix It* (2008) 152.

[173] Report of the CEPS High-level Group, *Shifting EU Institutional Reform into High Gear* (2014), at 1–24, available at https://www.ceps.eu/system/files/HLG%20report%20on%20EU%20Institutional%20Reform%20with%20covers%20rev.pdf (last visited 17 January 2017).

[174] Joint declaration on practical arrangements for the codecision procedure, *supra* note 101.

[175] See the House of Lords Report with Evidence, *supra* note 139, at 14.

[176] See Bressanelli, Héritier, Koop, and Reh, 'The Informal Politics of Codecision: Introducing a New Data Set on Early Agreements in the European Union', 64 *EUI Working Papers* RSCAS (2014).

[177] For a recent example, see Regulation (EU) 806/2014, *supra* note 51, where the institutions in practice settled a compromise concerning the limits of EU competence in the trialogues, reflected in paras 19–20 and Article 1 of the Regulation. This interpretation has not been challenged in the Court, even though the institutions and Member States disagree on the need of the separate international agreement between the Member States.

reached swiftly once the trialogues are launched, even if there is no Treaty-based time limit for first reading decision-making.

During the trialogue phase, the EU democratic process is in the hands of very few: the European Parliament rapporteur(s), the representatives of the Council Presidency, and a few Commission officials. This phase largely escapes public scrutiny. The joint declaration quoted earlier stipulates that 'trilogies taking place within the European Parliament and Council shall be announced, where practicable', and 'when conclusion of a dossier at first reading is imminent, information on the intention to conclude an agreement should be made readily available as soon as possible'. There is no mention of access to information while the process is in the substantive phase. Civil society representatives have pointed out how trialogues represent the victory of efficient law-making over the formal machinery of law-making, which results in a general lack of transparency.[178] The Parliament's 2011 report relating to the implementation of Regulation 1049/2001:

> Emphasises that trialogues and the conciliation procedures . . . are a substantial phase of the legislative procedure, and not a separate 'space to think'; believes especially that the current procedures as regards trialogues prior to a possible first reading agreement fail to ensure a satisfactory level of legislative transparency and access to documents both internally, to the Parliament, and externally in relation to citizens and public opinion; requests, therefore, that documents created in their framework, such as agendas, summaries of outcomes and the 'four column' documents drawn up for facilitating negotiations, should not in principle be treated differently from other legislative documents, and that they should be made public as regards trialogues prior to a possible first reading agreement.[179]

Many of these challenges were discussed during the attempts to reform Regulation 1049/2001, but so far there is no agreement on how access should be arranged. One would think that in today's world technical means to guarantee more direct access would exist, if there was a will to use them. To give a simple example, the legislative procedure is currently not backed up by any shared interinstitutional space where documents and meeting schedules would be recorded in real time, accompanied with relevant contact information.

Access to information by the members of the three institutions not present during these discussions is also limited. Information is power, and the trialogue format empowers those that possess it at the expense of those who do not. Political scientists have demonstrated how within the Parliament, first reading agreements emphasize the discretion given to its own rapporteur(s), who can present a first reading agreement with the Council as a 'take it or leave it' offer to the committee and the plenary. This allows a substantial amount of discretion to the rapporteur.[180]

[178] See, e.g. Bunyan, 'European Parliament: Abolish 1st [and 2nd] reading secret deals – bring back democracy "warts and all"', Statewatch analysis available at http://www.statewatch.org/analyses/no-84-ep-first-reading-deals.pdf (last visited 17 January 2017).

[179] EP Resolution of 14 September 2011 on public access to documents (Rule 104(7)) for the years 2009–2010, (2010/2294(INI)) P7_TA(2011)0378, at para. 29.

[180] Discussed in Hix and Høyland, 'Empowerment of the European Parliament', 16 *Annual Review of Political Science* (2013) 171, at 184. For rules concerning the Parliament's representation and position-building, see European Parliament Rules of Procedure, *supra* note 122, Rule 70.

First reading agreements stress the role of responsible committee in the Parliament, and reduce the effect on the meaningfulness of parliamentary debates. In practice, it is the Parliament's negotiating team consisting of the rapporteur and the shadows which establishes its positions. Handing out information to the public is in the hands of the rapporteurs, whose tweets commenting on the conduct of negotiations also create a practical avenue to information for many Member State governments. At the same time, tweeting is often limited by interinstitutional agreements on policy lines to be taken when communicating with the public.

As far as the Council is concerned, first reading agreement solutions mean in practice no political level debates in the Council. Deals are effectively concluded before they reach the ministers. The Council position is settled by Coreper. In principle, feedback from trialogues is given to the delegations either through working parties or Coreper. National parliaments often experience difficulties following decision-making in trialogues. This is also due to the extent to which Commission proposals may be amended during the legislative process and the speed at which legislation is adopted, which hinders effective scrutiny of the proposed amendments at national level.[181] Quick political agreements in first reading are particularly challenging for the Commission, which has a highly political top level and technically minded civil servants, who are in practice left to settle the deals with the politicians in the Parliament[182] and the Presidency representatives. Early agreements also reduce the powers of the Commission, which has difficulties hanging on to its proposal after the Parliament and the Council have already reached agreement on a text.[183]

F. The Culture of Political Deals

Efficient law-making is largely promoted through a by-passing of the formal machinery of law-making.[184] There is reluctance in the Council and among many MEPs to overhaul and formalize trialogue rules, visible also in the plans for a new Interinstitutional Agreement on Better Regulation, which seems to effectively settle the playing field for the next five years. The informal and flexible functioning of the current rules enhances not only the claimed efficiency of the procedures, but also the opportunities for key actors to influence the dossiers.[185] Efficiency ranks high among the EU values used to justify institutional solutions.[186] Informal institutions are also shaped by actors' different time horizons, sensitivities to failure, and levels of resources.[187] For example, the Parliament's time horizon is longer than that of a

[181] House of Lords Report with Evidence, *supra* note 139, at 15–16.

[182] Fuglsang and Olsen, 'Staying in the Loop. The Commission's role in first reading agreements', *EPIN Working Paper* No. 25, September 2009.

[183] Jacqué, *supra* note 52, at 390.

[184] Bunyan, *supra* note 178.

[185] Stie, *supra* note 124, at 182.

[186] See Leino, 'Efficiency, Citizens and Administrative Culture. The Politics of Good Administration in the EU', 4 *European Public Law* (2014) 681.

[187] Thomson and Hosli, *supra* note 13, at 393.

Council Presidency, which sets the Council legislative agenda. But not all matters discussed 'are as extremely urgent as they are said to be. There is an element of political pressure in this time factor.'[188]

The culture of political deals and interinstitutional compromises has consequences for the quality of legislation. There are many good reasons to question 'whether reaching a deal early in the process among only a handful of people who meet in secrecy, is actually a productive method of ensuring qualitatively good decisions'.[189]

These fears have produced a number of initiatives aiming to reverse the trend, including an interinstitutional agreement on better law-making, the Commission's REFIT and smart regulation initiatives, and subsidiarity-related initiatives by national parliaments.[190] While these attempts gain plenty of support at the level of principle, they weigh very little in the face of more urgent political necessities relating to the interest in closing individual dossiers. A closed legislative dossier gains plenty of political points for rapporteurs, Council Presidencies, and members of the Commission. Tight schedules, abstraction, and ambiguity thus also act as legislative techniques. Clarity and better law-making give way to efficiency and flexible outcomes that everyone can explain in their own way in their home states.

The risk is that the product becomes 'bad' legislation that is unclear, vague, and subject to various interpretations. This technique delays many of the relevant substantive decisions to the stage of implementation. Technical implementation then becomes subject to administrative and judicial politics. Substantive choices are pushed to the stage of implementation, which raises questions relating to democratic accountability. There would also seem to be a link between compromises, unclear obligations, and delays in implementation.[191] This increases the institutional role of the Commission in monitoring compliance with EU law. Infringement proceedings offer a second opportunity to discuss the true meaning of the vague provisions, which might have been intentionally left unclear during the legislative procedure in order to find a deal that everyone could live with. Solving substantive obligations also increases the desire of the European Parliament to urge that it should be given a role in the process of

[188] Legal, *supra* note 139, at 58. [189] Stie, *supra* note 124, at 184.

[190] Interinstitutional Agreement on Better Law-making, OJ 2003 C 321/1, available at http://eur-lex.europa.eu/LexUriServ/LexUriServ.do?uri=OJ:C:2003:321:0001:0005:EN:PDF (last visited 17 January 2017). See also the Commission 'smart regulation' initiative, available at http://ec.europa.eu/smart-regulation/index_en.htm (last visited 12 April 2017) and the European Parliament Directorate for Impact Assessment and European Added Value, available at http://www.europarl.europa.eu/the-secretary-general/en/activities/recent_activities/articles/articles-2012/articles-2012-october/articles-2012-october-2.html (last visited 17 January 2017).

[191] The general state of implementing EU law is assessed on an annual basis by the Commission. For the most recent report, see Report from the Commission, 31st Annual Report on Monitoring the Application of EU Law (2013), COM(2014) 612 final. In its report, the Commission argues that '[l]ate transposition of directives remains a persistent problem hindering delivery of tangible benefits for citizens'.

national implementation[192]—a process in which the current Treaties offer it no formal position.[193]

The legislative procedure formally ends with the adoption of a legal act. The discussion concerning its meaning may continue before the CJEU, if annulment proceedings are raised within the two-month deadline. But any EU legislative process today also involves questions relating to acts that complement the legal framework. The Lisbon changes on the restructuring of the typology of legal acts have resulted in the strengthening of the Commission in this respect, since it now has a role in legislative matters through the creation of the category of delegated acts.[194] Powers to develop or implement the legal framework are increasingly delegated to the Commission in order to escape complex and time-consuming legislative processes. While such choices appear merely technical, these questions often persist longest on the agenda. According to Article 290 TFEU '[t]he essential elements of an area shall be reserved for the legislative act and accordingly shall not be the subject of a delegation of power'. The expanded use of delegated powers also contributes to a greater complexity of legal frameworks. The Commission has used these powers expansively. In practice, highly significant questions have been left outside the legislative process to be later settled on the basis of delegated acts.[195] While it certainly makes the legislative procedure less painful if difficult matters are postponed, this strategy increases the role of the Commission, especially since the European Parliament and the Council have used their power to oppose delegated acts extremely seldom.

The current informal framework for closing legislative deals translates into a low level of transparency. In many instances direct access of citizens and NGOs to information concerning negotiations on legislative files remains limited, which weakens their possibilities of influencing them. The task of civil society is to influence the positions of the institutions, and it is difficult to do that without knowing what those positions are, and what they are based on. At the same time, there is widespread concern relating to uncontrolled access by lobbyists representing individual and business interests to the same process, and the influence that they have on the outcome.[196]

[192] See, e.g. the EP Resolution of 4 February 2014 on the 29th annual report on monitoring the application of EU law (2011), (2013/2119(INI)), where the Parliament '[c]alls on the Commission to make compliance with EU law a real political priority to be pursued in close collaboration with Parliament, which has a duty (a) to keep the Commission politically accountable and (b), as co-legislator, to make sure that it is itself fully informed with a view to constantly improving its legislative work' (para. 12).

[193] Under Article 291 TFEU, 'Member States shall adopt all measures of national law necessary to implement legally binding Union acts', but implementing powers can be conferred on the Commission or exceptionally on the Council, '[w]here uniform conditions for implementing legally binding Union acts are needed, those acts shall confer implementing powers on the Commission'.

[194] Hofmann, 'Legislation, Delegation and Implementation under the Treaty of Lisbon: Typology Meets Reality', 15(4) *European Law Journal* (2009) 482, at 504.

[195] See, e.g. the Regulation on the Single Resolution Mechanism and Fund No 806/2014, *supra* note 51, which empowers the Commission to adopt various delegated acts.

[196] See, e.g. the 2013 Global Corruption Barometer, where 60% of Europe's citizens consider their country's government being run to a large extent or entirely by a few big interests. The Report is available at http://www.transparency.org/whatwedo/publication/global_corruption_barometer_2013 (last visited 17 January 2017).

Lobbying activities raise risks of corruption and regulatory capture,[197] which affects trust in the legislative process producing fair, informed, and balanced acts. While technical outside expertise is often needed to respond to the demands of the complex world, lobbying may also be experienced as undue influence, which would be best dealt with through transparent mechanisms framing such activities. No effective mechanisms are today in place. The most frequently proposed way of dealing with these problems is the idea of a legislative footprint, which would record the influence of lobbyists' influence on legislative acts, and would be used by all participants in the EU policy-making process.[198]

The Court's jurisprudence clearly lays down the main principle of public access and its linkage with the principle of democracy:

> [I]ncreased openness . . . enables citizens to participate more closely in the decision-making process and guarantees that the administration enjoys greater legitimacy and is more effective and more accountable to the citizen in a democratic system. Those considerations are clearly of particular relevance where the Council is acting in its legislative capacity . . . Openness in that respect contributes to strengthening democracy by allowing citizens to scrutinize all the information which has formed the basis of a legislative act. The possibility for citizens to find out the considerations underpinning legislative action is a precondition for the effective exercise of their democratic rights.[199]

The Court set the threshold high in referring to 'all the information which has formed the basis for a legislative act': it is clearly not only quantity that is of relevance, but also quality. The legislature needs to provide access to information concerning the key elements on the legislative agenda while the relevant process is ongoing and there is a chance to influence it. It would seem that legislative transparency is anything but secured post-Treaty of Lisbon and remains just as much contested as before. While:

> [c]losed settings could be legitimate in situations where actors search for common ground and where a shielded setting is a means to reaching goals that can otherwise not be achieved . . . when the purpose of a setting is the adoption of public policy, secretly reached agreements must at some point be tested and justified in a publicly accessible manner.[200]

The EU decision-making framework builds on informal solutions that weaken the opportunities for participation. Participatory practices in the EU have so far been largely detached from normative considerations regarding the place of citizens in the Union political system.[201]

Currently, very few really know why certain legislative choices have been made, and even these few in the know often choose to remain silent. Justifying the current method would be difficult, for example, before the national parliaments. They

[197] Commission's Report, EU Anti-Corruption Report of 3 February 2014, COM(2014) 38 final.

[198] Berg, 'What's the real influence of lobbyists in Brussels?', posted on the Transparency International website on 12 March 2015, available at http://transparency.eu/whats-the-real-influence-of-lobbyists-in-brussels/ (last visited 18 January 2017).

[199] Joined Cases C-39/05 P and C-52/05 P, *supra* note 164, at paras 45–46.

[200] Stie, *supra* note 124, 189.

[201] See J. Mendes, *Participation in EU Rule-making. A Rights-based Approach* (2011).

experience the effects of secrecy in rather concrete terms when Member State governments are either not in the possession of relevant information, or do not have a realistic time frame in which to deliver this information to their parliaments before decisions have already been made in Brussels. Urgency and efficiency are overrated in EU decision-making. This points to a need to find another sort of a balance between a process which is efficient but secretive, on the one hand and slow but open and public, on the other.

4. Time for a New Sort of a Compromise?

The Laeken Declaration on the Future of Europe, adopted in December 2001, still bears great relevance for various questions discussed in this chapter. The Declaration stressed the aim of bringing the institutions closer to citizens by making them both more efficient and open at the same time. According to the Declaration, citizens feel that 'deals are all too often cut out of their sight and they want better democratic scrutiny'.[202] These concerns had a clear connection with the division of competence between the EU and its Member States, which needed to be made more transparent while not leading to 'a creeping expansion of the competence of the Union or to encroachment upon the exclusive areas of competence of the Member States'.[203]

It would seem that these concerns remain at least equally valid today. Even after a number of Treaty reforms relating to a clearer division of competence and wider openness in legislative matters, the EU Treaties continue to establish only some of the parameters of the EU legislative procedure. The key solutions rely on compromises and informal interinstitutional arrangements, which emphasize flexibility and aim at efficient law-making. The EU legislative process turns into a wonderful example of the interplay between law and politics. From within the process, law operates as 'a common language understood and shared by all'.[204] The rules of decision-making affect political choices and arguments used to defend them. Understanding law as language, or as 'rules of the game', links with the approach of many critical legal scholars, who find that:

> Legal doctrine not only does not, but also cannot, generate determinate results in concrete cases. Law is not so much a rational enterprise as a vast exercise in rationalization. Legal doctrine can be manipulated to justify an almost infinite spectrum of possible outcomes. Moreover, a plausible argument can be made that any such outcome has been derived from the dominant legal conceptions. Legal doctrine is nothing more than a sophisticated vocabulary and repertoire of manipulative techniques for categorizing, describing, organizing, and comparing: it is not a methodology for reaching substantive outcomes.[205]

[202] Laeken Declaration, Laeken Declaration on the Future of the Union, 15 December 2001, SN 273/01.

[203] *Ibid.* [204] Jacqué, *supra* note 15, at 43.

[205] Hutchinson and Monahan, 'Law, Politics and Critical Legal Scholars: The Unfolding Drama of American Legal Thought', 36 *Stanford Law Review* (1984) 199, at 206.

The legal rules concerning EU decision-making are often instrumentalized in order to promote particular institutional objectives. Power relations are affected by how well acquainted the key players are with the rules of law-making.

The relevant question is, who wins and who loses by the current arrangements? The informal nature of many arrangements currently empowers some key players in the legislative process, including in particular the rapporteurs of the European Parliament and the Council Presidency. The general assumption seems to be that the closed and informal setting is for the benefit of efficient law-making machinery that creates results in the form of the maximum number of closed legislative files for each Council Presidency and European Parliament's rapporteur. The quality of this legislation might not always be first class, and might be dependent on a high amount of delegated acts complicating the legal framework further, but does it matter as long as it is produced swiftly?

Who loses then? The informal rules of law-making bring to the fore many fundamental questions relating to participation and power in the adoption of EU legal acts. What is lost in the process are the possibilities of participation and openness, and result in legislation that might take longer to produce but that might be easier to implement and more carefully thought through. The drafters of REFIT and better regulation initiatives might actually have a point—sometimes less might actually be more. That these values are lacking is not a mistake but a result of an intentional balance made by the institutions, which have decided to vouch for efficiency instead of participation, and seem to believe that it is 'either/or', or that some loss of efficiency would not be worthwhile even if it would enable proper discussions and wider participation to take place.

The relevant political question is whether the balance created by today's informal law-making framework is the right one. Efficiency is not an absolute value, and it favours those currently in powerful positions. The Treaties would also allow a different balance. One would think that a slight loss in the efficiency part might not be fatal, if the end result was a more inclusive process enabling participatory practices at institutional level, at national level through the national parliaments, and at the level of civil society. Could the time be ripe for a new sort of a compromise?

3

Abnormal Sources and Institutional Actions in the EU Sovereign Debt Crisis—ECB Crisis Management and the Sovereign Debt Loans

Claire Kilpatrick

This analysis focuses on sources and institutional actions in the European Union (EU) sovereign debt crisis. By this I mean the large new and distinctive body of normative sources created or developed from 2008 onwards to provide assistance to EU Member States facing sovereign debt problems. This embraces two rather different sets of sources. On the one hand, there is the loan assistance itself (the 'bailout'). On the other, there is the use of special new sources and actions by the European Central Bank (ECB) directed towards banks and states on the brink of bailout or in actual receipt of bailout assistance. This includes the provision of Emergency Liquidity Assistance (ELA), the Securities Markets Programme (SMP) launched at the same time as the first eurozone bailout in May 2010 and the Outright Market Transactions (OMT) programme announced in September 2012.

The title of this chapter also signifies an intention to examine this large new body of sovereign debt sources and actions from a particular angle, by investigating different ways in which they might be considered to be *abnormal*. This requires us to consider when a source might be considered to be normal or abnormal both generally and in the specific legal context of the sovereign debt crisis. I take the position that abnormal is related to, but not the same as, other ways of describing sources which are out of the ordinary. On one side of abnormality are sources that are unusual or novel or unconventional. To conclude that a source or interaction is not simply unusual or novel or unconventional but also abnormal is to make a negative normative evaluation of that source or interaction in at least some respects. On the other side of abnormality are stronger claims of illegality and systemic mutation of the EU legal order. Such claims of normality—and counterclaims of constitutional mutation—have been a central feature of analyses of euro crisis sources. I argue that a source can be abnormal while still being found, more or less persuasively, to be lawful. However, one indicator of abnormality is the presence of normative EU instructions without those instructions being framed as legal sources. At the same time, the presence of abnormality does not in itself indicate systemic mutation.

Abnormal Sources and Institutional Actions in the EU Sovereign Debt Crisis: ECB Crisis Management and the Sovereign Debt Loans. First Edition. Claire Kilpatrick © Claire Kilpatrick 2018. Published 2018 by Oxford University Press.

Abnormality thus serves the useful function of permitting calibration of changes in sources, including institutional claims concerning those sources. When all the evidence of abnormality is assessed, it may then be that features such as the *institutional context* or the *accumulation* or the *interaction* or the *scale* or the *geographical concentration* or the *duration* of abnormal sources allow further claims to be made of sectoral or systemic mutation. Hence, it provides a productive alternative path, as well as a method for testing, assertions that, on the one hand, the euro-area crisis produced primarily institutional variation or, on the other, that it constitutes a mutation of the EU constitutional order.[1]

1. Two Areas Explored in Order to Test Abnormality

The claim of abnormality varies across the two issues explored in this analysis. While other issues could certainly also be examined,[2] these two appear both central and closely related. First, I claim that the EU sovereign debt sources are abnormal legal sources when measured against two particular liberal-legal conceptions of the rule of law: a formal conception and a procedural conception ('Abnormality 1').[3] This entails looking at how these sources are made and communicated to those who feel their effects, and how any shortfalls in their formal aspects have been remedied (or not) by courts and related accountability bodies, in particular the European Ombudsman. Both the sovereign debt loans and many ECB measures fall considerably short when measured against the rule of law in its formal and procedural variants.

Second, I claim that the *exercise* of its mandates by the ECB in sovereign debt episodes is abnormal in particular because of conditionality, contamination, and accumulation of mandates or the absence of a mandate ('Abnormality 2').

To lay the ground for considering these issues, the relevant sovereign debt crisis management sources will be outlined. As these sources and mechanisms are often unfamiliar and challenging for (EU) legal scholars, involving as they do sovereign debt loans and the relationships between the ECB and national banks and states, explaining them clearly is an important component of the analysis. The policy choices made by the EU during the crisis will then be set against other leading alternatives. This both clarifies the policy choices made by the EU institutions and provides

[1] For an excellent overview in the context of a claim of increased institutional variation, see De Witte, 'Euro-Crisis Responses and the EU Legal Order: Increased Institutional Variation or Constitutional Mutation', 11 *European Constitutional Law Review* (2015) 434. See further Section 6.

[2] See my argument that EU institutional denial of the EU law reviewability of the sovereign debt loan assistance mechanisms was abnormal: Kilpatrick, 'Are the Bailout Measures Immune to EU Social Challenge Because They Are Not EU Law?', 10 *European Constitutional Law Review* (2014) 393. As an instance of constitutional mutation, many focus on 'going outside the EU Treaties' in the many international agreements between EU Member States in the context of the euro-area crisis: the EFSM and ESM discussed later in this chapter as well as the Fiscal Compact Treaty and the Single Resolution Fund. I do not regard this as either unlawful or strongly abnormal.

[3] I draw in part on the argument developed in Kilpatrick, 'On the Rule of Law and Economic Emergency: The Degradation of Basic Legal Values in Europe's Bailouts', 35 *Oxford Journal of Legal Studies* (2015) 325. However, in this analysis I examine a much wider range of sources including the passage from Greece II to Greece III in 2015 as well as developing a fuller analysis of ECB measures.

an important steer away from the assumption that there was no alternative way to approach the crisis. On these foundations, I consider the two areas of abnormality: rule of law and the actions and mandates of the ECB.

2. Constructing the EU's Sovereign Debt Crisis Sources: ECB Crisis Management and Sovereign Debt Loan Assistance

A. The ECB and Crisis Management

At least six new crisis roles for the ECB can be ascertained,[4] and these will be considered briefly in turn. While all these roles have remained in play from their introduction they are presented here in chronological order of their introduction. It is worth noting that all these measures are officially considered by the ECB itself to be 'non-standard' or 'unconventional' in contrast to standard interest rate decisions directed towards its primary mandate of maintaining price stability; the extent to which they are also abnormal is considered under Abnormality 2.

One needs to understand first some features of the relationship between the banks, the ECB, and states in the eurozone. Banks operate by lending money they have obtained, primarily to businesses and individuals. Key sources from which they obtain the money to make loans are deposits and from issuing bonds. They operate on the basis that few of those with a claim to money in the bank (such as depositors and bondholders) will ask for their money to be returned at the same time, allowing almost all of that money to be loaned at interest by the bank. This allows banks, as De Grauwe summarizes it, to 'borrow short but lend long'.[5] Hence, many of their assets (their loans) are mortgages based on 30-year terms; however, many of their liabilities (what the bank itself owes) can be called in at short or no notice (think of depositors accessing their current accounts). Banks generally also hold large quantities of government bonds as part of their assets, which are usually considered to be safe assets. A specific feature of the euro area is that banks generally hold very large quantities of the government bonds of 'their' state rather than a pot of mixed government bonds from a wide range of euro-area states.

Banks can also raise further money to make loans through a variety of sources. One very important mode is lending to each other (interbank lending), which was especially important in the run-up to the financial crisis. Central banks also lend money to banks via auctions or tenders. When the financial crisis took hold, banks stopped lending to each other (the sudden stop of interbank lending) and asset holders began to take their money back from banks they saw as at risk. This meant

[4] See for the fullest legal analysis to date Beukers, 'The New ECB and its Relationship with the Eurozone Member States: Between Central Bank Independence and Central bank Intervention', 50 *Common Market Law Review* (2013) 1579. See also K. Tuori and K. Tuori, *The Eurozone Crisis: A Constitutional Analysis* (2013), especially at 102–104, 162–168, focusing mainly on relaxed collateral requirements and the Treaty-compatibility of bond-buying programmes; Wilsher, 'Ready to Do Whatever it Takes? The Legal Mandate of the European Central Bank and the Economic Crisis', 15 *Cambridge Yearbook of European Legal Studies* (2013) 503.

[5] P. De Grauwe, *Economics of Monetary Union* (10th edn, 2014).

the ECB was called upon to fulfil its role as lender of last resort to these banks, whose alternative sources of liquidity had diminished.

Because of the importance of functioning banks to states, and the increased reliance of banks on the ECB, the crisis opened up possibilities for the ECB to shape the choices of banks and states. It could require a bank, typically a central purchaser of government debt, not to buy its government's bonds as a condition of direct lending to the bank. It could adjust the terms on which direct lending would be made, or indeed no longer made, to banks. Stopping direct lending meant the ECB was no longer acting as a lender of last resort to the banking sector. This left the national central bank the possibility of fulfilling that function through the provision of ELA. However, the ECB exercised a veto over the national central bank's provision of ELA. In all these ways, the ECB could decide when a state with vulnerable banks could be moved towards bailout.[6] In this introductory section, I introduce the ECB's actions. In Abnormality 2 later in the chapter, I return to examine in more detail how the ECB used these actions in ways that can certainly be described as abnormal.

1. *Providing Enhanced Liquidity to Banks or Other Credit Institutions in the Eurozone*

In the crisis, three key instruments have been used by the ECB to provide enhanced credit to banks. We have seen that the banks typically obtain part of their funding from the ECB through short-term (called 'main refinancing operations' and which take place weekly) and long-term refinancing operations (LTROs). The ECB holds tenders or auctions in which a bank can obtain liquidity from the ECB in exchange for posting assets (also called collateral) equal to the amount it has been allotted by the ECB. The ECB sets a minimum bid rate for the tender (the cost of the borrowing by the bank from the ECB, also called the repo rate). However, before the crisis (2000–2008), the ECB auctioned a *pre-set amount* in a *variable-rate* tender procedure. Hence banks would frequently not get all the liquidity they wished from the ECB and obtained that liquidity at a cost higher than the minimum bid rate. During the crisis, a *full allotment* at *fixed rates* was adopted for all refinancing operations. This means that banks had unlimited access to central bank money (liquidity) at the minimum bid rate.[7] This filled in the liquidity gap created by the shortfall in interbank lending and the reduced appetite for risk seen from other traditional lenders to banks. In addition, the maturity of some LTROs by the ECB to national banks was extended from one year to three years, again to ease banks' refinancing concerns. In addition, the ECB announced in June 2014 that it would conduct a series of targeted longer-term refinancing operations (TLTROs) aimed at improving bank

[6] A recent and fascinating analysis of the euro-area crisis, on which my analysis draws, is M. Sandbu, *Europe's Orphan: The Future of the Euro and the Politics of Debt* (2015). The great strength of his analysis is its eye for the detailed history and many episodes of the crisis as well as setting out the alternative economic and political options available at any given moment.

[7] Cour-Thimann and Winkler, 'The ECB's Non-Standard Monetary Policy Measures: The Role of Institutional Factors and Financial Structure', *European Central Bank Working Paper* 1528, April 2013.

lending to the euro-area non-financial private sector, excluding loans to households for house purchases, over a window of two years. A third shift concerns changes to what the ECB accepts as collateral in its tenders to provide money to banks in the eurozone. The US decision to allow Lehman Brothers to go into bankruptcy in September 2008 is acknowledged as a pivotal moment in the global financial crisis, and Tuori and Tuori describe the ECB's actions post-Lehman as 'a U-turn in collateral policy'.[8] The ECB Statute[9] (Article 18.1) simply provides that 'adequate collateral' must be provided without specifying what qualifies as such. In the crisis the ECB both considerably extended what it would accept as eligible collateral and combined this with offering unlimited funding to banks which could offer such collateral. These three changes, when applied, had the effect of allowing banks to refinance a larger part of their balance sheet for a longer period and on easier terms with the ECB. These are classic features of a central bank acting as a lender of last resort to banks.

However, just as importantly, the ECB also made decisions to contract and expand what it accepted as collateral in order to shape states' choices. This is analysed fully later in Abnormality 2.

2. *Enhanced Liquidity to National Banks Via Emergency Liquidity Assistance*

ELA is used when the ECB decides that direct lending to national banks will no longer be undertaken. This means ELA succeeds the types of assistance considered earlier (such as auctions or tenders, LTRO, and relaxed collateral). It also means that when banks require ELA, that assistance is the life support for them and their state. As it is the state, not the ECB, that is the backstop for ELA by its national central bank when banks' liquidity is secured via ELA, the sovereign's financial strength is also placed into question. The ECB document on ELA procedures[10] describes it as follows:

> Euro-area credit institutions can receive central bank credit not only through monetary policy operations but exceptionally also through ELA... Responsibility for the provision of ELA lies with the NCB(s) [National Central Banks] concerned.
>
> ... However Article 14.4 [ECSB Statute] assigns the Governing Council of the ECB responsibility for restricting ELA operations if it considers that these operations interfere with the objectives and tasks of the Eurosystem. Such decisions are taken by the Governing Council by a majority of two-thirds of the votes cast.

The ECB then has a veto over the provision of ELA. By withholding or granting permission to the national central bank to provide ELA, a decision which importantly is renewed in periods of days and weeks, rather than months or years, the ECB

[8] Tuori and Tuori, *supra* note 4, at 102.

[9] Protocol 4 of the EU Treaties on the Statute of the European System of Central Banks and of the European Central Bank (OJ 2012 C 326/230).

[10] ECB, ELA Procedures, published on 18 October 2013, available at https://www.ecb.europa.eu/pub/pdf/other/201402_elaprocedures.en.pdf (last visited 13 January 2017). The emergence of this document is analysed later when we examine Abnormality 1: rule of law.

effectively controls the choices open to the state. How this power was used by the ECB during the crisis is analysed later.

3. *Bond-Buying Programmes Conditional on Policy Reforms and Asset Purchase Programmes*

Although the ECB mainly interacts with national systems through its tenders to purchase bank assets for money, as explained earlier, it can also directly buy and sell marketable instruments. These can include government bonds, provided they are purchased on the secondary bond markets and not directly from a national sovereign. Article 18(1) of the ECB Statute allows the ECB to, *inter alia*, buy and sell marketable instruments, and the purchase of government bonds as such instruments is justified by the ECB to ensure accurate transmission of its monetary policy. The bonds are bought on the secondary market because Article 123 Treaty on the Functioning of the European Union (TFEU) prohibits the direct purchase by the ECB of Member State debt instruments.[11]

The ECB has introduced two high-profile bond-buying programmes since the eurozone sovereign debt crisis. The first, the Securities Market Programme,[12] was introduced in May 2010 to accompany the first eurozone bailout in Greece. It operated in Greece, Ireland, and Portugal as well as in two states not in sovereign debt loan programmes, Italy and Spain, where it operated briefly from August 2011. The second, the OMT, was announced in September 2012,[13] preceded by the famous announcement of ECB President Mario Draghi on 26 July 2012: 'Within our mandate, the ECB is ready to do whatever it takes to preserve the euro. And believe me, it will be enough.' Both programmes entail purchase by the ECB of government bonds of eurozone states on the secondary bond market. A feature of these programmes is that they were directed towards the bonds of particular vulnerable states and were accompanied by conditionality. Features of this conditionality are highlighted when we look at the rule of law (Abnormality 1) and at the ECB's roles (Abnormality 2).

This distinguishes both these programmes from the broader Public Sector Purchasing Programme launched in January 2015.[14] This is aimed at all euro-area states except those in sovereign debt programmes, which are excluded unless they comply

[11] Article 123(1) TFEU provides: 'Overdraft facilities or any other type of credit facility with the European Central Bank or with the central banks of the Member States (hereinafter referred to as "national central banks") in favour of Union institutions, bodies, offices or agencies, central governments, regional, local or other public authorities, other bodies governed by public law, or public undertakings of Member States shall be prohibited, as shall the purchase directly from them by the European Central Bank or national central banks of debt instruments.'

[12] ECB Decision of 14 May 2010 establishing a Securities Markets Programme, OJ 2010 L 124/8.

[13] Note that OMT was announced only in a Press Release following the meeting of the ECB Governing Council on 5–6 September 2012. Legal instruments regulating OMT have not to date been adopted.

[14] ECB Decision 2015/10 of 4 March 2015 on a secondary markets public sector asset purchase programme, OJ 2015 L 121/20.

with their programmes.[15] Building on smaller, earlier, programmes, this is a large-scale purchasing programme of government bonds and EU institutions and government agency securities across the whole euro system, designed to combat deflationary tendencies in the euro area. This is usually called 'quantitative easing'.

4. *Member of the Troika Managing the Roll-Out of Sovereign Debt Loan Assistance*

The ECB is also given an important formal role in devising and monitoring the conditions imposed in return for sovereign debt loan assistance in the euro area. The various different loan instruments, set out and explained in more detail in the next section, all give the ECB roles alongside the Commission and the International Monetary Fund (IMF), together forming the troika of institutions monitoring EU sovereign debt programmes. As provided from 2013 in the EU Regulation accompanying all euro-area bailouts, whatever their source:

> Where a Member State requests financial assistance... it shall prepare, in agreement with the Commission, acting in liaison with the ECB, a draft macro-economic adjustment programme...[16]

In addition to drafting the loan conditions, the ECB liaises with the Commission to monitor its implementation and a programme state is placed under a legal obligation to fully cooperate with the Commission and the ECB.[17]

5. *Enhanced Surveillance of 'at Risk' States*

The overhaul of Economic Monetary Union (EMU) governance in the 'six pack' of 2011 and the 'two pack' of 2013 introduced many new features of economic governance.[18] One of these was a new regime of enhanced surveillance for euro-area states in receipt of precautionary financial assistance requiring policy changes or at risk of entering a sovereign debt programme. In this regime the Commission and ECB have more distinct roles, with the Commission deciding whether to place a euro-area state in the regime, while the ECB's role is linked to its role as a supervisor of the euro-area banking system so that it may, for example, carry out stress tests on banks as part of this regime. The Commission and ECB are empowered to carry out regular review missions.[19]

[15] *Ibid.*, Article 3(2)(d), 'In the event of a review of an on-going financial assistance programme, eligibility for PSPP purchases shall be suspended and shall resume only in the event of a positive outcome of the review'. The latter is defined in Article 2(5) as decisions by both the Board of Directors of the ESM and, where involved, the Executive Board of the IMF, to approve the next disbursement under the programme.

[16] Article 7(1), Regulation 472/2013 of 21 May 2013, OJ 2013 L 140.

[17] *Ibid.*, Article 7(4).

[18] See Kilpatrick, 'The New E in EMU: A Lawful and Effective Design?', *ADEMU Working Paper* 2016.

[19] See, in particular, Article 3 Regulation 472/2013, *supra* note 16.

B. Loan Assistance

Large-scale sovereign debt loan assistance is an entirely new EU activity developed following the 2007–2008 global financial crisis. Sovereign debtors are EU states which obtained loans ('bailouts') from EU and euro area organized financial facilities from 2008 onwards. The EU sovereign debtor group is a large one: to date, seven EU states (Cyprus, Greece, Hungary, Ireland, Latvia, Portugal, and Romania) entered into full bailouts while Spain had a partial (financial sector) bailout and other Member States have hovered close to requiring bailouts (Italy, Slovenia). The bailouts can helpfully be divided into two waves: an earlier non-eurozone wave from 2008 and a later, and financially much more significant, eurozone wave beginning with the first Greek Loan Facility in May 2010.

Hungary,[20] Latvia,[21] and Romania[22] have all, since autumn 2008, received assistance under an already existing Treaty provision (Article 143 TFEU) to set up a Facility to assist non-eurozone states with balance of payments difficulties liable to jeopardize the functioning of the internal market or the implementation of the Common Commercial Policy.[23]

For a series of reasons, set out in the following sections, the EU pedigree of the four eurozone bailouts is less straightforward. Some are partly based on EU Law (Ireland, Portugal) while others are entirely based on three distinctive kinds of international agreement made by the eurozone states (Greece, Cyprus). The banking sector loan to Spain was also provided under the two successive international loan agreements set up by the eurozone states.

[20] Council Decision 2009/102 of 4 November 2008 providing Community medium-term financial assistance for Hungary, OJ 2009 L 37/5. The EU balance of payments loan was up to €6.5 billion (while the IMF's was up to €12.5 billion). The actual loan amount was lowered (€5.5 out of €6.5 from the EU and €9.1 out of €12.5 from the IMF) and the loan period (November 2008–October 2010) was shortened by one year. In 2011, Hungary requested precautionary financial assistance; this was made politically conditional on Orbán's Government committing to central bank independence and the judicial reforms recommended by the Venice Commission: European Commission—IP/12/407, 25/04/2012. This financial assistance was not taken up.

[21] Council Decision 2009/290 of 20 January 2009 providing Community medium-term financial assistance for Latvia, OJ 2009 L 79/39. Again the loan period and amount was shortened (from three to two years) though most of the EU balance of payments loan on offer was used (€2.9 out of €3.1 billion on offer).

[22] Council Decision 2009/459 of 6 May 2009 providing Community medium-term financial assistance for Romania, OJ 2009 L 150/8 amended by Council Decision 2010/183 of 16 March 2010, OJ 2010 L 83/19. Romania was granted up to €5 billion under the facility alongside just under €13 billion from the IMF, €1 billion from the World Bank, and €1 billion from the European Investment Bank and the European Bank for Reconstruction and Development. The full EU loan facility amount was used during the loan period (May 2009–June 2011). A second programme of financial assistance (March 2011–June 2013) entailing a precautionary credit line of €5 billion (€3.6 billion from the IMF; €1.4 billion from the EU facility) but not drawn upon. A third precautionary programme of €2 billion was agreed in October 2013 (Decision 2013/513/EU, OJ 2013 L 279/73) to run until end-September 2015 but was not drawn upon. See for a review *Balance of Payments Assistance Programme. Romania 2013–2015*, European Economy Institutional Paper 012, European Commission, November 2015.

[23] Article 143 TFEU fleshed out in Council Regulation 333/2002, OJ 2002 L 53/4, establishing a facility providing medium-term financial assistance for Member States' balance of payments. Pre-crisis, the latter made the maximum total available €12 billion. Post-crisis this was increased to €50 billion. The Treaty explicitly envisions such EU assistance being accompanied by IMF assistance as well as bilateral assistance from other States: Article 143(2) TFEU.

1. No EU Loan Mechanism, No EU Money

When, in late 2009 and early 2010, Greece, a eurozone state, had a sovereign debt crisis, the decision was taken to offer Greece a loan. However, the EU possessed neither a legal mechanism nor the financial means to grant Greece a loan of the required size. This was resolved by agreeing on Saturday 8 May 2010 to loan Greece €80 billion on the basis of bilateral agreements with other eurozone states alongside €30 billion from the IMF.

2. Exceptional EU Loan Mechanisms: The EFSM and the EFSF

The EU immediately (Sunday 9 May 2010) remedied the lack of legal mechanism and lack of financial means by creating two new bailout mechanisms: the European Financial Stability Mechanism (EFSM) and the European Financial Stability Facility (EFSF). The EFSM is a creature of EU law. Article 122(2) TFEU is the legal basis for Council Regulation 407/2010 of 11 May 2010 establishing a European Financial Stability Mechanism:

> Where a Member State is in difficulties or is seriously threatened with severe difficulties caused by natural disasters or exceptional occurrences beyond its control, the Council, on a proposal from the Commission, may grant, under certain conditions, Union financial assistance to the Member State concerned.

However, this EU mechanism was suitable only for emergencies on a smaller financial scale than the eurozone crisis as the loan amount available was limited by the EU budget to €60 billion. Indeed, the difficulties of increasing the EU's budget drove all remaining foundational financial assistance instruments outside the EU Treaty framework.

To address this funding shortfall, the EFSF was contemporaneously established by an immediately effective international agreement. This much larger fund, initially €440 billion and later extended, operated as a private company established in Luxembourg under the control of the eurozone states. The bulk of Ireland's support scheme, €85 billion (November 2010–December 2013), and Portugal's €78 billion (May 2011–May 2014), came from these two sources. Greece's second 'eurozone' loan programme (Greece II) was exclusively EFSF-based: in March 2012 a €130 billion loan was agreed (planned to last until December 2014).[24]

In May 2012 Spain's largest bank Bankia announced a need for government support of €19 billion to survive. This initiated debates on Spain's ability to rescue its banking sector. In July 2012, Spain obtained EFSF assistance of up to €100 billion to recapitalize banks. However, this assistance was transferred to the European

[24] The Greek bailouts are the most difficult to unravel for a number of reasons. One is that the second bailout was required before the first one had run its course. Greece I was planned to run from May 2010 until 2014 with a eurozone contribution of €80 billion. In March 2012, a second Greek bailout was agreed of just under €110 billion (plus €34.6 billion relating to the private sector involvement deal—the Greek 'haircuts') while the non-utilized portion of Greece I was rolled-over. The end period of Greece II and the transition to Greece III is considered in more detail in the main text.

Stability Mechanism (ESM), which became operational in October 2012 before any disbursements were made.

3. *Permanent Funding Mechanism: The ESM*

EU Treaty amendment created an explicit authorization for the Member States (as opposed to the EU or the EU Council in eurozone composition) to have a funding mechanism.[25] The eurozone states contemporaneously established a permanent funding mechanism, the ESM, as an intergovernmental organization between the eurozone Member States.[26] It superseded the exceptional EFSM/EFSF mechanisms, although these continued to provide the basis for the pre-existing Irish, Portuguese, and Greek bailouts. Designed to have an effective lending capacity of €700 billion, the ESM's first use in full bailout mode was in relation to Cyprus in May 2013 (up to 9 billion from ESM; available until March 2016).

The financial sector Spanish loan assistance was first granted under the EFSF but transferred to the ESM before the first and principal disbursement was made in December 2012.[27] Spain exited the loan assistance programme on 31 December 2013. Overall, €41.3 billion was disbursed as a sovereign debt loan to Spain to re-capitalize and restructure its banks. Hence, it is not the banks but the Spanish state, that is to say its tax payers, which must repay the loan. Although the loans went to a number of Spanish banks the largest recipient was Bankia. Bankia is a large universal bank in Spain resulting from a crisis-driven merger of seven savings banks in 2010. During the crisis, it benefited from several state measures, mostly granted by the Spanish State Fund for the orderly restructuring of banks (FROB) including several recapitalizations, state guarantees on senior unsecured debt, and the segregation of a significant part of its impaired assets and loans to an asset management company. The total amount of state aid received by Bankia in the form of capital and impaired asset measures, including the aid disbursed under the ESM programme, amounted to approximately €36 billion. Just under half of Bankia's funding had come through a 2011 share issue through a stock matter flotation shortly before its collapse.

[25] Council Decision 2011/199 of 25 March 2011 amending Article 136 of the Treaty on the Functioning of the European Union with regard to a stability mechanism for Member States whose currency is the euro, OJ 2011 L 91/1. The amendment provides: '3. The Member States whose currency is the euro may establish a stability mechanism to be activated if indispensable to safeguard the stability of the euro area as a whole. The granting of any required financial assistance under the mechanism will be made subject to strict conditionality'. It required the agreement of all 27 Member States to enter into force which, after a late Czech ratification, finally occurred in April 2013.

[26] ESM Treaty agreed on 2 February 2012. Requiring ratification by its 17 eurozone signatories, it came into effect on September 27 2012. For details of its lending to date see: https://www.esm.europa.eu (last visited 26 September 2017). For an unsuccessful legal challenge to the compatibility of these two changes with the EMU Treaty provisions, see Case C-370/12, *Pringle*, judgment of 27 November 2012 (ECLI:EU:C:2012:756).

[27] Unlike the seven broader EU sovereign debt loans, the IMF made no financial contribution to the Spanish sovereign debt loan for its banks as it cannot make financial sector loans. In addition, Spain's obligations under the European Semester were not suspended for the duration of the programme as they were in the full sovereign debt programmes. The MoU containing the loan conditions can be found at: http://ec.europa.eu/economy_finance/eu/countries/pdf/mou_en. pdf (last visited 9 January 2017). See also Council Decision 2012/443 of 23 July 2012 addressed to Spain on specific measures to reinforce financial stability, OJ 2012 L 202/17.

This had been primarily aimed at its Spanish retail customers (those with deposits) as international institutional investors were uninterested; the loan assistance placed the loss on these small and inexperienced creditors rather than on larger professional creditors who had been covered by state guarantees.[28] Litigation by these minority shareholders concerning flotation fraud claims led the Spanish government to propose a compensation settlement.[29]

4. *Greece II—Greece III 2015: Distinct Loan Mechanisms and ECB Intervention*

The passage between Greece II and Greece III during 2015 is of great intrinsic interest. It also highlights the differences between these various loan mechanisms as well as the interactions between loan assistance and ECB interventions. Greece II was based on financial assistance of just under €165 billion (€145 billion from the EFSF and €20 billion from the IMF) until the end of 2014. The period was later extended until the end of June 2015. This extension resulted from the triggering of Greek elections in late December 2014 by the failure to indirectly elect a new Greek President and the resulting election of Syriza as the party of government with Alexis Tsipras as Prime Minister in January 2015. Just before expiry of Greece II, Greek Prime Minister Tsipras called a referendum on the possible terms of a bailout agreement based on documents circulated in late June 2015. Greece II expired on 30 June 2015. On 5 July 2015 the Greek referendum produced a strong 'No' vote to the bailout terms presented. The ECB had rejected Bank of Greece requests to increase ELA support to Greece immediately following announcement of the referendum and after its result. In addition, after the referendum result, it adjusted the haircuts on collateral accepted by the Bank of Greece for ELA.[30] Capital controls were introduced. On 8 July 2015 Greece requested a third round of financial assistance, this time from the ESM. After difficult negotiations, Greece III was agreed and makes up to €85 billion available under the ESM between August 2015–2018.

While the ESM request which became Greece III was under examination, on 17 July 2015, Greece was granted just over €7 billion in short-term financial assistance under the EFSM in order to meet July 2015 repayment obligations to the ECB (the redemption of bonds) and settling its arrears to the IMF.[31] The assistance was disbursed

[28] Extensive and useful details of Bankia's crisis management can be found in the Commission's state aid case decision on Bankia, especially (88) to (94): http://ec.europa.eu/competition/state_aid/cases/246568/246568_1406507_239_4.pdf (last visited 9 January 2017); see also Sandbu, *supra* note 6, at 145 and 154.

[29] Reuters, 'Spain may compensate Bankia's shareholders after flotation fraud claims', 5 February 2016.

[30] See ECB Press Releases of Sunday 28 June 2015, available at https://www.ecb.europa.eu/press/pr/date/2015/html/pr150628.en.html (last visited 10 January 2017), and Sunday 6 July 2015, available at https://www.ecb.europa.eu/press/pr/date/2015/html/pr150706.en.html (last visited 10 January 2017), both of which report the Governing Council's decision to maintain the provision of ELA at the level decided on 26 June 2015, before the referendum was announced. For analysis and criticism of this use of ELA, see Abnormality 2: the ECB.

[31] Council Implementing Decision 2015/1181 of 17 July 2015 on granting short-term financial assistance to Greece, OJ 2015 L 192/15.

in one instalment on 20 July 2015, and was linked to economic policy conditionality. The ESM assistance was, *inter alia*, to repay that short-term EFSM bridge loan.

This EFSM assistance was controversial. The UK and the Czech Republic were strongly opposed to using an EU, rather than a euro-area only, financial instrument to grant the bridging loan to Greece. As the EFSM is an EU-wide fund, backed by the EU budget, disbursements from it need the approval of all of the EU's 28 governments, rather than just the 19 of the euro area. However, decisions in the EFSM are taken by qualified majority voting,[32] which meant that the UK and the Czech Republic could be outvoted. The different situations of euro-area and non-euro-area states were, however, taken into account in both the Council Decision granting the bridging loan under the EFSM to Greece, and in an amendment to the EFSM regulation itself by providing:

> Union financial assistance under this Decision shall not be made available unless liquid collateral amounting to their exposure has been provided to those Member States whose currency is not the euro under legally binding arrangements such that it is immediately payable to them to the extent required to cover any liability they may incur as a result of any failure by Greece to repay the financial assistance in accordance with its terms.[33]

To summarize, five main distinctive mechanisms have been used to provide sovereign debt loans to EU Member States: balance of payments loans for non-euro-area states, bilateral loans between states, the EFSM, the EFSF, and the ESM.

It is also very important to understand that the foundational bailout instruments, as outlined earlier, are only one layer of bailout sources. The individual bailouts, and the conditions they contain, are the truly critical sources for affected EU citizens and professional norm-detectors,[34] and these will be a central focus when we look at rule of law abnormalities. Each bailout entails normative obligations unfolding over periods of years in three key stages: loan agreement; loan disbursement and conditionality; loan repayment and post-programme surveillance.[35] To fully evaluate its

[32] Article 3(2), Council Regulation 407/2010 of 11 May 2010 establishing a European financial stabilization mechanism, OJ 2010 L 118/1 (EFSM Regulation).

[33] Article 1(2), Council Implementing Decision 2015/1181 of 17 July 2015, *supra* note 31; new Article 3(2a) EFSM Regulation, Council Regulation 2015/1360 of 4 August 2015 amending Regulation 407/2010 establishing a European financial stabilization mechanism, OJ 2015 L 210/1.

[34] Waldron, 'The Concept of Law and the Rule of Law', 43 *Georgia Law Review* (2008) 1, at 26: 'the norms of a legal system should be public knowledge in the sense of being publicly available to anyone who is sufficiently interested and available in particular to those who make a profession of being public norm-detectors'.

[35] See, e.g. Ireland where the Commission summarizes as follows: 'Ireland is now subject to post-programme surveillance (PPS) until at least 75% of the financial assistance received has been repaid. So barring any early repayments, PPS will last at least until 2031.The objective of PPS is ultimately to measure Ireland's capacity to repay its outstanding loans to the EFSM, EFSF and bilateral lenders. Under PPS, the Commission, in liaison with the European Central Bank, will (i) conduct regular review missions in the Member State to assess its economic, fiscal and financial situation; and (ii) prepare semi-annual assessments of Ireland's economic, fiscal and financial situation and determine whether corrective measures are needed': http://ec.europa.eu/economy_finance/assistance_eu_ms/ireland/index_en.htm (last visited 10 January 2017). Of the bailout states, only Latvia has exited bailout governance: from 20 January 2012 to 16 January 2015 Latvia was subject to post-programme surveillance (PPS). The PPS has expired, as Latvia has repaid 75% of the EU loan. In March 2014, Latvia repaid the first tranche of €1 billion and the second tranche of €1.2 billion was repaid on 16 January 2015: http://ec.europa.eu/economy_finance/assistance_eu_ms/latvia/index_en.htm (last visited 10 January 2017).

legal structure and content, each bailout needs to be reconstructed individually. Take one strand of the Irish bailout, the EFSM loan, as an example. With its Treaty basis in Article 122(2) TFEU, this strand of the Irish bailout operated by Council Implementing Decisions (CIDs) being taken under the EFSM Regulation. The initial CID of 7 December 2010 set out the actions to be taken over each year of the loan period. Loan disbursements were made subject to the conditions set out in an MoU (Memorandum of Understanding) and the troika (i.e. the ECB, Commission and IMF) made regular checks (in practice three times a year) on progress. Just as importantly, the conditions for loan disbursement were amended throughout the life of the loan. This led to corresponding amendments to the Irish CID and the MoUs. There were nine further CIDs during the disbursement of the Irish loan.

This outline of sovereign debt sources gives a good sense of the span of measures over the crisis. Before proceeding to examine my two claims of abnormality I consider first the argument that it was impossible for the EU institutions and sovereign debt sources to act otherwise. A standard and therefore important response to evidence of abnormality such as the different elements presented in this analysis is that, regrettable though some of them may well be, there was no alternative to the measures outlined earlier in the face of the unanticipated events which led to the financial and sovereign debt crisis in Europe. The EU had to navigate the treacherous and rapidly changing waters of financial and sovereign debt crises and with appropriate respect for its constitutional and institutional limits. To my mind, this underemphasizes the choices made by the EU institutions and leaves those choices, and the mode of their exercise, inadequately scrutinized by legal scholars. Section 3 below sets the policy choices made by the EU during the crisis against other leading alternatives.

3. There is No Alternative? Law and Policy Choices and the Implications for Abnormality in EU Sovereign Debt

An important component of my argument is that there were alternative law and policy choices which would have avoided the abnormal legal manifestations explored in this analysis. Moreover, the policy choice made significantly shaped some of the abnormalities in this analysis. The alternatives I present here are backed by formidable evidence, arguments, and proponents. Nonetheless, even if one does not accept these alternatives, one might still feel deeply concerned about features of the sources used to execute EU policy choices during the sovereign debt crisis.

My starting point is that there was no normal or standard legal outcome. One way or another the Maastricht EMU framework would require re-reading and re-working to fit circumstances which had never been planned for. That framework was premised on the markets pricing national public and private debt accurately so as to obviate the need for either a sovereign or a muscular private bank lender of last resort. A lender of last resort can be needed for both sovereigns and also for private banks. While the latter function is an accepted part of the mandate of central banks, including the ECB, the former is not at first sight accepted by the Treaty framework.

Yet properly embracing both functions was necessary to approach the EU's public and private debt crises. The original framework was not designed for public debt difficulties of the kind that were faced by Greece in 2009–2010. More importantly, it had no system in place to resolve the issue of the many private banks facing insolvency across the EU, although nothing prevented individual states proceeding with resolution. Given the particular importance of banks as a source of lending within the EU, compared to the US,[36] struggling banks could rapidly place into question the strength of the sovereign, particularly if the latter supported them extensively (and expensively).

A. The Bank-Focused Alternative

As Martin Sandbu has convincingly argued,[37] one alternative is that the EU and its states could (and should) have chosen to rapidly and decisively resolve their 'zombie' banks (i.e. insolvent banks which are still operating). The costs of this would primarily have fallen on those holding the assets of these banks: 'burning the bondholders'. These effects would have been felt across Europe because, for example, German banks held many of the Irish zombie bank bonds. It would have distributed the costs of the bank failures very differently, spreading them over bondholders in many European states, rather than the costs being placed primarily on the taxpayers located in the same state as the failing banks. A focus on failing banks would have given support to a public narrative stressing that public profligacy and inadequate structural reform in states were not the driving cause of the unsustainable debt pricing of a range of sovereign debt states.[38] And a focus on failing banks would also have weakened the link between those banks and their sovereigns. It should be stressed that between 2008 and 2010 eurozone states had much more domestic freedom to decide whether or not to resolve their banks and some, such as Ireland, made unwise choices to try to keep failing banks afloat by guaranteeing to their bondholders that the debts of those banks would be honoured in full by the state. However, from 2010 onwards the policy space was occupied by the EU institutions, by the ECB, and by the European Commission. At a number of critical junctures, especially in 2010 and 2011, the choice was made by the EU institutions not to resolve the banks, and to pass the cost of keeping them afloat onto the taxpayers of the home states of those banks rather than onto their bondholders. Hence, the terms of the €85 billion Irish bailout included not only a €17.5 billion 'Irish contribution' from its pension fund but also €10 billion to immediately recapitalize its banks. Banks would be

[36] See Cour-Thimann and Winkler, *supra* note 7; Sandbu, *supra* note 6, at 85.

[37] Sandbu, *supra* note 6, at 85. His overall vision is of greater national fiscal autonomy within a collectively oriented euro-area fiscal framework, muscular debt restructuring for banks and sovereigns and, though as desirable rather than essential, debt mutualization by a coalition of the willing (excluding Germany).

[38] See, for an analysis making such a claim by an ECB member, 'The European Crisis and the role of the financial system', speech by Vítor Constâncio, Vice-President of the ECB, at the Bank of Greece conference on 'The crisis in the euro area', Athens, 23 May 2013.

recapitalized by Irish taxpayers rather than making those holding bonds in these banks face losses.[39]

A major bank resolution would have required the ECB to fully stand behind the banking system as a lender of last resort. While it is important for failing banks, or parts of banks, to be resolved, it is equally important to maintain the systemic features of the banking system while that process is occurring. This primarily means ensuring that those wishing to obtain their money deposited with the bank can continue to do so; that is to say, maintaining liquidity in the banking system. This is the role of a central bank as a lender of last resort to its banking system(s): to ensure liquidity flows at all times even when (indeed especially when) individual banks are malfunctioning. This is a core ECB function. Yet, as we shall see, the ECB did not play this role in a straightforward way during the crisis. Instead, it made liquidity support conditional on 'favourable' national political developments and used it as a tool to push states into sovereign loan debtor status under which the state (and its taxpayers) took on the weight of their failing banks and had to sign up to many other substantial conditions, unrelated to their banking system. This use of conditional liquidity by the ECB is absolutely critical to emphasize, as states cannot continue to function without banking system liquidity. Accordingly, states must do the ECB's bidding when confronted with this particular threat, and time after time during the crisis this was confirmed. Hence the ECB did actually create 'there is no alternative' moments for the sovereign debtor states.

B. The State-Focused Alternatives

There are also states whose debt crisis genuinely presented, at the outset, as a sovereign debt crisis rather than a failed bank crisis and where the banking failures flowed from the sovereign debt crisis rather than the other way around: Greece and, albeit much less straightforwardly, Portugal. Of course, a sovereign debt crisis rapidly led to banking crisis in these states too.[40] Focusing on Greece, Sandbu argues that, just as the EU fatally refused to accept restructuring of private (bank) debt, it also failed to accept restructuring of sovereign debt. The EMU framework neither prohibited nor mandated debt restructuring of any individual state. Restructuring Greek debt would have been entirely possible without Greece needing to leave the euro. A complementary prop could have been the ECB supporting Greece as a sovereign lender of last resort to give a breathing space in which the least painful and fairest way of achieving that debt restructuring could have been examined. Greece would still have needed a loan to help it through a painful and substantial debt restructuring but that loan would have been of an entirely different scale to what was paid out during the ongoing sovereign debt loan period.[41]

[39] Sandbu, *supra* note 6, at 98–101.

[40] See De Grauwe, *supra* note 5, at 203: 'Banks are the largest holders of government bonds. When as a result of the sovereign debt crisis of 2010 bond prices in a number of eurozone countries dropped, banks made large losses. As a result, a bank crisis erupted in a number of those countries'.

[41] Sandbu, *supra* note 6, at 68, estimates in the order of €25 billion: that is up to 90% less than what was borrowed by the Greek state.

Others more broadly stress sovereign debt, rather than bank failure, as the leading cause of the euro-area crisis and press for a federal solution. De Grauwe's influential analysis, for example, emphasizes the need for the ECB to stand firmly behind Member States as a sovereign lender of last resort; as much centralization of EMU fiscal policy as is politically feasible; and the importance of mutualization of debt issuance between states.[42] It could be argued that given the absence of the moral hazard[43] which underpinned the prohibition on monetary financing in Maastricht (Article 123 TFEU), the most effective, least harmful, and, on this reading, Treaty-compatible way to insulate eurozone states from sovereign debt crises is for the ECB to act as a lender of last resort to states.[44] It would also require accepting, at the very least, a gap in the Maastricht framework. The prohibition on monetary financing and the no bailout provision in Article 125 TFEU were geared at preventing national fiscal profligacy. The Treaty framework was not designed to prevent unsustainable debt pricing driven by other factors, such as banking failure, or market failure of the animal spirits kind, whereby the very absence of a sovereign lender of last resort itself becomes a key driver of unsustainable sovereign debt pricing in states seen as more vulnerable because of banking failures, actual or anticipated, as well as fears that countries might leave, or be required to leave, the euro area. The function of the sovereign lender of last resort in such circumstances is not to bail out weak states but rather to dampen fears of reversible euro membership which created redenomination risks, prevent contagion between banking failure and sovereign debt, and a breathing space for bank regulators to weed out failing banks. It should also be underlined that the need for the ECB to act as a sovereign lender of last resort would have been much less pressing had bank resolution been undertaken as a priority throughout the post-2008 period.

C. The EU Policy Choice: Conditional Life Support for 'Failing' States

Instead, however, the EU chose a path which initially rejected, and then subsequently only very partially accepted, banking and sovereign debt restructuring and cleaved as closely as possible to the prohibition of monetary financing in Article 123 TFEU and the no bailout clause in Article 125 TFEU. It can be summarized as a policy of conditional life support for 'failing' states, though in some cases it was not the state but its banks which were failing and in remaining unresolved weakened their sovereign too. Rather than absolutely standing behind these states as a lender

[42] See centrally De Grauwe whose stance is summarized in the latest edition of his *Economics of Monetary Union*, *supra* note 5.

[43] *Ibid.*, at 124: De Grauwe argues rather that the ECB role is to provide liquidity by acting as lender of last resort to banks and sovereigns while supervision of sovereigns should be viewed as a separate role in the hands of a separate institution.

[44] Sandbu, *supra* note 6, at 158, notes this more precisely means the ECB acting as a government bond buyer of last resort in the secondary market. He argues the Treaties do not prevent this and in fact this has always been an ECB activity: yet this seems to understate the different functions of ECB government bond-buying pre- and post-crisis and overlook, despite this being his core argument elsewhere in his analysis, the effect of failing banks on assessments of government bonds. This is what made the prohibition on monetary financing in Article 123 TFEU relevant. See Abnormality 2 later in the chapter for further discussion.

of last resort, the eurozone solution for these states was to provide conditional life support while very belatedly and partially proceeding with banking resolution and reform. Conditional life support was achieved primarily by subjecting those states benefiting from emergency assistance via ECB measures and bailouts to far-reaching conditionality. By showing that states would not get something (easing of collateral requirements for banks, liquidity assistance, purchase of their bonds, financial assistance) for nothing, but rather only through painful or even punishing socio-economic adjustments, and through setting the interest rate and terms of sovereign loans, the spirit of the prohibition of monetary financing and bailouts would be honoured.

Such conditionality was not tightly confined to the 'causes' of the sovereign debt crisis. Indeed, the main causes—the failure of the eurozone to provide a sovereign lender of last resort, the unresolved banking sector crisis, and fears of euro reversibility—were either inadmissible or not foregrounded in this narrative. Rather, conditionality essentially focused on fiscal consolidation, structural reform especially reforms to labour and social protection, and financial sector 'reform', while only the latter was centrally causally connected to the crisis in most states. And, in so far as the reform required states not to resolve failing banks but to continue to pour capital into them, the loan assistance aggravated rather than alleviated the crisis. Indeed, the very similar loan conditions applied to the three non-euro EU states, Hungary, Latvia, and Romania, which obtained EU balance-of-payments loan assistance from 2008 onwards, demonstrate the turn to a standard recipe (albeit applied with very differing degrees of detail and intensity in different states) of dramatic fiscal contraction and dismantling of social and labour protection, rather than a tailored conditionality matching the reasons which have necessitated the sovereign debt loan assistance.

Sovereign debt adjustment programmes have been adopted in four eurozone states since 2010. All four eurozone states in full bailouts had emergency ECB measures applied before and during the bailouts. Italy did not enter bailout but had emergency ECB assistance. Spain had emergency ECB assistance and a banking sector bailout. Conditionality could be pursued more intensively and with greater normative precision when a state was in bailout than when the normative pressure came, for euro-area states, via ECB emergency assistance.

Of course this policy choice and policy narrative can be seriously critiqued and subjected to very testing inquiry on any number of grounds: for endangering macro-economic security and GDP growth in Europe; for its unfair and unjustifiable distributive effects between the peoples of Europe and between bank bondholders and the taxpayers of certain states; for its frequent substitution of technocracy for democracy; for the policy-dependent consequences it continues to produce in proposals and actions towards a euro-area treasury and more centralized budget control; for its contribution to massive unemployment, especially among young people, and economic insecurity for individuals and families; and for its breach or shift away from a wide series of commitments enshrined in national laws, national constitutions, EU laws, and regional and international human rights guarantees. Yet its function in this particular analysis is more circumscribed. It is primarily to provide weight and detail to the claim that other choices were available to EU policy-makers in how to deal with banking and sovereign debt crises and to sharpen the specific features of the particular policy choice made which can be summarized as conditional life support for 'failing' states.

My focus is on how this policy choice shaped or was manifested through abnormal legal sources. Although this has some relationship to the broader constitutional critiques of euro crisis often found in current legal scholarship, it is less focused on how the euro crisis has altered the EU constitutional framework and more focused on sources and institutional mandates and actions. This more precise focus adds some quite distinct, less explored, and troubling new dimensions to how we consider the law of euro crisis.

The policy choice of conditional life support for 'failing' states shaped a series of developments pushing towards abnormality. These are particularly relevant when we turn to Abnormality 2, as this policy choice strongly shaped how the ECB exercised its mandates during the crisis. Yet the rule of law abnormalities with sovereign debt sources are not so directly linked to this policy choice and are more directly attributable to EU institutional choices and positions. Nonetheless, the policy frame which entailed opening up the bailout route for individual eurozone states when other measures are deemed no longer appropriate certainly led to an intense individual 'emergency' conditionality framework for each state. This may have fed into rule of law shortfalls and a reluctance to accept standard EU law review of such measures.

4. Abnormality 1: Rule of Law Measurement

A. Formal Rule of Law Measurement

A focus on the rule of law which attends to the formal qualities of the norms themselves proves especially well suited to characterizing problematic dimensions of the bailout instruments. As I have argued more fully elsewhere,[45] the approach most apt to capture rule of law concerns in EU bailouts is one broadly shared by legal philosophers but most famously and engagingly developed by Lon Fuller in *The Morality of Law*.[46] By taking the example of King Rex's inept legal regime he develops eight ways to fail, or conversely eight desiderata, in the enterprise of making law: generality, promulgation, prospectivity, clarity, absence of contradiction, asking the possible, constancy, and congruence between law and its application and enforcement. I argue that three of these—generality, promulgation, and clarity—are deeply problematic in the bailouts because of five features of these sources. It is noteworthy that both ECB crisis management sources and sovereign debt loan sources raise formal rule of law issues, making this a systematic issue across sovereign debt crisis sources.

[45] See Kilpatrick, *supra* note 3.

[46] L. Fuller, *The Morality of Law* (revised edn, 1969). See also H.L.A. Hart, 'Problems of the Philosophy of Law' in his *Essays in Jurisprudence and Philosophy* (1983) 88.

A first feature is legal *complexity*: the legal bailout norms are complex in manifold ways that 'normal' EU law is not. Our outline of the sovereign debt sources provides a good sense of this problem. We traced some features of the Irish bailout via the EFSM but of course one also needs to work through how that strand links to the other bases of the Irish loan: the EFSF and bilateral agreements. Just piecing all the sources together for any given bailout requires making sense of intricate, lengthy, and complexly interconnected chains of sources. And that is before turning to the legal difficulties that these hybrid EU/international sources present. Positions taken by a range of EU institutions denying the applicability of EU law constraints to sovereign debt sources have made the task of understanding these sources even more complex: the results have been legal confusion and stasis.[47]

Second, *inaccessibility*: those sovereign debt sources which are publicly available are incredibly difficult to find. Yet, as Deirdre Curtin argues,[48] transparency concerns not only the legal construction of individual rights to access documents but the 'much broader and more pro-active duty of the administration itself to ensure that information about its policy and actions is provided in an accessible fashion'.[49] Accordingly, the Internet is crucial as in practice transparency is all about 'the quality and scope and completeness of the information and documents that the institutions make available on the Internet . . . this is as far as most users get'.[50]

EU citizens, even professional norm-detectors, will understandably turn to the Europa website. The webpages on EU financial assistance contain plenty of press releases, and figures on disbursements and repayments, but precious little hard information about sovereign debt sources.[51] There is absolutely no chance that one could possibly reconstruct any bailout from what has been made available. You can find the traditional EU source elements in those bailouts which have them with proper navigation of EUR-LEX, but not the evolving MoUs. To locate those, one needs to know (but how?) that they are appended to the back of voluminous reports (each over 100 pages) in the European Economy Occasional paper series which contain reports on the ongoing surveillance by the Commission (and ECB for euro-area bailouts). There are 11 of these reports for Ireland, for instance. At the back of each of these are the changing MoUs.

In summary, accessibility has been a major problem. It is very difficult for even a specialized lawyer or national court to reconstruct the legal map of bailout measures so as properly to frame questions of constitutionality or fundamental rights' compliance. It has been nigh on impossible for EU citizens to find the legal sources which are having a major impact on their lives.

[47] See Kilpatrick, *supra* note 2.

[48] D. Curtin, *Executive Power of the European Union: Law, Practices, and the Living Constitution* (2009).

[49] *Ibid.*, at 207.

[50] *Ibid.*, at 218.

[51] For example, this is what was available in relation to each bailout state on 16 January 2014, at the height of the sovereign debt loan programme period, on the Commission website, http://ec.europa.eu/economy_finance/assistance_eu_ms/index_en.htm: Hungary—the original Council Decision, some MoUs, the 3rd post-programme review; Romania: some MoUs; Latvia—the initial Council Decisions, one amending Decision, the MoUs, staff reports on post-programme surveillance; Ireland—drafts of 3/10 Council Implementing Decisions and the initial MoU; Portugal—initial MoU; Greece—2 MoUs relating to the 2nd Greek loan; Cyprus—no official sources. Press releases and political statements by EU institutions predominate.

Third, *incomprehensibility*: for many of the central bailout sources, only English native speakers will be able to read them in their own language. Consider how far removed this is from the normal EU language regime. The Commission website on EU financial assistance is only in English; the EFSF and ESM are not available in the languages of the bailout countries; and MoUs are only available in English. Note the distance from the normal requirement that those who are subject to norms should be able to read them. This is why comprehensibility of legal sources has, in the special context of the EU polity, also entailed foundational language commitments. The European Economic Community's very first Regulation, No. 1 of 1958 (still in force), sets out the commitment to respect the official languages of each of the EU's Member States.[52] This includes specific commitments by EU institutions to send documents to Member States and any person subject to the jurisdiction of a Member State in the language of that state as well as requiring that '[r]egulations and other documents of general application shall be drafted in the official languages'.[53] Beyond the technicalities, surely the rule of law requires that major normative sources should be available in the languages of those subject to them.

An important though limited and belated move towards resolving in part the problems of complexity, accessibility, and comprehensibility, at least for euro states, is the introduction in the 'two pack' of May 2013 of a regulation requiring the loan assistance programme, whatever its provenance, to be mirrored in a Macroeconomic Adjustment Programme (MAP), under EU law.[54] Although this is welcome, it should be stressed that the MAPs for Ireland and Portugal came into effect just as those countries were exiting their programmes. The MAP for Greece, undoubtedly the most important given the special difficulties regarding the EU law status of the Greek bailout and its size, conditionality scope, and duration, was not made until 19 August 2015.[55] This was well over five years after Greece first obtained sovereign debt loan assistance managed by EU institutions and well over two years after the 'requirement' in the two pack to have such an MAP took effect. Moreover, it has only a limited effect on reducing problems of complexity, accessibility, and comprehensibility. Although the MAP is available in all EU languages, it contains only an outline of the programme measures and imposes a requirement of consistency between the MAP and the evolving MoUs. Clearly this leaves the possibility of gaps opening between what is actually required and the terms of the MAP.

[52] Council Regulation 1/1958 of 15 April 1958 determining the languages to be used by the European Economic Community, OJ 1958 L 17/385. It has been amended to add new official languages when enlargement so requires, most recently with the Croatian accession to the EU on 1 July 2013. Article 342 TFEU, by making Union language rules subject to unanimity in Council, also underlines the importance and sensitivity of this issue. For a recent strong commitment to the EU language regime see C-566/10P, *Italy v. Commission*, Grand Chamber judgment of 27 November 2012 (ECLI:EU:C:2012:752).

[53] See Articles 3 and 4 of Regulation 1/1958, *supra* note 52.

[54] Regulation 472/2013, *supra* note 16, on the strengthening of economic and budgetary surveillance of member states in the euro area experiencing or threatened with serious difficulties with respect to their financial stability. See especially Article 7.

[55] Council Implementing Decision 2015/1411 of 19 August 2015 approving the macroeconomic adjustment programme of Greece, OJ 2015 L 219/12.

Fourth, and perhaps underlining most forcefully the gap between 'normal' and 'bailout' EU norms, is the issue of *secret normative sources* in the form of letters from the ECB to the Irish, Spanish, and Italian governments. Although all these letters ultimately came to be in the public domain, this certainly did not occur with the ECB's prompt blessing. The Spanish and Italian letters of August 2011, linked to bond-buying by the ECB under the SMP, contained detailed requirements to modify national labour laws with a timetable for realization. They even told the national governments what kinds of laws to use. The Irish letter, of 19 November 2010, finally made public after the struggle described below, four years later, made the decision through the lever of ECB provision of ELA as discussed earlier, to send Ireland into a sovereign debt loan assistance programme. It is not necessary to settle the status, as 'law' or otherwise of these letters, to make evident the concerns they raise for those wishing to preserve a thin version of the rule of law in the EU. If they are law, then of course 'secret' laws are deeply problematic. But, importantly, simply asserting that these secret letters are not 'law' does not suffice to allay rule of law concerns. Should these letters be considered not to contain binding obligations, they evidence that national labour laws and other highly significant decisions about the use of ECB powers are being shaped in secret institutional structures with significant normative power outside the law. Yet the rule of law is not just a feature of the norms called law that exist, it is a commitment to govern through law and, as Neil Walker puts it, 'the avoidance of large zones of non-law (either in theory or in practice) where other forms of domination prevail'.[56]

Fifth, a further but distinct important manifestation of secret sources concerns the granting and withdrawal by the ECB of national central bank power to supply ELA to their banks. Beyond the voting procedure set out in Article 14(4) of the ECB Statute, what is most notable about the many individual ELA decisions that were taken in relation to sovereign debt national central banks is the absence of any public promulgation of those decisions.

Until late 2015 it was not possible to find out either the reasons for maintaining or withdrawing ELA or the level of ELA which has been authorized on any given occasion. Decisions of the greatest possible significance in the life of EU states were communicated via limited and opaque Press Releases by the ECB. Take the ECB Press Releases of Sunday 28 June and Sunday 6 July 2015 on Greece both of which report the Governing Council's decision to maintain (rather than permit any increase) the provision of ELA at the level decided on 26 June 2015, before the referendum [of 5 July] was announced. After the referendum result, the Press Release of 6 July 2015 reports that the Governing Council adjusted the haircuts on collateral accepted by the Bank of Greece for ELA. These Press Releases give outcomes but do not provide figures or reasons.

Yet this situation was still a marked improvement on the situation during the first phase of the sovereign debt crisis. Up until October 2013, ELA was truly secret, with

[56] Walker, 'The Rule of Law and the EU: Necessity's Mixed Virtue' in N. Walker and G. Palombella (eds), *Relocating the Rule of Law* (2009) 119, at 121. See also *ibid.* at 122, 'a high priority on rule *through* the modality of law, as opposed to other modalities of power such as threat, economic incentive or threat to first-order right reason' (emphasis in original).

economists and journalists scouring the balance sheets of national central banks, and unsuccessfully trying to obtain information in press conferences with the ECB President,[57] to try to find traces or clues of ELA provision. If we examine the ECB Press Releases of 2010, a year in which we know not only that exceptional amounts of ELA were disbursed but that its threatened withdrawal was used to send Ireland into bailout in November 2010, there is not one single mention of ELA. 2011 and 2012, years in which extensive ELA provision continued, are also notable for the absence of any reference to ELA in the ECB's Press Releases. While the financial situation of certain euro-area states made it a fairly safe bet that they were in receipt of ELA, nothing was officially communicated. It was so unclear what countries were using ELA that journalists leapt on a slip of the tongue in 2012 by the Belgian central bank governor implying that not just Cyprus, Greece, and Ireland (the known unknowns) but also Portugal (the unknown unknown) was using ELA.[58] In October 2013 the ECB decided to make publicly available a document on ELA procedures, announcing: 'In order to enhance the general understanding of the Governing Council's role in the provision of ELA by NCBs, the Governing Council decided on 16 October 2013 to make the related procedural rules public.' This two-page summary of the rules provides information about what and when the national central banks have to inform the ECB of in relation to their ELA provision. In addition, since that time, ECB Press Releases have provided information about the maintenance or withdrawal of ELA. However, no public information is provided on the sums of money involved or the reasons for the ECB decision. In late 2015, probably as a result of challenges to the ECB's failure to give reasons or details of its ELA decisions, which we will consider when we turn to the procedural rule of law, the ECB shifted position a little further to allow some light to be shed on ELA. Yet its stance is one of both extreme reluctance and acquiescence to a more open policy only when it considers that that instrument is unlikely to be of great future importance. This is EU institutional transparency only when pushed and when it is least needed.

Measuring the bailout sources against Fuller's eight desiderata three stand out. Two concern general promulgation—the need to generally publicize or make known the rules of law. He notes:

[57] See, e.g. ECB Press Conference, 2 December 2010, in which Mr Trichet was asked, 'I also have a technical question on the balance sheet of the Central Bank of Ireland. There has been an increase in other assets, which could mean some kind of emergency lending. Are national central banks able to make emergency loans outside the normal ECB financing operations? Is this something the ECB discusses or votes on?' He replied, '[W]e have a doctrine covering the emergency liquidity assistance (ELA) and I have nothing to add to it, it is a standing concept', available at https://www.ecb.europa.eu/press/pressconf/2010/html/is101202.en.html#qa (last visited 13 January 2017).

[58] Keohane, 'ELA stumble du jour', *Financial Times* 14 May 2012; see also FT Alphaville, 'Cypriots banks and some sneaky ELA' which shows the detective work, 'FT Alphaville has been very curious about the €18 billion of mystery ELA which showed up in the ECB's financial report at the end of April, but until now we weren't sure where the cash had ended up. We had a few guesses of course, but no proof. We finally have some solid evidence to back up our guess work. The central bank of Cyprus' latest balance sheet includes €3.8 billion marked as "other claims on euro area credit institutions denominated in euro". As we have noted before, [this] is code for ELA…' It goes on to note indirect signs of Portuguese ELA detected in the Bank of Portugal's balance sheet.

The laws should . . . be given adequate publication so that they may be subject to public criticism, including the criticism that they are the kinds of laws that ought not to be enacted unless their content can be effectively conveyed to those subject to them.[59]

The other is the need for clarity—to make rules understandable while maintaining their meaning and integrity. Fuller focuses mainly on the void-for-vagueness issue, arguing that 'obscure and incoherent legislation can make legality unattainable by anyone'.[60] He does not imagine sources in languages people subject to them cannot read. Of course EU bailout law has a different constitutional structure to the inept legal regime of Rex in his kingdom depicted by Fuller. Those living in bailout states can feel the effects of the national law applied to them. But they cannot easily access, read, or make legal sense of the 'EU law' behind that law. This analysis of bailout sources also strongly confirms another hypothesis of Fuller's—that failure in relation to one essential legal value tends to become cumulative.[61] We have seen that complexity is a problem which is substantially aggravated by the different facets of the accessibility problems with these sources: the difficulties of finding them, their availability only in English, or their non-public availability.

Although legal sources are extensively deployed, what seems best to capture how bailout states are treated by the EU is Fuller's distinction between 'managerial direction' and law:

Law is not, like management, a matter of directing other persons how to accomplish tasks set by a superior, but is basically a matter of providing the citizenry with a sound and stable framework for their interactions with one another.[62]

Unlike law, managerial direction focuses on achievement of managerial goals. While managerial direction may often wish to follow the same desiderata as the principles of legality, this is expedient and collateral to the overall goal of achieving managerial objectives. Hence, should the means to best achieve such goals require secret pressures, unpublished norms, and large discretion for decision-makers to change the rules, there is no intrinsic managerial reason to object. Moreover, while norms still need to be promulgated in managerial mode, they need only be made public to the subordinate charged with their execution (national governments or central banks of bailout or ECB-managed states) rather than more generally. The bailouts make more sense when viewed as pursuing the managerial goal of sending EU states into bailout when deemed necessary and applying conditionality to try to achieve re-entry into the sovereign debt markets as soon as possible and by whatever means necessary.

[59] Fuller, *supra* note 46, at 51. He also later notes (at 97): 'Each of the demands of legality can be outraged in ways that leave no doubt. Caligula, for example, is said to have respected the tradition that the laws of Rome be posted in a public place, but saw to it that his laws were in such fine print and hung so high that no-one could read them.'

[60] *Ibid.*, at 61.

[61] *Ibid.*, at 91: 'infringements of legal morality tend to become cumulative. A neglect of clarity, consistency or publicity may beget the necessity for retroactive laws. Too frequent changes in the law may nullify the benefits of formal, but slow-moving procedures for making the law known.'

[62] *Ibid.*, at 210; see generally at 207–214.

B. Procedural Rule of Law Measurement

Waldron argues that a *procedural* rather than the norm-based approach generally adopted by legal philosophers better addresses the rule of law concerns citizens typically have. While legal philosophers focus on formal qualities for the general norms on which public action is based, such as publicity and clarity, popular uses of the rule of law tend instead to focus on ensuring due process before independent courts.[63] He argues that a legality or rule-based focus accordingly gives insufficient weight to the distinctive attributes of justice before courts which are central to popular understandings of the Rule of Law.

Waldron's analysis signals attention to important linkages between legality concerns and procedural concerns in the EU bailout context. As he notes, procedural rule of law concerns stress access to justice as 'a mode of governance that allows people a voice, a way of intervening on their own behalf in confrontations with power'.

My particular focus is on how the ECB, the Court of Justice, and the Ombudsman responded, or not, to the formal rule of law problems identified earlier. The formal rule of law problems with the bailout sources evidently made it very difficult for national courts properly to frame preliminary references. When Portuguese and Romanian courts made preliminary references on the compatibility of bailout measures with the EU Charter of Fundamental Rights (EUCFR), they did not specifically mention the EU law sources underpinning all or part of their bailouts. The Court of Justice, as a rule of law defender, could have acknowledged and alleviated these deep deficiencies. Instead, it summarily rejected all these references on the basis that the national courts had provided no evidence that the challenged measures were implementing EU law as required under Article 51 EUCFR.[64] EU judicial accountability in the face of rule of law problems has been lacking.

The secret letters were also challenged before the European Ombudsman after unsuccessful attempts to obtain them using access to documents requests before the ECB.[65] With regard to both the Spanish and Irish letters, the Ombudsman relied on the broad margin of discretion for institutions to define the public interest, here as regards the monetary and economic policy of the EU or a Member State. However, the new Ombudsman dealing with the Irish case, while finding the public interest exception applied at the time of the request in 2011, asked the ECB to release it in spring 2014 as a 'friendly solution'. When the ECB refused, she:

[63] Waldron, 'The Concept of Law and the Rule of Law', 43 *Georgia Law Review* (2008) 1.

[64] Romania and Court of Justice: Case C-434/11, *Corpul Național al Polițiștilor*, Order of 14 December 2011, [2011] ECR I-00196 (ECLI:EU:C:2011:830); Case C-134/12, *Corpul Național al Polițiștilor*, Order of 10 May 2012 (ECLI:EU:C:2012:288); Case C-462/11, *Cozman*, Order of 14 December 2012, ECR I-00197 (ECLI:EU:C:2011:831). Portugal and Court of Justice: Case C-128/12, *Sindicato dos Bancários do Norte and Others*, Order of 7 March 2013 (ECLI:EU:C:2013:149); Case C-264/12, *Sindacato Nacional dos Profissionais de Seguro e Afins*, Order of 26 June 2014 (ECLI:EU:C:2014:2036).

[65] Spanish letter: Decision of the European Ombudsman closing his inquiry into Complaint 2016/2011/AN against the European Central Bank, Opened on 11 November 2011, Decision of 19 July 2012. Irish letter: Case 1703/2012/(VIK)/CK, Decision of 24 April 2014. The complaint is 'The ECB wrongly refused access to its letter, dated 18 November 2010, addressed to the Irish Finance Minister, Mr Brian Lenihan'. A new European Ombudsman, Emily O'Reilly, decided this case. She took office in October 2013 replacing Nikiforos Diamandouros.

expressed publicly her regrets that the Governing Council of the ECB had wasted the opportunity to demonstrate its commitment to the principles of transparency and accountability and to further enhance its legitimacy in the eyes of the EU citizens, at a time when so many of them have been suffering as a result of the economic crisis.[66]

Several months later, the Irish letter was released by the ECB on 6 November 2014. Its release is presented by the ECB on its website as follows:

With this decision, the ECB honoured the European Ombudsman's call for the Governing Council to re-consider the release of the letter. The Governing Council also decided to disclose a further three letters that were part of correspondence between the ECB and the Irish authorities in the run-up to the official application of Ireland for support under an EU/IMF adjustment programme.[67]

The content of the actions contained in the letter is analysed further in Abnormality 2 later in the chapter.

The limited and opaque communication via Press Release of decisions on ELA provision by the ECB has also been challenged in the context of an ongoing annulment action before the Court of Justice under Article 263 TFEU in which a Greek firm (Alcimos) is challenging the validity of the June/July 2015 ELA decisions taken for Greece.[68] As part of its action, Alcimos made a request for public access to ECB documents asking precisely for the details of how much ELA had been granted to which banks and the percentage of the haircut the ECB had imposed on Greek government bonds being used as collateral by the banks.[69] Disclosure of the ELA ceiling was refused, relying on the terms of the ECB decision on public access because it would 'harm the financial, monetary or economic policy of the Union or Member State' and 'the stability of the financial system in the Union or in a Member State'.[70] Nonetheless the access request still provides us with the longest and fullest information on ELA ever provided by the ECB, showing the utility of even unsuccessful public access requests in situations exhibiting an extreme lack of accountability and transparency combined with an exceptionally high public interest in the non-disclosed information. According to the ECB, publication of the amount of

[66] European Ombudsman, 'Ombudsman: Governing Council of the ECB has wasted an opportunity for openness and transparency', Press release no. 7/2014, 7 March 2014, available at http://www.ombudsman.europa.eu/en/press/release.faces/it/53710/html.bookmark (last visited 13 January 2017).

[67] European Ombudsman, 'Ombudsman welcomes ECB decision to release "Irish ECB letter"', Press release no. 22/2014, 6 November 2014, available at https://www.ombudsman.europa.eu/en/press/release.faces/en/58279/html.bookmark (last visited 13 January 2017).

[68] Case T-368/15 R, *Alcimos Consulting v. ECB*, Order of the President of the General Court of 1 September 2015 (ECLI:EU:T:2015:584). An application for interim measures was refused in an Order by the President of the General Court of 1 September 2015. Alcimos holds a bank account with a Greek bank, which had a balance of €10,582.84 on the day the capital controls were imposed. It sustains that the ECB decisions resulted immediately in capital controls and a bank holiday so that Alcimos was not able to freely use the funds available for transactions outside Greece. I am grateful to Nicholas Lee, an EUI researcher, for bringing this litigation to my attention.

[69] Request for public access to ECB documents under ECB Decision 2004/3 of 4 March 2003 on public access to ECB documents, OJ 2004 L 80/42, 30 July 2015. Alcimos used its right under the Decision to appeal to the ECB Executive Board which rejected its appeal on 24 September 2015.

[70] Article 4(1)(a) second and seventh indents of ECB Decision 2004/3 of 4 March 2003 on public access to ECB documents, OJ 2004 L 80/42.

ELA, of the banks to which it was supplied, or of the haircut imposed on Greek bonds collateral would permit computation of banks' liquidity situation and could aggravate their liquidity problems and cause financial instability. Much less convincingly, even *ex post* publication of ELA and the banks in receipt of ELA could, according to the ECB, have detrimental effects on the Governing Council's opinion-building and decision-making in future similar situations.

Nonetheless, the outcome of such lack of disclosure is that the General Court, in considering whether interim measures should be granted in the proceedings by Alcimos against the ECB, presents the dispute in the following quite exceptional way:

By those two decisions ('the contested decisions'), the ECB left the ceiling to the provision of emergency liquidity assistance unchanged, despite requests by the Bank of Greece, which, *according to press reports*, had submitted a request for an increase of the ceiling to ELA by EUR 6 billion, from a previous level of EUR 89 billion.[71]

Two weeks after this decision, and while the ECB Executive Board was considering Alcimos' public access to ELA documents appeal, on 16 September 2015 the ECB announced that henceforth ELA figures and the banks to which it is paid could be made public by the national central banks. It is hard to square this with the reasons given just two weeks earlier by the ECB to deny public access to that information. Additionally, and crucially, this change of policy does not extend to the ECB's deliberations on ELA which will apparently remain secret:

The Governing Council of the European Central Bank has decided that national central banks will from now on have the option to communicate publicly about the provision of Emergency Liquidity Assistance (ELA) to the banks in their country, in cases where they deem that such communication is necessary.[72]

This part of my analysis has provided a detailed set of examples to evidence its claim that measured by both aspects of the rule of law, formal and procedural, the sovereign debt sources are deeply problematic. Secrecy, inaccessibility, and the avoidance of legal sources governed by the standard EU language regime are the hallmarks of the sovereign debt sources created and used by the EU institutions. While there have been some belated and limited moves to resolve some of these problems, and these are not entirely meaningless, for the most part they are the sovereign debt equivalent of locking the stable door after the horse has bolted. Importantly, such foundational legal abnormalities are not a necessary corollary of the particular policy choices made by the EU institutions in managing the banking and sovereign debt crises. While arguments may properly be made for limited disclosure in some of these cases, the net is cast much too widely and for much too long for that to be a convincing explanation.

[71] Case T-368/15 R, *supra* note 68, at para. 2 (emphasis added).

[72] ECB Press Release, 'Communication on Emergency Liquidity Assistance', 16 September 2015, available at https://www.ecb.europa.eu/press/pr/date/2015/html/pr150916.en.html (last visited 13 January 2017).

5. Abnormality 2—ECB Mandates Are Abnormal Because of Conditionality, Contamination, Accumulation, and Absence

As noted when introducing the ECB measures, the ECB measures are explicitly 'non-standard', 'unconventional' or even expressly, in the case of liquidity assistance via national central banks with ECB veto, 'emergency' measures. Such measures are to be distinguished from its *standard* measure of adjusting interest rates so as to achieve its primary mandate of price stability.

Much of the discussion surrounding these measures has focused on whether they are 'constitutional'. In this regard, almost all legal discussion[73] has focused on the Treaty prohibition on monetary financing in Article 123TFEU, the monetary policy mandate of the ECB, and the bond-buying programmes of the ECB, especially the OMT programme following the preliminary reference made on this point by the German Federal Constitutional Court. The outcome of this challenge has, unsurprisingly, confirmed the EU legality of the OMT programme.[74]

Yet this is but one, and arguably not the most compelling, candidate in assessing whether the ECB did not stick to its institutional mandate. I will revisit the ECB activities introduced earlier, but this time with an eye to abnormal features. My argument is that the ECB exercised its institutional mandates abnormally in four ways. It imposed inappropriate conditions on some of its mandates. It contaminated features of one mandate with exercise of others. It has an inappropriate accumulation of mandates. It has no mandate for fiscal and economic intervention in the Member States. Many of the examples below demonstrate a number of these abnormal features. I look first at the ECB's function as a lender of last resort to banks and then at its more contested sovereign lender of last resort actions.

A. The ECB as a Lender of Last Resort to Banks

The ECB did not respect or fulfil its central crisis role of acting as a lender of last resort to banks. It inappropriately used its powers as the lender of last resort to banks to decide when states should enter bailouts. To put this another way, central bank provision of liquidity to banks should be subject to only one condition: that it is for providing liquidity to the banking system rather than protection of bank investors through capital injections to failing banks. States should resolve failing banks while being able to rely on their central bank to provide systemic banking liquidity while they do so. Instead, the ECB provided liquidity to national banking systems in a way that made choices about which states would be pushed into sovereign debt loan assistance or punished for refusing to accept, or trying to renegotiate, the terms of that sovereign debt loan assistance. It is worth underlining that this central abnormality has nothing to do with the ECB acting as a *sovereign* lender of last resort. Here we are focusing only on how it executed its accepted and uncontroversial mandate as a

[73] Beukers' analysis, *supra* note 4, is a notable exception.

[74] Case C-62/14, *Gauweiler and Others*, Judgment of the Court (Grand Chamber) of 16 June 2015 (ECLI:EU:C:2015:400).

central banker to the euro-area banks. This means returning to its provision of enhanced liquidity in its direct lending to banks and its oversight of national central banks provision of emergency liquidity assistance.

1. *Providing Enhanced Liquidity to Banks or Other Credit Institutions in the Eurozone*

As analysed earlier, in the crisis the ECB overall and appropriately acted as a classic lender of last resort to provide liquidity to banks. However, much less classically or appropriately, it used its powers in this respect to move certain states along the road to bailout or to send hefty warning signals to states.

In 2012 the ECB's refusal to suspend its normal collateral requirements in loans to Cypriot banks triggered a request for financial assistance from the state of Cyprus. One important source of collateral banks can offer is government bonds. By refusing to accept government bonds as eligible collateral, banks in a particular state can rapidly be pushed into requiring ELA and from there, as explained later, it is easy to require a state to enter bailout, no matter how unorthodox that may be as a matter of central bank practice. Hence, as Beukers notes, relying on newspaper reports, in April 2011 the ECB allegedly pressured Portuguese banks to stop using the ECB's liquidity to buy Portuguese bonds, producing the effect of pressuring Portugal into a request for financial assistance.[75]

In return for bailout entry, the ECB can then reverse its decision and accept as collateral the government bonds of the bailout state. When Greece agreed its first bailout, the ECB agreed to accept as collateral for loans to Greek banks, Greek government bonds with junk status.[76] Irish and Portuguese[77] bonds subsequently received the same treatment. This mode of operation was set out more fully by the ECB in Guidelines, the most recent of which dates from July 2014.[78]

That this process can also be reversed is perfectly illustrated by Greece in 2015. A few weeks after the election of Syriza as the Greek party of government, the ECB revisited the acceptance of Greek government bonds as collateral irrespective of the credit quality rating. Its decision to no longer exempt Greek government bonds from standard collateral requirements is explained as follows:

> On the basis of the information available, the Governing Council has made an assessment, according to which it is not currently possible to assume a successful conclusion of the review of the European Union/International Monetary Fund programme for the Hellenic Republic. Consequently, the Hellenic Republic is no longer deemed to be in compliance with the conditionality of the programme and, as a result, the conditions for the temporary suspension

[75] Beukers, *supra* note 4.

[76] ECB Decision 2010/3 of 6 May 2010 on temporary measures relating to the eligibility of marketable debt instruments issued or guaranteed by the Greek Government, OJ 2010 L 117/102.

[77] ECB Decision 2011/10 of 7 July 2011 on temporary measures relating to the eligibility of marketable debt instruments issued or guaranteed by the Portuguese Government, OJ 2011 L 182/31.

[78] Guideline ECB/2014/31 of 9 July 2014 on additional temporary measures relating to Eurosystem financing operations and eligibility of collateral and amending Guideline ECB/2007/9, OJ 2014 L 240/28.

of the Eurosystem's credit quality thresholds in respect of such instruments... are no longer fulfilled.[79]

The effect of this Decision was to make Greek banks dependent on ELA from February 2015.

2. The ECB and the Provision of Emergency Liquidity Assistance

ELA by national central banks occurs when the ECB has stopped its direct lending operations to banks. It is important to understand that by refusing or modifying the provision of ELA by national central banks, the ECB effectively requires states to request bailouts. This is because withdrawal of the lender of last resort function to the banking system means the banking system can no longer operate: there is effectively speaking no money in the banks and extensive capital controls are unsustainable for long. The only 'choice' given to euro-area states placed in this situation by the ECB is to regain their power to print money to provide liquidity to their banks by exiting the single currency.

Hence, even when states do have public finance reserves, and therefore do not for that reason need to enter bailout at that time, as was the Irish case in 2010 and the case for Greece, which was running a primary surplus in 2015, they can be bounced into bailout by ECB actions. Hence, while Ireland was denying it would have a bailout, the Irish member of the ECB, Mr Patrick Honohan, speaking from Frankfurt announced on Irish national radio on the morning of 18 November 2010 that it would.[80] There was no way out of bailout in that particular context for the Irish state. The freeze on ELA to Greek banks in July 2015 had the same effect.[81]

It should once again be stressed that there is no quarrel with the ECB refusing ELA if it is of the view that banks are insolvent rather than simply illiquid. But this does not tally with the use and withdrawal of ELA simply as a reward for states accepting bailout entry or bailout terms or as a penalty for not doing so. We should, of course, not forget the ECB's role in setting and monitoring those very bailout terms, an issue we assess below.

[79] ECB Decision 2015/300 of 10 February 2015 on the eligibility of marketable debt instruments issued or fully guaranteed by the Hellenic Republic, OJ 2015 L 53/29.

[80] The text of the interview is available at http://www.theguardian.com/business/ireland-business-blog-with-lisa-ocarroll/2010/nov/18/ireland-central-bank-governor-transcript (last visited 13 January 2017). Sandbu's book, *supra* note 6, has a chapter on Ireland (Ch. 4) which begins with a discussion of the Honohan interview. The Irish Banking Inquiry Report of January 2016, Volume 1, contains a Chapter (10) on 'Ireland and the Troika Programme': https://inquiries.oireachtas.ie/banking/wp-content/uploads/2016/01/02106-HOI-BE-Report-Volume1.pdf (last visited 13 January 2017). This makes clearer still the decision by the ECB on 12 November 2010 that its exposure to Irish banks was too high and its subsequent off-the-record briefing that Ireland would enter a programme. The ECB declined to appear before the Inquiry: for the correspondence between the inquiry and the ECB in which President Draghi declines ECB participation, see Report of the Joint Committee of Inquiry into the Banking Crisis, Volume 2, Appendix 7, Correspondence with the ECB.

[81] See the analysis of Sandbu, *supra* note 6, for Greece at 77–78 and for Ireland at 94 for an analysis of the still sustainable public finances of the Irish state when it entered bailout.

Hence, in the originally secret letter sent to Ireland on 19 November 2010,[82] ECB President Trichet made clear that it would extend ELA to Irish banks only if the Irish government accepted a bailout:

> [I]t is the position of the Governing Council that it is only if we receive in writing a commitment from the Irish Government vis-à-vis the Eurosystem on the four following points that we can authorize further provision of ELA to Irish financial institutions:
>
> 1. The Irish government shall send a request for financial support to the Eurogroup;
> 2. The request shall include the commitment to undertake decisive actions in the areas of fiscal consolidation, structural reforms and financial sector restructuring, in agreement with the European Commission, the International Monetary Fund and the ECB;...[83]

Ireland entered bailout immediately thereafter. On 21 March 2013, the ECB ended the long period of discussion between Cyprus and the EU on the terms of a possible bailout by stating that ELA would only be available after 25 March 2013 if Cyprus entered bailout. Cyprus then entered bailout. In the highly sensitive transition between Greece II and Greece III in the summer of 2015, as discussed earlier, the provision of ELA was again a central issue. The decisions of the ECB not to allow an increase of ELA, and to adjust the haircuts on collateral accepted by the Bank of Greece for ELA after the referendum result on 5 July 2015, were decisive contributors to the Greek decision to seek a third bailout on 8 July 2015. Repayment of the ECB in July via the EFSM funds led to a subsequent increase in the ELA ceiling. Hence rather than acting as a lender of last resort to banks, the ECB operated a strongly conditional liquidity stance. Liquidity provision was used as a lever to send states, when deemed appropriate by the ECB, along the road or into bailout. This contaminates the liquidity provision function with other concerns: programme compliance or the alignment of the preferences of governments with those of the central bank. The accumulation of mandates between the ECB as an institution monitoring and setting the terms of bailouts is also relevant here: while there is no straightforward or inevitable policy connection between the conditionality in loan assistance and the decision to accept government bonds of that state as collateral from banks in that state, such a connection is mechanically operated by the ECB.

[82] Trichet, Letter of the ECB president to the Irish Minister for Finance dated 19 November 2010 on the large provision of liquidity by the Eurosystem and the Central Bank of Ireland to Irish banks and the need for Ireland to agree to an adjustment programme, available at http://www.ecb.europa.eu/press/shared/pdf/2010-11-19_Letter_ECB_President_to%20IE_FinMin.pdf?31295060a74c0ffe738a12cd9139f578 (last visited 13 January 2017). This letter was only made public in November 2014 in a process discussed earlier under Abnormality 1: Rule of Law.

[83] *Ibid.* The other two points concerned *recapitalizing banks* and *ensuring ELA repayment*, both highly controversial. In relation to the latter, although Ireland had been lent very large amounts, a central bank system is very different from a private bank in its functions. It cannot go bankrupt, has a licence to print money, and its mandate, at minimum, is to ensure a functioning banking system and guarding against excessive inflation or deflation.

B. The ECB and Sovereign Debt

This is where we get closest to the Treaty constraints on ECB action, as a bond buyer and as an EU institution deciding on the conditions to apply to euro-area states receiving loan assistance. Conditional government bond-buying and stringent loan terms were imposed to provide reassurance that the measures taken respected the prohibitions on bailouts and monetary financing. Hence, abnormalities here, it may be argued, came as part and parcel of the policy choice adopted.

1. *Bond-Buying and Troika Membership: The Acceptability of Fiscal and Social Conditionality*

By buying government bonds, the ECB lowers the interest that Member States have to pay for government debt. This makes it controversial in relation to Article 123 TFEU.[84] The ECB's insistence that such purchases are necessary to safeguard appropriate monetary policy transmission and the singleness of monetary policy is contested by many, with such arguments being made before the Court of Justice in the *Gauweiler* preliminary reference by the German Constitutional Court.[85] As Tuori and Tuori state:

> The telos of the exception made in Article 123(1) [TFEU] in favour of secondary market purchases is to facilitate 'normal' liquidity operations and not emergency measures amounting to the bailout of a Member State threatened by insolvency.[86]

The ECB's first bond-buying programme, the SMP, operated in two phases, in the few months following the first eurozone bailout (Greece I in May 2010) and in August 2011 at which time the ECB purchased Italian and Spanish bonds. OMT was announced in September 2012; its real power came through its announcement effect on government bond markets. By stating that the ECB would buy unlimited amounts of government bonds on secondary markets, it became much less likely that any such bond purchases under the programme would in fact be needed, a classic sovereign lender of last resort signal. As noted when considering policy alternatives in this analysis, whether such a sovereign lender of last resort stance by the ECB breaches Article 123 TFEU depends on one's reading of that provision. An evidence-based but teleological argument, based on preparatory sources,[87] can be made that

[84] Article 123(1) TFEU provides: 'Overdraft facilities or any other type of credit facility with the European Central Bank or with the central banks of the Member States (hereinafter referred to as "national central banks") in favour of Union institutions, bodies, offices or agencies, central governments, regional, local or other public authorities, other bodies governed by public law, or public undertakings of Member States shall be prohibited, as shall the purchase directly from them by the European Central Bank or national central banks of debt instruments.'

[85] See Case C-62/14, *supra* note 74.

[86] Tuori and Tuori, *supra* note 4, at 166.

[87] See, for such evidence, the *Gauweiler* judgment, *supra* note 74, at para. 100: 'It is apparent from the preparatory work relating to the Treaty of Maastricht that the aim of Article 123 TFEU is to encourage the Member States to follow a sound budgetary policy, not allowing monetary financing of public deficits or privileged access by public authorities to lead to excessively high levels of debt or excessive Member State deficits (see the Draft Treaty amending the Treaty establishing the European Economic Community with a view to achieving economic and monetary union, *Bulletin of the European Communities*, Supplement 2/91, at 24 and 54).'

the moral hazard rationale underpinning that provision was not what was driving unsustainable bond yields in certain euro-area states. Accordingly, the crisis drive towards debt unsustainability in certain states was not the result of state 'misbehaviour' and could not be corrected by good state behaviour; accordingly ECB government bond purchases did not fall foul of that prohibition.

This is not the stance that the ECB took. Mindful of the counter-arguments that OMT was not about monetary policy transmission but rather that OMT, by lowering debt costs, reduced the pressure on states to restore market confidence through fiscal and structural reform, it tried to square the circle. It did this by on the one hand, insisting the bond purchases were focused on ensuring the singleness of monetary policy and its appropriate transmission and, on the other, accompanying bond purchases with conditionality. Hence the ECB conditions for the Spanish and Italian SMP purchases were laid down in secret (but leaked) letters and included fiscal and labour market reforms. As Beukers states in relation to Italy, 'formally the adoption of structural reforms by Italy was not a condition of the ECB's acquisition of Italian bonds. But *de facto* there was conditionality providing a clear instance of ECB pressure on Italy to adopt structural reform through a – potentially – powerful instrument'.[88] OMT makes conditionality a formal requirement so that bond-buying under this programme will only occur if the state has accepted conditionality within an ESM programme, in which, of course the ECB has a role in agreeing and monitoring those conditions.[89]

Assuming, as the Court of Justice did in *Gauweiler*,[90] that such bond purchases are to allow appropriate transmission of monetary policy, does not exhaust the questions about the ECB mandate. Two questions are raised about the ECB's mandate to impose fiscal and structural conditionality.[91]

The first concerns their redundancy to the expressed monetary policy objective. If the bond-buying programmes are there simply to restore broken monetary policy transmission, there is no need and no justification for conditionality. The ECB argument is that policy mistakes by states as well as broken monetary policy transmission lead to declining investor appetite for government bonds.[92] This argument was

[88] Beukers, *supra* note 4, at 1599.

[89] The ECB Press Release, 'Technical features of Outright Monetary Transactions', 6 September 2012, states with regard to conditionality: 'A necessary condition for Outright Monetary Transactions is strict and effective conditionality attached to an appropriate ESM programme… The Governing Council will consider Outright Monetary Transactions to the extent that they are warranted from a monetary policy perspective as long as programme conditionality is fully respected, and terminate them once their objectives are achieved or when there is non-compliance with the macroeconomic adjustment or precautionary programme.'

[90] *Gauweiler* judgment, *supra* note 74, at para. 50.

[91] Such questions are not fully addressed by the Court of Justice in *Gauweiler*, *ibid.*: it considers only whether making OMT conditional on an ESM programme means OMT itself falls outside monetary policy. It finds it does not as OMT can only indirectly encourage states to comply with ESM programmes, at paras 57–59; nor is ESM compliance a sufficient condition for OMT access, at para. 62; and the condition falls within the ECB's Treaty obligation (Article 119(3) and 127(1) TFEU) to ensure that public finances are sound, at para. 61.

[92] The 'two legs' argument of ECB President Draghi, Press Conference, 6 September 2012: '[W]e should not forget why countries have found themselves in a bad equilibrium to start with. And this is because of policy mistakes if the central bank were to intervene without any actions on the part of governments, without any conditionality, the intervention would not be effective and the Bank would lose

accepted by the Court of Justice in *Gauweiler* when it considered that such measures are amongst those that ensure the ECB does not breach Article 123 by ensuring that OMT does not substantially affect state incentives to run a sound budget.[93] Yet questions can be raised about the normality of conditionality accompanying bond-buying. We can first refer back to the alternative narratives of euro-area crisis outlined earlier, which suggest mistakes not just by these states but by other states too and by the EU institutions, such as suggesting that the euro was reversible, were a large contributor to the bond difficulties faced by states during the crisis. This would suggest a much less neat fit between bond-buying and imposing conditionality only on the state whose bonds will be purchased. We can also link this policy decision to what we might call 'ECB conditionality creep', a prevailing mindset that no ECB 'help' can be given to a 'failing state' without getting something in return.

The second concerns the absence of an ECB mandate to impose fiscal and structural reforms on euro-area Member States. As Beukers comments in relation to the ECB's troika roles:

> In giving the ECB these new tasks, the Eurozone Member States do not seem to have been concerned with delineating the ECB's responsibility substantively to negotiating or monitoring only on matters closely related to its monetary policy mandate.[94]

Bond-buying conditionality, alongside that imposed by the ECB as a troika member in the euro-area sovereign debt programmes, exemplify the concerns expressed by AG Cruz Villalón in his Opinion in *Gauweiler*. Although the ECB, alongside its primary mandate, has a mandate in Article 127(1) TFEU to support the economic policies of its Member States, it requires quite a stretch of the imagination for that to cover the interventions outlined in this analysis, which were neither soft enough to be considered simply supportive nor in any sense supportive of economic choices those Member States wished to make. The Court of Justice has not considered the conditionality of the SMP which was fully decided by the ECB and it kept separate in *Gauweiler* the bond-buying in the OMT from the conditionality in the ESM, not considering the role played by the ECB in the latter. Yet as the Advocate General notes in *Gauweiler*:

> Unilaterally making the purchase of government bonds subject to compliance with conditions when those conditions have been set by a third party is not the same as doing so when the 'third party' is not really a third party. In those circumstances, the purchase of debt securities subject to conditions may become another instrument for enforcing the conditions of the financial assistance programmes.[95]

its independence. At the same time, we see that we are in a bad equilibrium and, therefore, policy action, though convincing, does not seem to produce – at least not in the relatively medium term – the results for which it is geared. So that is why we need both legs for this action.'

[93] *Gauweiler* judgment, *supra* note 74, at para. 120.

[94] Beukers, *supra* note 4, at 1590. However, ultimately he sustains that legally the ECB can undertake all the actions my analysis argues are more legally problematic.

[95] Case C-62/14, *Gauweiler and Others*, Opinion of AG Cruz Villalón delivered on 14 January 2015 (ECLI:EU:C:2015:7), at para. 145.

His proposed solution to the dual role is to require the ECB to withdraw from monitoring financial assistance when OMT is activated. Only this will allow OMT to retain its character as a monetary policy measure. While the Advocate General rightly identifies the institutional abnormality of these particular cumulating mandates, there is also the broader question of the basis of the ECB mandate for intervening in a precise, directed, and normatively powerful fashion in Member States' fiscal and structural reforms. This feature of ECB action in bond-buying and troika membership remains difficult to convincingly justify on the basis of the Treaties or the ECB Statute.

Nonetheless the OMT decision by the ECB, set against its other actions, while undoubtedly an 'atypical' EU measure,[96] actually counts as one of its least abnormal. It was made fully public, accompanied by reasons and was plausibly based on the Treaties and the ECB Statute. The accumulating mandates were open, not secret.

2. *The Telling Examples of Ireland in 2010 and Greece in 2015*

We have already noted that the ECB pushed Ireland into bailout by denying access to direct lending or ELA for Irish banks. However, at the same time, in its secret letter of 19 November 2010 in which it tellingly anticipates its official role as a troika member, it also took away Ireland's choice to reduce the costs of its bailout by restructuring and resolving its banks. A bailout condition was to continue providing capital to its failing banks. This meant the costs of bank failure were allocated not to the investors in the banks but rather to the taxpayers of Ireland.[97] While ELA could appropriately have been refused if Ireland misdirected it to propping up insolvent banks rather than providing banking system liquidity while it resolved them, instead ELA was refused unless Ireland accepted that it would use the loan to prop up those insolvent banks in its bailout and not make bondholders shoulder losses. It is hard to think of a more telling example of an abnormal use by the ECB of its mandates.

While the ESM request which became Greece III was under examination, on 17 July 2015, Greece was granted just over €7 billion in short-term financial assistance under the EFSM in order to meet its July 2015 repayment obligations to the ECB (the redemption of bonds) and settling its arrears to the IMF.[98] The assistance was disbursed in one instalment on 20 July 2015, and was linked to economic policy conditionality. The ESM assistance will be used, *inter alia*, to repay that short-term EFSM bridge loan. It is particularly worth underlining how this particular arrangement illustrates well the tensions between the various roles of the ECB in sovereign debt loan states. The EFSM loan was needed to repay the ECB for bond redemptions. Yet, in its role as a troika member, it fell to the ECB to decide, in liaison with the Commission, whether Greece should be granted the EFSM loan which would

96 See the numerous references to its atypical nature in AG Cruz Villalón's Opinion, *ibid.*, at paras 75, 76, and 82.

97 See Irish Banking Inquiry Report of January 2016, *supra* note 80, Volume 1, Chapter 11, which gives extensive details of the repeated ECB imposition of its view that bondholders could not be touched under the loan assistance programme.

98 Council Implementing Decision 2015/1181 of 17 July 2015, *supra* note 31.

be used to repay itself. Hence the preamble to the decision granting EFSM loan assistance to Greece in July 2015 provides that 'the assessment by the Commission, in liaison with the European Central Bank... is that Greece needs financing of a total amount of EUR 7 160 million over the month of July 2015'.[99]

Even if the ECB withdraws from the troika during episodes of bond-buying, as the Advocate General in *Gauweiler* suggests, there is still a risk that its mandates will be *contaminated* by external concerns. The examples in this analysis show time and time again a cross-contamination in the ECB's banking operations with its concerns about the behaviour of particular governments in sovereign debt or sovereign debt vulnerable states and a use of banking system levers to place pressure, sometimes irresistible in the case of ELA, on the political choices of states.

6. Abnormality of Legal Sources in the EU Sovereign Debt Crisis as an Alternate Means of Calibrating the Presence of Institutional Variation or Constitutional Mutation

This chapter has examined two axes of abnormality of EU sovereign debt crisis measures—the rule of law and the ECB's roles in states which are in crisis. This analysis differs from most euro-area crisis analysis to date both in its focus and in its arguments. In its focus, it goes beyond the major attention paid to date, including by those who claim constitutional mutation, on the EMU/EU law compatibility of the loan assistance mechanisms (EFSM/EFSF/ESM) and bond-buying by the ECB. Indeed, it argues that the major legal abnormalities lie not with the more examined issue of the Treaty compatibility of loan assistance mechanisms and ECB bond-buying programmes. In these areas, those policy abnormalities which exist are largely a function of the contestable meta-policy decision discussed at the beginning of this chapter, to cleave as closely as possible to the prohibition on monetary financing, bailouts, and the ECB mandate in Articles 123, 125, and 127 TFEU.

This analysis shows that a different light, of particular legal interest, can be shed by instead examining how the bailouts and ECB measures were actually carried out and institutionally placed within the EU framework. This reveals lesser-known and examined stories of secrecy, inaccessibility, managerialism, attempts to block and deny accountability and to present the dubious law and policy pathways the EU institutions followed in the sovereign debt crisis as regrettable but unavoidable—when they were almost always anything but.

This focus allows a very different set of arguments to be made about the significance for legal scholars of the sovereign debt crisis sources. Importantly, it suggests that some manifestations are not primarily questions of EU constitutional transformation but rather, more foundationally, of legal malformation and inappropriate institutional actions.

Moreover, this analysis sets the ECB measures and sovereign debt measures in a broader context of policy alternatives and considers how institutional roles interact.

[99] *Ibid.*

In so doing, it particularly raises questions about how the ECB conducted its role as a lender of last resort to banks. We can also see that searching questions need to be asked of the ECB and the Commission about their commitment to ensuring compliance with (EU) legal values and requirements in sovereign debt management.

We further suggest that this method of proceeding is a way of reconsidering whether the sovereign debt crisis is an instance of EU institutional variation or constitutional breach or mutation. The more fine-grained assessment of different manifestations of abnormality allows particular patterns or concentrations of abnormality to be more clearly discerned, investigated, and contextualized. When all the evidence of abnormality is assessed, it may then be that features such as the *accumulation* or the *interaction* or the *scale* or the *geographical concentration* or the *duration* or the *effects* of abnormalities allow further more fully specified and located claims to be made of systemic mutation, sectoral mutation, or legal and institutional shortfalls. If one measures the situation of Greece, for example, against these features over the period from 2010 onwards, a strong case can be made that there is more than simply institutional variation in the EU sources and actions applied to this particular state. We may also assess the withdrawal of ELA to Ireland differently when we consider the role of the ECB as lending of last resort to banking systems, when we add that it was achieved via secret letter and a surprise announcement to the Irish media by the Irish member of the ECB, and when we further consider that the ECB, as a troika member, blocked Ireland from restructuring its insolvent banks by imposing losses on bondholders. The burden of this analysis has been to lay the groundwork for a richer legal reconstruction and assessment of the sovereign debt crisis by connecting and linking ECB and loan assistance sources to foundational legal issues of public promulgation, transparency, accountability, and respect for institutional mandates.

4

New Governance in the EU after the Euro Crisis—Retired or Reborn?

Mark Dawson

1. Introduction—New Governance in 2017

At the dawn of the twenty-first century, 'new governance' (NG) was at the forefront of academic debates about the transformation of EU legal acts.[1] The ambitious goals of the EU's central Lisbon Strategy—and the choice of a novel, non-binding instrument, the Open Method of Coordination (OMC)—to deliver it, suggested a new pivot in the legal and political machinery through which EU integration was to advance. If the 1960s and 1970s had been the era of 'integration through law', with the 1980s and 1990s using 'mutual recognition' to further the legal liberalization of a single European market, Lisbon heralded a new era. Integration to achieve central EU objectives—a 'knowledge-based' economy, or a renewed 'European social model'—was no longer to be delivered through binding rules but through the soft coordination of 'new governance'. These instruments were posited not only as supplementing, but as 'transforming' EU law, questioning the centrality of institutions like the Court of Justice of the European Union (CJEU) to the EU's future political and legal order.[2]

Some 15 years on, it is worth considering how premature the heralding of a 'new governance' era was. On the one hand, many of the original hopes of those most optimistic about NG's advance have been dashed. The EU's central 'Lisbon Strategy' failed to achieve its economic and social targets, with its 'Lisbon 2020' successor on course to fare even worse.[3] Policy processes delivered via the OMC—such as the once-heralded OMC for Social Inclusion and Social Protection—are withering, with academic prophecies of their limited effectiveness backed up by an increasingly poor national compliance record.[4] At the same time, the CJEU seems

[1] G. de Búrca and J. Scott (eds), *Law and New Governance in the EU and the US* (2006).

[2] See the special issue, 'New Governance and the Transformation of Law', *Wisconsin Law Review* (2010) 227; M. Dawson, *New Governance and the Transformation of European Law* (2011).

[3] Dawson, 'Learning from Past Failures? New Governance in the European Union from Lisbon 2000 to Lisbon 2020', 17 *Maastricht Journal of European & Comparative Law* (2010) 107.

[4] Daly and Copeland, 'Poverty and Social Policy in Europe 2020: Ungovernable and Ungoverned', 42 *Policy and Politics* (2014) 351.

to wield more substantive influence than ever, with ambitious rulings in areas from social policy to EU citizenship to consumer protection demonstrating the Court's obstinate ability to frame EU policy-making. If the 2000s seemed the era of 'soft law', the last half decade has seen an apparent reassertion of the EU legal order's 'harder' edge.

In spite of this, there are recent developments that seem to forward rather than challenge the idea of a continued 'new governance' era. The key development doing so—and the policy area that will be the primary focus of this chapter—is changes in EU economic governance. While EU economic governance after the euro crisis would seem to carry hard law elements,[5] a key empirical claim of this chapter is that post euro-crisis economic governance has generalized central elements of the NG paradigm into an increasingly central domain of EU policy-making. While economic governance post-crisis has been designed to significantly centralize national fiscal policy,[6] its attachment to 'rolling' and revisable regulation and its strong 'proceduralization' of EU and national policy-making bind it closely to the NG model. Policy-makers have turned to an enhanced form of NG as a way of managing complex, multilevel problems which traditional command and control regulation could not solve.

Finally, the chapter will advance a more contested, and explicitly normative, argument. As well as tracing the similarities and differences between economic governance and the NG paradigm, the chapter will also consider the suitability of NG instruments to achieve the goals desired by policy-makers seeking to respond to the crisis. As the chapter will argue, the EU may be using NG tools to achieve tasks to which they are wholly unsuited. While the lessons of previous experience with NG suggests that these methods work poorly in achieving harmonization and policy convergence, particularly in costly, distributive areas of policy, these are precisely the tasks that the new forms of economic governance are being asked to achieve. At the same time, some of the more promising aspects of the NG legacy—its experimental focus on policy innovation and mutual learning between states—is precisely the aspect of the NG paradigm that post-crisis economic decision-making seems to have left behind. Learning the lessons of NG's past may be vital in securing a central (and positive) place for NG instruments among the EU's future legal acts.

2. What was 'New Governance'?

One of the core difficulties in determining whether 'post-crisis' economic governance should be conceptualized under the rubric of NG is the high level of doubt and contestation surrounding NG itself.[7] 'Governance' suggests a de-centring of the

5 See more generally on constituent features of post-crisis economic governance, Dawson, 'Legal and Political Accountability Structure in Post-Crisis EU Economic Governance', 53 *Journal of Common Market Studies* (2015) 976.

6 On the impact of the crisis on the EU's institutional and decision-making structure, see Dawson, *ibid.*

7 See Möllers, 'European Governance: Meaning and Value of a Concept', 43 *Common Market Law Review* (2006) 313, at 314.

state as the primary means of exercising public authority. Its 'newness' suggests a departure from traditional forms of regulation. Beyond this, however, the term seems to beg as many questions as it answers, potentially bringing together disparate processes of European policy-making from the binding directives of the social dialogue to the soft steering of voluntary standards or codes of conduct.

The core consensus of the NG literature seems to be negative rather than positive: academics are much clearer about what NG is *not* than what it is.[8] What it clearly precludes is 'command and control' regulation, guided by central institutions, and epitomized by the 'Classical Community Method' (CCM) of directives, regulations, and decisions.[9] While there are many ways to characterize the CCM, three features stand out: (i) the importance of review institutions (like courts and parliaments) in ensuring norms are supervised and obeyed; (ii) the presence of norms as binding law; and (iii) the divide under the CCM between rule formation and rule application.[10] In the latter case, CCM rules carry a lengthy process of institutional deliberation but are not to be politically contested once they are formed. The primary duty of national institutions is to 'apply' CCM rules domestically (such that significant deviance from given norms, even under directives, is categorized as 'non-compliance', resulting in suitable penalties and enforcement mechanisms).

NG procedures, in their various guises, seem to depart from these central tenants, and in diverging ways. As shown by a central example—the process of 'open coordination' used by Lisbon to coordinate social and education policies—it significantly relegates traditional review institutions like courts and parliaments.[11] Neither play a significant role in the formulation or review of OMC guidelines and recommendations. As a result, norms under the OMC are not adopted as binding law, with persuasion rather than legal coercion seen as the primary instruments of inducing policy change. Finally, the CCM's bright line between the formation and application of norms is thoroughly eroded in most NG processes.[12] In the case of the OMC for example, objectives and guidelines are formed as a policy cycle, with domestic experience of what 'works', or of new regulatory issues and problems, feeding into central norms later in the policy cycle. Deviance from norms is not seen as non-compliance but either as experimentation or as evidence that the original norms were not adequately framed in the first place. Under this account, if the CCM is from Mars, NG is from Venus.

[8] Dawson, *supra* note 2, at 72–77; Dawson, 'Three Waves of New Governance in the European Union', 36 *European Law Review* (2011) 208, at 211–213.

[9] Scott and Trubek, 'Mind the Gap: Law and New Approaches to Governance in the European Union', 8 *European Law Journal* (2002) 1; de Búrca, 'The Constitutional Challenge of New Governance in the European Union', 28 *European Law Review* (2003) 814.

[10] Deakin and de Schutter, 'Reflexive Governance and the Dilemmas of Social Regulation' in S. Deakin and O. de Schutter (eds), *Social Rights and Market Forces: Is the Open Coordination of Employment and Social Policies the Future of Social Europe?* (2005).

[11] Dawson, *supra* note 2, at 203–206.

[12] Deakin and de Schutter, *supra* note 10.

The main problem with this 'negative' definition of NG is that, in practice, the binary distinction is not so clear.[13] If one takes any of these three variables, NG processes often seem to interrelate with hard law alternatives.[14] To take the economic governance example that this chapter will focus on, the Broad Economic Policy Guidelines, which were the pre-cursor to the current regime of fiscal policy coordination, operated as an OMC process.[15] At the same time, it was embedded in a series of directives and regulations and included the possibility of 'hard' fiscal penalties if states deviated from the famous Maastricht deficit criteria. Many hard law directives carry soft law elements, particularly in the social policy field from which NG sprang, such as optional articles or provisions whose content is to be elaborated by social partners or other non-conventional bodies. If NG was whatever hard law was not, how could this be reconciled with hard law's very 'softness', or the continuities between NG and more traditional modes of regulation?[16]

An alternative approach is to seek a more 'positive' definition of NG or to see NG as embodying particular concepts or modes of rule.[17] Two schools of thinking are important in considering this second alternative (and, indeed, both are useful when analysing whether present economic decision-making can be seen as a category of NG). The first of these emerges from the US context. In an influential essay from 2008 (building from earlier work) Jonathan Zeitlin and Charles Sabel have associated the development of NG with a shift in the EU towards 'democratic experimentalism'.[18]

The experimentalist model is based on scepticism towards the idea that contemporary regulatory problems can be solved by central actors. NG mechanisms seek to solve problems of limited or 'bounded' rationality on the part of policy-makers by delegating policy-making responsibilities to lower-level actors within relatively wide mandates.[19] Within these mandates, local actors are encouraged to experiment with policy solutions but on the premise that they will report to the central level on their performance. By so doing, central policy-making may benefit from experience of which policy options are successful, which are not, and which may be generalized to other policy or territorial contexts.

In this sense, experimentalism combines two crucial elements of what this chapter will term the 'new governance paradigm'.

[13] This point is evident in the significant literature on 'hybridity' between hard and soft law. See Kilpatrick, 'New EU Employment Governance and Constitutionalism', in G. de Búrca and J. Scott (eds), *supra* note 1, at 124; Armstrong, 'The New Governance of EU Fiscal Discipline', 38 *European Law Review* (2013) 601.

[14] See Terpan, 'Soft Law in the European Union – the Changing Nature of EU Law', 21 *European Law Journal* (2014) 68, at 79.

[15] See Hodson and Maher, 'The Open Method of Coordination as a New Mode of Governance: the Case of Soft Economic Policy Coordination', 39 *Journal of Common Market Studies* (2001) 719.

[16] D. Trubek and L. Trubek, 'Hard and Soft Law in the Construction of Social Europe: The Role of the Open Method of Coordination', 11 *European Law Journal* (2005) 343, at 355–361.

[17] Dawson, *supra* note 5, at 214. For a different typology, focused on the OMC case and its relation to particular general principles of EU law, see Armstrong, 'The Open Method of Coordination: Obstinate or Obsolete?', 45 *University of Cambridge Faculty of Law Research Paper* (2016).

[18] Sabel and Zeitlin, 'Learning from Difference: The New Architecture of Experimentalist Governance in the European Union', in C.F. Sabel and J. Zeitlin (eds), *Experimentalist Governance in the European Union* (2010) 1; J. Zeitlin, 'EU Experimentalist Governance in Times of Crisis', 39 *West European Politics* 5 (2016).

[19] *Ibid.*, at 6.

(a) The first of these is revisability. NG in this sense is associated with the erosion of the application/formation distinction mentioned earlier. Rules are not formed 'once and for all' but are to be revised according to practical experience, and on an ongoing iterative basis. Normally, this revision is to be conducted by executive actors (e.g. in the OMC case, committees are made up of governmental officials but other actors such as civil society or technical agencies may also be tasked with revision). One shifts from universal rules to revisable 'decisions' (a category to which Section 4 of this chapter will return).

(b) The second is differentiation. Experimentalism rejects the idea of 'one size fits all' policy-making, or the notion that the primary goal of EU legal acts should be to harmonize national rules in order to establish a unitary European standard. Substantive difference is not only permitted under the experimental model but seen as a useful policy tool: an opportunity to use the diversity of different national contexts to 'experiment' and thereby build more innovative and effective policies.

While democratic experimentalism has had significant influence on the academic and institutional debate about NG, it is a framework that has been questioned,[20] and that should be complemented by other approaches. A second potential conceptual basis for a 'positive' definition of NG comes from procedural theory.

The common starting point between proceduralism and experimentalism is a shared interest in the de-centring of public authority. For architects of the procedural approach, such as Jürgen Habermas, one can no longer in a democratic polity see the authority of the law as emerging from its formal pedigree, nor from its ability to achieve particular material public goods. Rather, the validity of the law emerges from the ability of addressees of the legal order to carry a say in the law's formation.[21] This implies a strong role for law, not so much in the elaboration of substantive goals for citizens, but rather in creating a procedure within which goals can be deliberated and determined. Law in this sense must play a secondary role, addressing disparities of power between participants, ensuring the free flow of information and executing the norms thereby produced.

While Habermas' account is not directly tied to the multilevel context of the EU—and contains a strongly normative dimension—some scholars have connected procedural ideas to the notion of EU law as a 'reflexive' procedural device.[22] EU law does not only proscribe substantive outcomes, but may play a role in encouraging Member States, and domestic institutions, to consider the impact of their policies on neighbouring states and seek out commonly agreed upon solutions to collective problems. EU law need not always 'replace' or harmonize national standards but may guide national policy-making, encouraging it to internalize the preferences and view-points of outsiders.[23]

[20] See in particular Scheuerman, 'Democratic Experimentalism or Capitalist Synchronization: Critical Reflections on Directly-Deliberative Polyarchy', 17 *Canadian Journal of Law and Jurisprudence* (2004) 101.

[21] See Habermas, 'Paradigms of Law', 17 *Cardozo Law Review* (1996) 771.

[22] Deakin and de Schutter, *supra* note 10; Smismans, 'Reflexive Law in Support of Directly-Deliberative Polyarchy', in S. Deakin and O. de Schutter (eds), *supra* note 10.

[23] This idea of EU law as compensating for the external democratic deficits of national democracies is also a key insight in the work of Christian Joerges. See Joerges, 'Deliberative Supra-nationalism: Two Defences', 8 *European Law Journal* (2002) 133.

Proceduralism in this sense speaks to two further elements of the NG paradigm that have been influential in the existing academic literature.[24]

(c) The third of these is procedural constraint. While many approaches to NG seem to place it outside of 'classical' EU law, NG in fact provides the law with a crucial but different role. Law is designed to bind participants in a common *process* of decision-making without thereby presupposing that processes' substantive outcomes.

(d) The fourth element is 'domesticization' of EU policy. Whereas classical EU law often saw domestic institutions primarily as actors who could 'implement' EU policy under a formal hierarchy of norms, a procedural approach to NG sees domestic institutions as themselves engaged in the process of EU policy-making. NG in this sense both seeks to devolve to domestic and 'local' institutions significant decision-making power and encourages those institutions themselves to adopt 'other-regarding' or (in the common political science vernacular) 'Europeanized' norms and procedures.[25]

It is of course a generalization to talk of a single NG paradigm. These four (inter-related) features of an 'ideal type' in NG may, however, be helpful in considering to what extent post-crisis governance has adopted the NG framework. It is to that subject which this chapter now turns.

3. New Governance and the Euro Crisis

While this section of the chapter will argue that 'post crisis' economic governance has carried over much of the NG paradigm, the crisis response can also be seen as an explicit critique of NG instruments, or at least a central perception of them. The key perception is the 'weakness' of NG or its perceived inability to affect meaningful policy change.[26]

This perception is closely related to the evolution of the Maastricht settlement for the governance of the euro area. The Post-Maastricht economic and monetary union (EMU) carried certain hierarchical 'command and control' elements. The central example was the decision to centralize monetary policy within the monopoly power of the European system of central banks. Famously, however, this monetary centralization was accompanied by a decentralization of responsibility for fiscal policy. Member States were themselves primarily responsible for their budgets, subject to two overarching conditions: that deficits and debt were restricted to 3 and 60 per cent of GDP respectively.

To enforce these targets, two main instruments of supervision were intended. The first was the 'invisible hand' of market discipline. The fierce current debate about

[24] For more detail on NG's theoretical origins, see Dawson, *supra* note 2, at 103–162.

[25] Olsen, 'The Many Faces of Europeanization', 40 *Journal of Common Market Studies* (2002) 921.

[26] See, on this critique at an institutional level, the 2004 Kok Report, *Facing the Challenge: The Lisbon Strategy for Growth and Employment* (2004), available at https://ec.europa.eu/research/evaluations/pdf/archive/fp6-evidence-base/evaluation_studies_and_reports/evaluation_studies_and_reports_2004/the_lisbon_strategy_for_growth_and_employment__report_from_the_high_level_group.pdf (last visited 1 September 2017).

Article 125 TFEU's no bailout clause reflects the idea that the Maastricht settlement prohibited states from free-riding on the fiscal performance of others. As neither the EU nor other governments could assume government debt from other states, national governments would thereby (in theory at least) be incentivized to manage their debt and deficits responsibly. Better debt and deficit ratios would lead to lower rates of interest on government bonds and thereby better national fiscal performance (and more money to spend on popular social and other programmes).[27]

The second instrument was the Stability and Growth Pact (SGP). Its two main elements were a preventative arm, established via Regulation 1466/97 and a dissuasive arm (Regulation 1467/97).[28] The preventive arm was designed as a process of budgetary surveillance *ex ante*. It obliged Member States to submit annual Stability and Convergence programmes with the possibility of warnings and recommendations from ECOFIN where national budgets were clearly likely to exceed the 3 per cent deficit limit. This also included annual recommendations in the areas of fiscal and employment policy, monitored both by the Commission and the Member States.

The SGP's dissuasive arm was more coercive, permitting sanctions against Member States with excessive deficits, with a qualified majority vote needed in the Council to determine that an excessive deficit existed, to issue a formal warning and, finally, to impose a non-interest-bearing deposit or fine. The SGP was in this sense formed as a series of instruments that mixed traditional regulation with 'NG' elements, in which fiscal policies would be flexibly coordinated.[29]

The principal critique of NG from political science literature has often centred on the limited evidence for its effectiveness.[30] Without binding force, instruments of 'soft' policy coordination were likely to be manipulated: obeyed by states when it suited them and flouted where the costs of compliance were too high. The experience of the SGP in the 2000s bears out some of this critique. While the decision to leave the 'dissuasive arm' in the hands of the Council clearly reflected the political salience of penalizing excessive deficits, it also left sanctioning decisions open to political bargaining between the Member States. Only two years after the first euro notes were issued, in 2003 France and Germany were themselves the subject of Commission recommendations for sanction under the SGP but used their political influence to place the procedure in abeyance (a procedural irregularity that was later questioned by the Court of Justice).[31] The inability of the Commission to enforce

[27] Dawson, 'Economic and Monetary Union: Maastricht's Great Failure', in M. de Visser and A.P. van der Mei (eds), *The Treaty on European Union 1993–2013: Reflections from Maastricht* (2014) 475.

[28] Council Regulation (EC) 1466/97 of 7 July 1997 on the strengthening of the surveillance of budgetary positions and the surveillance and coordination of economic policies, since amended, OJ 1997 L 209/1 and Council Regulation (EC) 1467/97 of 7 July 1997 on speeding up and clarifying the implementation of the excessive deficit procedure, since amended, OJ 1997 L 209/6.

[29] Schelkle, 'EU Fiscal Governance: Hard Law in the Shadow of Soft Law?', 13 *Columbia Journal of European Law* (2007) 705.

[30] See, e.g. Eckhardt, 'The Open Method of Coordination on Pensions: An Economic Analysis of its Effects on Pension Reforms', 15 *Journal of European Social Policy* (2005) 3; M. Dawson, *New Governance and the Transformation of European Law* (2011), at 175–183.

[31] Case C-27/04, *Commission v. Council*, [2004] ECR I-06649 (ECLI:EU:C:2004:436). While the Court agreed with the Commission that the deficit procedure could not be placed in abeyance, it rejected another, equally important, Commission argument, i.e. that the Council's failure to adopt the

and pursue sanctions against the Union's larger Member States—in the face of a qualified majority voting (QMV) requirement—was seen by many as making a mockery of the SGP's credibility in withstanding political pressure.[32]

By early 2008, the inability of fiscal policy coordination to either promote economic convergence among the Member States or to limit public debt and deficits was already apparent. By 2008, Greece already carried a public debt standing at 99.2 per cent of its GDP, a full 40 per cent above the Maastricht criteria, and a public deficit of 7.7 per cent.[33]

While the SGP could hardly be blamed as the sole culprit for the euro crisis (other states affected by the crisis, such as Spain, carried positive budgetary conditions in 2008), the immediate crisis response was full of rhetoric of 'strength', and of the need to create more robust and automatic fiscal rules.[34] Elements of the 'six' and 'two' pack legislation designed to 'strengthen' EMU can in this sense be seen as an explicit critique of NG's reliance on non-binding or persuasive norms.[35]

A central example is the set of reforms undertaken to the excessive deficit procedure (EDP). To address the debacle of 2003, the revised EDP now includes a novel 'Reversed' QMV system, whereby Council recommendations, including those involving fiscal penalties, shall be adopted unless explicitly overturned via a qualified majority.[36] This has been coupled with further centralizing provisions, ranging from the possibility of adopting sanctions earlier in the procedure, to the provisions under the 'two pack' regulations to supervise and provide recommendations for the national budget prior to its domestic adoption.[37]The heightened review powers of both the Commission and ECOFIN over national budgets post-crisis seems to suggest a move away from flexibility towards more traditional 'command and control' regulation.

Before coming to such a conclusion, we should take pause. There is much in the post-crisis economic governance framework that fits well within the NG paradigm. This begins at the explanatory level. The 'rise' of NG has often been explained in terms of a 'constitutional compromise'.[38] According to this account, processes

Commission's recommendations under the procedure was a decision capable of review under then Article 230 EC.

[32] Heipertz and Verdun, 'The Dog that Would Never Bite? What We Can Learn from the Origins of the Stability and Growth Pact', 11 *European Journal of Public Policy* (2004) 765.

[33] Eurostat News Release/Euro Indicators no. 149/2009 of 22 October 2009.

[34] See, e.g. the report of the 'four Presidents' (H. Van Rompuy, J.M. Barroso, J.-C. Juncker, and M. Draghi), 'Towards a *Genuine* Economic and Monetary Union', 5 December 2012, available at http://www.consilium.europa.eu/uedocs/cms_Data/docs/pressdata/en/ec/134069.pdf (last visited 5 January 2017).

[35] The six- and two-pack regulations, established in 2011 and 2013 respectively, were designed to develop a more robust monitoring framework for EU economic governance. The regulations establish a new procedure for monitoring macroeconomic imbalances, allow earlier monitoring of national budgets and place constraints on the ability of governments to overturn Commission recommendations on sanctions for fiscal deficits and debt.

[36] On its legality, see Palmstorfer, 'The Reverse Majority Voting under the Six Pack: A Bad Turn for the Union?', 20 *European Law Journal* (2014) 186.

[37] Regulation (EU) 473/2013 of the European Parliament and of the Council of 21 May 2013 on common provisions for monitoring and assessing draft budgetary plans and ensuring the correction of excessive deficit of the Member States in the euro area, OJ 2013 L 140/11, Articles 6–7.

[38] Zeitlin, 'Social Europe and Experimentalist Governance: Towards a New Constitutional Compromise?', in G. de Búrca (ed.) *EU Law and the Welfare State: In Search of Solidarity* (2005) 213.

such as the OMC were forwarded as a compromise between national leaders who recognized the need for greater supranational action in particular domains, but feared the sovereignty loss implied by regulation through the normal CCM. Desiring greater EU steering, but recognizing legal and political limitations on traditional EU law in the social field, the OMC was adopted as an alternative solution.

Fast-forwarding to the post-crisis landscape, we see related pressures. Once the crisis struck, a strong (albeit not uniform) academic consensus emerged that the divide between a centralized monetary policy and de-centralized fiscal policy had to be addressed.[39] A credible eurozone required far greater centralization and stronger safeguards against 'beggar thy neighbour' fiscal decisions, which could destabilize the common currency area.

Against this consensus, however, was ranged a myriad of legal and political obstacles. Legally, the Treaty structure not only seemingly prohibited the assumption of national debt but also limited the EU's ability to harmonize national fiscal policies, or to create new institutions for that purpose.[40] Politically, the common obligations and arduous decision-making process of the CCM seemed unsuitable for governing a euro area with both divergent economic challenges faced by participating states and a need for rapid and changing fiscal intervention.

The outcome of these conflicting demands was once again a form of constitutional compromise, in which many of the features of the NG paradigm were maintained or even embellished (albeit with some significant departures thrown in).[41] Once again, NG models acted as a 'lowest common denominator' allowing supranational steering without overriding entirely national prerogatives (particularly those of more debt-free Member States). This can be seen by returning to the four features of the NG paradigm described in Section 2 earlier.

4. The EU's 'New' Economic Governance

A. Revisability

The link between post-crisis economic governance and the revisability aspect of the NG paradigm should be seen in light of debates regarding conflicts between NG and classical notions of the 'rule of law'. The rule of law has often been associated with the need for stable, general, and universal rules that can guide official and individual conduct alike and be used to judge conformity with the law *ex post*.[42] The corollary of this is that the law must remain relatively static, with complex legislative procedures required for its revision. Where executives are given discretion to apply

[39] See, e.g. H. Enderlein *et al.*, 'Completing the Euro: A Roadmap Towards Fiscal Union in Europe', (2012), available at http://www.institutdelors.eu/media/completingtheeuroreportpadoa-schioppa-groupnejune2012.pdf?pdf=ok (last visited 5 January 2017).

[40] De Witte and Beukers, 'The Court of Justice Approves the Creation of the European Stability Mechanism Outside the EU Legal Order: Pringle', 50 *Common Market Law Review* (2013) 805, at 805.

[41] A related argument, based on the 'hybridity' of soft and hard law under new economic governance has been developed by Kenneth Armstrong, see Armstrong, 'The New Governance of EU Fiscal Discipline', 38 *European Law Review* (2013) 601.

[42] L. Fuller, *The Morality of Law* (2nd edn, 1969).

legal standards, their discretion is limited—in the EU case, for example, executive rule-making power has been seen to extend only to 'non-essential' elements of the legislative act.[43]

Part of NG's advance has been due to the ability of its norms to adapt quickly to changing regulatory demands and perceptions. The appeal of the OMC lay partly in the ability of its norms to change as pressing new issues came to the political table. These norms could also be interpreted flexibly, including within their ambit structures from a variety of European welfare states (such as collective bargaining, contributory insurance, single-payer health systems, and many other national peculiarities).[44] EU norms could in this sense accommodate significant differences in the means by which EU states delivered social and employment goals, without one method of delivery being seen as automatically superior to another.

Inevitably, with this flexibility came significant discretion. The decision, under the OMC for employment for example, whether to issue a country-specific recommendation was a genuine 'decision': however, clear and universal criteria were not available to guide the executive on when a decision should or should not be issued. This flexibility allowed executive actors like the Council significant leeway to adapt their norms to different national environments.

In doing so, however, these decisions created a significant 'discretionary space' in EU politics. NG's emphasis on revisability seemed in direct conflict with the notion of a stable and independent rule of law.[45] To paraphrase John Adams' famous definition, NG seemed to be built on a government 'of men, not laws', with few clear expectations as to when and how particular rules would be applied.

Post-crisis economic governance's preference for decisions over rules may be the key element joining its procedures to the NG paradigm.[46] One must not confuse 'rules' here with 'legislation'. Legislation under post-crisis economic governance abounds, from the regulations revising the EDP to those establishing the EU's new Macroeconomic Imbalances Procedure (MIP). Crucially, however, these two sets of legislative frameworks create procedures within which important budgetary decisions are made. In both cases (the EDP and MIP), the Commission and Council (in the form of ECOFIN) is vested with decision-making authority at numerous stages of the policy-making process.

As explained recently by the Commission, this discretion is seen by policy-makers as necessary to effectively apply fiscal rules in a diverse economic area:

> Equal treatment does not mean 'one-size-fits-all' and must be combined with the economic assessment that is required by every situation. It is on purpose that the [Stability and Growth] Pact envisages flexibility in the way its rules should be applied, both over time and across

[43] Article 290 TFEU.

[44] See Scharpf, 'The European Social Model: Coping with the Challenges of Diversity', 40 *Journal of Common Market Studies* (2002) 645.

[45] See on this question, Dawson, 'Soft Law and the Rule of Law in the European Union', in A. Vauchez and B. De Witte (eds), *Lawyering Europe: European Law as a Trans-national Social Field* (2013) 221, at 224–228.

[46] Chalmers, 'The European Redistributive State and a European Law of Struggle', 18 *European Law Journal* (2014) 667, at 682–684; Menéndez, 'Editorial: A European Union in Constitutional Mutation', 20 *European Law Journal* (2014) 127, at 136–137.

countries. It is also on purpose that some discretion is left, within the agreed rules, for the Commission and the Council to assess the soundness of public finances in the light of country-specific circumstances, in order to recommend the best course of action based on the latest developments and information.[47]

In the MIP, for example, the Commission and Council make at least eight such decisions. They must decide: (i) whether to conduct an in-depth review of an at-risk Member State;[48] (ii) whether to adopt preventative recommendations;[49] (iii) whether to declare the opening of an excessive imbalances procedure (EIP);[50] (iv) whether to accept or demand revision to any corrective plan issued by a Member State under an EIP;[51] (v) whether a Member State has adequately implemented its corrective plan;[52] (vi) whether to apply an interest-bearing deposit where that plan is not adequately implemented;[53] (vii) whether to vary the fine 'on grounds of exceptional economic circumstances';[54] and (viii) whether to close the procedure.[55] The sheer length of this procedure already tells us something significant—norms under the MIP and EDP never seem to crystallize into a 'once and for all' agreement but are based on repeated and rolling 'micro-assessments' by the EU institutions of national fiscal performance.

While the legislation gives the Commission and Council some guidance, the level of precision in the legislative text is highly variable. For many of the decisions above, the Commission and Council have near total decision-making discretion. This begins with the Directive's very material scope. A macroeconomic imbalance is defined as:

> Any trend giving rise to macroeconomic developments which are adversely affecting, or have the potential adversely to affect, the proper functioning of the economy of a Member State or of the economic and monetary union, or of the Union as a whole.[56]

It is difficult to perceive of any national measure that would be excluded from the ambit of this definition. In essence, the definition rests, as others have argued,[57] on a contentious economic definition of which policies and spending decisions are or are not likely to adversely affect the functioning of either national economies *or* the EU economy as a whole.

This imprecision also extends to the temporal scope of the procedure. A particularly significant example may be the decision whether to disapply sanctions in times of 'exceptional circumstance'. This is defined as circumstances 'resulting from an unusual event outside the control of the Member State concerned and which has a major impact on the financial position of the general government, or when resulting from a severe economic downturn'.[58] This is further specified to require an unforeseeable GDP loss of at least 2 per cent per annum. If this definition is applied to recent events, one can see the high level of discretion and ambiguity involved. In the

[47] Commission Communication, 'Making the best use of the flexibility within the existing rules of the stability and growth pact', COM(2015) 12 final, 13 January 2015.
[48] Regulation (EU) 1175/2011, OJ 2011 L 306, Article 5(1).
[49] *Ibid.*, Article 6(1).
[50] *Ibid.*, Article 7(1)–(2).
[51] *Ibid.*, Article 8(2)–(3).
[52] *Ibid.*, Article 10(1)–(4).
[53] Regulation (EU) 1174/2011, OJ 2011 L 306, Article 3(1).
[54] *Ibid.*, Article 3(6).
[55] Regulation (EU) 1175/2011, *supra* note 48, Article 11.
[56] *Ibid.*, Article 2(1).
[57] See Menéndez, *supra* note 46.
[58] Regulation 1467/97, OJ 1997 L 209, Article 1.

case of Spain, for example, was the collapse in that state's housing market (which had a significant bearing on its financial crisis) a 'usual' and 'foreseeable' event or was it instead something entirely out of the government's control (given that extensive housing devaluation also occurred during the crisis in a number of other Member States)?

While no sanctioning decisions have yet been made under the MIP, the capacity for uneven decision-making has already been demonstrated with reference to the operation of its sister procedure, the EDP.[59] France's government deficit, for example, has been subject to an EDP since 2013. In spite of its failure to reduce its deficit, the Commission has consistently placed the EDP against France in abeyance, deciding in March 2015 to delay a sanctioning decision until 2017.[60] Notable are possible disparities in treatment vis-à-vis other, smaller, Member States: as Chalmers and Chivas have pointed out, Belgium was asked in 2013 to rectify its excessive deficit immediately, whereas France was given an extended deadline to address its own deficit (in spite of the fact that the Belgian budget deficit stood at 2.9 per cent in 2012, compared to a French deficit of 4.8 per cent).

This aspect of EU economic governance illustrates well how economic governance procedures share NG's emphasis on discretionary and revisable rules and standards. In place of universal and relatively clear legal standards, decisions under economic governance are adaptable in response to a range of political, social, and economic factors.

B. Differentiation

The presence of revisability under post-crisis economic governance already implies the importance of a second aspect of the NG paradigm—the differentiation of legal and political standards.[61] This, too, was an important point of departure between NG and the CCM. The CCM carried the possibility in some cases of national opt-outs or 'optional' elements of legislation. The norm, however, was a legislative regime that produced relatively uniform obligations between European states. This uniformity reflected both the sovereign equality of states, that is, that they were equally subject to both the benefits and duties of EU integration, and the functional need to promote the single market through the application of common regulatory conditions.[62] If NG's emphasis on flexibility in rule-making and country-specific recommendations was a break from this, post-crisis economic governance goes much further.

The most obvious type of differentiation is between euro and non-eurozone states. The six-pack legislation establishing the revised EDP and new MIP procedure

[59] See on this, the excellent paper by Chalmers and Chivas, 'EU Law-Making and the State of European Democratic Agency', in O. Cramme and S. Hobolt (eds), *Democratic Politics in an EU under Stress* (2014), at 99.

[60] See Robert, 'Commission Delays French Deficit Procedure', 27 November 2014, available at http://www.euractiv.com/sections/euro-finance/commission-delays-french-deficit-procedure-310395 (last visited 5 January 2017).

[61] On the desirability of differentiation, see J.C. Piris, *The Future of Europe: Towards a 2-speed EU?* (2012); Craig, 'Two-speed, Multi-speed and Europe's Future', 37 *European Law Review* (2012) 800.

[62] R. Dehousse, *The Community Method: Obstinate or Obsolete?* (2011).

applies to all EU states; its sanctioning regime, however, only applies to the eurozone.[63] Similarly, the two-pack legislation creates a regime for domestic budgetary surveillance that applies only to eurozone states. This division is further complicated by new instruments such as the Fiscal Compact and the newly enacted provisions for banking regulation. All Member States, barring the UK, are committed to ratification of the Compact. Similarly, the EU's new Single Supervisory Mechanism (SSM) for banking regulation applies formally only to eurozone states. At the same time, a number of other EU states have indicated their preference to come within the SSM's ambit under a 'close cooperation' agreement with the European Central Bank.[64] In this sense, while differentiation between euro and non-eurozone is real, the preference of most Member States has been to gravitate towards the regulatory regime of the eurozone.

Even *within* the eurozone, however, a second type of differentiation is at play. In place of the CCM's idea of a relatively uniform set of procedural and substantive obligations under EU law, post-crisis economic governance offers a highly uneven regime. The level of EU supervision to which states are subject, and the extent of their reporting and procedural obligations, is heavily dependent on their fiscal status. In this sense, we see differentiation in the form of uneven sovereignty loss.[65] States with positive fiscal conditions can expect relatively light review of domestic policies; states with higher debt and deficits (and arguably those with less political bargaining power too) can expect increasingly cumbersome EU-level supervision.

One way of seeing the EDP process is thus as a series of stages of EU-level review.[66] The first level is the experience of states with positive budgetary conditions—such states already have significant reporting obligations under the EDP's 'preventative' arm, but are not subject to significant EU correction. The second level concerns states deemed to have an excessive deficit. These states still retain significant sovereignty in the sense that they themselves must establish a corrective plan for alleviating their deficit; at the same time, this plan is subject to EU-level monitoring and recommendations. The third level concerns those states repeatedly in breach of EU deficit rules, or those states whose budgetary plans are unlikely to lead to exit from the procedure. For these states, the 'two-pack' legislation[67] envisages the co-agreement between the Member State and Council of a far more detailed 'economic partnership programme'. The Council's 2013 opinion on Spain's programme indicates the level of detail obligations under such programmes entail:

> Even though the Economic Partnership Programme stops short of presenting plans for a comprehensive systematic review of major spending items, measures to rationalize spending

[63] See Regulation (EU) 1173/2011 of the European Parliament and the Council of 16 November 2011 on the effective enforcement of budgetary surveillance in the euro area, OJ 2011 L 306/1.

[64] See, e.g. Konstantinova and Groendahl, 'Bulgaria asks ECB to supervise banks as crisis festers', 15 July 2014, available at https://www.bloomberg.com/news/articles/2014-07-15/bulgaria-asks-ecb-to-supervise-banks-as-crisis-festers (last visited 1 September 2017).

[65] On the association of the crisis with 'asymmetrical sovereignty transfer', see M. Dawson, 'Legal and Political Accountability in Post-Crisis EU Economic Governance', 53 *Journal of Common Market Studies* (2015) 976.

[66] Applying this analysis to the Fiscal Compact regime, see Chalmers, *supra* note 46, at 677–682.

[67] Article 9 of Regulation (EU) 473/2013, OJ 2013 L 140/11.

on health, employment policy (see also recital 14 on fighting tax fraud) and on public administration give information on some key expenditure items. Regarding health expenditure, the revision of the basket of benefits and of reference prices of pharmaceutical products and the introduction of a centralized purchasing platform for health supplies, could result in a more efficient use of public resources. Regarding public administration, reforms are expected to generate savings over a three-year period from increasing overall efficiency, notably by eliminating duplicated administrative structures, streamlining overheads, rationalizing the so-called 'institutional' administration, as well as reforming local entities. Strict monitoring and enforcement of all these measures will be required to realize expected savings.[68]

While such 'programmes' already evidence significant EU-level steering, the final and fourth level of EU supervision involves much greater sovereignty loss. This level concerns those states subject to economic adjustment programmes as a result of EU/IMF financial assistance. While at the time of writing Greece has resisted a number of its obligations under this programme, states receiving financial assistance, as well documented by other work,[69] face 'co-government' with the Troika, with that institution carrying an effective veto over the most significant elements of the national budget.[70]

Differentiation in this example, as will be explored in Section 5 later, is utilized for a very different purpose under EU economic governance than it was used for older NG procedures. By contrast with the OMC, less differentiation is needed to accommodate structural differences between Member States—what Fritz Scharpf once termed 'legitimate diversity'[71]—than to produce more *convergent* economic outcomes, in particular vis-à-vis the government deficit. In terms of substantive policy outcomes, differentiation is (somewhat ironically) used under the EDP to foster policy convergence (around austerity principles) across a diverse eurozone.[72]

When considered from the perspective of legal acts, however, economic governance shares with the NG paradigm a rejection of the *form* of universal legal standards. As put by an influential group of economists, in the post-crisis EU, 'sovereignty runs out with solvency'.[73] The very obligation to apply particular rules and procedures has become increasingly differentiated between EU states.

C. Domesticization and Procedural Constraint

If differentiation is the order of the day under post-crisis economic governance, what unity is left in the legal framework? To find this unity, we may have to look at a further

[68] See Proposal for a Council Opinion on the Economic Partnership Programme for Spain, COM(2013) 902 final, available at http://eur-lex.europa.eu/LexUriServ/LexUriServ.do?uri=COM:2013:0902:FIN:EN:PDF, indent (9) (last visited 5 January 2017).

[69] See, e.g. the special issue of the Industrial Law Journal edited by S. Deakin, 'The Sovereign Debt Crisis and European Labour Law', 41 *Industrial Law Journal* (2012) 3; J. Pisani-Ferry, G.B. Wolff, and A. Sapir, 'EU-IMF Assistance to Euro Area Countries: An Early Assessment', 19 Bruegel Blueprint (2013).

[70] 'The Troika' refers to the three institutions—the European Central Bank, the European Commission, and the IMF—managing financial assistance to debt-stricken eurozone states during the financial crisis.

[71] Scharpf, 'Legitimate Diversity: The New Challenge of European Integration', *Les Cahiers européens de Sciences Po* (2002) 1.

[72] On this substantive convergence, see Dawson, *supra* note 65.

[73] Enderlein *et al., supra* note 39.

'procedural' element of the NG paradigm. This procedural element speaks to the idea of law not simply as a set of substantive and behavioural norms, but rather as a device within which substantive deliberation is conducted. Procedural law in this sense seeks to guide the institutions and procedures through which policies are made.

In the EU context, while post-crisis economic governance contains plenty of 'substantive' policy steering—see Section 5 later in the chapter—it also displays a heightened attention to procedural norms. Economic governance shares with the NG paradigm a focus on seeking to influence domestic processes, encouraging them to internalize and reflect upon EU-level targets and objectives. In this sense, it makes sense to consider the NG 'features' of domesticization and procedural constraint together. Primarily, this chapter discusses the steering, via EU economic governance, of domestic rules and institutions (with EU law acting as a procedural 'umbrella' within which such steering takes place).

Economic governance's procedural turn begins with the unusual (or 'abnormal' as Claire Kilpatrick has put it[74]) legal sources through which post-crisis reform has been advanced. One of these is the Fiscal Compact's 'golden' balanced budget rule. As an international treaty, the framers of the Compact operated within significant institutional constraints as to how the golden rule could be domestically applied and enforced. While, on the one hand, the treaty's framers were keen to ensure that national signatories complied with its standards; on the other, this Treaty—operating outside of normal EU law—would not necessarily enjoy the benefit of EU law's traditional enforcement mechanisms.

An example of the compromise produced by this is the empowerment of the CJEU under Article 8 of the Compact. That article provides the Court with jurisdiction to determine whether Member States have implemented the golden rule, but provides that standing to bring such an action is restricted to the contracting parties, that is, the Member States. As a non-EU treaty, the framers were in this sense unsure of the legality of the Commission taking on its traditional guardian role in ensuring that EU standards are domestically complied with.[75]

The main focus of the Compact is therefore on domestic rather than EU institutions. The domestic government is given three primary duties under the Compact: to establish a balanced budget rule within the national legal order (preferably one of a constitutional nature);[76] to establish a domestic 'corrective' mechanism to ensure the rule is domestically complied with;[77] and to support Commission recommendations for the application of EU fiscal rules.[78] Clearly, the first two of these at least speak to a desire to domesticize existing goals under both EU primary and secondary law within the domestic legal order. Reflecting the fear that EU intervention may be too late to rectify economic imbalances, the national order itself is encouraged to induce its domestic policy-making process to consider the impact of spending deci-

[74] See the chapter by Claire Kilpatrick in this volume.

[75] Nonetheless, the use of the EU institutions seems frequent under both the ESM and the Fiscal Compact Treaties. See on this, Dimopoulos, 'The Use of International Law as a Tool for Enhancing Governance in the Eurozone and Its Impact on EU Institutional Integrity', in M. Adams, F. Fabbrini, and P. Larouche (eds), *The Constitutionalization of European Budgetary Constraints* (2014), at 43–47.

[76] Treaty on Stability, Coordination and Governance, Article 3(2).

[77] *Ibid.*, Article 3(1)(e). [78] *Ibid.*, Article 7.

sions on the viability of the eurozone (as a prior step to the possibility of EU intervention under the SGP later on where fiscal rules are not effectively complied with).

This domesticization impulse is also reflected in overlapping secondary legislation. The reforms established by the six- and two-pack legislative frameworks to fiscal coordination have already been discussed. A more neglected aspect of those legislative packages is Directive 2011/85 and Regulation 473/2013, which seek to establish budgetary frameworks for the Member States. Just as an important element of the NG paradigm, as already discussed, was its focus on creating a procedural framework within which substantive policies can be equitably elaborated and determined, so these pieces of legislation mandate an elaborate common EU procedural frame for national budgeting.

The overriding goal of the Directive is to ensure that national budgetary planning is based on accurate and independently verifiable data. For the Regulation, the principal goal is to connect national and EU budgetary processes. To achieve these ends, the legislation demands that states: (i) make national fiscal data, and its underlying methodology, publicly available;[79] (ii) establish Medium Term Budgetary Frameworks projecting major items of expenditure three years in advance;[80] (iii) establish a common budgetary timeline synchronized to the European Semester (the EU cycle for budgetary monitoring);[81] and (iv) establish independent bodies to monitor compliance with national and EU fiscal standards, including the 'occurrence of circumstances leading to the activation of the correction mechanism' laid down in the Fiscal Compact.[82]

The latter element speaks to a tendency evidenced in other areas of EU secondary law (such as equality[83] and data protection[84] law) to mandate specific domestic bodies tasked with ensuring respect for EU standards. These particular mandated bodies are independent Fiscal Councils; bodies which were on the rise in the Member States independently of EU action, yet have been further promoted in the wake of the crisis.[85] While the Regulation does not specify the structure of Fiscal Councils in detail, the requirement that they are operationally independent—and therefore able to credibly monitor and supervise state fiscal performance—is specified.

Examining other EU legislative instruments which mandate specific domestic institutions, the Commission has been willing to play an active role in policing the independence of such institutions. The Commission successfully, for example, brought an infringement action against Hungary, beginning in January 2012, for

[79] Council Directive 2011/85/EU of 8 November 2011 on requirements for budgetary frameworks of the Member States, OJ 2011 L 306/41, Article 3(2).

[80] *Ibid.*, Article 9.

[81] Regulation (EU) 473/2013, OJ 2013 L 140/11, *supra* note 37, Article 4.

[82] *Ibid.*, Article 5(2). The remaining aspects of this Regulation (relating to the monitoring of budgetary plans) have already been discussed in Section 4(A) above.

[83] See Directive 2000/43/EC implementing the principle of equal treatment between persons irrespective of racial or ethnic origin, OJ 2000 L 180/22, Article 13.

[84] Directive 95/46/EC of the European Parliament and of the Council of 24 October 1995 on the protection of individuals with regard to the processing of personal data and on the free movement of such data, OJ 1995 L 281, Article 28.

[85] See (particularly on the pre-crisis rise of fiscal councils and fiscal rules), M. Hallerberg, R.R. Strauch, and J. von Hagen, *Fiscal Governance in Europe* (2010).

failing to adequately protect the independence of both the national central bank and the national data supervisor.[86] This could be seen as a peculiarly 'procedural' aspect of EU law, and of the Commission's infringement power. The goal of EU action here is not to enforce particular substantive EU policies per se but rather to guarantee a domestic policy-making or monitoring framework that is itself mandated by EU law. In this case, EU law acts to ensure that functioning independent institutions can be maintained in the national sphere that may serve to domestically foster EU goals and concerns.

While national Fiscal Councils may not be the most obvious host for the kind of thick normative and substantive discourse that Jürgen Habermas had in mind when he penned his procedural account of modern law, they speak to NG's embrace of procedural and institution building norms, and its view of EU governance as a medium to link European and national policy-making. To this extent, economic governance may carry more commonality with the NG paradigm than first thought.

5. New Economic Governance's Normative Core: Experimentalism or Harmonization?

How are we to view these empirical developments in EU governance from a more normative perspective? 'New governance' was never merely a descriptive project. While part of its academic agenda was to describe empirically the directions into which the EU's legal and political framework was moving, NG also produced an intense normative debate.[87] While on one side of this debate were those who saw NG as part of a 'managerial' turn away from democratic and law-mediated rule,[88] others saw NG as heralding an experimental, or even participatory turn in EU decision-making.[89] While, for example, processes like the OMC rejected EU-level parliamentary scrutiny of their activities, they also provided new structural opportunities for civil society actors, increasingly organizing at a transnational level, to enter policy discussions previously closed off to them at both the EU and national levels.[90]

At the same time, the differentiation of NG carried the possibility for states to 'experiment' with different policy solutions to seemingly intractable public policy

[86] See EC Press Release, *European Commission launches accelerated infringement proceedings against Hungary over the independence of its central bank and data protection authorities as well as over measures affecting the judiciary*, 17 January 2012, available at http://europa.eu/rapid/press-release_IP-12-24_en.htm (last visited 5 January 2017).

[87] See, e.g. Magnette, 'European Governance and Civic Participation: Beyond Elitist Citizenship?', 51 *Political Studies* (2003) 1; Büchs, 'How Legitimate is the Open Method of Co-ordination', 46 *Journal of Common Market Studies* (2008) 765.

[88] See, e.g. Joerges, 'Integration Through De-Legalisation?', 33 *European Law Review* (2008) 235; Dawson, 'New Governance and the Managerial Sensibility in Modern Law', 2 *Wisconsin Law Review* (2010) 389.

[89] Sabel and Zeitlin, *supra* note 18; C. de la Porte and P. Pochet, 'Participation in the Open Method of Coordination: The Cases of Employment and Social Exclusion' in P. Pochet and J. Zeitlin (eds), *The Open Method of Coordination in Action* (2005).

[90] Dawson, *supra* note 2, at 192–195.

problems.[91] To give one example, while the poverty and social exclusion of the late 1990s seems tame by the standards of today, the OMC SPSI allowed states to compare best practice on a number of novel schemes to reintegrate the socially excluded, ranging from minimum income schemes to 'sure-start' programmes for disadvantaged children.[92] The ideal of mutual learning and national 'scoreboarding' under the OMC was designed to provide EU policy-makers with a better sense of how EU-level policy-making was applied at the domestic level, and to encourage states to learn from the good practices of their neighbours (while avoiding the pitfalls of poor performers). Under such an experimental model, the EU's significant diversity could be seen not as an obstacle to 'harmonized' EU standards but as an opportunity to test (and later perhaps generalize) different policy solutions.[93]

Returning to the present day, 'experimentalism' still has much to commend itself, particularly when considering the outlook for the European economy. While Europe's economic downturn has not been evenly shared between states, there are a number of common problems. One in particular is spiralling youth unemployment; reaching endemic levels in Greece, Spain, Portugal, and Italy, and seemingly immune to EU-level initiatives designed to tackle the problem.[94] Another is growing income inequality.[95] In the face of these problems, there may be some advantage to an experimental model, which encourages states to try out novel policy solutions. While no state is likely to find a magic bullet to tackle the EU's anemic growth and employment outlook, successful schemes in particular states, such as on youth unemployment, could prove useful models for adoption (and adaptation) in other national contexts.

It is on this point that the differences, rather than similarities, between the 'new economic governance' and the NG paradigm become important. While, as highlighted earlier, the EU has heavily relied on elements of NG following the crisis, it has been to achieve a different ultimate goal. The purpose of flexible governance processes, like the European Semester, has not been to experiment with policy solutions but to achieve a particular pre-defined goal: fiscal prudence and balanced budgets. In this sense, even if economic governance entails significant differentiation and flexibility in how specific norms are framed, this flexibility is (as already discussed) used to foster policy *convergence* around a particular social and economic model.

This point can be demonstrated by examining the operation of the European Semester since the establishment of the 'six pack' in 2011. Analysing the set of 'country-specific recommendations' (CSRs) and in-depth reviews issued to Member States in the 2011–2014 round of economic coordination, one can begin to identify

[91] See Kerber and Eckardt, 'Policy Learning in Europe: the Open Method of Coordination and Laboratory Federalism', 14 *Journal of European Public Policy* (2007) 227.

[92] Heidenreich and Bischoff, 'The Open Method of Co-ordination: A Way to the Europeanization of Social and Employment Policies?', 46 *Journal of Common Market Studies* (2008) 497.

[93] Sabel and Zeitlin, *supra* note 18.

[94] See, e.g. the limited impact of the EU's much heralded 2012 employment package, available at http://ec.europa.eu/social/main.jsp?catId=1039 (last visited 6 January 2017).

[95] See, e.g. the OECD Report on 'Income Inequality in the European Union', *OECD Economics Department Working Paper Series* 952, available at http://www.oecd.org/officialdocuments/publicdisplaydocumentpdf/?cote=ECO/WKP%282012%2929&docLanguage=En (last visited 6 January 2017).

the degree of uniformity present in EU-level recommendations.[96] In the CSRs, it is possible to identify consistently a strong focus on budgetary consolidation as an anchor point for recommendations across a wide range of policy areas. While this policy focus is to be expected in recommendations relating to fiscal policy, it is also apparent in other areas.[97]

One example is pensions policy. Of the 24 countries for which the Commission compiled specific recommendations from 2011–2013, 17 received recommendations on pensions reform; 15 of them detailed, and all of them remarkably uniform in their substantive prescriptions. While systems of pension delivery vary significantly between the states to which recommendations are made, recommendations aimed at all 15 Member States from 2011 to 2013 have recommended increasing the statutory retirement age and linking retirement age to life expectancy. At the same time, aspects of the national pension regime, which could inhibit long-term fiscal sustainability, were rejected. Recommendations on invalidity pension schemes (a regular way to take into account different capabilities especially when increasing the pension age) emphasize their possible abuse and call for their restriction (Austria, Bulgaria). Where differentiated retirement ages for men and women (Bulgaria, Slovenia, Poland) exist, their abandonment is demanded. Finally, countries which carry income indexation of pensions, designed to ensure that they rise along with general income (Slovakia and Slovenia), are criticized.

The demand for convergence is also apparent in other areas of policy covered by the CSRs. Recommendations on tax and social security between 2011 and 2013 were received by 23 Member States.

Of these states, 19 were asked to change their tax system in order to boost its 'growth friendliness' and ability to contribute to fiscal consolidation. The Commission's favoured method of doing so is to alter the burden of taxation: Member States consistently received recommendations on shifting tax from labour to consumption (e.g. of energy, property, and other goods).[98] Little mention is made of the distributional impact of this choice (consumption taxes, which typically do not take into account a person's income, tend, of course, to fall far harder on the poor than labour taxes). In the place of the OMC's emphasis on diversity and flexible implementation, recommendations under the European Semester seem to advance a uniform policy agenda.[99] While states are subject to different degrees of scrutiny and intervention, they are asked to *substantively* converge around a highly particular economic and social model.

The difficulty with using NG methods for this purpose is the significant gap between this goal and the record of NG mechanisms to date. While political scientists

[96] This element of this chapter is drawn on empirical research from Dawson, 'The Legal and Political Accountability of "Post-Crisis" EU Economic Governance', 53 *Journal of Common Market Studies* (2015) 976.

[97] European Commission, 'Annual Growth Survey 2013', COM(2012) 750 final.

[98] *Ibid.*, at 10.

[99] The final element worthy of mention here is the increasing level of prescriptiveness in CSRs. This is well documented in Bekker, 'The EU's Stricter Economic Governance: A step towards a more binding coordination of social policies?', *WZB Discussion Paper* (2013). For a counterview, emphasizing greater flexibility in more recent rounds of the European Semester, see Zeitlin and Vanhercke, 'Socializing the European Semester: EU Social and Economic Policy Coordination in Crisis and Beyond', *Journal of European Public Policy* (forthcoming, 2017).

now have 15 years of experience cataloguing the trials and tribulations of open coordination in social policy, there is no real evidence that NG processes in that domain have led to significant policy convergence between EU states (or even that convergence was a significant policy goal in the first place).[100] This is unsurprising—when states are faced with conflicts between the 'recommendations' of NG and policies supported by entrenched domestic interests, their incentives to follow those recommendations are limited.[101] Incentives to engage in non-compliance may be even greater in the fiscal field, where budgetary recommendations carry significant financial and political costs. These costs may outweigh the burden of EU-level penalties (which, as will be seen, have rarely been applied).

At most, the experience of NG in social policy suggests, as discussed earlier, a 'mutual learning' effect. Even mutual learning, however, has tended to be selective; a tool for nudging policy change, rather than for harmonization.[102] Unsurprisingly, practices and models adopted for one state can never be completely transported to another without significant modification. The more cynical interpretation of this effect is that states 'learn' selectively, adopting those elements of EU policy that fit within existing domestic programmes and rejecting those that do not.

While there are important differences between both social and economic policy; as well as between the OMC and the more intrusive form of NG seen in the fiscal field; EU leaders would be wise to heed some of these lessons. The experience of fiscal coordination since the crisis began bears out the need for caution in predicting the ability of NG to transform national fiscal structures. One can observe this, for example, in the experience of the European Semester since its inception.[103] Tracking the operation of the Semester in the 2011 and 2012 rounds, Hallerberg, Marzinotto, and Wolff also detect elements of a selective convergence effect:

> The evidence for a sample of six EU countries indicates that there is a problem in domestic implementation. More precisely, EU recommendations were found to have not altered dramatically the national process of policy formulation, especially when the suggested reforms are likely to erode rents and dominant positions in product and service markets. The German case demonstrates that Member State governments generally 'implement' recommendations they were already doing anyway and ignore recommendations that would involve truly new reforms.[104]

The point that Hallerberg, Marzinotto, and Wolff make illustrates an important paradox in the use to which EU policy-makers are trying to put NG procedures. The

[100] See, e.g. Visser, 'Neither Convergence Nor Frozen Paths: Bounded Learning, International Diffusion of Reforms, and the Open Method of Coordination', in M. Heidenreich and J. Zeitlin (eds), *Changing European Employment and Welfare Regimes: The Influence of the Open Method of Coordination on National Reforms* (2009); Kerber and Eckardt, *supra* note 91.

[101] Lodge, 'Comparing Non-Hierarchical Governance in Action: The Open Method of Coordination in Pensions and Information Society', 45 *Journal of Common Market Studies* (2007) 343.

[102] See Visser, 'The OMC as a Selective Amplifier for National Strategies of Reform. What the Netherlands wants to learn from Europe' in Pochet and Zeitlin (eds), *supra* note 89.

[103] M. Hallerberg *et al.*, *An Assessment of the European Semester*, European Parliament Directorate General for Internal Policies Study (2012), available at http://www.europarl.europa.eu/meetdocs/2009_2014/documents/econ/dv/studybruegel_/studybruegel_en.pdf (last visited 6 January 2017).

[104] M. Hallerberg *et al.*, 'On the Effectiveness and Legitimacy of EU Economic Policies', *Bruegel Policy Brief* (2012), available at http://bruegel.org/wp-content/uploads/imported/publications/pb_2012-04_final.pdf (last visited 6 January 2017), at 5.

very design of NG is intended to accommodate structural diversity, that is, to allow EU goals to be 'filtered' through diverse national systems of policy delivery, whether that diversity comes from 'varieties of welfare' or 'varieties of capitalism'.[105] For that very reason, however, the same instruments should not be expected to erode economic diversity or to create convergence around a shared European economic or fiscal model.

To this more structural point could be added other political difficulties in using NG instruments to affect economic change. One, for example, is the use of fiscal penalties as an inducement for governments to take recommendations under EU economic governance seriously. In effect, there are a number of interrelated problems likely to prevent fiscal penalties from being applied.

First, penalties may only be applied to states facing significant economic distress—it is unclear how a further financial sanction is likely to improve the state's fiscal performance; indeed, the opposite may be the case (i.e. that such states require greater investment). Second, there are no guarantees that applying a fiscal penalty will affect meaningful change. A state, facing the powerful 'rent-seeking' domestic constituencies referred to by Hallerberg, Marzinotto, and Wolff, may find it politically more advantageous to accept a penalty than to affect the desired structural change.[106] Finally, the Commission, as initiator of such a penalty, must weigh up the costs to itself of levying such a fine. Alienating a large and powerful Member State, for example, may produce costs later on if that state is needed for the purposes of advancing the Commission's political agenda (arguably, the shift towards a more politicized Commission re-enforces this dynamic, by giving 'Spitzenkandidaten' an incentive to court large domestic constituencies).[107]

The result of these factors is that fiscal penalties are 'the dog that barks but does not bite' in recent EU integration. While the post-crisis period has seen more states than ever placed under an EDP, fiscal penalties are yet to be applied in *any* such procedure post-crisis. In this sense, the hardness of the EU's post-crisis economic governance may be less effective than assumed.

In the face of these limits, the best chance of achieving policy change may yet lie in bargaining and negotiation—seeking to *persuade* Member States of the long-term benefits of structural and fiscal reform—rather than upon strengthened fiscal rule-making. The OMC's development of tools for information sharing, benchmarking, and mutual learning may yet be instructive in this regard. For all the talk of strength, NG was not designed to produce substantive centralization and convergence. We should not expect it to do so.

[105] On the importance of structural diversity—an insight from varieties of capitalism literature—to understanding the possibilities for an effective crisis response, see Scharpf, 'No Exit from the Euro-rescuing Trap?', 14 *MPIfG Discussion Paper* (2004). See also, Leino-Sandberg and Saarenheimo, 'Sovereignty and Subordination: On the Limits of EU Economic Policy Coordination', 2 *European Law Review* (2017) 166.

[106] The need, and obstacles, facing structural change in the EU economy is a theme of Dariusz Adamski's work. See Adamski, 'The Evolving Constitutional Relationship Between Economic Competitiveness and the Euro Area', unpublished manuscript, on file with the author.

[107] On this problem in the context of human rights law, see M. Dawson, E. Muir, and M. Claes, 'Enforcing the EU's Rights Revolution: The Case of Equality', 3 *European Human Rights Law Review* (2012) 276, at 285.

6. The Future of New Governance among the EU's Legal Acts

What place is NG likely to carry among the EU's future legal acts? Tying EU economic governance to the general NG paradigm raises the question of whether 'rules' under EU economic governance deserve the label of legal acts at all. If we are to take seriously the decision-like nature of the EDP and MIP procedures, for example, perhaps we ought not to consider these procedures as belonging within legal categories at all. Returning to the earlier NG debate, if NG departs so far from rule of law standards, what does it mean to talk of NG as 'law'? Alternatively, is EU economic governance simply 'against the law'; a clear breach of legal standards?[108]

While such a conclusion is tempting, there remain important reasons to maintain a place for NG-like instruments within the field of EU legal acts themselves. The first reason is a conceptual one. Arguing that NG is something outside of the law necessarily presumes a particular conceptual account of law itself. Our very definition of what constitutes law, particularly in a post-national setting, is contested and evolving. As earlier NG literature has pointed out, one should not preclude the ability of functional evolution and institutional change to transform our very understanding of what is meant by 'EU law' in the first place.[109]

The second reason is more practical. Excluding NG from legal categories could also mean excluding it from the EU's existing mechanisms of legal and political review. Returning to a theme brought up by other contributors to this volume, the EU courts have been reluctant to conduct full judicial review of new economic governance measures, often on the grounds that they 'fall outside of the scope of EU law' (and in spite of their clear coercive effects).[110] Seeing NG as outside of the EU's legal acts also carries a considerable capacity to dilute the ability of individuals to contest economic governance measures that deeply affect their lives.[111]

As this chapter has argued, it may be preferable to see 'new' economic governance as within (or at least in relation to) legal categories. This requires, however, a keen sense of its recent past. It is one thing to use NG instruments—insulated from the democratic input of the European Parliament, and operating parallel to the official division of competences between the EU and its Member States—as a mechanism of mutual learning and cooperation. It is quite another to use these instruments to forcibly converge national budgets around a particular economic, and arguably social, model. As this chapter has highlighted, quite apart from these normative queries, the record of NG processes in achieving such harmonization goals is limited at best. Recognizing the creation of 'new' economic governance should not be equated with celebrating its re-birth.

108 See Claire Kilpatrick's chapter in this volume.

109 Walker, 'Constitutionalism and New Governance in the European Union: Rethinking the Boundaries', in de Búrca and Scott (eds), *supra* note 1.

110 See Case C-370/12, *Thomas Pringle v. Government of Ireland*, judgment of 27 November 2012, (ECLI:EU:C:2012:756). See also Barnard, 'The Charter, the Court and the Crisis', 18 *Cambridge Legal Studies Research Paper Series* (2013).

111 See also Dawson, *supra* note 65.

5

The Social Dialogue as a Source of EU Legal Acts—Past Performance and Future Perspectives

Aukje A.H. van Hoek

1. Introduction

The bodies that represent the two sides of industry, commonly referred to as social partners, enjoy a special position in European Union (EU) law. At the EU level, organizations of employers and workers are privileged stakeholders within the system of information and consultation regarding EU social policies. They may enter into negotiations, leading up to contractual relations, which may in turn be transformed into EU law by Council decisions. At the national level, social partners may be responsible for implementation of EU law, but may also jointly or on their own accord be held accountable for violations of the EU Treaty provisions on non-discrimination and freedom of movement.

The Treaty on the Functioning of the European Union (TFEU) provisions, the European Commission, and the European Court of Justice (ECJ) recognize the (*de jure* and/or *de facto*) regulatory function of the social partners, both at national and European level. Hence, it makes sense to study the role of the social partners as EU legal actors in the context of this volume. But studying the role of private actors as regulators poses a challenge, both with regard to the issue of definition (what exactly is meant by 'private regulation'?) and as to the question of legitimacy. On both topics the literature is immense and cannot even be summarized here. Hence the goal of this chapter can be no more than modest. What I aim to do is first to provide an overview of the role of social partners in EU law. It will be concluded that EU law does recognize the regulatory role of the social partners, but provides neither a legal nor a fully developed conceptual framework (Section 2). The second point to be addressed concerns the output of the social dialogue at EU level (Section 3). Here the conclusion will be that the social partners fulfil a variety of functions, both as stakeholder and co-regulator. However, only a small percentage of the documents produced in the social dialogue have the status of collective agreement. It is the latter group which is most interesting from the point of view of regulation. Hence in the

The Social Dialogue as a Source of EU Legal Acts – Past Performance and Future Perspectives. First Edition.
Aukje A.H. van Hoek © Aukje A.H. van Hoek 2018. Published 2018 by Oxford University Press.

sections following, the route from agreement to binding decision is analysed. How do the activities of the social partners interact with the EU legislative architecture (Section 4)? Can these acts be measured by the existing model(s) of good governance at EU level (Sections 5 and 6)?

The question is topical, as there is currently a debate on the role of the Commission with regard to the procedure of Article 155 TFEU. This debate was triggered by the refusal of the Commission to put a collective agreement entered into by the social partners in the hairdressing sector before Council. The refusal was part of the REFIT package in which the Commission announced its strategy to reduce red tape.[1] Hence, the result of negotiations between the social partners was tested against the policy agenda of the Commission. This chapter puts that decision in a wider perspective in order to assess its implications for the future (Section 7).

2. Social Partners in EU Law—Not Just Any Stakeholder

The history of association building and collective bargaining at EU level spans well over half a century by now.[2] A first recognition of the social partners as relevant actors at the European level is to be found in the now defunct Treaty on the European Coal and Steel Community of 1952, in which a Consultative Committee brought together representatives of employers', workers', and consumer organizations. The 1958 Rome Treaties established an advisory Economic and Social Committee which also gathered representatives of various categories of economic and social activities. During the following years, several joint advisory committees were created by the European Commission to give advice on social and employment aspects in specific sectors.[3] These developments enabled the social partners to assume their role as privileged stakeholders in the consultation process.[4] Social partners are currently active in a myriad of consultation and decision-making bodies at EU level, ranging from the Economic and Social Committee, the European Social Fund and the Standing Committee on Employment to the Management Board of the European Center for the Development of Vocational Training, and the Expert Committee on Transnational Company Agreements.

[1] European framework agreement of 26 April 2012 between Coiffure EU and UNI Europa Hair & Beauty on the protection of occupational health and safety in the hairdressing sector. See, *inter alia*, http://corporateeurope.org/sites/default/files/attachments/red_tape_crusade.pdf (last visited 8 March 2017).

[2] C. Barnard, *EU Employment Law* (2012), at 711; B. Bercusson, *European Labour Law* (2nd edn, 2009), at 126; Treu, 'European Collective Bargaining Levels', in P. Davies *et al.* (eds), *European Community Labour Law: Principles and Perspectives, Liber amicorum Lord Wedderburn of Charlton* (1996) 169–187, at 171.

[3] Barnard, *supra* note 2, at 711. The structure of the sectoral social dialogue was revised in 1998. See Communication from the Commission of 20 May 1998 adapting and promoting the social dialogue at Community level, COM(98) 322 final and Commission Decision 98/500 of 20 May 1998 on the establishment of Sectoral Dialogue Committees promoting the Dialogue between the social partners at European level, OJ 1998 L 225/27.

[4] Barnard, *supra* note 2, at 711.

An important starting point for the official recognition of collective bargaining at EU level is to be found in the Single European Act of 1986, followed by the Social Charter of 1989. These instruments conferred a duty on the Commission to promote social dialogue at EU level and specifically acknowledged that this dialogue may lead to 'relations based on agreement' (Single European Act) or 'contractual relations' (Charter). The text of the relevant provisions was prepared by the social partners themselves in what became known as the 'Val Duchesse dialogue', that is, the cross-sectoral social dialogue which first took place at Val Duchesse in January 1985.[5] In 1991, the social partners reached an agreement on both consultation and collective bargaining which was introduced almost verbatim into EU law by the Treaty on European Union and can now be found (in a slightly altered format) in Article 154 and 155 TFEU.[6]

Article 154 (ex-Article 138 EC) obliges the European Commission to consult with management and labour both as to the general direction of any Union action in the social policy field and on the content of any proposal to be submitted. Hence, on any proposed EU action in this field, the social partners have to be consulted at least twice.[7] On the occasion of this consultation, management and labour may inform the Commission that they prefer to enter into negotiations amongst themselves with the object of reaching agreement on the issue put forward for regulation.[8] The period available for negotiations, which is set at nine months, may be extended by joint decision of the Commission and the organizations of management and labour concerned.

In Article 155 (ex-Article 139 EC) the TFEU confirms that the dialogue between management and labour may lead to contractual relations, including agreements. The provision further stipulates that agreements concluded at EU level shall be implemented either in accordance with the procedures and practices specific to management and labour and the Member States or, in matters covered by Article 153, at the joint request of the signatory parties, by a Council decision on a proposal from the Commission. In the latter case, the European Parliament has no power of co-decision but is merely informed. Several European directives, with both cross-sectoral and sectoral coverage, are based on such EU collective agreements.[9]

The consultative and co-legislative role of the social partners under Article 154/155 takes place both at the cross-sectoral and the sectoral level. But management and labour also meet at the level of the company. The promotion of social dialogue within the company is part of the European Employment Strategy. The

[5] *Ibid.*, at 712. [6] Bercusson, *supra* note 2, at 146 ff.

[7] In addition, the social sector committees have a privileged position in the preparation of impact assessments as they are to be consulted whenever a proposal may impact significantly on social relations in their sector. See European Commission, *Industrial Relations Report* (2012), at 205.

[8] Barnard, *supra* note 2, at 71 claims that the social partners may only intercept the process at the second stage of consultation. This position is based on the Communication from the Commission of 14 December 1993 concerning the application of the Agreement on social policy presented by the Commission to the Council and the European Parliament, COM(93) 600 final, para. 29. For the opposite opinion, see Bercusson, *supra* note 2, at 149–150 and 534. In the material studied, the social partners did intervene at the stage of the second round of consultations.

[9] See below, Sections 3 and 4.

European involvement in this area is based on a theory of corporate governance in which collaboration and joint responsibility replaces a more hierarchical management style.[10] This led to the introduction of information and consultation rights at national level,[11] but also to the introduction of a special consultative body at the European level in transnational companies having subsidiaries in more than one Member State—the European Works Council (EWC).[12] The first European Works Council Directive was adopted in September 1994 and the current directive dates from May 2009.[13] According to Simitis and Lyon-Caen, 'the guiding principle behind the European Works Council Directive of 22 September 1994 was to encourage the establishment of multinational companies operating across the Community as centres or sites of industrial relations'.[14] The establishment of a system of information and consultation at the European level has indeed contributed to the establishment of a company-based structure for social dialogue which in turn increasingly leads to the conclusion of transnational agreements between management and labour. Though not regulated by EU law,[15] transnational company agreements have become a relevant factor in the governance of transnational companies in Europe and in particular in the management of change within such companies.[16]

In this context, in which the EU legal base for social dialogue is discussed, it is interesting to note that the EWC Directive attributes a specific norm-setting role to management and labour. The establishment of an EWC, the composition thereof, and its prerogatives are first and foremost subject to negotiations between manage-

[10] Barnard, *supra* note 2, at 658 and Proposal for a European Parliament and Council Directive of 2 July 2008 on the establishment of a European Works Council or a procedure in Community-scale undertakings and Community-scale groups of undertakings for the purposes of informing and consulting employees (Recast), COM(2008) 419 final.

[11] See Council Directive 2001/23 of 12 March 2001 on the approximation of the laws of the Member States relating to the safeguarding of employees' rights in the event of transfers of undertakings, businesses or parts of undertakings or businesses, OJ 2001 L 82/16 and Council Directive 98/59 of 20 July 1998 on the approximation of the laws of the Member States relating to collective redundancies, OJ 1998 L 225/16.

[12] Directive of the European Parliament and of the Council 2009/38 of 6 May 2009 on the establishment of a European Works Council or a procedure in Community-scale undertakings and Community-scale groups of undertakings for the purposes of informing and consulting employees (Recast), OJ 2009 L 122/28. Article 2 lays the threshold for the requirement to establish a European Works Council at more than 1000 employees within the EU. The undertaking should have at least two establishments in different Member States employing at least 150 people each. The signatures of at least 100 employees from at least two different Member States are needed to request the creation of a European Works Council—Article 1(2) juncto Article 5(1).

[13] Directive 2009/38 recast, *supra* note 12.

[14] Simitis and Lyon-Caen, 'European Community Labour Law: A Critical Introduction to its History', in P. Davies *et al.* (eds), *supra* note 2, at 11.

[15] I. Schömann, 'Transnational Collective Bargaining: In Search of a Legal Framework', in I. Schömann *et al., Transnational Collective Bargaining at Company Level. A New Component of European Industrial Relations?* (2012) 219–232, at 219–220; E. Pataut, 'Collective Agreements in Europe: European Social Dialogue and Contractual Autonomy', in J. Basedow *et al.* (eds), *Employee Participation and Collective Bargaining in Europe and China* (2016); O. Deinert claims that Article 155 TFEU gives binding effect to European collective agreements, but this is a minority opinion. See O. Deinert, *Internationales Arbeitsrecht* (2013), at 80–81 with references.

[16] See the Commission database on transnational company agreements, available at http://ec.europa.eu/social/main.jsp?catId=978 (last visited 8 March 2017) and Schömann, 'Transnational Company Agreements: Towards an Internationalisation of Industrial Relations' in Schömann *et al.* (eds), *supra* note 15, at 200.

ment and labour. Only when no agreement can be reached between central management and the 'special negotiation body' consisting of workers' representatives from the national subsidiaries, national law is called upon to regulate the composition and powers of the EWC, subject to a set of supplementary provisions in the EWC Directive itself.[17] Hence the substantive provisions in the EWC provide a background regulation which will only apply in absence of an agreement between management and labour. This system is akin to that of opening clauses in national labour law in which social partners are allowed to deviate from otherwise mandatory provisions by way of collective agreement.[18] Such opening clauses pose a strong incentive for collective negotiations as well as offering the possibility to reach solutions that are specifically adapted to the sector or company concerned. Several directives in the field of labour law allow the national social partners to deviate from the rules given therein by way of collective agreement or even autonomously set standards.[19] The EWC Directive, however, seems to be the only European instrument given such far-reaching powers to the social partners at union level.[20]

The norm-setting capacity of social partners at the national level is also recognized in primary EU law and the case law of the ECJ. In the 1974 *Walrave v. Koch* judgment[21] the ECJ considered that the ban on discrimination on grounds of nationality would have to apply to all types of regulation at the national level, both private and public, in order to be effective. Hence both the treaty provisions and Article 7(4) of Regulation 1612/68 were deemed to be applicable to collective labour agreements and other 'rules aimed at regulating in a collective manner gainful employment and the provision of services'.[22] This was sometimes referred to as the extended vertical effect of the Treaty provision, emphasizing the role of the social partners as quasi-legislators.[23] On the positive side, the regulatory function of collective agreements is recognized in Article 153(3) of the TFEU where it is stipulated: that '[a] Member State may entrust management and labour, at their joint request, with the implementation of directives adopted pursuant to paragraph 2, or, where appropriate, with the implementation of a Council decision adopted in accordance with Article 155'. Accordingly, directives and European-level collective agreements transposed

[17] Directive 2009/38 recast, *supra* note 12, Article 7; Barnard, *supra* note 2, at 667; COM(98) 322, *supra* note 3, at 21: Following the adoption of the 1994 Directive on the establishment of a European Works Council, the social partners in the companies concerned concluded more than 400 agreements before it came into force.

[18] For terminology see, *inter alia*, Barnard, *supra* note 2, at 714 and Bercusson, *supra* note 2, at 21–22; See Sciarra, 'Collective Agreements in the Hierarchy of European Community Sources', in P. Davies *et al.* (eds), *supra* note 2, at 207 for the radically different character of the derogation clause in the EWC Directive.

[19] Compare Bercusson, *supra* note 2, at 22; Barnard, *supra* note 2, at 65 and 714; Sciarra, *supra* note 18, at 206–207 with regard to working time.

[20] Sciarra, *supra* note 18, at 207; Barnard, *supra* note 2, at 668.

[21] Case C-36/74, *Walrave and Koch v. Association Union Cycliste Internationale and Others*, [1974] ECR 01405 (ECLI:EU:C:1974:140).

[22] *Ibid.*, at para. 17. The ECJ later confirmed the horizontal effect of the relevant Treaty provisions with regard to individual employers as well: Case C-281/98, *Angonese*, [2000] ECR I-04139 (ECLI:EU:C:2000:296). However, collective agreements and collective action may be considered particularly apt to influence the market freedoms. Compare Barnard, *supra* note 2, at 157; Sciarra, *supra* note 18, at 205–206.

[23] Barnard, *supra* note 2, at 157.

into EU law by a Council decision may be implemented by way of national collective agreements. Through this provision EU law recognizes the role of social partners as co-regulators (or even primary rule-makers in certain fields) at the national level. However, as is evident both from the provision of Article 153(3) itself and from the case law of the ECJ, such implementation is only sufficient when the national system of collective bargaining can ensure full and effective coverage of all workers concerned as well as individual remedies in case of breach.[24] In practice this is never the case. Implementation through collective bargaining is invariably accompanied by legislative or administrative measures.

This overview shows that EU law recognizes the regulatory function of social dialogue, both at EU and national levels. Article 143(3) articulates the role of the national social partners in the implementation of EU directives. However, in that case, the Member States retain final responsibility for full implementation. At the EU level, we find that collective agreements can supplement or replace EU legislation in specific instances. But the latter power is often mediated by way of Council decision. It is this specific regulatory function which is discussed in more detail in the following sections.

3. Social Dialogue in the EU—An Output Analysis

Barnard defines collective bargaining as 'a process of interest accommodation which includes all sorts of bipartite and tripartite discussions relating to labour problems directly or indirectly affecting a group of workers'. In a more narrow sense the term refers to negotiations between trade union representatives/organizations of workers on one side and employers, whether organized or on an individual basis on the other, which may lead to the conclusion of agreements, which may or may not qualify as legally binding agreements.[25] These definitions already indicate that the outcome of social dialogue may take different shapes and may take on different degrees of legal relevance.

As discussed earlier, the social dialogue at EU level takes place at different levels of organization. In this it is no different from social dialogue at the national level. The EU Member States differ in the make-up of social dialogue in their country, but generally the dialogue may take place at a cross-sectoral level, encompassing all sectors of the economy, be confined to a specific sector, or take place within a specific company or group of related companies. In addition, some Member States have

[24] The second full sentence of section 3 provides: 'In this case, it [= the Member State] shall ensure that, no later than the date on which a directive or a decision must be transposed or implemented, management and labour have introduced the necessary measures by agreement, the Member State concerned being required to take any necessary measure enabling it at any time to be in a position to guarantee the results imposed by that directive or that decision.' Barnard, *supra* note 2, at 70–71; Bercusson, *supra* note 2, at 20 and 541; Sciarra, *supra* note 18, at 197. See also Case C-143/83, *Commission v. Denmark*, [1985] ECR 00427 (ECLI:EU:C:1985:34) and Case C-235/84, *Commission v. Italy*, [1986] ECR 02291 (ECLI:EU:C:1986:303); Case C-187/98, *Commission v. Greece*, [1999] ECR I-07713 (ECLI:EU:C:1999:535).

[25] Barnard, *supra* note 2, at 709. Compare Bercusson, *supra* note 2, at 127.

systems of negotiations both at the national or federal level and at a more local level. The latter distinction is irrelevant for present purposes, but the former is not.

The cross-sectoral and sectoral social dialogue at EU level is closely linked to policy-making and regulation at EU level. The outcomes of these types of social dialogue share the characteristics of law in that they claim to be 'generally applicable': the norms contained in EU collective agreements at these levels contain general rules and principles which are meant to apply to an open group of norm addressees. This rule-making capacity is specifically recognized in Article 155 TFEU, which allows the social partners to put their agreement to the Commission for endorsement by Council decision. Only cross-sectoral and sectoral agreements qualify for this type of extension.[26] The scope of application of the norms thus extended is not restricted to cross-border situations, but rather is general in its application.[27] In contrast, the social dialogue within undertakings at the EU level specifically targets transnational undertakings and is closely linked to the activities of the European Works Councils. The agreements entered into affect the workforce of a specific company or group of companies and do not purport to have a general effect within a sector of economy or on the EU labour market as such. Extension under Article 155 is not possible. Hence, the legal framework for either activity is different and their output is weighed differently.

The European Commission monitors the outcome of the social dialogue, both at the cross-sectoral and sectoral level and as regards the dialogue within transnational companies.[28] In both cases the output of the social dialogue is characterized by a wide variety of texts and by a degree of unclarity as to their legal status.[29] The texts at sectoral and cross-sectoral level can be subdivided into three different groups.[30] The first group consists of procedural texts relating to the EU social dialogue itself. These may be binding or non-binding in character, but a common characteristic is the reciprocal character and the *inter se* effect of the content thereof. A second group of texts consists of joint opinions and declarations aimed at EU institutions. These texts are part and parcel of the policy-influencing role of the social partners as privileged stakeholders in the political debate. Given this role, their legal character is necessarily

[26] Treu, *supra* note 2, at 178–179.

[27] However, the social partners may limit the rules to cross-border situations, as they did in, e.g. the Agreement of 27 July 2005 between the Community of European Railways (CER) and the European Transport Workers' Federation (ETF) on certain aspects of the working conditions of mobile workers engaged in interoperable cross-border services in the railway sector.

[28] The European Commission maintains a database on social dialogue text at sectoral and multisectoral level (http://ec.europa.eu/social/main.jsp?catId=521&langId=en (last visited 8 March 2017)) as well as a database on transnational company agreements (http://ec.europa.eu/social/main.jsp?catId=978 (last visited 8 March 2017)).

[29] For transnational company agreements, see, *inter alia*, the Commission's database on transnational company agreements (TCAs), available at http://ec.europa.eu/social/main.jsp?catId=978 and their main page on TCAs, available at http://ec.europa.eu/social/main.jsp?catId=707&langId=en&intPageId=214 (last visited 8 March 2017). See also Commission Staff Working Document, *Transnational company agreements: realising the potential of social dialogue*, SWD(2012) 264 final. For present purposes the company agreements are less relevant and hence will not be further discussed here.

[30] Vademecum, *A Practical Guide for European Social Partner Organisations and their National Affiliates* (2014), available at http://ec.europa.eu/social/main.jsp?catId=329&langId=en (last visited 8 March 2017).

non-binding for the addressee. The third and most complex group targets the national level and aims to impact on the policy-making and/or legal position of the stakeholders there—government, social partners, and/or individual employers.[31] This latter group is the most interesting one for the present debate.

The European Commission, in its reports on social dialogue, subdivides this last group into three different subgroups, depending on their character and the follow-up measures they engender.[32] A first subgroup consists of tools and declarations aimed at the national level. Examples thereof are guides and handbooks explaining the meaning of certain texts, as well as websites and promotional activities meant to support the implementation or enforcement of certain rules or policies.[33] They do not require any particular follow up. The second subgroup consists of process-oriented texts, again aimed at the national level: frameworks of action, guidelines, codes of conduct, and policy orientations. These non-binding instruments, which are similar to the soft law instruments of the European Commission itself (as part of the open method of coordination[34]) typically are monitored as to their effect in follow-up reports. Lastly, the social partners may enter into agreements that contain rules to be applied to individual employment relations at the national level. In other words: they may enter into EU collective labour agreements. A collective agreement typically contains obligatory provisions dealing with the relationship between the signatory parties themselves and normative provisions aimed at regulating the individual employment relationships in the sector(s) covered by it. It is the latter aspect which turns collective agreements into a system of private regulation.[35] The follow up on these kinds of instruments is typically the implementation report: were the rules contained therein effectively implemented at the national level?[36]

Hence the output of the social dialogue can be evaluated against different standards. Whose behaviour does the instrument seek to affect? Is it *inter se* aimed at the EU institutions or rather stakeholders and parties at the national level? The regulatory character of social dialogue is essentially aimed at the national level: it tries to impact on the individual employment relationships in the Member States. But the instruments aimed at the national level may be quite diverse in character. A first distinction would be between tools and rules: does the instrument provide tools for

[31] A special case is the agreement of 19 April 2012 between UEFA, EPFL, ECA, and FIFPro Division Europe regarding the minimum requirements for standard player contracts in the professional football sector in the European Union and in the rest of the UEFA territory. This agreement is not targeting the national level but, rather, aims to impact the policy of UEFA.

[32] See, e.g. Communication from the Commission of 12 August 2004—Partnership for Change in an enlarged Europe—Enhancing the contribution of European social dialogue, COM(2004) 557 final, Annex 2.

[33] See, e.g. the database on posting of workers set up by the social partners in the construction industry and sponsored by the EC (http://www.posting-workers.eu/ (last visited 8 March 2017)) and the agreement of 3 December 2009 between Eurociett and UNI Europa to set up a European observatory on cross-border activities within the temporary agency work sector (to be found in the EC database on social dialogue texts).

[34] Compare Simitis and Lyon-Caen, *supra* note 14, at 20 and COM(2004) 557, *supra* note 32, at 9.

[35] Treu, *supra* note 2, at 177–178.

[36] See, e.g. European Social Partner, *Report on the Implementation of the European Autonomous Framework Agreement on Work-related Stress*, adopted at the social dialogue committee of 18 June 2008. Available at the Commission database on social dialogue.

implementation and enforcement or does it contain the rules to be implemented or enforced?[37] Finally, even when the instruments contain rules or policy directions, the binding character thereof may differ widely: from merely expressing policy directions, through soft law, to hard and fast rules. Only the latter represent collective agreements in the narrow meaning of that term.

Under Article 155 TFEU collective agreements may be implemented either according to the industrial relations traditions of the Member States or by binding Council decision. This puts collective agreements on the axis between upward and downward orientation: in order to impact on national employment relations, the social partners may directly involve the law-making architecture of the EU institutions. But the opposite is also true: the EU institutions may want to use the social partners as a means to further their policy goals. Collective bargaining at EU level can be used to bypass deadlocks in the legislative procedure.[38] A recent case in point was the attempt to revise the Working Time Directive by way of collective agreement after the ordinary legislative procedure failed to render a positive result.[39]

The two implementation routes create yet another distinction within the group of collective agreements which corresponds to a division in the Commission database on social dialogue texts. In February 2015, when the inventory for this chapter was made,[40] the database contained 12 collective agreements which were nominated by the social partners for conversion into a Council decision.[41] Eight agreements were categorized by the Commission as 'autonomous agreements'. In the context of the Commission database, this term refers to the manner of implementation, rather than to the question whether negotiations were a response to a legislative initiative of the Commission or autonomous from the outset.[42] The framework agreement on telework, for example, is deemed to be an autonomous instrument, though the social partners themselves explicitly state that the initiative for the proposal lay with the Commission.[43] In contrast, the hairdressers' agreement figures in the Council decision category although this agreement is autonomous in origin. However, it was

[37] See for an example of the former: J. Pillinger, *The Toolkit Demographic Change, Age Management and Competencies in the Gas Sector in Europe* (2009); the agreement between Eurociett and UNI Europa, *supra* note 33 (both to be found in the Commission database).

[38] See, for a description of the historical development of the European social dialogue as a reaction to the UK deregulatory agenda from 1979 onwards, Bercusson, *supra* note 2, at 126–128.

[39] See http://ec.europa.eu/social/main.jsp?catId=706&langId=en&intPageId=205. The legislative attempt was made in 2009: http://www.europeansundayalliance.eu/site/law/article/68.html. Negotiations between the social partners took place in 2012, but these likewise failed and were officially abandoned in 2013: http://www.worker-participation.eu/EU-Social-Dialogue/Latest-developments/Failure-of-the-revision-of-the-working-time-Directive-negotiations. In December 2014 a new round of consultations were opened: http://ec.europa.eu/social/main.jsp?catId=333&consultId=14&visib=0&furtherConsult=yes&langId=en. (All websites last visited 8 March 2017). For a similar strategy employed in the 1980s, see Barnard, *supra* note 2, at 761.

[40] The inventory is based on the content of the website in February 2015, http://ec.europa.eu/social/main.jsp?catId=521&langId=en (last visited 8 March 2017).

[41] In 2015 ten of those were implemented in the form of a directive; two were pending. In March 2017 the database contains 14 agreements registered as Agreement/Council Decision.

[42] The origin of the agreement does impact the procedure for making it binding through Council decision: discussed later in the chapter and in particular Section 5.

[43] Framework agreement of 16 July 2002 between ETUC, UNICE, UEAPME, and CEEP on telework.

put before the Commission in an attempt to make it binding by Council decision—a process which was halted by the Commission in the REFIT project.

The EU database further distinguishes Codes of Conduct (10); frameworks of action (9); guidelines (35); declarations (110); joint opinions (450); policy orientations (18); procedural texts (47), consisting mainly of rules of procedure for the social dialogue itself plus one Memorandum of Understanding on the development and maintenance of an online risk assessment tool; 'tools' (84); and follow-up reports (41). In 2010 the sectoral dialogue alone had produced more than 500 texts of varying legal status.[44] Only 11 of those are labelled as sectoral collective agreements.

It may be concluded from this overview that the strictly regulatory instruments in which social partners formulate rules that are meant to be binding at the national level, constitute a small minority within the multitude of outcomes of the social dialogue. This allows for a more detailed description of both the interaction between EU collective agreements and the legislative framework of the EU and the route these instruments have to follow in order to be implemented by way of Council decision.

4. Interaction between EU Legislation and EU Collective Bargaining

As was mentioned earlier, the Commission database distinguishes between autonomous agreements and Council decision agreements. The distinction employed by the Commission is crucial in understanding the way the agreement is transposed into the national legal system (by law, government decree, and/or national collective agreements). And, as discussed later in the chapter, the distinction also predicates the European governance tests that the agreement has to pass. However, on closer scrutiny, the interaction between the social dialogue and the EU legislative infrastructure is much more complex than that. To fully understand the role of social partners within the EU regulatory framework, it is necessary to take a closer look at those interactions.

An interesting subgroup within the group of Council decision agreements consists of the sectoral agreements on working time. The database on social dialogue contains four such agreements (out of a total of 20 collective agreements) all of which relate to working time in international transport. The original Working Time Directive of 1994 excluded the transport sector from its scope of application.[45] The 2000 revision of the Directive did extend the scope to include, in particular, the office workers of transport companies but only partially applied to mobile employees.[46]

[44] EC Press Release of 23 July 2010, 'Social affairs: Commission report on the sectoral social dialogue at European level', MEMO/10/354, available at http://europa.eu/rapid/press-release_MEMO-10-354_en.htm?locale=en (last visited 8 March 2017).

[45] Council Directive 93/104 of 23 November 1993 concerning certain aspects of the organization of working time, OJ 1993 L 307/18, Article 1(3). See also Barnard, *supra* note 2, at 535. Special rules for the transport sector already existed before the first Working Time Directive was adopted. These measures were based on the transport title of the EC Treaty. See, e.g. Council Regulation 3820/85 of 20 December 1985 on the harmonization of certain social legislation relating to road transport, OJ 1985 L 370/1.

[46] Directive 2000/34 of the European Parliament and of the Council of 22 June 2000 amending Council Directive 93/104/EC concerning certain aspects of the organization of working time to cover sectors and activities excluded from that Directive, OJ 2000 L 185/41.

Moreover, the Directive contained a provision which opened up the possibility to take special measures for specific sectors. This possibility was retained in the recast Directive 2003/88. Article 14 thereof specifies: 'This Directive shall not apply where other Community instruments contain more specific requirements relating to the organisation of working time for certain occupations or occupational activities.'[47]

Before the 2000 extension took place the social partners in merchant shipping concluded an agreement on working time of seafarers, which was put into effect by means of a Council directive in 1999.[48] When the Working Time Directive was extended to transport workers in 2000 (taking effect in 2003), merchant shipping was explicitly excluded from the scope of application of the Directive. This exclusion is retained in the current Working Time Directive (recast) 2003/88.[49] In reaction to the 2000 extension, social partners in the different transport sectors started negotiations in order to reach specific agreements for their sector. Between 2000 and 2012 they concluded agreements for civil aviation (2000), interoperable cross-border services in the railway sector (2004), and inland waterways (2012) respectively.[50] All of these were implemented by way of EU directive[51] and rely on Article 14 of the Working Time Directive for their priority over the rules of the general directive. Transport by road likewise has a special regime, which is, however, contained in a directive adopted under the normal legislative procedure.[52]

The negotiations on the agreements for both seafarers and civil aviation were started after a second-stage consultation by the European Commission.[53] At that stage of the legislative procedure the Commission has already decided it is necessary to take action at EU level. The agreement in the rail sector was not preceded by a two-stage consultation, but nevertheless had the full support of the Commission. The agreement for inland waterways in contrast came into being on the initiative of the social partners themselves, hence independent of any prior analysis as to subsidiarity,

[47] Directive 2003/88 of the European Parliament and of the Council of 4 November 2003 concerning certain aspects of the organization of working time, OJ 2003 L 299/9.

[48] Council Directive 1999/63 of 21 June 1999 concerning the Agreement on the organization of working time of seafarers concluded by the European Community Shipowners' Association (ECSA) and the Federation of Transport Workers' Unions in the European Union (FST), OJ 1999 L 167/33.

[49] See Directive 2003/88, *supra* note 47, preamble para. (12) and Article 1.

[50] Implemented by Council Directive 2000/79 of 27 November 2000 concerning the European Agreement on the Organisation of Working Time of Mobile Workers in Civil Aviation concluded by the Association of European Airlines (AEA), the European Transport Workers' Federation (ETF), the European Cockpit Association (ECA), the European Regions Airline Association (ERA), and the International Air Carrier Association (IACA), OJ 2000 L 302/57 and Council Directive 2005/47 of 18 July 2005 on the Agreement between the Community of European Railways (CER) and the European Transport Workers' Federation (ETF) on certain aspects of the working conditions of mobile workers engaged in interoperable cross-border services in the railway sector, OJ 2005 L 195/15.

[51] The Council formally accepted the European agreement between the European Barge Union (EBU), the European Skippers Organisation (ESO), and the European Transport Workers' Federation (ETF) concerning certain aspects of the organization of working time in inland waterway transport on 19 December 2014. See Procedure 2014/0212/NLE.

[52] Directive 2002/15 of the European Parliament and of the Council of 11 March 2002 on the organisation of the working time of persons performing mobile road transport activities, OJ 2002, L 80/35.

[53] Council Directive 1999/63, *supra* note 47, preamble (5)–(7).

proportionality, and political priority.[54] In the case of transport by road the deviation from the general directive took the form of a 'normal' directive after the negotiations between the social partners had failed.[55] Accordingly, the sectoral social dialogue plays a crucial role in formulating special sectoral regimes. However, for the effectiveness of these special rules the social partners depend on the Commission and Council. The agreements themselves are not 'Community instruments' in the meaning of Article 14 of the Working Time Directive.[56] And, as will be discussed in more detail later, when the initiative for the agreement rests entirely with the social partners, the Commission may scrutinize the result more intensely for appropriateness.

There are two agreements which relate to occupational safety and health. This is again an area in which there is extensive pre-existing legislation at the EU level.[57] In this arena, the social partners in the healthcare sector adopted a framework agreement on prevention from sharp injuries in the hospital and healthcare sector, which was converted into a directive in 2010.[58] The agreement was a response to an initiative of the European Parliament, which adopted a resolution in 2006 calling upon the Commission to submit a proposal on this issue. The negotiations started in 2008, after extensive two-stage consultations.[59] In contrast, the hairdressers' agreement of 2012[60] was entered into at the initiative of the social partners themselves without support from the Commission. Hence there were no prior consultations within the EU legislative framework as to the necessity of EU action in the field and no impact assessment.

In the area of working time, collective agreements are used to develop specialized regimes within the context of a pre-existing European legislative framework. Also, agreement in the area of occupational safety and health operate within such a pre-existing framework. However, in the case of the Working Time Directive the specialized regimes constitute a deviation from the rules of the Directive, in order to take

[54] Proposal for a Council Directive of 7 July 2014 implementing the European Agreement concluded by the European Barge Union (EBU), the European Skippers Organisation (ESO), and the European Transport Workers' Federation (ETF) concerning certain aspects of the organization of working time in inland waterway transport, COM(2014) 452 final, at 5.

[55] Directive 2002/15, *supra* note 52, preamble para. (3).

[56] See COM(2014) 452, *supra* note 54, at 9, Sciarra, *supra* note 18, at 200–201 and Däubler, 'Instruments of EC Labour Law', in P. Davies *et al.* (eds), *supra* note 2, at 164–165. However, the UK House of Commons Library Standard Note SN/BT/1377 seems to put directives and special agreements at a par with regard to Article 14 of the Working Time Directive.

[57] Notably Council Directive 89/391 of 12 June 1989 on the introduction of measures to encourage improvements in the safety and health of workers at work, OJ 1989 L 183/1 (European Framework Directive on Safety and Health at Work) and the directives that build upon this framework: see https://osha.europa.eu/en/legislation/directives/the-osh-framework-directive/the-osh-framework-directive-introduction (last visited 8 March 2017) and K. Riesenhuber, *European Employment Law* (2012), at 365–369.

[58] Council Directive 2010/32 of 10 May 2010 implementing the Framework agreement on prevention from sharp injuries in the hospital and healthcare sector concluded by HOSPEEM and EPSU, OJ 2010 L134/66.

[59] EC Press Release of 8 March 2010, 'New legislation to reduce injuries for 3.5 million healthcare workers in Europe', IP/10/243, available at http://europa.eu/rapid/press-release_IP-10-243_en.htm?locale=en (last visited 8 March 2017) and Proposal for a Council Directive of 26 October 2009 implementing the Framework Agreement on prevention from sharp injuries in the hospital and healthcare sector concluded by HOSPEEM and EPSU, COM(2009) 577 final.

[60] Hairdressers' agreement, *supra* note 1.

the special characteristics of the sector into account. The agreements on occupational safety and health do not detract from the obligations contained in the relevant framework directive. They rather add specific duties or provide for specific interpretations of and ways to implement certain already existing duties.[61]

A different role is fulfilled by the agreements in which special European diplomas and/or certificates are created. Such agreements exist(ed) in both the hairdressing sector and with regard to locomotive drivers in the railway sector. In these cases, the social partners developed a common licensing model in order to enhance free movement of persons and services. But that's about where the similarity between the two ends. The European agreement on the Implementation of the European Hairdressing Certificates 2009 is autonomous in both start and implementation and does not in any way refer to or build upon a European legislative framework.[62] The negotiations on the CER-ETF Agreement on a European Locomotive Driving Licence 2004[63] started at the initiative of the social partners, but the social partners had intended the agreement to be implemented by Council decision.[64] Instead, the voluntary system was largely replaced by a directive,[65] which, however, did by and large follow the outline provided by the agreement.[66] The Commission explains its choice of not simply submitting the agreement under Article 155 TFEU (then Article 139 EC) by the fact that, contrary to the agreements on working time which are fully covered by Article 153 TFEU, the question of licences relates to safety and interoperability of the railway system. According to the Commission this calls for a clear EU legislative framework which should be fully coordinated with the other elements of the European legislative framework regarding interoperability and safety of railway networks. Hence the choice for a directive of the European Parliament and the Council, adopted under the normal legislative procedure and based on the competences related to transport policy.[67] After adoption thereof the social partners issued a statement on

[61] Article 16(3) Directive 89/391, *supra* note 57: The provisions of this Directive shall apply in full to all the areas covered by the individual Directives, without prejudice to more stringent and/or specific provisions contained in these individual Directives.

[62] See http://ec.europa.eu/social/main.jsp?catId=521&langId=en&agreementId=5126 (last visited 8 March 2017). The certificate does, however, fit into the system of Directive 2005/36 of the European Parliament and of the Council of 7 September 2005 on the recognition of professional qualifications, OJ 2005 L 255/22, consolidated text Eurlex 2005L0036 – EN – 17.01.2014 – 010.003. This Directive is not based on the social policy paragraph of the TFEU.

[63] Agreement of 27 January 2004 between the European Transport Workers' Federation (ETF) and the Community of European Railways (CER) on driving licence, available at http://www.cer.be/publications/charters-and-agreements/cer-etf-agreement-driving-licence (last visited 8 March 2017).

[64] *Ibid.*: 'The Agreement shall be implemented by the CER-affiliated companies pending a European Directive. For the part covering the scope of this Agreement, both parties want the Directive to be written on the basis of this Agreement.'

[65] Directive 2007/59 of the European Parliament and of the Council of 23 October 2007 on the certification of train crews operating locomotives and trains on the railway system in the Community, OJ 2007 L 315/51.

[66] The Commission proposal formulates the interaction between the Directive and the agreement slightly differently and states that the agreement was established in anticipation of the adoption of the Directive. See Proposal for a Directive of the European Parliament and of the Council of 3 March 2004 on the certification of train crews operating locomotives and trains on the Community's rail network, COM(2004) 142 final.

[67] Article 71 ECT (now Article 91 TFEU). It is interesting to note that the purpose of both agreements and of the Directive is also related to free movement. Compare the legal base for the Directive on

the interaction between the two instruments, both of which were deemed to apply, albeit on different grounds.[68]

Yet another role is performed by the agreements which implement International Labour Organization (ILO) Conventions. The conventions of the ILO are atypical in that they are concluded in a tripartite organization, in which management and labour are also represented. The conventions thus adopted require the Member States, within the limits of their jurisdiction, to ensure full implementation of the standards contained therein, through national laws or regulations, through applicable collective bargaining agreements, or through other measures or in practice.[69] Hence, implementation by way of collective agreements is already part of the ILO framework.[70] In 2006 the General Conference of the ILO adopted the Maritime Labour Convention (MLC).[71] This highly complex Convention regulates a variety of issues relating to employment in merchant shipping, ranging from social security and repatriation rights to working time, on board recreational facilities and holiday allowances. The structure of the MLC is unique in its layered set up of articles, regulations, and standards, which carry with them different obligations for the contracting states.[72] Due to its wide-ranging subject matter, both the Member States and the EU are involved in its implementation.[73] Implementation through an EU collective agreement was seen as a way to smoothen the ratification process, and the social partners reached such an agreement in 2008. Their agreement was converted into a directive in 2009 and entered into force simultaneously with the MLC itself on 20 August 2013.[74] Both the agreement and the directive are limited in scope: they only implement the binding provisions of the MLC as it was not deemed possible to also include the non-binding standards in a directive.[75] Moreover, they only implement the provisions which deal with topics covered by Article 153 TFEU. Both the agreement and the directive contain amendments to the agreement (and ensuing directive) on working time of seafarers discussed earlier.

Work in fishing is excluded from the MLC. However, in 2007 a special Work in Fishing Convention was concluded in the context of the ILO. As (parts of) this Convention fell within the exclusive competence of the EU,[76] the Council authorized

the recognition of professional qualifications. This was, however, not used as a separate argument by the Commission for not using the procedure of Article 155 TFEU. On the choice of legal basis for measures having social policy implications, see also Bercusson, *supra* note 2, at 145.

[68] Agreement on driving licence, *supra* note 63.

[69] See, e.g. Article IV(5) MLC, 2006.

[70] See ILO Convention C144 of 21 June 1976 concerning tripartite consultations to promote the implementation of international labour standards.

[71] See http://ilo.org/global/standards/maritime-labour-convention/text/lang--en/index.htm (last visited 8 March 2017).

[72] Memorie van Toelichting (explanatory note to the implementation of the MLC in the Netherlands) *Kamerstukken II* 2010/2011 32 534 nr 3, at 1.

[73] Hence, it is a mixed agreement.

[74] Council Directive 2009/13 of 16 February 2009 implementing the Agreement concluded by the European Community Shipowners' Associations (ECSA) and the European Transport Workers' Federation (ETF) on the Maritime Labour Convention, 2006, and amending Directive 1999/63/EC, OJ 2009 L 124/30, preamble (9) and Article 7.

[75] Memorie van Toelichting, *supra* note 72, at 2. The standards are not fully binding but do carry obligations as they operate on a 'comply or explain' basis.

[76] Proposal for a Council Decision of 27 May 2008 authorizing Member States to ratify, in the interests of the European Community, the Work in Fishing Convention, 2007, of the International Labour Organisation, COM(2008) 320 final, at 3.

the Member States to ratify the convention on behalf of the EU in 2010.[77] Based on the experience with the implementation of the MLC, the Commission invited the social partners to reach an agreement on the implementation of the ILO Convention in the EU Member States.[78] In May 2012 an agreement was signed in the presence of Commissioner Damanaki.[79] In the following year this text was revised to make it compatible with the *acquis communautaire* and the social dialogue provisions in the TFEU and to accommodate the expectations expressed by the Commission. The revised text was signed in May 2013 but the Commission was slow in forwarding a proposal to implement the agreement to Council.[80] On several occasions, the social partners have expressed their concern at this delay.[81]

Lastly, most early collective agreements at EU level were cross-sectoral in character and were related to work-life balance and atypical employment. They related to parental leave (1995, recast 2009), part-time work (1996), and fixed-time work (1999). These agreements broke new ground in EU labour law. In the 1980s the Commission set out to regulate atypical employment, that is, labour relationships which deviate from the standard model of employment which is based on a contract of indeterminate duration and involves integration of the worker within the work organization of the employer. Accordingly the Commission put forward proposals on part-time work, temporary agency work, and fixed-term work. However, none of these proposals were adopted by Council, where at the time they still required unanimity.[82] After the adoption of the Social Protocol to the 1997 Maastricht Treaty, the topics were once more put on the agenda, this time as part of the (newly established) social dialogue. The social partners managed to reach agreement on part-time work and fixed-term work in 1996 and 1999. The negotiations on temporary agency work, however, failed in 2001.[83] In 2002 the Commission submitted a proposal which built upon the work done by the social partners. However, it took until 2008 for a directive to be adopted—through the normal legislative procedure. The two collective agreements were transposed into a directive

[77] Convention C188 of 14 June 2007 concerning work in the fishing sector. See, *inter alia*, Council Decision 2010/321 of 7 June 2010 authorizing Member States to ratify, in the interests of the European Union, the Work in Fishing Convention, 2007, of the International Labour Organisation (Convention No. 188), OJ 2010 L145/12 and COM(2008) 320.

[78] Communication from the Commission of 10 October 2007 to the European Parliament, the Council, the European Economic and Social Committee, and the Committee of the Regions—Reassessing the regulatory social framework for more and better seafaring jobs in the EU (first phase consultation of the social partners at Community level provided for in Article 138(2) of the Treaty), COM(2007) 591.

[79] See https://osha.europa.eu/en/legislation/guidelines/sector_specific/index_html/1/1/the-fishing-agreement-title-unknown (last visited 8 March 2017).

[80] The Commission did announce a costs/benefit analysis to be performed: see below, note 139.

[81] See, e.g. Statement of the EU social partners in Sea Fishing in support of the right that social partners' agreements are made legally binding, 14 February 2014, EP(14)12, available at http://www.etf-europe.org/files/seealsodocs/42083/EP12%20SSDCF%20Statement%20in%20support%20of%20SPA%20hairdressing.pdf (last visited 8 March 2017). In May 2016 a proposal transposing the agreement (COM(2016) 0235) was sent to the European Parliament. See *infra* note 141.

[82] Riesenhuber, *supra* note 57, at 415 with references.

[83] *Ibid.*, at 417.

in 1997[84] and 1999.[85] Another form of atypical employment, telework, was regulated in an autonomous agreement in 2012.[86]

The overview in Section 3 shows the social partners at EU level to be active in a variety of ways. Collective bargaining as an instrument of regulation, however, is intimately linked to the regulatory framework of the EU. The possibility to have an agreement made binding through Council decision plays an important role in this interrelationship. When collective agreements are made binding by EU directive, the rules contained in the agreement have to be implemented in the Member States in a manner which ensures effective enforcement of the rights and obligations contained therein. This means, *inter alia*, that the implementation measures should guarantee full coverage of the targeted workforce, individual legal protection if the directive contains individual rights, and an enforcement mechanism which effectively deters breaches. These requirements make it *de facto* impossible to implement the EU collective agreements through national collective agreements only. EU horizontal subsidiarity could hence preempt national horizontal subsidiarity.[87]

When a collective agreement is not made binding, but relies on the autonomous implementation route, implementation studies show that the effect in the Member States is likely to be divergent.[88] For example the 2012 agreement on telework was implemented through a legislative procedure in Hungary and by way of collective agreement in Denmark, whereas in the UK the agreement was not implemented in any binding way at all.[89] This lack of consistent implementation seems to rule out implementation of conventions through the autonomous route when the EU itself is a signatory to the convention.[90] However, also in the case of ILO Conventions in which the Member States ratify on behalf of the EU, implementation through the

[84] Council Directive 97/81 of 15 December 1997 concerning the Framework Agreement on part-time work concluded by UNICE, CEEP and the ETUC, OJ 1998 L 14/9.

[85] Council Directive 1999/70 of 28 June 1999 concerning the Framework Agreement on fixed-term work concluded by UNICE, CEEP and the ETUC, OJ 1999 L 175/43.

[86] Framework agreement on telework, *supra* note 43.

[87] Branch, 'The Evolution of the European Social Dialogue Towards Greater Autonomy: Challenges and Potential Benefits', *International Journal of Comparative Labour Law and Industrial Relations* (2005) 321, at 329.

[88] Treu, *supra* note 2, at 173. Larsen and Andersen, 'A New Mode of European Regulation? The Implementation of the Autonomous Framework Agreement on Telework in Five Countries', 13/2 *European Journal of Industrial Relations* (2007) 181. Branch, *supra* note 87, at 327–329. Bercusson, *supra* note 2, at 154–155.

[89] European Social Partners, *Report on the Implementation of the European Framework Agreement on Telework*, adopted by the social dialogue committee on 28 June 2006; Larsen and Andersen, *supra* note 88. See in general on the problem of implementing the soft law instruments of EU social dialogue: Léonard, 'European Sectoral Social Dialogue: An Analytical Framework', 14/4 *European Journal of Industrial Relations* (2008), at 408 and Branch, *supra* note 87, at 333.

[90] In its 2004 Communication on social dialogue the Commission stated its position on the choice between autonomous implementation and implementation by Council decision in the following manner: 'While recognising the broad scope of the social partners' competences, in line with the previous concerns of the Commission, where fundamental rights or important political options are at stake, or in situations where the rules must be applied in a uniform fashion in all Member States and coverage must be complete, preference should be given to implementation by Council decision. Autonomous agreements are also not appropriate for the revision of previously existing directives adopted by the Council and European Parliament through the normal legislative procedure': COM(2004) 557 final, *supra* note 32, at 10. See for a critical assessment of this position: Bercusson, *supra* note 2, at 560.

autonomous route would create difficult problems of state liability if the implementation is deemed to fall short of Treaty obligations.

Where collective agreements amend a directive or deviate from one, the autonomous route might also be excluded. This seems to be the case with the sectoral working time agreements. The Working Time Directive does specifically allow for deviation by EU instrument, but this term refers to official instruments only, collective agreements not being considered as such.[91] Hence, the sectoral collective agreements cannot become operational without the help of the EU institutions. Similarly, it does not seem possible to amend the Working Time Directive itself by autonomous agreement.[92] An even more complicated issue concerns the power of the social partners to amend or withdraw agreements once these are implemented by way of Council directive. In the case of the revision of the Parental Leave Directive, the update of the existing agreement turned directive took place in close cooperation between the social partners and the EU institutions.[93] However, there is no indication in the agreements and/or the directives to suggest that the directives lose their binding force when the social partners decide to terminate the underlying agreement. In this respect, the social partners seem to lose control of their agreement upon adoption thereof by Council.[94] This makes it all the more urgent to inquire into the procedure that leads to the implementation of collective agreements by way of Council decision and the tests performed within that procedure.

5. Testing the Outcome of Social Dialogue

Under Article 155 TFEU the signatory parties to an EU collective agreement may request the Commission to put their agreement before Council in order to make it binding in EU law. However, as soon as the signatory parties involve the EU regulatory framework, the EU institutions regain responsibility for the process and the provisions agreed upon are tested against that framework. The CFI decided as much in the UEAPME case.[95] In this case, an organization of employers made up of small

[91] Däubler, *supra* note 56, at 164–165. Sciarra, *supra* note 18, at 200–201.

[92] It is interesting to note that the Commission did, however, call upon the social partners to start negotiations on the revision of the Working Time Directive after the legislative procedure failed to render a positive result: see Communication from the Commission of 21 December 2010 to the European Parliament, the Council, the European Economic and Social Committee, and the Committee of the Regions—Reviewing the Working Time Directive (Second-phase consultation of the social partners at European level under Article 154 TFEU), COM(2010) 801 final, at 2 and 16.

[93] See Proposal for a Council Directive of 30 July 2009 implementing the revised Framework Agreement on parental leave concluded by BUSINESSEUROPE, UEAPME, CEEP, and ETUC and repealing Directive 96/34/EC, COM(2009) 410 final.

[94] See, in contrast, the mechanisms to make collective agreements generally binding in the Netherlands: the extension is limited in time and will in any case expire with the collective agreement. The extension can also be retracted on request of the social partners when they withdraw from or change their collective agreement: *Toetsingskader AVV*, Staatscourant 2013, nr 34009-n1, at 6.

[95] Case T-135/96, *UEAPME v. Council*, [1998] ECR II-02335 (ECLI:EU:T:1998:128). See also Written Question 3402/98 by Catherine Lalumiere to the Commission. Possibility for the European Union of Association for Craft and Small and Medium-Sized Enterprises (UEAPME) to participate in European consultations between management and labour as a full-fledged social partner, OJ 1999 C 297/70.

and medium-sized enterprises (SMEs) objected to the conversion of the framework agreement on parental leave into a directive, as they had not been admitted to the negotiation table. In its judgment the CFI decided that the social partners are free to choose not only whether to enter into negotiations, but also with whom. However, when they involve the EU legislative architecture, it is incumbent upon the Commission to check whether the agreement conforms to the requirements of EU law. As the procedure of Article 155 TFEU excludes any meaningful input from the European Parliament—which is only informed[96]—the principle of democracy on which the Union is founded requires that the participation of the people be otherwise assured, in this instance through a check of the representativeness of the signatory parties. Moreover, all EU action based on Article 153 TFEU should avoid imposing administrative, financial, and legal constraints in a way which would hold back the creation and development of SMEs. This requirement can also—if necessary—be checked by the courts.

The *UEAPME* case is the only case to date in which the application of Article 155 TFEU has been challenged. The lack of open conflict and the absence of case law also imply that the question to what extent the EU framework applies unmodified to the outcome of the social dialogue is still largely untested. In the last couple of years a fierce debate has arisen as to the question whether the Commission actually enjoys discretion as to whether or not to put an agreement before Council.[97] The trigger for this debate is the position taken by the Commission on the European framework agreement on the prevention of health risks in the hairdressing sector (2010).[98] On the official website of the Commission, the agreement is hailed as 'regulation by social partners for social partners' and 'tailor-made for small businesses'.[99] However, while the Commission's services were assessing the framework agreement, opposition was voiced against the agreement by a number of Member States, led by the Netherlands and the UK.[100] These states officially asked the European Commission not to forward the framework agreement to the Council of Ministers for adoption as a legally binding decision. The same approach was pursued by Member States and parts of the Commission against two other sectoral social dialogue agreements concluded by ETF, one on working time in inland waterway transport and one on the implementation of the 2007 ILO 'Work in Fishing Convention'. In the REFIT communication of 6 June 2014 the Commission announced its decision not to

[96] Article 155(2) TFEU.

[97] See Bercusson, *supra* note 2, at 152–153 with regard to the uncertain meaning of the Treaty provision and their historical development.

[98] See https://osha.europa.eu/en/legislation/guidelines/sector_specific/index_html/1/1/european-framework-agreement-on-the-protection-of-occupational-health-and-safety-in-the-hairdressing-sector (last visited 8 March 2017).

[99] Hairdressing sector agrees on new measures to boost health and safety, 24 February 2012, available at http://ec.europa.eu/social/main.jsp?langId=en&catId=329&newsId=1286&furtherNews=yes (last visited 8 March 2017).

[100] See, *inter alia*, https://www.cnvvakmensen.nl/caos/kappers/cao-kappers/nieuws/europese-commissie-gooit-veiligheid-kappers-te-grabbel; http://www.fnvmooi.nl/persbericht-zzpers-tot-stoppen-gedwongen/; http://www.rethinkrefit.eu/docs/VAKBEWEGING-792_tcm22-304705.pdf. (All websites last visited 8 March 2017.)

present a proposal on the hairdressing agreement during its current mandate.[101] The 2015 Work Programme of the new Commission contains no further information on this issue. As mentioned earlier, despite previous reluctance, the agreement on working time in inland waterway transport has by now been submitted to Council, which made it binding in December 2014. The agreement on the Work in Fishing Convention followed suit in 2017.

Meanwhile the EU social partners consider the hairdressing agreement a test case for social dialogue and the EU's commitment towards social Europe.[102] On 14 February 2014, the Sectoral Social Dialogue Committee on Sea Fisheries (SSDC-SF) adopted a statement urging the Commission to respect the autonomy of the social partners and assist them, when so requested, in making social partners' agreements legally binding.[103] This statement was a response to the refusal of the Commission to submit the hairdressers' agreement to Council, but also reflects the concern of the social partners as regards the other agreements which were halted by the Commission during that period.[104]

The debate on the role of the Commission in the procedure of Article 155 TFEU has two distinct elements: a first one relates to the question which tests should be performed on the outcome of social dialogue before any agreement can be turned into EU law. This question immediately affects the autonomy of social dialogue versus the EU institutions. The second question addresses the role of the Commission in this: should the Commission be able to halt the progress by simply not submitting a proposal or is the test to be performed by Council or even exclusively in Court? I do not purport to formulate a definitive answer to the ongoing debate. However, I will try to give an overview of the checks which the Commission performs before putting a proposal before Council and how these operate in practice.

This analysis is complicated by the fact that the framework in which legislative proposals are tested has changed considerably over time. In 2015 only one collective agreement had been implemented by Council decision under the full application of the Lisbon Treaty whereas two were adopted under a transitional regime.[105] Under the Lisbon Treaty, national parliaments are involved in the legislative procedure through the early warning mechanism. Through this mechanism the parliaments can perform a subsidiarity check on Commission proposals. The mechanism only

[101] Communication from the Commission of 18 June 2014 to the European Parliament, the Council, the European economic and social committee and the Committee of the regions—Regulatory Fitness and Performance Programme (REFIT): State of Play and Outlook, COM(2014) 368 final, at 4 footnote 8. Uni Global Union, 'EU Commission says no to social partner agreement of hairdressers', 2 October 2013, available at http://www.uniglobalunion.org/news/eu-commission-says-no-social-partner-agreement-hairdressers (last visited 8 March 2017). For the term of appointment of the Commission, see https://ec.europa.eu/info/about-european-union/organisational-structure/political-leadership_en#term-of-office (last visited 8 March 2017).

[102] See, *inter alia*, Uni Global Union, 'Barroso must stop playing with workers' health and safety', 24 October 2013, available at http://www.uniglobalunion.org/news/barroso-must-stop-playing-workers-health-and-safety (last visited 8 March 2017).

[103] Statement of the EU social partners in Sea Fishing, *supra* note 81.

[104] See the Statement of the EU social partners in Sea Fishing, *supra* note 81.

[105] See Communication from the Commission of 2 December 2009 to the European Parliament and the Council—Consequences of the entry into force of the Treaty of Lisbon for ongoing interinstitutional decision-making procedures, COM(2009) 655 final with annexes.

applies to legislative procedures, excluding the input of national parliaments into other decision-making and/or regulatory processes.[106] Interestingly enough, the adoption of a Council directive under Article 155 TFEU is labelled as a 'non-legislative procedure' in the post-Lisbon system[107] though the outcome of the procedure is clearly legislative in character.[108] Hence, whereas under the procedure of Article 155 TFEU the influence of the European Parliament is reduced to the possibility of giving an opinion, the influence of national parliaments seems to be completely excluded.

The roles of Commission and Council are likewise limited, as both feel bound by the contents of the agreement between the social partners. In several proposals for implementation the Commission has stressed that neither the Commission nor Council can amend the agreement in any way. Though this point is not unequivocally agreed upon in literature, it seems common ground between the institutions that the transposition of a collective agreement by Council decision is basically a 'yes or no' decision: the agreement is implemented as it stands or it is rejected.[109]

Impact assessments became standard procedure only in 2003. Though impact assessments are not required in the case of a request under Article 155 TFEU,[110] the model of testing applied in the assessments may also influence the test performed by the Commission in procedures not subject to assessment.[111] Likewise, the arguments used by the Commission are influenced by the protocols on subsidiarity and better regulation which were developed between the adoption of the first social partner agreement and the implementation of the most recent one.

With only a small sample, spread widely in time, it is not possible to draw too absolute a conclusion from the overview given below. Moreover, as I mentioned before, there is currently hardly any case law on the role of Commission and Council under Article 155 TFEU. Nevertheless, a description of the tests performed and the way they operate in practice may shed some light on the way the Commission perceives the relationship between the autonomy of the social partners and the responsibility of the EU institutions.

[106] C. Barnard and S. Peers (eds), *European Union Law* (2014), at 113.

[107] See COM(2014) 452 final, *supra* note 54, procedure 2014/0212/NLE.

[108] Barnard and Peers, *supra* note 106, at 98. The extension of collective agreements in Germany, the Netherlands, and Belgium likewise has this mixed character of an administrative procedure resulting in regulation with all the characteristics of (private law) legislation. See, e.g. the Dutch *Toetsingskader AVV* 2014, Staatscourant 2013, nr 34009-n1, at 3 which contains the government's position and policy on extension of collective agreements, Christiaanse and Joosten, 'De andere Zalm-norm: loonpolitiek via de Wet AVV', 9 *Nederlands Tijdschrift voor Sociaal Recht* (2004), 63 ff and Deinert, *supra* note 15, at 420–421.

[109] COM(93) 600 final, *supra* note 8; Council legal service, Opinion of 31 March 1994, Council Doc 6116/94; COM(2014) 452 final, *supra* note 54, at 4–5; Proposal for a Council Directive of 8 February 2005 on the agreement between the Community of European Railways (CER) and the European Transport Workers' Federation (ETF) on certain aspects of the working conditions of mobile workers assigned to interoperable cross-border services, COM(2005) 32 final, at 9 (paras 45–48). See also Bercusson, *supra* note 2, at 158–160.

[110] See for example COM(2009) 410, *supra* note 93, at para. 2.3 and COM(2009) 577, *supra* note 59, at para. 2.3.

[111] For an overview of the tests performed, see European Commission, Impact Assessment Guidelines 15 January 2009, SEC(2009) 92, available at http://ec.europa.eu/smart-regulation/impact/commission_guidelines/docs/iag_2009_en.pdf (last visited 8 March 2017).

6. Representativeness, Legality, and Appropriateness

In its Communication on adapting and promoting the social dialogue at Community level of 20 May 1998, the Commission formulated which tests it would perform before any legislative proposal implementing a collective agreement is presented to the Council. This formulation is repeated almost verbatim in each proposal of the Commission with regard to a specific agreement. Accordingly, the Commission will carry out an assessment 'involving consideration of the representative status of the contracting parties, their mandate, and the legality of each clause in the collective agreement in relation to Community law, and the provisions regarding small and medium-sized enterprises'.[112] But the test applied in practice also pertains to subsidiarity and proportionality. The proposal is also assessed in the light of the overall EU policy in the field. The latter three tests are taken together as a test for the 'appropriateness' of the proposed action.

A. Representativeness

The proposals in which agreements are submitted to Council all contain a check on representativeness. The basic requirements which EU social partners must fulfil to be admitted to the social dialogue are that they are organized at European level while being made up of organizations which are themselves an integral and recognized part of the Member States' social partner structures.[113] They should have the capacity to negotiate agreements and have the structures required to enable them to participate effectively in the framework of the EU social dialogue. The Commission delegates the basic representativeness test to Eurofound, a tripartite European Union agency, which regularly publishes updates on the representative status of social partners.[114] When an agreement is entered into, the representativeness of the signatory parties is tested for the sector to which the agreement is meant to apply. In that sector they should be representative both as regards the number of employees and employers covered and as regards the number of Member States represented.[115] In this assessment the presence or absence of other, non-included representatives of management and labour is also weighed as a factor.

An illustrative example of how the test is performed in practice can be found in the proposal on the implementation of the agreement on working time in inland waterway transport. The Commission, *inter alia*, stated the following:

[112] COM(98) 322, *supra* note 3, at 19.

[113] COM(93) 600 final, *supra* note 8 and COM(98)322, *supra* note 3. Riesenhuber, *supra* note 57, at 156.

[114] Eurofound was established by Council Regulation 1365/75 of 26 May 1975 on the creation of a European Foundation for the improvement of living and working conditions, OJ 1975 L 139/1. See http://www.eurofound.europa.eu/observatories/eurwork/representativeness-studies (last visited 8 March 2017). COM(2004) 557 final, *supra* note 32, at 9: 'The Commission proposes that the representativeness studies should be carried out by the European Industrial Relations Observatory of the Dublin Foundation.'

[115] Riesenhuber, *supra* note 57, at 156.

Given that the [signatory parties] do not have affiliates in all EU Member States, to make the negotiation process transparent they sent a joint letter to the transport and labour ministries of all Member States in November 2009 informing them of the core content of their negotiations and asking them to forward the information to the relevant national social partner organisations. It appears there was no official response to this letter. The representativeness study carried out by Eurofound did not identify any other sectoral social partner organisation organised at European level. The Commission therefore concludes that the [signatory parties] are the only EU-wide organisations representative of both sides of industry in IWT.[116]

As the 'signatories to the Agreement have sufficient representative status with regard to IWT in general and to the workers and employers who may be covered by the Agreement's provisions, and they have had a mandate from their national members to negotiate and conclude the Agreement', the requirements for transposition were met.[117] Earlier in the document the Commission had already asserted that '[d]uring negotiations on the Agreement, SMEs were well represented by the ESO and their representatives were amongst the strongest supporters of the Agreement'.[118]

The UEAPME case mentioned earlier related to the framework agreement on parental leave. This agreement was revised in 2009, this time with the participation of UEAPME. In the proposal regarding the revised framework agreement the Commission starts with the assessment that the 1995 Framework Agreement on parental leave was signed by the European cross-industry social partners ETUC, CEEP, and UNICE (today called 'BUSINESSEUROPE'). At the time, these organizations were deemed to meet the representativeness test. Studies commissioned by the Commission in 1999 and 2004 showed that their representativeness has not substantially changed and that their membership now includes the main cross-industry social partners in the new Member States.[119] According to the Commission, they are by far the most representative organizations of management and labour at EU level. All four organizations had a specific mandate from their national members for the negotiations on parental leave and concluded the agreement on behalf of their members. All four approved the outcome of the negotiations in accordance with their internal decision-making procedures. The conditions of representativeness were therefore met.

B. The Legality Test

The representativeness test is procedural in character and is not related to the content of the agreement; however, the other tests performed by the Commission are. As far as these tests contain policy decisions and/or leave discretionary powers to the Commission, they may encroach upon the autonomy of the social partners to decide what and how to regulate within their own domain. Accordingly the less the test restricts itself to a pure legality check, the more likely it is to be contested whenever it leads to a refusal to implement. As Lo Faro already remarked in 2000: 'One cannot help wondering (even though the hypothesis seems somewhat remote) what the consequences would be, if quite apart from possibly deeming an agreement to be

[116] COM(2014) 452, *supra* note 54, at 8. [117] *Ibid.* [118] *Ibid.*, at 6. [119] *Ibid.*

contrary to Community law, the Commission gave a negative assessment of the substantive choices made by the social partners'.[120] With the refusal of the Commission to submit the hairdressers' agreement to Council this hypothesis is now a reality. What then are the tests the Commission performs before proposing the implementation of an agreement?

First, to be admissible for conversion under Article 155 TFEU, the agreement must relate to matters open for regulation under Article 153 TFEU.[121] Additionally, the Commission will check whether any of the provisions of the agreement violate pre-existing EU law. And, lastly, Article 153(4) stipulates that measures in this area of EU policy should have a minimum character: they 'shall not prevent any Member State from maintaining or introducing more stringent protective measures compatible with the Treaties'.[122] A standard assessment will check all three aspects as part of the 'condition of legality'. The instrument of choice for implementation of collective agreements is the directive. Under Article 153(2)(b) directives in the field of social policy 'shall avoid imposing administrative, financial and legal constraints in a way which would hold back the creation and development of small and medium-sized undertakings'. In the UEAPME case the CFI implied that this requirement is not at the discretion of the social partners and/or the Commission but is open for scrutiny by the courts. The several proposals submitted by the Commission show that the Commission will take the requirement into consideration when assessing a specific agreement.

C. The Appropriateness of Legislative Action at EU Level

It is widely accepted that neither the Commission nor Council can amend the provisions of the agreement as it is going through the transformation process of Article 155 TFEU. It is basically a 'yes or no' decision for both institutions.[123] As discussed in the previous section, the Commission often cooperates at close quarters with the social partners in the wording of an agreement, especially when the negotiations start at the initiative of the Commission and depend on transformation into a directive for their effectiveness. The agreement on work in fishing offers a clear example of this close collaboration, as the original agreement was amended to make it eligible for submission to Council. The close collaboration smoothens the way for implementation

[120] A. Lo Faro, *Regulating Social Europe* (2000), at 114–115.

[121] As collective agreements are implemented through directives, their scope is limited to the topics mentioned in Article 153(1) under a-i. See, e.g. Riesenhuber, *supra* note 57, at 158. Dissenting: Bercusson, *supra* note 2, at 156.

[122] Barnard, *supra* note 2, at 55.

[123] Barnard, *supra* note 2, at 76. This is not based on the text of the provision, but it is standard practice and reiterated in several documents. See, *inter alia*, Opinion of 31 March 1994, *supra* note 109: while the Commission and Council could introduce rules for implementation they cannot amend the essence of the agreement. For a different opinion, see Riesenhuber, *supra* note 57, at 159: he states that the Commission is obliged to submit an agreement to Council without any amendments. However, in his opinion Council should be allowed to make changes and amendments as it would be inconsistent to hold it more strictly bound with regard to proposals of the social partners than with regard to autonomous proposals of the Commission (Article 193(1) TFEU). The Dutch government supports the reading of the Council legal service. See *Kamerstukken II* 21 501–31 Nr. 361: Letter of the Dutch Minister of Social Affairs.

by Council decision as any problems regarding the contents of the agreement can be addressed beforehand. The situation is different when the social partners open negotiations at their own initiative.[124] In those cases the Commission might be faced with a fait accompli and any checks against the standards of better governance would have to be performed after the fact.

Moreover, when the social partners start their negotiations in the second stage of consultation, their negotiations take place within a predetermined EU policy. The decision to regulate has already been taken and a preliminary impact assessment has been performed. Under the current practice, a collective agreement is not subject to a separate impact assessment. This is true for both autonomous agreements and agreements resulting from prior consultation. However, if the agreement was the result of private initiative, rather than EU policy, an extensive scrutiny of the appropriateness of EU action is in fact performed. The Commission already announced as much in its 1998 Communication.[125] In the proposal on the agreement concerning certain aspects of the organization of working time in inland waterway transport they made good on this 'promise':

> As the European Agreement concerning certain aspects of the organisation of working time in IWT was concluded at the social partners' own initiative, the Commission needs to assess the appropriateness of EU action in the area... Commission staff prepared an analytical document which accompanies this proposal in line with the guidelines on impact assessment. It provides a proportionate analysis which assesses the socio-economic impact of implementing the Agreement.[126]

However, this analysis is not restricted to autonomous agreements.

In its proposals the Commission routinely checks for consistency with other policies and addresses the issues of subsidiarity and proportionality. The latter test is based on the fact that all EU legislative action is bound by the principles of subsidiarity and proportionality.[127] The principle of proportionality prescribes that 'the content and form of Union action shall not exceed what is necessary to achieve the objectives of the Treaties'. The principle regulates the scope of EU action, once this can validly be taken. It also affects the choice of instruments by favouring those instruments which impact the least on the prerogatives of other relevant stakeholders. Hence, the choice between binding legislative measures and self-regulation is part of the proportionality analysis. This suggests that a preference for collective bargaining over top-down legislation also follows from the proportionality principle. However, in the labour law literature, the powers of the social partners vis-à-vis the legislature is traditionally coined in terms of subsidiarity.

The principle of subsidiarity impacts at an earlier stage of the regulatory process as it concerns the legitimacy of EU action as such. Its principle purpose is to delineate

[124] Barnard seems to suggest that negotiations under Article 153 always have to take place in reaction to a Commission consultation. This is not the leading opinion, however (see, e.g. Riesenhuber, *supra* note 57, at 158), and not supported by practice.

[125] 'In addition, before proposing a decision implementing an agreement negotiated on a matter within the material scope of Article 2 ASP, but outside the formal consultation procedure, the Commission has the obligation to assess the appropriateness of Community action in that field.' Communication from the Commission of 20 May 1998, *supra* note 3.

[126] COM(2014) 452, *supra* note 54, at 5.

[127] Article 5 TEU.

the respective powers of the Union and the Member States. In this context subsidiarity refers to vertical subsidiarity—the legislative assumption that the EU should act only and insofar as the objectives of the proposed action cannot be sufficiently achieved by the Member States. In labour law, however, subsidiarity operates at the horizontal level. There, the term refers to a mechanism where legislative intervention is deemed subsidiary to regulation by the social partners themselves. EU law recognizes the role of social partners in Article 154, where the social partners are given the power to substitute proposed legislative action by collective negotiations. The impact assessment guidelines of 2009 recognize this aspect of subsidiarity by requiring the Commission to pay attention to the choice between self-regulation and EU action.[128] However, in contrast to the situation in some of the Member States, the social partners at EU level do not seem to have a reserved domain in which the legislator should not intervene.[129] EU collective agreements—linked as they are to the mechanism of Article 155 TFEU—largely cover the topics that are open for EU regulation and hence rarely pertain to those issues which are traditionally the prerogative of the social partners (such as pay and collective labour relations).[130] The interrelationship of collective agreements with the overall EU framework—as described in Section 4—further enhances the legislative character of collective bargaining, which is sometimes referred to as 'bargaining in the shadow of the law'.[131]

An analysis of the proposals submitted by the Commission demonstrates that the Commission does consider it to be its duty to assess whether the agreement meets the tests of subsidiarity and proportionality and overall appropriateness. The test performed has, however, developed over time.[132] In the proposals on the agreements on part-time work and fixed-term work specific assessment of the subsidiarity requirements is lacking, in line with the overall legislative framework of the time. The

[128] SEC(2009) 92, *supra* note 111.

[129] On the different models of labour law in the Member States, see, e.g. Barnard, *supra* note 2, at 58 ff.

[130] Bercusson, *supra* note 2, at 156 ff argues that the social dialogue itself is not limited to the competence catalogue of Article 153 TFEU.

[131] Riesenhuber, *supra* note 57, at 157; Bercusson, *supra* note 2, at 147–148.

[132] See for the current framework: Report from the Commission, Annual Report on Subsidiarity and Proportionality 2013, COM(2014) 506 final. The documents studied are COM(2014) 452, *supra* note 54; COM(2009) 577, *supra* note 59; COM(2009) 410, *supra* note 93; Proposal for a Council Directive of 2 July 2008 implementing the agreement concluded by the European community shipowners' associations (ECSA) and the European transport workers' federation (ETF) on the maritime labour convention, 2006 and amending Directive 1999/63/EC, COM(2008) 422; COM(2005) 32, *supra* note 109; Proposal for a Council Directive of 23 June 2000 concerning the European Agreement on the Organisation of Working Time of Mobile Workers in Civil Aviation concluded by the Association of European Airlines (AEA), the European Transport Workers' Federation (ETF), the European Cockpit Association (ECA), the European Regions Airline Association (ERA) and the International Air Carrier Association (IACA)COM(2000) 382; Proposal for a Council Directive of 28 April 1999 concerning the Framework Agreement on Fixed-term Work concluded by UNICE, CEEP and the ETUC, COM(1999) 203; Communication from the Commission of 18 November 1998 to the Council, the European Parliament, the Economic and Social Committee and the Committee of Regions on the organization of working time in the sectors and activities excluded from Directive 93/104EC of 23 November 1993, COM(1998) 662, PRT 98/0320; Proposal for a Council Directive of 23 July 1997 concerning the framework agreement on part-time work concluded by UNICE, CEEP and ETUC, COM(97) 392.

proposals contain a more general assessment of the agreements against the EU social policy. For example: the proposal on the implementation of the agreement on part-time work specifies that the agreement 'contributes to implementing the conclusions of the Essen European Council' after having already concluded that the negotiations took place after the second round of consultation by the Commission and fitted the priorities expressed in the Commission's White Paper on the future of European Social Policy.[133] An almost identical assessment was made with regard to the proposal on fixed-term work. In both cases, the negotiations between the social partners started after the legislative process failed.

In the case of the agreements on working time, the special regimes are based on Article 14 of the Working Time Directive. In its proposal on the special agreement in inland waterway transport of 2014 the Commission states with regard to subsidiarity that 'Article 14 refers to "Community instruments" as necessary to lay down such provisions. Therefore, the objective of the proposal can only be achieved at EU level.'[134] The need for a specific regime is substantiated with the transnational character of the sector involved and the need to establish minimum standards in order to avoid unfair competition.[135] The fact that the social partners deemed it necessary to reach a specific agreement is not mentioned as such. And as the agreement was entered into at the initiative of the social partners themselves, the Commission performed an impact assessment before putting the agreement before Council. The proposals on the older working time agreements contain little information on this point. As regards the agreement in the railway sector the Commission merely states that it has already given its support to the negotiations between the social partners in this field during the Transport Council's deliberations on the 'second railways package' on 28 March 2003. Hence, the agreement fitted into the work plan of the Commission.[136]

A more straightforward reference to the autonomy of the social partners can be found in the proposal implementing the agreement on prevention from sharp injuries of 2009. In its assessment of the subsidiarity requirement the Commission largely defers to the social partners: 'The fact that the substantive provisions of the Agreement incorporated in the proposal were drafted by the legitimate representatives of workers and employers acting at EU level (i.e. those most concerned by the various measures on the ground) is another guarantee of respect for the principle of subsidiarity.'[137] However, as is evidenced by the word 'another', this argument is apparently not conclusive in and by itself. A similar reference to the social partners' assessment of the need for action is made in the proposal regarding the revision of the Parental Leave Directive of the same year.[138] However, in that case the Commission also checks whether the agreement is overly prescriptive and detailed

[133] COM(97) 392, *supra* note 132, at 6.

[134] COM(2014) 452, *supra* note 54, at 9.

[135] SEC(2009) 92, *supra* note 111.

[136] COM(2005)32, *supra* note 109. The published proposals on the other agreements do not contain an explanatory memorandum.

[137] COM(2009) 577, *supra* note 59, para. 3.3, at 10.

[138] COM(2009) 410, *supra* note 93, para. 3.3, at 7–8.

and starts with stating that goals of the agreement can only be attained at EU level. The arguments used here refer to the fact that the agreement is meant to update an existing directive and aims to create a level playing field in a crucial aspect of reconciling work, private, and family life. The proposal on the Maritime Labour Convention of 2008 again mentions the agreement between the social partners as (only) one of the arguments in assessing subsidiarity, together with arguments regarding the international character of the economic sector covered by the agreement and the need for minimum standards in order to avoid social dumping.

With regard to the most recent agreement in our sample, the work in fishing agreement of 2012, it is interesting to note that even though negotiations started at the invitation of the Commission and the legal services delivered a positive legal opinion as regards compliance with EU law, the Commission announced it would perform a full costs/benefits analysis before submitting a proposal to Council. It did so in the progress report on occupational health, first semester 2014.[139] In the same report the Commission announced that it had contracted an external study with regard to the hairdresser agreement of 2010, in order to better assess the added value of the agreement. Both collective agreements were meant to become operational in areas prioritized by the Commission in its 2007 Action Plan for reducing administrative burdens.[140] Both were put on hold by the previous Commission pending further investigation and at the time the manuscript was written still awaited implementation.[141]

Accordingly, one may conclude from the materials available that the Commission does check the agreements between the social partners against the requirements of appropriateness, subsidiarity, and proportionality. The fact that the social partners agreed on the need for EU action is important but not in itself deemed to be conclusive. In recent cases, this scrutiny seems to have intensified. The Commission pays less deference to the social partners but will perform a cost/benefit analysis and some form of impact assessment in case these have not already been performed in the earlier stages of consultation. This strict scrutiny of the content of EU collective agreements is in line with a stricter assessment of all types of EU regulation and also fits the deregulatory agenda of the Commission, but seems to clash with the autonomy of the social partners at EU level.

[139] Information from the Commission, Progress report on OSH activity—First Semester 2014, 22 May 2014.

[140] See Communication from the Commission of 24 January 2007 to the Council, the European Parliament, the European Economic and Social Committee and the Committee of the Regions—Action Programme for Reducing Administrative Burdens in the European Union, COM(2007) 23, in which both working environment/employment relations and fisheries are listed as priority areas.

[141] Since then, the Council adopted Directive (EU) 2017/159 of 19 December 2016 implementing the Agreement concerning the implementation of the Work in Fishing Convention, 2007 of the International Labour Organisation, concluded on 21 May 2012 between the General Confederation of Agricultural Cooperatives in the European Union (Cogeca), the European Transport Workers' Federation (ETF) and the Association of National Organisations of Fishing Enterprises in the European Union (Europêche) (Text with EEA relevance)—not yet in force.

7. Outlook

The social partners at EU level play an important role both as stakeholders and as co-regulators. The output analysis of the social dialogue shows that the strictly normative, regulatory instruments referred to as EU collective agreements are a small minority within the overall production of texts and instruments. Within the group of collective agreements, the agreements put before council for implementation by Council decision form an important subgroup. These latter instruments interact with the overall EU legislative framework in a variety of ways: they may implement international obligations taken on by the EU and/or the Member States, they may derogate from a general framework directive or specify the obligation contained in such. In those cases, the collective agreements need to be transposed into an EU instrument in order to be effective. This reliance on Article 155 TFEU is caused in part by the almost complete absence of genuine opening clauses at European level. For this reason the sectoral agreements on working time could not attain the required legal effect but for a Council decision transposing them into an EU instrument; however, in the areas where the existing EU legislative framework does not intervene with national implementation, the social partners may rely on the extension mechanism to ensure an even level of implementation. Research has shown that, to date, the autonomous implementation route has not resulted in full implementation in all Member States.

In the past, the Commission has used the social dialogue to further EU social policy and circumvent political deadlocks in Council. In its policy documents of the time, social dialogue is described as an important element of EU governance. However, this happy cohabitation relied on converging interests between the social partners and the Commission. Currently, this convergence seems to have come to an end. In its REFIT communication the Commission stressed that the way in which the Commission prepares regulation has changed significantly over recent years. Reduction of the administrative burden imposed on businesses, and in particular SMEs, is one of the key policy objectives and a touchstone for any regulatory proposal. One of the areas which are prioritized for screening within the REFIT agenda is safety and health in the workplace.[142] This domain also includes the regulation of working time. As the overview of EU collective agreements has shown, it is particularly this domain which has been regulated by EU collective agreements. This explains the current clash between the Commission and social partners: their policies might well be at cross-purposes.

The discrepancy between the agenda of the social partners and the policy agenda of government is a phenomenon which is also known in those national systems in which collective agreements are extended by government decree. For example, in the Netherlands a fierce debate took place in 2004 when the government's wage policy

[142] Communication from the Commission of 2 October 2013 to the European Parliament, the Council, the European Economic and Social Committee and the Committee of the Regions—Regulatory Fitness and Performance (REFIT): Results and Next Steps, COM(2013) 685 final, at 2.

was not followed by the sectoral social partners in their negotiations. At the time the Minister threatened not to extend the agreements which were contrary to official policy—in this case by not respecting the wage ceiling proposed by the government and the trialogue.[143] The EU social dialogue has specific characteristics which make the problem even more difficult. Both the absence of direct norm-setting competence for the social partners at EU level and the absence of effective autonomous implementation increase the pressure on the route of Article 155 TFEU. Meanwhile the Commission, when evaluating the agreement between the social partners, is caught between horizontal and vertical subsidiarity.

Subsidiarity in EU law is a judiciable principle which lies at the heart of EU competence. But it is also a highly politicized concept often leading to an overall assessment of the 'appropriateness' of a specific action. Several authors have stressed that it is not up to the Commission to make a final judgement on this—the social partners should decide on the appropriateness of their action.[144] However, that conclusion does not sit well with the overall structure of EU competence. But even if we acknowledge that a Council decision ex-Article 155 TFEU is bound by the requirements of subsidiarity and proportionality as well as the requirement regarding SMEs, it is questionable whether the Commission should have a power of veto in this regard. We know from the UEAPME case that representative organizations may challenge a Council decision to make an agreement binding. However, there is no decision yet on the question whether these organizations may also challenge the decision by the Commission not to submit a proposal to the Council. And if so, whether the European courts would be willing to overrule the assessment of the Commission both as regards subsidiarity and as to the impact of the agreement on SMEs. This may be tested if and when the Commission actually does decide not to submit a proposal on the hairdressers' agreement. There are interesting times ahead.

[143] Christiaanse and Joosten, *supra* note 108. A similar discussion took place in the 1990s: Zalm, 'Betekenis en toekomst van de AVV', *ESB* (1992), 364 ff. See in a comparative perspective Dorssemont, 'De binding van werkgevers aan collectieve arbeidsovereenkomsten – Enkele beschouwingen over juridische factoren die binding bevorderen of verzwakken', 13/2 *Arbeidsrechtelijke Annotaties* (2014), at 37.

[144] B. Bercusson, *European Labour Law* (1996), at 542–543; Riesenhuber, *supra* note 57, at 159; Dorssemont, 'Some Reflection on the Origin, Problems and Perspectives of the European Social Dialogue', in M. De Vos (ed.), *A Decade beyond Maastricht* (2003) 3, at 27.

6

Treaties between EU Member States as Quasi-Instruments of EU Law

Bruno De Witte and Thibault Martinelli

1. Introduction

This chapter deals with international treaties concluded between Member States of the European Union (EU), but limited to the cases where such treaties can be considered as *quasi-instruments* of EU law. In some other cases, treaties between EU Member States are, instead, an *integral part* of the EU legal order. This applies, quite obviously, to the so-called founding Treaties, namely the current Treaty on European Union (TEU) and Treaty on the Functioning of the European Union (TFEU) and all their predecessors since the Treaty of Paris establishing the European Coal and Steel Community; they form the bulk of EU primary law, and will not be considered here. In still other cases, situated at the other end of the spectrum, there are bilateral and multilateral treaties concluded between EU Member States (with or without some third states) that *stand apart* from EU law; the Member States conclude such treaties in their capacity as sovereign states to deal with subject matter which is either entirely outside EU competence or within the shared competence of the EU and its Member States. Since the scope of the EU's shared competence has expanded with each Treaty revision, most of those inter-state treaties will have *some* connection with EU law. For example, if riparian states conclude an agreement to protect the aquatic quality of a common river basin, they will need to take into account the rules of EU environmental law;[1] if EU states conclude one of many bilateral treaties to avoid double taxation of companies and individuals, that bilateral convention may not unduly discriminate against EU citizens;[2] and if they conclude agreements on

[1] See the *Accord international sur la Meuse*, signed in Gent in 2002 between France, Germany, Luxembourg, the Netherlands, Belgium, and the three Belgian Regions, which refers to EU environmental law standards. The text of the agreement is published on the website of the *Commission Internationale de la Meuse*, created by the agreement and established in Liège; http://www.meuse-maas.be/Accueil.aspx (last visited 27 February 2017).

[2] See T. O'Shea, *EU Tax Law and Double Tax Conventions* (2008); Maitrot de la Motte, 'Les conséquences de la subsidiarité des conventions fiscales internationales dans leur rapport avec le droit de l'Union européenne', in L. Burgorgue Larsen *et al.* (eds), *Les interactions normatives, droit de l'Union européenne et droit international* (2012) 211. One among the several cases in which the ECJ examined

educational cooperation, benefits granted to each other's nationals must, in principle, be extended to the resident citizens of other EU states.[3] In relation to those treaties, the normal rules on the relation between EU and national law apply: the EU states can freely conclude them, as long as they do not deal with matters that come within the EU's exclusive competence, and as long as they contain no rules that conflict with EU law. Those two rules of thumb are generally accepted in principle, but their practical application is sometimes complex and controversial. A recent example of such controversy is the fate of the bilateral investment treaties concluded between what are current EU Member States, but at a time when one of the two parties was not yet a Member State; this category typically includes investment treaties concluded by Central and East European states before they joined the EU. There are major issues not only of substantive conflict between their content and EU internal market law, but the Commission also claims that the entire subject matter of those instruments now falls, since the entry into force of the Lisbon Treaty, within exclusive EU competence.[4] These interesting legal issues will not be explored further here. This chapter will, rather, focus on an intermediate category of Member State treaties that are neither an integral part of EU law (as the founding Treaties are) nor completely outside the EU legal order, but can be considered as *quasi-instruments of EU law*. They fulfil a functional role that is similar to genuine EU law instruments such as regulations and directives, but they do not formally belong to secondary EU law, since the source of their existence is an international agreement between states, rather than a decision by one or more EU institution(s). Their close ties with EU law manifest themselves in various ways which will be illustrated in this chapter. For example, those agreements might have been concluded in connection with the founding Treaties; the EU institutions might have collaborated in their negotiation or implementation; primary EU law may have provided for their conclusion or referred to their existence; or they may have been integrated later on within the EU legal order.

Two broad types of agreements that thus gravitate around or towards the EU legal order can be distinguished: parallel or *complementary agreements*[5] (concluded by all EU Member States) and *partial* or *inter se* agreements (concluded by a subset of them).[6] These two types of agreements have a different underlying *raison d'être*. On the one hand, parallel agreements 'complement' the EU legal order. This complementarity can take different forms: ensuring the functioning of EU institutions, implementing EU objectives in ways foreseen by the founding Treaties, or supplementing EU rules. On the other hand, partial agreements are a means of differentiated

the compatibility with EU law of a bilateral tax convention is Case C-336/96, *Robert Gilly v. Directeur des services fiscaux du Bas-Rhin*, [1998] ECR I-02793 (ECLI:EU:C:1998:221).

[3] See Case C-235/87, *Annunziata Matteucci v. Communauté française of Belgium et al.*, [1988] ECR 05589 (ECLI:EU:C:1988:460), at para. 23. See discussion of the implications of this judgment by M. Klamert, *The Principle of Loyalty in EU Law* (2014), at 282–286.

[4] For discussion of those legal issues, see Dimopoulos, 'The Validity and Applicability of International Investment Agreements between EU Member States under EU and International Law', 48 *Common Market Law Review* (2011) 63.

[5] This expression is used by T.C. Hartley, *The Foundations of European Community Law* (5th edn, 2003), at 98, and will be adopted in this chapter.

[6] The term '*inter se* agreement' is used in international law to indicate agreements concluded by some but not all of the parties to an earlier treaty relating broadly speaking to the same subject matter.

integration: they allow a subset of like-minded states to pursue objectives of European integration among themselves and outside the EU constitutional framework. Those two categories will be examined in turn in Sections 2 and 3 below, after which Sections 4 and 5 will explore in somewhat more detail two areas in which partial agreements were recently, and rather controversially, used: the legal response to the euro-area crisis (Section 4) and the long-expected creation of an EU patent protection system (Section 5). Section 6 will draw some general conclusions. The analysis, it should be emphasized, is limited to agreements which Member States conclude *among themselves*. The much more numerous agreements which the EU Member States conclude *with third countries* will not be covered, even though they, too, may occasionally constitute instruments of EU law, namely when the states act on behalf of the EU on the international plane.[7]

2. Complementary Agreements

Our analysis of the category of complementary agreements will adopt an evolutionary perspective, since those agreements have followed a distinct historical trajectory with phases of abundant use followed by phases (such as the present one) of rather limited use.

Historically, one type of complementary agreement that emerged soon after the entry into force of the European Economic Community (EEC) Treaty was that of 'the decisions or acts of the representatives of the Member States meeting within the Council'. They are still being concluded today on various occasions. Legally, they are distinguishable from regular acts of the Council even though they are approved during (or, as the expression goes, 'in the margin of') sessions of the Council. Even though they are designated as 'acts' or 'decisions', they are in fact international agreements concluded in simplified form. The Council is merely used as a forum within which the representatives of the Member States, 'taking off their hat' as members of the Council, negotiate and conclude those international agreements. Since those 'decisions of representatives' are not part of the list of institutional acts mentioned in the founding Treaties, the rules on the adoption and implementation of Council acts do not apply to them and they fall outside the founding Treaties' system of judicial review.[8] There is no reference to them on the Council's rules of procedure either. As instruments of public international law, their effect is defined by the national legal order of each Member State and not by EU law.[9]

[7] See the analysis by Cremona, 'Member State Agreements as Union Law', in E. Cannizzaro, P. Palchetti, and R. Wessel (eds), *International Law as Law of the European Union* (2012) 291; and by Rosas, 'The Status in EU Law of International Agreements Concluded by EU Member States', 34 *Fordham International Law Journal* (2011) 1304.

[8] Joined Cases C-181/91 and C-248/91, *Parliament v. Council and Commission (Emergency Aid)*, [1993] ECR I-03685, at para. 15: 'acts adopted by representatives of the Member States acting, not in their capacity as members of the Council, but as representatives of their governments, and thus collectively exercising the powers of the Member States, are not subject to judicial review'.

[9] Pescatore, 'Remarques sur la nature juridique des "décisions des représentants des Etats membres réunis au sein du Conseil"', *Sociaal Economische Wetgeving* (1966) 579.

These 'decisions of representatives' are frequently used in the EU's external relations, in particular to express the common views of the EU states whenever they engage in the negotiation or conclusion of mixed agreements alongside the EU.[10] 'Decisions' or 'acts of the representatives' were also used as a 'domestic' legal tool since the early days of the EEC. In several cases, the founding Treaties require (or did require) the Member States to take a specific collective decision, for example, to define the seat of the EU institutions,[11] to appoint members of the European Court of Justice,[12] or to organize the diplomatic and consular representation of European citizens abroad.[13] In these cases, the 'acts of the representatives', despite being formally instruments of international law, have a very strong connection with EU law: Member States are under an EU law obligation to adopt them and they can even prove to be essential to ensuring the institutional functioning of the EU. Another indication of their strong link with EU law is the fact that they form part of the *acquis communautaire.* New Member States accede to them automatically by virtue of the Act of accession to the EU.[14]

In addition to those international agreements in simplified form, EEC law also provided, from the start, for the conclusion of fully fledged international treaties which were called *conventions* (a term frequently used for treaties elaborated within the framework of an international organization, e.g. in the Council of Europe). In its Article 220 EEC, the original version of the Treaty of Rome set out a framework for the negotiation of such conventions in four domains in particular: (i) the abolition of double taxation; (ii) the mutual recognition of companies; (iii) the mutual recognition and enforcement of judgments; and (iv) the protection of persons and the enjoyment and protection of rights under the same conditions as those accorded by each state to its own nationals. At the time of drafting the EEC Treaty, those 'Community conventions' were seen as a more suitable instrument for unifying the Member States' laws in those areas, rather than the EEC regulations and directives whose nature and use were not yet clearly established.

Article 220 EEC left a wide margin of appreciation to the Member States. They were invited to enter into negotiations on those subjects, but not compelled to do so.[15] Since this soft obligation was placed upon all Member States collectively, it was generally admitted that only parallel agreements (i.e. signed by all Member States) could be concluded on the basis of Article 220 EEC. The framework set out by that

[10] See, for their use in external relations practice, and some of the legal controversies this recently caused, the chapter by Alan Dashwood in this volume, Section 6.

[11] Article 341 TFEU ('by common accord of the governments of the Member States').

[12] Article 253 TFEU ('by common accord of the governments of the Member States').

[13] Previously provided for by Article 8c EEC. See Decision of the Representatives of the Government of the Member States meeting within the Council of 19 December 1995 regarding protection for citizens of the European Union by diplomatic and consular representations, OJ 1995 L 314/73. Today, Article 23 TFEU provides for the adoption of EU directives on this matter.

[14] Articles 3 or 4 of the Acts of accession to the EU of the new Member States contain a standard language for that purpose. See for example Article 3(1) of Act of accession of Bulgaria and Romania ('Bulgaria and Romania accede to the decisions and agreements adopted by the Representatives of the Governments of the Member States meeting within the Council'), OJ 2005 L 157/29.

[15] See Case C-137/84, *Mutsch*, [1985] ECR 02681 (ECLI:EU:C:1985:335), at para. 11: Article 220 'merely defines a number of matters on which the Member States are to enter into negotiations with each other "so far as is necessary"'.

provision was incomplete; in particular, the role that European Community (EC) institutions would play in the conclusion or implementation of Community conventions was left undefined. In practice, though, there was combined action by the Member States and the EC institutions which reinforced the informal and legal links between Community conventions and the EC legal order. As a result, Community conventions bore the characteristics of EC law and displayed a high degree of 'supranationality'.[16] At the negotiation stage, Community conventions largely relied on the EC institutional structure. Although it had no legal right of initiative, the European Commission instigated the implementation of the programme set out in Article 220 EEC. The Council provided the setting within which the representatives of the Member States signed the conventions. Consequently, the procedure leading to their conclusion was close to the one followed, at that time, for the adoption of EC secondary law. This was especially so considering the low degree of involvement of the then Assembly in the integration process, and the fact that directives for the harmonization of laws under Article 100 EEC also had to be adopted unanimously, like the conventions.

In 1968, when negotiating the Brussels Convention on jurisdiction and enforcement,[17] the first and most successful case of an Article 220 convention, the Member States were concerned that a standalone convention would be a weak harmonizing instrument without an authoritative interpreter responsible for ensuring its uniform application across the Community. To remedy this problem, it was decided to extend the preliminary ruling jurisdiction of the European Court of Justice to the Brussels Convention via an additional Protocol annexed to the Convention. As soon as cases were brought before it under that Protocol, the Court of Justice reinforced the 'hybrid' character of the Brussels Convention. The Convention was to be interpreted in the same way as EC legal acts[18] 'having regard both to its principles and objectives and *to its relationship with the [EEC] Treaty*'.[19] In view of the aim pursued by the Convention, it must, according to the Court, override any conflicting national legislation.[20] As a result of this process, initiated by the Member States through the conclusion of a protocol and later refined by the Court of Justice, the Brussels Convention displayed two of the distinct constitutional characteristics of

[16] Schütze, 'EC Law and International Agreements of the Member States – An Ambivalent Relationship', 9 *Cambridge Yearbook of European Legal Studies* (2006–2007) 387, at 418–419.

[17] Convention 90/C 189/02 on Jurisdiction and the Enforcement of Judgment in Civil and Commercial Matters, OJ 1990 C 189/2 (consolidated version incorporating several revisions of the original Convention from 1968).

[18] See Rasmussen, 'A New Generation of Community Law? Reflections on the Handling by the Court of Justice of the Protocol of 1971 Relating to the Interpretation of the Brussels Convention on Jurisdiction and Enforcement of Judgements', 15 *Common Market Law Review* (1978) 249, at 261. Later on, the Court of Justice ruled that the interpretation given to the Brussels Convention was also valid for the interpretation of the equivalent provisions of the Regulation which succeeded the Convention in 2001, thereby 'retroactively' confirming the similarity of the methods of interpretation used. See, *inter alia* Case C-180/06, *Renate Ilsinger v. Martin Dreschers*, [2009] ECR I-03961 (ECLI: EU:C:2009:303), at para. 41.

[19] Case C-12/76, *Industrie Tessili Italiana Como v. Dunlop AG*, [1976] ECR 01473 (ECLI:EU: C:1976:133), at para. 9 (emphasis added).

[20] Case C-288/82, *Ferdinand M.J.J. Duijnstee v. Lodewijk Goderbauer*, [1983] ECR 03663 (ECLI: EU:C:1983:326), at para. 14.

the EC legal order: use of the preliminary ruling mechanism and primacy of European over national law.

In the 1970s, a growing number of Community conventions were drafted and negotiated even beyond the scope of Article 220 EEC.[21] Commentators saw in this movement the rise of a 'new Community law' beyond the strict limits of the EEC legal order.[22] The Court of Justice recognized that the source of its jurisdiction over a Community convention was not to be found in Article 220 EEC itself but in the additional protocol annexed to that convention. It was thereby confirmed that Community conventions remained creatures of international law and that Article 220 EEC, unlike other provisions of the Treaty of Rome, was not a legal *basis* entrusting powers upon the common institutions created by the Member States but only a legal *reference* to their pre-existing treaty-making power.[23]

When the Community method came 'under increasing pressure'[24] in the 1990s, complementary agreements were used to fulfil a different function: pushing integration forward in politically sensitive areas where the recourse to the Community method would not have been a politically acceptable solution. Article 220 EEC had originally been used to further the completion of the internal market in fields where it was perceived that the Community had no competence to act under the EEC Treaty. With the conclusion of the Arbitration Convention on the abolition of double taxation in 1990, that original understanding changed.[25] The Commission had first proposed a directive on this subject, on the basis of the harmonization clause of Article 100 EEC.[26] In order to unblock the negotiation process, the proposed directive was turned into a convention based on Article 220 EEC.[27] In this way, a specific issue closely related to the fiscal sovereignty of the Member States was made subject to a different, less 'supranational' regime, so that a political agreement could more easily be reached. Far from sharing the characteristics of EU law, the Arbitration Convention displays the 'traditional traits' of an international treaty. The idea of granting jurisdiction to the European Court of Justice was rejected in this case. Instead, an arbitration body settles disputes over the interpretation of the Convention.

[21] See, e.g. Draft Convention on the International Merger of *Sociétés Anonymes*, 27 September 1972, *Bulletin of the European Communities*, Supplement 13/73; Preliminary Draft of a Convention on Bankruptcy, Winding-Up, Arrangements, Composition and Similar Proceedings, 4 June 1973, Commission Document No J.J27/1/XIV/70. For a Community convention falling outside the scope of Article 220 EEC, see in particular, Convention 76/76/EEC for the European Patent for the Common Market, OJ 1976 L 17 (which never entered into force).

[22] See, for an author insisting on the importance of the Community conventions for the European integration process, Rasmussen, *supra* note 18; and Hauschild, 'L'importance des conventions communautaires pour la création d'un droit communautaire', in 11 *Revue trimestrielle de droit européen* (1975) 4.

[23] Schütze, *supra* note 16, at 418.

[24] R. Dehousse, 'The Community Method at Sixty', in R. Dehousse (ed.), *The 'Community Method'– Obstinate or Obsolete?* (2011) 3, at 3.

[25] Convention 90/436/EEC on the elimination of double taxation in connection with the adjustment of profits of associated enterprises, OJ 1990 L 225/10.

[26] Proposal for a Council Directive, OJ 1976 C 301/4.

[27] For a critical analysis of this process, see Scholsem, 'EC: The Proposal for a Council Directive on the Elimination of Double Taxation (Arbitration Procedure)', 11–12 *Intertax* (1982) 424.

Shortly afterwards, alternative methods to the Community method were formalized by the pillar structure put in place by the Maastricht Treaty. Within the third pillar of Justice and Home Affairs, a new legal reference to complementary agreements was added to the founding Treaties, in what was then Article K.3 TEU. Similarly to the Arbitration Convention, the choice for inter-state conventions was inspired by the wish to preserve the control by the Member States on the adoption and application of these instruments dealing with areas at the core of Member State sovereignty. Article K.3 conventions differed from their Article 220 EEC counterparts in the way they related to 'mainstream' Community law. Their regime remained governed by a separate Treaty (the Treaty on European Union). There was therefore no ground for relying on the principles enshrined in the EC Treaty so as to confer EC-like primacy to Article K.3 conventions.[28] In addition, institutional connections between Article K.3 conventions and the EU institutions were much more formalized: on the initiative of the Member States, the Council was entrusted with the tasks of establishing those conventions and of adopting their implementing measures. The Commission was not part of that process.

While the normative production of the EU continued to increase over the years, the number of new Community conventions sharply declined after the 1970s.[29] Major legal weaknesses made them unattractive instruments of European cooperation compared to regulations or directives.[30] First, the ad hoc negotiation of a mechanism of preliminary references to the Court proved time consuming. Second, the entry into force of conventions was subject to unanimous ratification by the Member States. The failure of one signatory state to ratify them could prevent their entry into force. Third, conventions proved to be ill-suited for a dynamic EC legal order that was expanding geographically. New Member States had to accede to 'decisions or acts of the representatives' by virtue of the Acts of accession to the EC, but their accession to Community conventions was made subject to further negotiations with the other Member States.[31] As a result, accession agreements to each Community convention had to be ratified by national parliaments upon each accession of a new state to the EC.[32] The Rome Convention on the law applicable to contractual

[28] Müller-Graff, 'The Legal Bases of the Third Pillar and its Position in the Framework of the Union Treaty', 31 *Common Market Law Review* (1994) 493, at 495.

[29] On average, around 50 directives and 1000 regulations were adopted every year in the 1970s. This increased to 80 directives and 1400 regulations in the 1980s and to 95 directives and 2100 regulations in the 1990s (calculations made on the basis of the data compiled by Dimiter Toshkov, 'Legislative production in the EU 1967–2012', available at http://www.dimiter.eu/Data.html (last visited 6 January 2017). In contrast, while a dozen Community conventions were negotiated in the 1970s, only two were concluded in the 1980s and 1990s.

[30] For a detailed explanation of the legal advantages of EEC legal acts over Community conventions, see Schwartz, 'Voies d'uniformisation du droit dans la Communauté européenne: règlements de la Communauté ou conventions entre les États membres', 105 *Journal du droit international* (1978) 751.

[31] See, e.g. Article 3(1) of the Act of Accession of Denmark, UK and Ireland to the EEC, OJ 1972 L 73/14.

[32] For the accession of Bulgaria and Romania in 2005 and of Croatia in 2013, the system was simplified. Those states have acceded to the then still in force Community conventions and Article K.3 conventions in virtue of the Acts of accession to the EEC Treaty at a date determined by a Council decision. See Article 3(3) of the Act of Accession of Bulgaria and Romania, OJ 2005 L 157/29; Article 3(4) of the Act of Accession of Croatia, OJ 2012 L 112/21.

obligations signed in 1980 illustrates all those deficiencies.[33] It took 24 years for the Member States to negotiate, sign, and ratify a Protocol granting jurisdiction over the Convention to the European Court of Justice.[34] In between, four agreements had to be negotiated to allow incoming Member States to accede to the Rome Convention.[35] In the first case that reached the Court in 2008,[36] the Court was placed in a situation where it was not really giving a first interpretation of the Convention rules but, rather, arbitrating between diverging interpretations developed by national courts over the years.[37] In the 1990s, the elaboration of Article K.3 conventions ran across the same difficulties as those negotiated on the basis of Article 220 EEC. As a result of the unanimous ratification requirement, only five of the ten 'third pillar' conventions have ever entered into force.[38] In an attempt to address this problem, Member States used ingenuous legal techniques designed to allow the provisional application of a convention pending its entry into force. In addition, intense discussions took place to define the scope of the Court of Justice's jurisdiction.[39] So far, though, the Court has never been called to interpret any of the Article K.3 conventions, even among those that remain in force today.

The Treaty of Amsterdam, in 1999, considerably reduced the scope of the third pillar (now limited to police cooperation and criminal justice, and no longer including immigration, asylum, and civil justice), and thereby also the areas in which Article K.3 conventions could be concluded. In addition, the competences of the EU were extended to encompass almost all the areas previously covered by Article 220 EEC (renumbered at Amsterdam as Article 293 EC). The Brussels and the Rome Conventions were subsequently turned into EU regulations.[40] Some of the Article K.3 conventions that never entered into force served as the basis for the adoption of EU legal acts.[41] The Treaty of Lisbon further confirmed this downward trend by

[33] Convention 80/934/EEC on the law applicable to contractual obligations, OJ 1980 L 266/1.

[34] Protocol on the interpretation by the Court of Justice of the Rome Convention of 19 June 1980 on the law applicable to contractual obligations, OJ 1989 L 48/1.

[35] Convention 84/297/EEC, OJ 1984 L 146/1; Convention 92/529/EEC, OJ 1992 L 333/1; Convention 97/C 15/02, OJ 1997 C 15/10; Convention 2005/C 169/01, OJ 2005 C 169/1.

[36] Case C-133/08, *Intercontainer v. Balkenende Oosthuizen*, [2009] I-09687 (ECLI:EU:C:2009:617).

[37] In this regard, the Opinion of the Advocate General in the case is revealing. The AG surveys the varying national interpretations of the provisions of the Convention at stake in the case and distinguishes between majority and minority positions taken by the highest national courts. See Case C-133/08, *Intercontainer v. Balkenende Oosthuizen*, Opinion of AG Bot, [2009] I-09687 (ECLI:EU: C:2009:319), at paras 71–73.

[38] E.g. some Article K.3 conventions were equipped with early application mechanisms. Member States, which had already ratified a convention, could declare that they would apply them in relation to the other Member States that had made the same declaration. See, e.g. Article 13(4) of the Convention drawn up on the basis of Article K.3(2)(c) of the Treaty on European Union on the fight against corruption involving officials of the European Communities or officials of Member States of the European Union, OJ 1997 C 195/2.

[39] S. Peers, *EU Justice and Home Affairs Law*, (3rd edn, 2011), at 15.

[40] Council Regulation 44/2001, OJ 2001 L 12/1 (Brussels Regulation); Regulation 593/2008, OJ 2008 L 177/6 (Rome I Regulation).

[41] See, e.g. Council Regulation (EC) 1348/2000 on the service in the Member States of judicial and extrajudicial documents in civil or commercial matters, OJ 2000 L 160/37 (whose substance is in essence taken over from the Convention on the service in the Member States of the European Union of judicial and extrajudicial documents in civil or commercial matters, OJ 1997 C 261).

abolishing the 'pillar structure' and by removing the former Articles 220 EEC and K.3 from the text of the founding Treaties.

The repeal of those Treaty provisions does not affect the validity of the few conventions that have not been 'readopted' as EU law instruments. They remain in force, as the source of their existence is the treaty-making power of the Member States, and not the reference made to their conclusion in the (previous text of the) founding Treaties.[42] Nor does the repeal of those Treaty provisions mean that Member States are no longer allowed to conclude parallel agreements in connection with the operation of the EU. It only means that these agreements are no longer mentioned as a normal category of instruments of EU cooperation. Indeed, even without being invited to do so by a specific provision of the TEU or the TFEU, the Member States are free in principle to regulate certain matters which are connected to the substance of the founding Treaties and which are important for the achievement of their objectives, in the form of an international agreement concluded between them, provided that, by doing so, they do not disregard their EU obligations. Member States have sometimes opted for this instrument for political reasons (absent any obligation or encouragement to do so under the founding Treaties); namely, where a formal Council act did not seem appropriate to them. A good and longstanding example of this is the agreements on financial contributions allocated to developing countries of the ACP group within the framework of the European Development Fund (EDF). The original reason for this 'escape' from EU law seems to have been that the Member States could thus decide to use a specific contribution key for the EDF that was different from their general contribution key to the EU budget, so as to reflect the 'historical ties' of some EU states (mainly France and the UK) with a large number of beneficiaries of EDF funding. The Court of Justice in the *Bangladesh* case[43] confirmed the validity of this technique and there is no reason why this would be different today. Indeed, the Member States concluded a further 'internal agreement' (as it is called) on their EDF contributions in post-Lisbon times.[44]

Still, complementary agreements may seem problematic when concluded in policy areas in which the EU possesses (shared) law-making competence, and where therefore an act of secondary EU law could instead have been adopted. By 'reverting' to international law without it being legally necessary, Member States escape the procedural and substantive guarantees of EU law. The institutional balance between the Council, the Parliament, and the Commission is swept aside and the EU regime for the protection of fundamental rights and for access to information does not apply. In any case the existence of this 'rival' option of concluding parallel international agreements has become a largely theoretical issue. Apart from the 'decisions' or 'acts

[42] Article 9 of the Protocol No 36 on transitional provisions annexed to the Treaty of Lisbon (OJ 2012 C 326/322) confirms, quite unnecessarily, that the legal effects of Article K.3 conventions that are still in force will be preserved.

[43] Joined Cases C-181/91 and C-248/91, *supra* note 8.

[44] The internal agreement currently in force for the financial framework period 2014–2020 was published in OJ 2013 L 210/1.

of the representatives' designed to ensure the proper institutional functioning of the EU, very few complementary agreements are still being concluded today.[45]

One can draw two conclusions from this historical overview. First, due to the superior normative qualities of 'real' EU law, complementary agreements have fallen into almost complete disuse. Their historical impact on the EU legal order is nevertheless not negligible. The establishment of the third pillar, within which Article K.3 conventions were a prominent legal instrument, paved the way for later EU legislative activities in the policy domain of Justice and Home Affairs.[46] Similarly, key EU legislative texts in force today such as the Brussels and Rome I Regulations have their origin in older Community conventions. Second, the trajectory of those complementary agreements has followed the expansion of the EU policy agenda and of the scope *ratione materiae* of the EU legal order. Originally, they were aimed mainly at furthering the completion of the internal market, whereas they later dealt with the policy field of Justice and Home Affairs. During the 'constitutionalization' era of the EU legal order of the 1960s and 1970s, Community conventions adopted one of the EC legal order's most distinctive features: the preliminary ruling procedure. The doctrines that marked the emerging constitutional nature of EC law (direct effect and primacy) were extended to the most successful of the Community conventions, namely the Brussels Convention. In the 1990s, when the Community method was viewed as too constraining to be extended to new policy domains, the Arbitration Convention and the Article K.3 conventions were used as an alternative, non-supranational, mode of pursuing the European integration process.

3. Partial Agreements

The political dynamics of the European integration process has always been marked by the existence of clubs of Member States that acted as 'subregional groupings'[47] through the conclusion of treaties. As exemplified by the Benelux Union,[48] such

[45] Among those rare examples one could mention (in addition to the one mentioned in the previous footnote): Convention on centralized customs clearance concerning the allocation of national collection costs retained when traditional own resources are made available to the EU budget, OJ 2009 C 92/1; Agreement between the Member States of the European Union, meeting within the Council, regarding the protection of classified information exchanged in the interests of the European Union, OJ 2011 C 202/13.

[46] On the importance of the third pillar as created by the Maastricht Treaty for the subsequent development of the field of Justice and Home Affairs, see Monar, 'Justice and Home Affairs: The Treaty of Maastricht as a Decisive Intergovernmental Gate Opener', 34 *Journal of European Integration* (2012) 717.

[47] This term was coined by J. Wouters and M. Vidal to designate the Benelux Union: 'Towards a Rebirth of Benelux?', 2 *Revue belge de droit international* (2007) 533.

[48] Treaty instituting the Benelux Economic Union 1958, 381 UNTS 167 amended by Treaty revising the Treaty instituting the Benelux Economic Union 2008, 2868 UNTS n°A-5471. Within this category, one can also mention the Franco-German bilateral alliance formalized early on by the Elysée Treaty of 1963, but which spread into a number of domains not covered by that Treaty; for a general view of this evolution, see U. Krotz and J. Schild (eds), *Shaping Europe: France, Germany, and Embedded Bilateralism from the Elysée Treaty to Twenty-First Politics* (2012). Further cases are the Nordic Cooperation and the Visegrad Group composed of the four Central European countries. The Nordic Cooperation is not a genuine *inter se* subsystem as it involves two third countries (Norway and Iceland) whereas the Visegrad Group has not been established by a formal treaty but by a mere 'declaration'.

'regional agreements' formalize alliances between like-minded states in consideration of their historical, geographical, or cultural proximity. Those regional *fora* are used to discuss policy issues related to the EU or to establish closer forms of cooperation in a wide variety of other domains, including by means of the conclusion of treaties. But those treaties are mostly kept quite separate, politically and institutionally, from the EU frame.

Starting in the 1980s, though, the practice of concluding partial agreements emerged. Such agreements were increasingly used as a means of differentiated integration to handle the growing heterogeneity of EU membership and the diverging aspirations of the EU Member States. The most prominent examples of such agreements, until recently, were the Schengen Agreement on the abolition of borders[49] concluded in 1985, its implementing Convention of 1990,[50] and the Prüm Convention on the stepping up of cross-border police cooperation in 2005.[51] Those treaties were characterized by the creation of an intergovernmental structure independent from the EU's institutional framework, and by their openly temporary character. Whereas Article 220 and K.3 conventions fulfilled a role that was functionally equivalent to EU secondary law by implementing the 'programme' laid down in the founding Treaties, the Schengen treaties and the Prüm Convention pursued EU objectives in ways that were not so clearly anticipated by the founding Treaties. In both instances, a subset of Member States pursued, by means of extra-EU agreements, the achievement of an EU objective on an intergovernmental basis with the openly admitted purpose to play 'a pioneering role' and to favour further integration within the EU framework. From that perspective, the Schengen Agreement and Convention, and the Prüm Convention, were thought to be temporary arrangements providing a testing ground for subsequent measures to be taken at the level of the EU. The Schengen Agreement did not include an expiry clause setting a time limit for its existence, but, in a separate declaration, the Schengen states announced that the content of the agreement they had concluded would serve them as a basis for the negotiation of equivalent measures to be adopted within the EU framework.[52] The Prüm Convention was also concluded for an indefinite duration[53] but its temporary character was embodied in one of its provisions according to which an initiative would be taken to incorporate the Convention into the EU framework on the basis of an assessment of its functioning.[54]

Whereas complementary agreements rely partly or entirely on the institutional machinery of the EU, the existence and implementation of the Schengen Agreement

[49] Agreement between the Governments of the States of the Benelux Economic Union, the Federal Republic of Germany and the French Republic on the gradual abolition of checks at their common borders, OJ 2000 L 239/13.

[50] Convention implementing the Schengen Agreement of 14 June 1985 between the Governments of the States of the Benelux Economic Union, the Federal Republic of Germany and the French Republic on the gradual abolition of checks at their common borders, OJ 2000 L 239/19.

[51] Prüm Convention of 27 May 2005 on the stepping up of cross-border cooperation, particularly in combating terrorism, cross-border crime, and illegal migration 2005, 2617 UNTS 3.

[52] This declaration is cited and discussed by Schutte, 'Schengen: its Meaning for the Free Movement of Persons in Europe', 28 *Common Market Law Review* (1991) 549, at 567–568.

[53] See Article 52(1) of the Prüm Convention, *supra* note 51.

[54] See Article 1(4) of the Prüm Convention, *supra* note 51.

and the Prüm Convention was independent from the EU institutions. The Court of Justice had no authority to interpret them.[55] Those two partial agreements were equipped with their own intergovernmental structure. The oversight and the implementation of the gradual abolition of checks at the borders operated by the Schengen Agreement and its Implementing Convention was left in the hands of an Executive Committee composed of Member State representatives. This implementation method gave rise to an entire set of legal instruments that remained for a large part unpublished.[56] Likewise, a Committee of Ministers was tasked to ensure the implementation of the Prüm Convention.[57]

Both 'Schengen' and 'Prüm' were indeed integrated within the EU legal order but through different legal techniques. The Schengen area was first set up by five countries but was very quickly enlarged to other Member States.[58] The Treaty of Amsterdam then brought the Schengen Agreement and its implementing measures within the boundaries of the EU legal order on the basis of an additional Protocol.[59] The Protocol empowered the Council to designate the legal bases for the measures forming the Schengen *acquis* without specifying which specific EU legal form they would take.[60] This left some uncertainties as to the effects of the Schengen rules and the way they would be interpreted by the Court of Justice post-Amsterdam.[61] In contrast, the substance of the Prüm Convention was directly transferred into a Council decision.[62]

When the Schengen Agreement was signed in 1985, there was not yet a built-in mechanism of differentiated integration within the EU constitutional framework. Around that time, systems of informal cooperation between subgroups of Member States were mushrooming in fields as varied as foreign affairs, defence, migration, and border controls. The Schengen model, in particular, raised criticism because its institutional structure had important deficits in terms of transparency, democratic

[55] The idea of conferring jurisdiction to the Court of Justice over the Convention implementing the Schengen Agreement had been supported by some Schengen States, but it did not happen. See Groenendijk, 'The Competence of the EC Court of Justice with Respect to Intergovernmental Treaties on Immigration and Asylum', 4 *International Journal of Refugee Law* (1992) 531, at 536.

[56] Yet, a large number of those Decisions of the Schengen Executive Committee formed part of the 'Schengen *acquis*' which was transported into the EU legal order after the Amsterdam Treaty's entry into force. They take over 300 pages in the 'Schengen *acquis*' collection published in OJ 2000 L 239.

[57] See Article 43 of the Prüm Convention, *supra* note 51.

[58] Agreements on the accession to the Convention implementing the Schengen Agreement of Italy (27 November 1990), Spain (25 June 1991), Portugal (25 June 1991), Greece (6 November 1992), Austria (28 April 1995), Denmark (19 December 1996), Finland (19 December 1996), and Sweden (19 December 1996), OJ 2000 L 239.

[59] Protocol No 19 on the Schengen *acquis* integrated into the framework of the European Union, OJ 2012 C 326/290.

[60] Council Decision 1999/436/EC, OJ 1999 L 176/17.

[61] On the complex issues raised, at the time, by this Schengen integration operation, see among others: Peers, '*Caveat Emptor?* Integrating the Schengen *Acquis* into the European Union Legal Order', 2 *Cambridge Yearbook of European Legal Studies* (2000) 87; Leidenmühler, 'The Incorporation of the Schengen *acquis* into the Framework of the EU by Example of the 'Ne Bis in Idem' Principle', 5 *The European Legal Forum* (2002) 253.

[62] Council Decision 2008/615/JHA (so-called 'Prüm Decision'), OJ 2008 L 210/1. Some elements of the Prüm Convention have not been incorporated in the EU framework via the Prüm Decision. See on this, Answer given by Ms Malmström on behalf of the Commission (22 February 2013) to the Question E-011693/12, OJ 2013 C 340 E/463.

control, and judicial protection.[63] Those concerns would be all the more serious if those legal constructions were to become effectively permanent rather than temporary. In reaction to this evolution, the Treaty of Amsterdam put in place the *general* enhanced cooperation procedure in order to provide an intra-EU alternative for intergovernmental *avant-gardes* that could develop in the future. Upon the fulfillment of rather onerous procedural requirements, a minimum number of Member States could henceforth engage in cooperation among themselves *within* the four corners of EU law rather than outside. In addition, the integration of the Schengen *acquis* into the EU legal order gave rise to a specific mechanism of differentiated integration within the EU legal order, organized by the (so-called) Schengen Protocol.

What is now, post-Amsterdam, the legal interplay between the enhanced cooperation procedure and extra-EU systems of variable geometry? Could one argue that enhanced cooperation should have priority over extra-EU agreements, meaning that a group of Member States should first try to use the former mechanism before engaging in the latter?[64] To date, the European Court of Justice has never directly addressed that question. In any case, the introduction of the enhanced cooperation procedure was not explicitly framed as prohibiting schemes of closer cooperation on EU-related matters outside the EU framework. It should rather be seen as an attempt by Member States to discipline their own behaviour in order to avert the risk of proliferation of those extra-EU regimes. Despite the successive Treaty reforms of the enhanced cooperation procedure (in both the Nice and Lisbon Treaties) designed to facilitate its use, the temptation to leave the EU framework and set up a separate *inter se* regime under international law has continued to exist to date. This is especially the case (but not only) when the number of Member States willing to go further in the integration process is lower than the minimum number required for launching an enhanced cooperation. The subsequent practice of Member States confirmed that view. In 2005, seven Member States signed the Prüm Convention, which was one country less than the minimum required at that time to initiate an enhanced cooperation.[65]

In any case, it has always been clear that a group of EU states cannot resort to the conclusion of a separate *inter se* treaty in order to escape from their obligations under EU law. The practical importance of the principle of primacy of EU law over partial agreements between Member States was illustrated by a judgment of the European

[63] See Curtin and Meijers, 'The Principle of Open Government in Schengen and the European Union: Democratic Retrogression?', 32 *Common Market Law Review* (1995) 391.

[64] For a discussion of this question in which the author proposes a positive answer: Martínez Capdevila, 'Son los acuerdos *inter se* una alternativa a la cooperación reforzada en la UE? Reflexiones al hilo del Tratado de Prüm', 40 *Revista española de derecho europeo* (2011) 419. See also K. Tuori, *European Constitutionalism* (2015), at 208: 'a powerful case can be made for Member States not being allowed to resort to international agreements where enhanced cooperation is legally possible'.

[65] On the Prüm Convention, see Ziller, 'Le traité de Prüm. Une vrai-fausse coopération renforcée dans l'Espace de sécurité, de liberté et de justice', *EUI Working Paper LAW* No. 2006/32 (2006), available at http://cadmus.eui.eu/bitstream/handle/1814/6401/LAW-2006-32.pdf?sequence=1&isAllowed=y (last visited 6 January 2017). On the Convention's negotiation history, see Gaillard and Wissmann, 'Der Vertrag von Prüm – Ergebnis einer engen Zusammenarbeit zwischen Deutschland und Frankreich?', in C. Demesmay, M. Koopmann, and J. Thorel (eds), *Die Konsenswerkstatt. Deutsch-französische Kommunikations- und Entscheidungsprozesse in der Europapolitik* (2013) 195.

Court of Justice in 2006 that found the application of a Schengen Convention rule to be incompatible with the rights of free movement which third-country nationals who are family members of EU citizens derived from Community law.[66] The Court's finding was facilitated by the fact that Article 134 of the Schengen Convention contained an express conflict rule giving priority to Community law, but the Court would no doubt have come to the same conclusion with regard to an agreement that does not contain such an express primacy rule.

One can conclude from this overview that partial agreements have incentivized the creation of systems of variable geometry within the EU legal order, so that variable geometry has now become one of its stable and pervasive characteristics.[67] In particular, the Schengen Agreement stimulated the establishment of a *specific* and of a *general* mechanism of differentiated integration within the European constitutional framework. Yet, their role was not exhausted by this 'pioneering' function. In the last decade, we have witnessed a rather striking, and perhaps surprising, revival of partial agreements concluded in the margins of, but closely linked to, the EU legal order. Those recent developments will be examined in the following sections.

4. International 'Side Agreements' in the Euro-Area Crisis Context: the EFSF, the ESM, the Fiscal Compact, and the SRF Agreement

Many authors have noted the considerable variety of legal instruments used when formulating the collective responses to the euro-area crisis in the period 2010–2015.[68, 69] Some important elements of the reformed legal regime were put in place by means of EU legislation: the eight pieces of EU legislation on economic governance known as the 'six pack' (2011) and 'two pack' (2013), and the three pieces of legislation forming together the Banking Union. Soft law (e.g. the Euro Plus Pact of March 2011) and informal institutional practice (e.g. the calling of Eurozone summits and changes in European Central Bank (ECB) lending policies) were abundantly used. More unusual was the conclusion of four international law treaties 'on the side' of the EU legal order, each of which were concluded between many, but less than all, the EU Member States:[70] the Decision of the Representatives of the euro-area countries

[66] Case C-503/03, *Commission v. Spain*, [2006] ECR I-01097 (ECLI:EU:C:2006:74), particularly paras 33–35.

[67] A. Rosas and L. Armati, *EU Constitutional Law: An Introduction* (2010), at 98.

[68] This section of the chapter borrows, in part, from an earlier publication by one of the authors: De Witte, 'Using International Law in the Euro Crisis – Causes and Consequences', 4 *ARENA Working Papers* (2013), available at http://www.sv.uio.no/arena/english/research/publications/arena-working-papers/2013/wp4-13.pdf (last visited 6 January 2017).

[69] For a synthetic overview of those legal instruments with references to their source, see A. Hinarejos, *The Euro Area Crisis in Constitutional Perspective* (2015), ch. 3.

[70] Those four are not the only *inter se* agreements that were used in the context of the unfolding euro-area crisis. One could also add the coordinated bilateral agreements between Greece and all the other euro-area states, signed in 2010, which constituted the first instrument of financial support for Greece before the EFSF entered the picture.

of 10 May 2010 to set up the European Financial Stability Facility (EFSF);[71] the Treaty establishing the European Stability Mechanism (ESM Treaty), signed on 1 February 2012 between the (then) 17 euro-area countries, and entered into force in September 2012;[72] the Treaty on Stability, Coordination and Governance in the Economic and Monetary Union (commonly known as the 'Fiscal Compact'), signed on 2 March 2012, between the 17 euro-area countries and eight further EU Member States, and entered into force on 1 January 2013;[73] and finally the Agreement on the Single Resolution Fund (SRF) signed by 26 Member States (all except the UK and Sweden) on 21 May 2014, which has not yet entered into force.[74]

The seemingly arbitrary nature of those actions by the governments is illustrated by what happened on Sunday 9 May 2010, on the day of the sixtieth anniversary of the Schuman Declaration. At a special urgent meeting of the Council, composed of ministers of Economy or Finance (the so-called Ecofin Council), a regulation was adopted to create the European Financial Stabilisation Mechanism, a new EU law instrument to confront the unfolding sovereign debt crisis. In the margin of that meeting, the members of the Council from the 17 euro-area countries 'switched hats' and transformed themselves into representatives of their states at an intergovernmental meeting; in that capacity, they adopted a decision by which they committed themselves to establish the EFSF outside the EU legal framework.[75] From the point of view of the EU institutional balance, one could say that the Council (or at least a large fraction of it) parted company with the Commission and the European Parliament in order to adopt separate measures in a purely intergovernmental context in which they were not 'hindered' by the presence of the supranational EU institutions and by the cumbersome decision-making procedures of EU law.

It could be tempting to explain the conclusion of all four international treaties dealing with the euro-area crisis as the expression of a general return to intergovernmentalism in the European integration process. Whereas there is some truth in that observation, there are also other, more specific and contingent, reasons that explain the use of international treaties in each of those cases. Very roughly speaking, and subject to more detailed explanations in the following paragraphs, those reasons can be summarized as: *urgency and money* (in the case of the EFSF), *money and path dependency* (in the case of the ESM), *political symbolism* (in the case of the Fiscal Compact), and *distrust among EU states* (in the case of the SRF agreement).

[71] Decision of the Representatives of the Governments of the Euro Area Member States Meeting within the Council of the European Union. The text can be found in the (public) Council document 9614/10 of 10 May 2010, available at http://register.consilium.europa.eu/doc/srv?l=EN&f=ST%20 9614%202010%20INIT (last visited 6 January 2017).

[72] The current version of that treaty (after later accessions of new euro-area states) can be found on the ESM's website: https://www.esm.europa.eu/sites/default/files/20150203_-_esm_treaty_-_en.pdf (last visited 6 January 2017).

[73] The text of this treaty can be found at http://europa.eu/rapid/press-release_DOC-12-2_en.htm (last visited 9 January 2017).

[74] Agreement on the Transfer and Mutualisation of Contributions to the Single Resolution Fund, Council document 8457/14 of 14 May 2014.

[75] As was shown in Section 2 above, there is a long-standing practice of such 'decisions of representatives' concluded in the margins of the Council. What was unprecedented, in this case, is the fact that the decision was adopted by the governments of the euro-area countries only, making it a partial rather than a parallel agreement.

As mentioned earlier, the European Financial Stability Facility (EFSF) was created in May 2010, at the very same time as a new EU law instrument serving the same purpose of giving financial support to countries facing a severe sovereign debt crisis, namely the European Financial Stability Mechanism (EFSM) established by a Council Regulation based on Article 122(2) TFEU.[76] In fact, both instruments have been used simultaneously and cumulatively with respect to Ireland and Portugal (Greece being dealt with at first by bilateral agreements and later by the EFSF). The decisive reason for this bifurcated approach seems to have been the perceived inability of the EU-law instrument (the EFSM) to deal conclusively with the crisis. In view of its limited and strongly earmarked budgetary resources, the European Union itself did not possess sufficient 'firepower' to deal with a massive sovereign debt crisis. The €60 billion earmarked for the EFSM was the upper limit available at that time,[77] whereas the EFSF's financial capacity was made many times larger, since it could tap the national budgetary resources of the participating countries. Also, when the EU budget is used, non-euro-area countries are indirectly called upon to fund an operation which aims at ensuring the stability of the euro area. The UK, in particular, was less than keen to spend large amounts of EU money to support Greece or other euro-area countries. Hence, the decision to 'go outside' the institutional framework of the European Union, and to build a more powerful financial guarantee instrument by means of a separate agreement between the euro-area countries themselves and, therefore, without requiring financial guarantees from the side of the non-euro-area countries. It would not have been practical, though, to start negotiating a fully fledged international agreement, in view of the perceived *urgency* of the policy response. Therefore, rather than concluding a formal treaty, the euro-area states set in place a complex legal regime consisting of three elements. First, there was an *executive agreement*, that is, an international agreement immediately operational upon signature by the representatives of the governments without the need to go through ratification by their national parliaments (this was the above-mentioned Decision of the Representatives). Second, a *private company* was established under Luxembourg law, of which the 17 euro-area states were the only shareholders (this company was called the EFSF).[78] Third, a *Framework Agreement* between the EFSF and its 17 'high shareholders' set out the decision-making rules of the Facility and substantive guidance for its operation (this is *not* a formal treaty under international law, because

[76] Council Regulation 407/2010 of 11 May 2010 establishing a European financial stabilization mechanism, OJ 2010 L 118/1.

[77] See *ibid.*, Article 2(2), referring to an upper limit of the loans or credit lines constituted by 'the margin available under the own resources ceiling for payment appropriations'. What this sibylline phrase means is that only those 60 billion were available for serving as a loan guarantee, with all the rest of the EU budget being committed to other purposes. The Commission's original idea of making the euro-area Member States guarantors of EFSM loans beyond those 60 billion appeared incompatible with the fact that the Member State contributions to the EU budget have a multiannual upper limit. See, for this explanation, Middleton, 'Not Bailing Out... Legal Aspects of the 2010 Sovereign Debt Crisis', in *A Man for All Treaties—Liber Amicorum en l'honneur de Jean-Claude Piris* (2012) 421, at 436.

[78] The text of the articles of incorporation of the EFSF can be found at https://www.esm.europa.eu/sites/default/files/efsf_status_coordonnes_23avrl2014.pdf (last visited 9 January 2017).

it was concluded between states and a private company).[79] In this manner, the EFSF could operate almost immediately without the need for ratifications which a formal international treaty would have triggered. It was then left to each state to 'sort out' the domestic legal conditions for its financial participation in the EFSF. What has been used, in this case, is a curious mixture of public international law (the original decision) and private law, supported by a 'creative' but largely uncontested use of the national constitutions of the participating states;[80] but all this to support an essentially EU policy, the preservation of the financial stability of the euro area.

The European Stability Mechanism (ESM), the permanent successor of the temporary EFSF, was established by means of a fully fledged treaty between the 17 euro-area states. The path towards the conclusion of the ESM Treaty was laid out by the European Council Decision of 25 March 2011 by which it approved an amendment of Article 136 TFEU. The choice of establishing the permanent stability mechanism by means of an international treaty followed logically from the TFEU amendment, which stated: 'The Member States whose currency is the euro may establish a stability mechanism to be activated if indispensable to safeguard the stability of the euro area as a whole.'[81] Why was the authorization contained in the additional clause of Article 136 TFEU addressed to the Member States and not to the European Union itself? In other words, why did the ESM have to be established as a separate international organization rather than as an EU agency? There seems to have been a mix of reasons for this. One reason is that of path dependency, with the ESM being constructed as the 'natural successor', in its mode of operation, of the intergovernmental EFSF. A second, very important, reason is the continued insufficiency of EU budgetary resources in view of the vast amount of funds that was thought needed for the ESM; as well as the continued unwillingness of the non-euro-area Member States to shoulder part of the financial contributions and associated risks. However, the closeness of the new organization to the European Union was expressed in various ways: by means of references in the Preamble to the EU's economic governance rules and to the amendment of Article 136 TFEU, and by several provisions of the treaty entrusting supporting roles to three EU institutions: the Commission, the ECB, and the Court of Justice. The governance system of the ESM thus forms a curious hybrid: all formal decision-making powers are entrusted

[79] To remove any doubt about this, one may turn to point 16 of the Agreement which makes it subject to English law (and therefore not to public international law). The text of the Framework Agreement is available at https://www.esm.europa.eu/sites/default/files/20111019_efsf_framework_agreement_en.pdf (last visited 6 January 2017).

[80] Except for two constitutional challenges before the German Constitutional Court, which led the court, each time, to adjust the way in which the role of the *Bundestag* had been designed in the German laws that were adopted to implement the EFSF arrangements. Judgments of 7 September 2011 and of 28 February 2012 (2 BvE 8/11). See the comment by A. von Ungern-Sternberg on the former judgment, in 'German Federal Constitutional Court Parliaments—Fig Leaf or Heartbeat of Democracy? Judgment of 7 September 2011, Euro Rescue Package', 8 *European Constitutional Law Review* (2012) 304.

[81] As for the reason why an amendment of the TFEU was considered necessary for the creation of the ESM, see De Witte, 'The European Treaty Amendment for the Creation of a Financial Stability Mechanism', 6 *SIEPS European Policy Analysis* (2011) available at http://www.sieps.se/en/publications/2011/the-european-treaty-amendment-for-the-creation-of-a-financial-stability-mechanism-20116epa/Sieps_2011_6epa.pdf (last visited 26 September 2017).

to organs composed of representatives of the members; but those representatives happen to be the same persons who represent their country in the EU's informal Eurogroup and Euro working group; and major tasks in preparing and implementing those decisions are entrusted to supranational EU institutions, that is, the European Commission and the ECB.

As for the third international agreement concluded in the context of the sovereign debt crisis, namely the *Fiscal Compact*,[82] the reasons for concluding it outside the EU institutional framework are much less apparent. Most of what it contains in terms of economic governance at the European level could have been adopted through EU legislation or by means of a modification of Protocol No. 12 on the excessive deficit procedure. In particular, the obligation to introduce into national law (preferably at the constitutional level) the new budgetary limits defined in Article 3, para. 1, could have been achieved, legally speaking, by means of EU legislation, if necessary adopted by means of the enhanced cooperation mode of decision-making in which not all EU states must participate. However, it was made very clear by the German government (that acted once more as the agenda setter for this treaty), in the course of the autumn of 2011, that the circumstances required nothing less than a treaty. The new commitment to budgetary stability seemed more solemn and more permanent if contained in a treaty which cannot be 'bent' later on, whereas EU legislation would be more liable to be 'softened' through later amendments. Therefore, making a treaty seemed to be the appropriate symbolic message of strong resolve which the unruly financial markets required, in the autumn of 2011.

The kind of treaty norm that the German government, and later also the French government, had in mind was a formal amendment of the TFEU like the one adopted in March 2011 on the financial stability mechanism. But this would have required the unanimous agreement of all EU Member States and probably a prior debate at a convention, in accordance with the EU's cumbersome ordinary revision procedure. At the December 2011 summit, that process was stopped short from the very start when the UK government refused to agree on such a TFEU amendment given that the (unrelated) conditions which it had put forward had not been accepted by the other governments. During the European Council meeting itself, the other governments, led by the French-German tandem, decided instantaneously to 'exit' from the EU institutional framework, and to go for a separate international agreement instead, so as to circumvent the British veto. They did not take time to consider whether, given the impossibility of a TFEU amendment, the wisest course might have been to adopt EU *legislation* through enhanced cooperation, rather than take the risk of engaging in this new and unpredictable treaty game.[83] So, one could say that the states *accidentally* stumbled into the conclusion of a separate international agreement, for a mix of reasons including the rigidity of the TFEU amendment process, the belief (especially on the German side) in the symbolic power of a

[82] We use, in this chapter, the common informal denomination of an instrument which is formally called the Treaty on Stability, Coordination and Governance in the Economic and Monetary Union.

[83] For an evocation of the political circumstances of the December meeting of the European Council that eventually led to the choice for a separate treaty, see 'The European Union and the Euro – Game, Set and Mismatch', *The Economist*, 17 December 2011, 43.

treaty, and also—admittedly—the wish to avoid going through the cumbersome and lengthy procedures of EU legislation. The Parties did, however, agree to incorporate the substance of the agreement 'into the legal framework of the Union' at a later stage, thereby echoing the 'integration' operation that had happened with the Schengen and Prüm conventions earlier on (see Section 3 above).

As for the Single Resolution Fund Agreement, concluded a few years after the others, the reasons for its conclusion were not clearly spelled out. The original Commission proposal for a Europe-wide banking resolution mechanism, based on Article 114 TFEU, was split in two by the Council, with one part (the resolution mechanism itself) forming the object of an EU regulation (namely Regulation 806/2014 on a single resolution mechanism), whereas the other part (the building of a fund to be used for resolution operations) was left to be created by the Member States by means of a separate international agreement. This splitting was requested by Germany, which invoked as its main legal argument that a measure imposing financing contributions by banks is a 'fiscal provision' which is excluded from the scope of Article 114 by paragraph 2 of that article;[84] but there were also important political reasons which were not discussed in a transparent way. It seems that the German government sought to ensure that it could abandon the Resolution Fund if the resolution rules themselves were to be later modified (under the qualified majority rule obtaining for Article 114-based measures) in contrast with German interests; for instance, by removing or reducing the bail-in provisions in the regulation on a single resolution mechanism. This aim would explain the explicit reference made to the 'fundamental change of circumstances' as a reason for terminating the agreement (this being a well-known, though controversial, rule of international treaty law) in Article 9(2) of the Agreement; a similar termination clause would obviously not have been available in an EU legal instrument. Again though, and as with the Fiscal Compact, the Contracting States agreed to incorporate a clause expressing their commitment to incorporate the substance of the Agreement into EU law at a later stage.[85]

Beyond the specific reasons explaining the recourse to international law in each of the four cases discussed earlier, there is a general feature of *inter se* treaties that make them an attractive tool, and that is, of course, the flexibility they offer at the time of their conclusion. Indeed, participation in the treaty negotiations is not predetermined by membership of the EU: the 'willing and able' states can decide to conclude a treaty with each other without having to ask the permission of the others. Also,

[84] In its press release on the day of the signature of the agreement, the Council enigmatically stated that 'using an intergovernmental agreement to establish rules on the transfer and mutualisation of contributions is intended to provide maximum legal certainty. The Council decided on this approach in December [2013], given legal and constitutional concerns in certain member states', in *Member states sign agreement on bank resolution fund*, Council Press Release 10088/14, 2014. For an articulation of the legal argument against the use of Article 114 for this part of the banking union project, see Calliess and Schoenfleisch, 'Die Bankenunion, der ESM und die Rekapitalisierung von Banken– Europa- und verfassungsrechtliche Fragen', *Juristenzeitung* (2015) 113, at 119 ff. For criticism of the intergovernmental solution, see Fabbrini, 'On Banks, Courts and International Law – The Intergovernmental Agreement on the Single Resolution Fund in Context', 21 *Maastricht Journal of European and Comparative Law* (2014) 444.

[85] Article 16(2), Agreement on the Transfer and Mutualisation of Contributions to the Single Resolution Fund 2014.

once the negotiation is successfully concluded, the entry into force of the treaty need not depend on ratification by *all* contracting parties. In fact, the creation of the EFSF did not depend on any country's ratification, since it was adopted as an executive agreement and brought into operation through an instrument of private law. As for the other three, the states provided for flexible entry-into-force rules, so as to mitigate the hazards of the national ratification process which all national governments were painfully familiar with from earlier revisions of the EU Treaties.[86] The Fiscal Compact offers a spectacular example of this flexibility, in that it provided that the treaty would enter into force if ratified by merely 12 of the 25 signatory states, provided that those 12 were all part of the euro area. The fact that the authors of the Fiscal Compact moved decidedly away from the condition of universal ratification for its entry into force created a 'ratification game' that was very different from that applying to amendment of the European treaties, where the rule of unanimous ratification gives a strong veto position to each individual country.[87] Here, instead, the cost of a negative decision could not be 'externalized' to the other countries, and would moreover mean that the country could not benefit from the potential support of the ESM.[88] The ESM Treaty, as well, had removed the veto power at least of the smaller euro-area states by providing that it would enter into force if ratified by states that, together, contributed 90 per cent of the funds for the Mechanism. In this way, the four largest countries (who contributed more than 10 per cent each) still had a 'ratification veto', but the smaller euro-area states did not. As for the Agreement on the Single Resolution Fund, it can enter into force upon ratification by countries possessing together 90 per cent of the weighted votes (according to the usual weighting applying to the adoption of EU acts).

Now, the ease with which EU Member States repeatedly used *inter se* treaties in their efforts to deal with the euro-area crisis may give the impression that there are no legal limits to such use. But, in fact, they are not entirely free to do so as and how they wish. As was pointed out earlier, in Section 3, *inter se* international agreements between two or more Member States are allowed, but only within the limits set by EU law obligations. The Fiscal Compact and the Single Resolution Fund Agreement, in fact, contain in their Article 2 a clear, and similarly worded, rule recognizing the primacy of EU law. The ESM Treaty does not have such a rule—but this does not change the legal reality, which is the undisputed precedence of EU law over conflicting provisions in treaties between Member States. Indeed, a number of serious allegations of conflict with EU law were made, in relation to the ESM Treaty[89] and/or the Fiscal Compact: interference with the exercise of (exclusive) EU competences;

[86] See now, for an overall perspective, C. Closa, *The Politics of Ratification of EU Treaties* (2013).

[87] For a discussion of those differences, see Closa, 'Moving Away from Unanimity. Ratification of the Treaty on Stability, Coordination and Governance in the Economic and Monetary Union', 38 *RECON Online Working Paper* 2011, available at http://papers.ssrn.com/sol3/papers.cfm?abstract_id=2005894 (last visited on 9 January 2017).

[88] The linkage between ratification of the Fiscal Compact and benefiting from ESM support is expressly made in both the preambles of the ESM treaty and of the Fiscal Compact.

[89] In fact, many of the legal criticisms of the ESM Treaty could be made of the EFSF arrangements too, but we will not examine those separately. The analysis relating to the ESM Treaty can be applied, *mutatis mutandis,* to the EFSF legal regime.

conflict with specific norms of primary and secondary EU law; and the unjustified 'use' of EU institutions in the implementation of those international agreements.[90] Some of those allegations were examined and rejected by the Court of Justice in the *Pringle* case, decided in November 2012.[91]

The applicant in that case had argued, among other things, that (i) the very conclusion of the ESM Treaty was in breach of primary EU law, and (ii) that some of its content was incompatible with primary EU law. Indeed, *inter se* agreements can conflict with EU law for a variety of reasons, but there is a major distinction to be made, depending on the area of EU law that is involved: in certain areas, the very fact that an *inter se* agreement is concluded is in breach of the EU's exclusive competence; in other areas—those outside the EU's exclusive competence—*inter se* agreements are permissible in principle but they should not contain institutional or substantive provisions that are incompatible with specific norms of EU law.[92] In its *Pringle* judgment, the Court basically followed this distinction in dealing with the complex preliminary questions relating to the ESM treaty: it first examined those EU Treaty provisions that were argued, by Mr Pringle, to preclude the very *possibility* for the Member States to conclude an agreement such as the ESM treaty,[93] and after having rejected those arguments, it turned to examine the various provisions of EU law which were, still according to the applicant, breached by the *content* of the ESM treaty.[94]

First, the fact that *inter se* agreements are not allowed in matters falling within the EU's exclusive competence would have been problematic if the Stability Mechanism were to be considered as a *monetary* policy instrument, as Pringle's lawyers argued. Indeed, monetary policy is, in relation to euro-area countries, an exclusive competence of the EU, according to Article 3(1) TFEU. However, in the system of the TFEU, the question of financial assistance to Member States, and budgetary matters generally, are clearly located in the Economic Policy chapter (Articles 120 to 126) rather than in the Monetary Policy chapter (Articles 127 to 133), and economic policy is—unlike monetary policy—a *shared* competence, in which the Member States have preserved the right to develop their own policies, alone or together with

[90] For discussions of these issues in the legal literature, see among others: Craig, 'The Stability, Coordination and Governance Treaty: Principle, Politics and Pragmatism', 37 *European Law Review* (2012) 231 (who finds a number of inconsistencies between the Fiscal Compact and EU law); de Gregorio Merino, 'Legal Developments in the Economic and Monetary Union During the Debt Crisis: The Mechanisms of Financial Assistance', 49 *Common Market Law Review* (2012) 1613, esp. at 1635–1640 (who concludes on the absence of conflict with EU law); and Dimopoulos, 'The Use of International Law as a Tool for Enhancing Governance in the Eurozone and its Impact on EU Institutional Integrity', in M. Adams, F. Fabbrini, and P. Larouche (eds.), *The Constitutionalization of European Budgetary Constraints* (2014) 41 (who highlights the long-term negative impact of those *inter se* treaties on the EU's institutional system).

[91] Case C-370/12, *Thomas Pringle v. Government of Ireland, Ireland, The Attorney General*, judgment of 27 November 2012 (ECLI:EU:C:2012:756).

[92] For a more elaborate discussion of the conditions under which *inter se* agreements are permissible, and of the requirement of substantive compatibility with EU law, see De Witte, 'Old-Fashioned Flexibility: International Agreements between Member States of the European Union', in G. de Búrca and J. Scott (eds), *Constitutional Change in the EU: From Uniformity to Flexibility* (2000) 31; and Schütze, *supra* note 16.

[93] *Pringle* judgment, *supra* note 91, at paras 93–107.

[94] *Ibid.*, at paras 108–182.

others. So, the Court of Justice concluded rightly that, although the creation of the ESM may have an impact on the common currency, its central importance is as a rescue mechanism for national fiscal crises. This is not an area of exclusive EU competence, and therefore an agreement between the euro-area states was permissible in principle.

On the question of substantive incompatibility with EU law, it had been argued by Mr Pringle that the ESM Treaty violated the no bailout clause of Article 125 TFEU, or at least that it allowed for its violation. Indeed, Article 125 states that EU Member States shall not be liable for the financial commitments of other Member States. But the Court ruled that loans and guarantees subject to strict conditionality (which is the nature of the rescue instruments contemplated under the ESM treaty) do not amount to states becoming liable for each other's debts. This somewhat optimistic interpretation (relying on the promise that the loans will eventually be paid back) allowed the Court to conclude that, in this regard, there was no conflict between the ESM treaty and EU law.

This left one other major argument against the ESM treaty which goes to the heart of the coexistence between the EU legal order and international side agreements, namely the fact that the ESM treaty, whilst not being an EU-law instrument, nevertheless gave specific roles to the EU institutions. Indeed, one of the most controversial issues in the *Pringle* case was whether the EU institutions can be 'borrowed' by the Member States when concluding and applying an international agreement situated outside the EU legal framework.[95] The text of the ESM treaty repeatedly refers to action to be taken by the EU institutions. The Court of Justice is mentioned only once, namely in Article 37, which states that disputes between ESM members about the interpretation of the ESM treaty that cannot be resolved by the ESM organs themselves will be submitted to the Court of Justice. The Commission and the ECB figure more prominently in several articles of the treaty. They are given important roles as 'agents' of the ESM organs, both in preparing the operations of the ESM (in particular, through the negotiation of a memorandum of understanding with the country applying for ESM financial assistance), and in coordinating the implementation of the rescue operation.

The allocation of extra tasks to the Court of Justice was the least problematic element, since Article 273 TFEU, whose text had figured in the EEC Treaty from the very beginning, allows the Member States to submit to the Court 'under a special agreement between the parties', 'any dispute between Member States which relates to the subject matter of the Treaties', and thereby to extend the jurisdiction of the Court beyond EU law proper. This trigger provision had been used much earlier in the EU's history in order to grant the European Court of Justice jurisdiction under some of the 'Art 220 conventions', most prominently under the Brussels Convention (see Section 2 above). The subject matter of the ESM treaty is indeed closely connected to the TFEU, and the ESM treaty is expressly declared to be a 'special agreement'

[95] See the detailed examination of this question by Peers, 'Towards a New Form of EU Law? The Use of EU Institutions outside the EU Legal Framework', 9 *European Constitutional Law Review* (2013) 37.

in the sense of Article 273 TFEU in recital 16 of its preamble, so that conclusively settled the issue.

Things were more complicated with respect to the 'borrowing' of the Commission and the Central Bank. Pringle invoked Article 13(2) TEU in this context. According to this provision, the EU institutions shall act within the limits of the powers given to them under 'the Treaties' (meaning the TEU and the TFEU, and no other treaties). On a literal interpretation, this could mean that it is not possible to give any additional functions to the Commission or the ECB (or indeed the Parliament and the Council) under separate international agreements such as the ESM treaty. Yet, the Court of Justice had accepted, in a couple of low-profile judgments of the 1990s dealing with development aid, that the Commission could perform tasks entrusted to it by all the Member States under a separate international agreement. The EC Treaty, it held in the *Bangladesh* case, 'does not prevent the Member States from entrusting the Commission with the task of coordinating a collective action undertaken by them on the basis of an act of their representatives meeting in the Council'.[96] And it repeated shortly afterwards, in the *Lomé* case that 'no provision of the Treaty prevents the Member State from using, outside its framework, procedural steps drawing on the rules applicable to Community expenditure and from associating the Community institutions with the procedure thus set up'.[97]

The case of the ESM Treaty was different, though, from those earlier cases in that the attribution of extra tasks was made, not by all the Member States acting together, but by a limited group of 17. This is a hypothesis which the Court of Justice had not addressed prior to the *Pringle* case. However, the non-participating Member States had, in fact, given their agreement for the use of the EU institutions. Already at the time the EFSF was created, in May 2010, the Council legal service, probably in consideration of the Court's *Bangladesh* judgment, had prepared a short text which was adopted as a Decision of the representatives of the governments of the 27 EU Member States and simply stated: 'The 27 Member States agree that the Commission will be allowed to be tasked by the euro area Member States in this context.'[98] The same thing happened when the ESM Treaty was signed, as is mentioned in recital 10 of the preamble of the ESM Treaty: 'On 20 June 2011, the representatives of the Governments of the Member States of the European Union authorized the Contracting Parties of this Treaty to request the European Commission and the European Central Bank to perform the tasks provided for in this Treaty.'

The importance of the tasks entrusted to the Commission and the ECB in the ESM treaty, compared to the rather anodyne administrative tasks of the Commission which had been challenged in the *Bangladesh* and *Lomé* cases, prompted the Court to add an additional condition for any institutional borrowing: the extra tasks should not 'alter the essential character of the powers conferred on those institutions

[96] Joined Cases C-181/91 and C-248/91, *supra* note 8, at para. 20.

[97] Case C-316/91, *European Parliament v. Council*, [1994] ECR I-00625 (ECLI:EU:C:1994:76), at para. 41.

[98] Council document 9614/10 of 10 May 2010, *supra* note 71. The words 'in this context' refer to the other Decision of the same day, and published in the same document, through which the *euro state governments* (rather than *all 27 governments*) had agreed to set up the EFSF.

by the EU and FEU Treaties'.[99] This formula stems from some Opinions given by the Court in the context of the conclusion of international agreements by the EU, in which it had emphasized, by the use of that formula, that such agreements should not alter the institutional identity of the Union.[100] The formula is here transposed from the context of the EU's external relations to the context of *inter se* agreements between the Member States. In applying the test, the Court finds—without surprise—that the ESM tasks entrusted to the Commission and the ECB do not affect the essential character of those institutions' powers.

One way to understand and justify the Court's rather liberal attitude towards the ancillary use of EU institutions in an intergovernmental framework, despite the strict language used by Article 13 TEU, is to distinguish between 'powers' and 'tasks'. What Article 13 TEU seeks to convey is that the powers of the institutions are fixed by the Treaties; it does not exclude that extra tasks may be given to the institutions as long as those tasks fit within their existing competences, and as long as all EU Member States agree to 'lend' the EU institutions. Crucially, the Court noted that 'the duties conferred on the Commission and ECB within the ESM Treaty, important as they are, do not entail any power to make decisions of their own. Further, the activities pursued by those two institutions within the ESM Treaty solely commit the ESM.'[101] Thus, the integrity of the EU legal and institutional order is preserved in two cumulative ways. First, because of the absence of decision-making powers under the ESM treaty there is no danger that the Commission and ECB will resort to law-making outside the constitutional constraints imposed by EU law (such as transparency, democratic accountability, and respect for fundamental rights). And, second, because their ESM-related activities will have no effects within the EU legal order, but only within the separate legal order of the ESM, the EU *acquis* (and its primacy over ESM law) will not be affected.

A borrowing of EU institutions also took place, but to a much minor extent, in the Fiscal Compact. One major difference, in that case, is that no formal text was adopted through which the two non-participating states, the United Kingdom and the Czech Republic, gave their authorization to the use of the EU institutions. Whether such an authorization, either explicit or implied, is a necessary requirement, is still unclear.[102] The Court of Justice saw no need to address that question in its *Pringle* judgment.

The Court's rather lenient approach to the compatibility of *inter se* treaties with EU law may be explained by the fact that the stakes were very high in *Pringle*, so that arriving at a negative verdict on the ESM treaty was, despite the arguments of many legal scholars, never a realistic option. It remains to be seen whether the ECJ will be similarly well disposed to other *inter se* treaties whose role in the European integration process is less prominent or less sound from a legal perspective. Beyond the

[99] *Pringle* judgment, *supra* note 91, at para. 158.

[100] Opinions 1/92, [1992] ECR I-02821 (ECLI:EU:C:1992:189), 1/00, [2002] ECR I-03493 (ECLI:EU:C:2002:231), and 1/09, [2011] ECR I-01137 (ECLI:EU:C:2011:123), referred to by the Court in the same para. 158 of the *Pringle* judgment, *supra* note 91.

[101] *Pringle* judgment, *supra* note 91, at para. 161.

[102] See, for discussion of that question in the context of the Fiscal Compact, the articles by Peers, *supra* note 95, and Craig, *supra* note 90.

question of legal compatibility, though, the recent adoption of a series of *inter se* treaties in the euro-area crisis context raises serious questions as to their impact on the general institutional balance in the European Union. That assessment is different for the Fiscal Compact or the Single Resolution Fund than for the ESM Treaty. The former two may be deeply problematic for other reasons, but they do not have a major effect on the EU institutional system, for the simple reason that they do not create new institutions or organs with decision-making powers.[103] The ESM Treaty is more problematic in that it creates its own parallel institutional structure of decision-making outside the EU framework. Even though, as we saw, there is some borrowing of the EU institutions, the formal decision-making power relating to stability support schemes is put in the hands of the Board of Governors or the Board of Directors. In personal terms, the members of these Boards are the very same people who compose the Ecofin formation of the Council and its working groups, but when acting within the ESM framework they are not subject to the normal constraints of EU law, such as the Commission's power of initiative, parliamentary control, and judicial review. The financial rescue regime of European economic governance is, indeed, marked by a high degree of intergovernmentalism which contrasts with the steady advance of supranational elements in other areas of Economic and Monetary Union (EMU) law.

5. The Agreement on the Unified Patent Court

Entirely apart from the treaties arising from the euro-area crisis, a further *inter se* agreement closely connected with the functioning of the European Union was signed on 19 February 2013, namely the Agreement on a Unified Patent Court (the 'UPC Agreement').[104] This agreement is part of a package of legal instruments designed to establish a system of unitary patent protection for the European Union: two regulations adopted under the enhanced cooperation procedure (to which all the Member States participate except Spain and Croatia) and the UPC Agreement concluded between 25 Member States (all except Croatia, Poland, and Spain). That package is the latest development in a long-lasting effort to establish a European-wide legal regime for patent law.[105]

By virtue of the Patent Regulation,[106] the 'European' patents granted by the European Patent Organisation (which is a separate international organization unconnected with the EU) will benefit from a unitary protection regime in the EU

[103] The Fiscal Compact does provide for meetings of the Heads of State or government of the contracting parties, but that collective organ does not have any decision-making powers, and involves just another form of 'hat switching' at European Council meetings.

[104] Agreement on a Unified Patent Court 2013/C 175/01, OJ 2013 C 175/1 ('UPC Agreement').

[105] The general literature on the latest package, situated in the perspective of the evolution of European patent law, includes: A. Ilardi, *The New European Patent* (2015); and the contributions in J. Pila and C. Wadlow (eds), *The Unitary EU Patent System* (2015).

[106] Regulation (EU) 1257/2012 of the European Parliament and of the Council of 17 December 2012 implementing enhanced cooperation in the area of the creation of unitary patent protection, OJ 2012 L 361/1 ('Patent Regulation').

states participating in this enhanced cooperation initiative. A 'twin' regulation with a separate legal basis provides for the translation arrangements for this new patent protection system.[107] The international agreement, for its part, establishes a judicial institution, the Unified Patent Court, which is given competence to adjudicate disputes between individuals relating to the European patents with unitary effect ('unitary patents') as well as those relating to the traditional 'European' patents that do not benefit from such an effect.

As we saw (in Section 3 above), the enhanced cooperation procedure was primarily designed to be an intra-EU alternative for the conclusion of partial agreements outside the constitutional framework of the EU. What we observe in the patent field is therefore rather unexpected, namely the combined use of those two mechanisms of differentiated integration which were thought to be alternative to one another. This combination leads to some legal problems, though, the most immediate of which is the divergent entry-into-force rules. Whereas the UPC Agreement, like most international treaties, has to undergo a process of ratification by its contracting states before it can enter into force, the two regulations enter in principle into force upon their adoption by the EU institutions and publication in the EU's Official Journal. The solution for this problem was to provide that the Patent Regulation and its twin Regulation on Translation Arrangements would, indeed, enter into force immediately but that their *application* would be delayed until the time of entry into force of the UPC Agreement,[108] which will happen once it is ratified by 13 of its contracting parties.[109]

How did such a baroque legal edifice come into being? There is a clear basis in the TFEU enabling the adoption *within* the EU legal order of a patent protection regime coupled with a judicial system to adjudicate it. In particular, Article 118 TFEU provides a specific legal base for 'the creation of European intellectual property rights to provide uniform protection of intellectual property rights throughout the Union'. On the basis of Article 262 TFEU, the European Court of Justice (or a specialized court within it)[110] could be granted jurisdiction over private disputes related to such intellectual property rights. How, then, can we explain that the Member States and the EU institutions came to develop such a complicated package of measures, including the conclusion of an agreement under international law?

[107] Council Regulation (EU) 1260/2012 of 17 December 2012 implementing enhanced cooperation in the area of the creation of unitary patent protection with regard to the applicable translation arrangements, OJ 2012 L 361/89 ('Regulation on Translation Arrangements').

[108] See Article 18(2) of the Patent Regulation, *supra* note 106, and Article 7(2) of the Regulation on Translation Arrangements, *supra* note 107.

[109] See Article 89 of the UPC Agreement, *supra* note 104 (which provides that the treaty will enter into force once ratified by 13 Contracting Parties 'including the three Member States in which the highest number of European patents' are in effect, namely France, Germany, and the United Kingdom). Note once again, as with the euro-crisis treaties, the use of a flexible entry-into-force rule, avoiding the requirement of ratification by all contracting states. Similarly to the ESM Treaty, the largest countries retain a 'ratification veto'. In this case however, the size of the country is not calculated on the basis of the size of its financial contribution to a fund but in terms of number of patents in effect on its territory.

[110] See Article 257 TFEU.

Separate sets of reasons lie behind the initiation of the enhanced cooperation procedure and the conclusion of a separate treaty. The founding Treaties require that the language arrangements for the unitary system of patent protection be decided by unanimity in the Council.[111] No unanimous agreement could be found on this point and an enhanced cooperation initiative was launched to bypass the veto of Italy and Spain who considered that their national languages had unjustifiably been excluded from the regulation's regime.[112] As regards the UPC Agreement, the recourse to an extra-EU treaty was guided by a general unwillingness on the part of the patent community, supported by the Member States, to involve the European Court of Justice in the adjudication of the unitary patents.[113] The view of the patent community seems to be that the Court of Justice does not have the required expertise to deal with such a technical area of the law. Its involvement via the mechanism of preliminary ruling would have slowed down the patent litigation process and entailed additional costs for litigants, so the argument goes.[114]

Back in 2009, the Commission had proposed a different legal route, namely the negotiation of a mixed *external* agreement to be concluded by the EU, its Member States, and third states participating in the European Patent Organisation (EPO), such as Switzerland and Turkey. Creating a system of patent adjudication with such a broader international scope would have had distinct advantages. It would have made it possible to involve third countries as well as to have one integrated adjudication mechanism for both 'European' (EPO) patents and 'unitary' (EPO-EU) patents, thereby avoiding the existence of two parallel systems of litigation. However, in 2011, the Opinion 1/09 rendered by the Court of Justice put a stop to this project.[115] The patent court contemplated would have been 'an organization with a distinct legal personality under international law' and was situated therefore 'outside the institutional and judicial framework of the European Union'.[116] By conferring exclusive power to that international court to apply EU law in proceedings related to unitary patents, the national courts of EU Member States would have been divested of their jurisdiction to apply and interpret EU law, and the European Court of Justice would have been deprived of its corresponding power to reply, by preliminary rulings, to questions referred by those courts.[117] Opinion 1/09 thereby precluded the option of an external agreement through which third countries could

[111] Article 118(2) TFEU.

[112] Council Decision 2011/167/EU of 10 March 2011 authorizing enhanced cooperation in the area of the creation of unitary patent protection, OJ 2011 L 76/53. This process was controversial and the two countries unsuccessfully attempted to torpedo the procedure by challenging before the Court the Council decision authorizing the enhanced cooperation procedure. See Joined Cases C-274/11 and C-295/11, *Spain and Italy v. Council*, judgment of 16 April 2013 (ECLI:EU:C:2013:240).

[113] Dehousse, 'La juridiction unifiée du brevet: le nouvel oxymoron du droit européen', in I. Govaere and others (eds), *The European Union in the World. Essays in Honour of Marc Maresceau* (2013) 259, at 269.

[114] For a summary of the arguments put forward by patent judges and lawyers in favour of limiting the involvement of the European Court of Justice in patent litigation, see House of Commons European Scrutiny Committee, *The Unified Patent Court: help or hindrance? Sixty-fifth Report of Session 2010–2012* (2012), available at http://www.publications.parliament.uk/pa/cm201012/cmselect/cmeuleg/1799/1799.pdf (last visited 9 January 2017).

[115] Opinion 1/09, *supra* note 100. [116] *Ibid.*, at para. 71. [117] *Ibid.*, at para. 88.

be associated to the patent adjudication mechanism.[118] Which alternatives were available after this? On the basis solely of Article 262 TFEU, it would not have been legally possible to grant the European Court of Justice (or a specialized court within it) jurisdiction over both 'European' patents and patents with unitary effect. The possibility of resorting to alternative or additional legal bases (such as the flexibility clause of Article 352 TFEU) was not investigated further because the 'ECJ option' did not 'meet the political requirements of the Member States and the interests of the users of the patent system'.[119] Instead, the Commission suggested turning the EU external agreement into an agreement to be concluded between the Member States only. In Opinion 1/09, referring to its prior case law, the European Court of Justice had mentioned the Benelux Court as a valid model of a separate judicial body created by some Member States in an *inter se* agreement. The intergovernmental negotiations on the design of the Unified Patent Court took the Benelux Court as their reference point. Similarly to the Benelux Court, the idea was to establish a court 'common to a number of Member States, situated within the judicial system of the Union and whose decisions are subject to mechanisms capable of ensuring the full effectiveness of the rules of the European Union'.[120] So, the Unified Patent Court is both an international court (since it is created on the basis of an international treaty) and a 'collective Member State court' for the purposes of the application of EU patent law.

The general reluctance to involve the European Court of Justice in patent litigation is further illustrated by the direct intervention of the European Council in the ordinary legislative procedure that led to the adoption of the Patent Regulation. While the Council and the Parliament had already found an informal agreement on the content of the Patent Regulation, the European Council 'suggested' removing from the Regulation the substantive provisions defining the acts against which the unitary patent provides protection.[121] Letting those provisions in the Regulation could have opened the floodgate of preliminary rulings on the scope of the patent protection. By an ingenious technique, those substantive provisions were transferred to the UPC Agreement, over which the European Court of Justice has no authority.[122] The final version of the Patent Regulation refers to the 'applicable national law' of the Member States in order to define the acts against which the patent provides protection;[123] but this reference to national law includes the UPC Agreement.[124]

[118] For an analysis of the legally available options to establish a common patent litigation system after Opinion 1/09, see Peers, 'The Constitutional Implication of the EU Patent', 7 *European Constitutional Law Review* (2011) 229, at 257–266.

[119] Commission non-paper, 'Solutions for a unified patent litigation system – The way forward after the Opinion 1/09 of the CJEU', annexed to Council document 10630/11 of 26 May 2011.

[120] Opinion 1/09, *supra* note 100, at para. 82; see also Case C-337/95, *Parfums Christian Dior v. Evora*, [1997] ECR I-6013 (ECLI:EU:C:1997:517).

[121] Desantes Real, 'Le "paquet européen des brevets", paradigme du chemin à rebours : de la logique institutionnelle à la logique intergouvernementale', *Cahiers de droit européen* (2013) 577, at 597–598. See European Council conclusions of 28/29 June 2012, EUCO 76/12.

[122] See Articles 25–29 of the UPC Agreement, *supra* note 104.

[123] Article 5(3) of the Patent Regulation, *supra* note 106.

[124] On the transfer of the provisions on the scope of the patent protection to the UPC Agreement, see Tilmann, 'The Compromise on the Uniform Protection for EU Patents', 8 *Journal of Intellectual Property Law and Practice* (2013) 78; Wadlow, '"Hamlet without the Prince": Can the Unitary Patent Regulation Strut its Stuff without Articles 6–8?' 8 *Journal of Intellectual Property Law and Practice* 207.

Like for the treaties concluded in the field of EMU, this highly 'creative' construction has been criticized and challenged for being incompatible with the EU constitutional framework. Spain brought unsuccessful challenges before the Court against the two regulations.[125] Although the rulings in those two cases deal with the validity of the EU legal acts composing the unitary patent package, they also touch upon the curious linkage between the Patent Regulation and the UPC Agreement. The Court upheld Article 18(2) of the Patent Regulation which provides that, in derogation from the general rule of the Patent Regulation, the unitary effect of the 'European patents' will only apply in the territory of the participating Member States that have ratified the UPC Agreement. In the Court's view, it is a valid arrangement to link the application of an EU legal act to the entry into force of an extra-EU agreement. A regulation can task the Member States with the adoption of the necessary measures to ensure its effective application.[126] In this instance, such measure was not to be adopted by each Member State individually but by the Member States collectively via the establishment of the Unified Patent Court.

Does this ruling entail that the Member States are under an EU obligation to ratify the UPC Agreement? Does it turn the ratification requirement into a mere formality? Advocate General Bot argued that the principle of sincere cooperation enshrined in Article 4(3) TFEU reinforces the link between the Patent Regulation and the UPC Agreement. In his view, pursuant to this principle, 'the participating Member States must take all appropriate measures to implement the Unitary Patent Regulation, including the ratification of the Agreement, as the Agreement is necessary for its implementation'.[127] This begs the question as to the possible legal consequences of this argument. Could the Commission initiate infringement proceedings against a Member State participating in the enhanced cooperation for failure to ratify the UPC Agreement, as this would violate the Patent Regulation read in conjunction with Article 4(3) TFEU?[128] The answer would essentially turn on the interpretation to be given to Article 18(2) of the Patent Regulation. On the one hand, that provision insists on the fact that such ratification is of 'a paramount importance' for a proper functioning of the system of unitary patent protection,[129] so that one

[125] Case C-146/13, *Spain v. Parliament and Council*, judgment of 5 May 2015, not yet reported (ECLI:EU:C:2015:298); Case C-147/13, *Spain v. Council*, judgment of 5 May 2015, not yet reported (ECLI:EU:C:2015:299).

[126] Case C-146/13, *supra* note 125, at paras 94–95. See also Case C-147/13, *supra* note 125, at paras 94–95 (in which the Court adopted an identical reasoning for the equivalent provision in the Regulation on Translation Arrangements).

[127] Case C-146/13, *Spain v. Parliament and Council*, Opinion of AG Bot of 18 November 2014 (ECLI:EU:C:2014:2380), at paras 180–181 ('By refraining from ratifying the UPC Agreement, the participating Member States would infringe the principle of sincere cooperation in that they would be jeopardising the attainment of the Union's harmonisation and uniform protection objectives').

[128] Note that in the context of Community conventions, similar arguments have been raised. The Commission recognized that it did not have the power under the then Article 169 EEC Treaty to start infringement proceedings against a State for failure to ratify a Community convention. See Answer given by Lord Cockfield on behalf of the Commission to the Written Question No 2171/84 by Mrs Jacqueline Thome-Patenôtre (RDE-F) to the Commission of the European Communities (8 May 1985), OJ 1985 C 189/41 ('it must point out that in regard to the ratification of conventions based on Article 220 of the EEC Treaty, it does not enjoy the powers conferred on it by Article 169') cited by P.-E. Partsch, *Le droit international privé de Rome à Nice* (2003), at 132.

[129] See Recital 25 of the Patent Regulation, *supra* note 106.

could argue that the Patent Regulation was adopted under the assumption that the Member States (and their national parliaments) retain a margin of appreciation in deciding to ratify the UPC Agreement. On this view, Article 18(2) allows the possibility of an 'enhanced cooperation within enhanced cooperation':[130] 25 Member States participate in the enhanced cooperation but the unitary effect of the 'European patents' could apply permanently in a subset of them only, depending on whether or not they decide to ratify the Agreement. On the other hand, the Court defined the derogation set out by Article 18(2) as a '*temporary*' one.[131] In the Court's view, it seems that this provision is to be understood as relating only to the application *ratione temporis* of the Regulation. Member States are not allowed to delay indefinitely the application in their territory of the Patent Regulation by not ratifying the UPC Agreement.

Through this action for annulment directed against the Patent Regulation, Spain also attempted indirectly to cast doubt on the legality of the UPC Agreement itself. As the Court recognized it, those points were beyond its jurisdictional reach. In an annulment action, the Court does not have jurisdiction to examine the compatibility with EU law of an agreement concluded by the Member States.[132] For such a challenge to be considered, another procedural route would have had to be followed by Spain: an infringement action based on Article 259 TFEU should have been brought against the Member States that are contracting parties to the UPC Agreement. As a result, the Court's ruling did not dispel all uncertainties as to the compatibility of the UPC Agreement with EU law. In particular, Spain argued that, in designing the Unified Patent Court, Member States had not sufficiently taken into account the criticisms formulated by the European Court of Justice in Opinion 1/09.[133] Significant steps had been taken to put the UPC Agreement in line with the requirements set forth in that earlier ruling.[134] The UPC Agreement indeed states that the UPC is 'a court common to the Contracting Member States' and provides for a mechanism of joint and several liability of the Contracting Member States for damage resulting from an infringement of EU law by the Unified Patent Court.[135] Yet, the Unified Patent Court remains a very idiosyncratic legal construction for which there is no clear precedent and which has not, as such, been validated by the European Court of Justice. There are differences with its most proximate model, the Benelux Court of Justice. Procedures before the Benelux Court are 'merely a step in the proceeding before the national courts'.[136] The Benelux Court is competent to answer preliminary ruling requests from the Benelux national courts on the interpretation of Benelux law only. In contrast, there exists no procedural link between the judicial system of the Member States and the adjudication mechanism set up by the UPC Agreement. In proceedings that are independent from procedures before national

[130] Desantes Real, *supra* note 121, at 641. [131] Case C-146/13, *supra* note 125, at para. 107.

[132] *Ibid.*, at para. 101 (the Court does not have 'jurisdiction to rule on the lawfulness of an international agreement concluded by the Member States').

[133] *Ibid.*, at para. 92. [134] Dehousse, *supra* note 113, at 265.

[135] See in particular Articles 20–23 of the UPC Agreement, *supra* note 104.

[136] Case C-337/95, *supra* note 120, at para. 22. See also Case C-196/09, *Miles and Others*, [2011] ECR I-05105 (ECLI:EU:C:2011:388), at paras 41–42.

courts, the Unified Patent Court will directly be tasked to apply, *inter alia*, EU law, including the Patent Regulation.[137]

If the compatibility of the UPC Agreement with the EU constitutional framework were ever to be considered by the European Court of Justice, it would only be indirectly in the context of post-ratification challenges[138] and in a procedural setting similar to the one of the *Pringle* case. On the occasion of the ratification, a national court would be asked whether a Member State would be in breach of its obligations under EU law by ratifying the UPC Agreement. The national court would then subsequently refer that question back to the European Court of Justice via the mechanism of preliminary ruling.

6. Conclusion

Treaties between the Member States form the foundation of the EU legal order, and every now and then those States, acting as 'Masters of the Treaties' revise these foundational rules, the last major occasion being the conclusion of the Lisbon Treaty. In addition, though less prominently, international treaties between EU Member States play an important role in the day-to-day operation of the European Union. In the panoply of law-making instruments that were made available to the Community institutions, treaties concluded by the Member States jointly were expressly included from the start, in 1957. They are a curious legal phenomenon that fits oddly with the vision of the European Union as an autonomous legal order with its own legal instruments, its own system of decision-making, enforcement, and judicial control. The reference to complementary international agreements signified that the Member States sought to preserve the possibility to exit from the 'autonomous legal order' and revert to traditional international law-making in order to perform certain tasks connected with the European integration project. Whereas these *complementary agreements* were much used in the first decades of European integration, and were revived after Maastricht for use in the 'third pillar', they no longer play an important role today. In contrast with this, we have seen a recent revival of *partial agreements*, concluded between less than all the EU Member States, which have recently become (in the context of the euro-area crisis and in relation to patent protection, in particular) an important but highly unorthodox legal instrument allowing for a differentiation of rights and obligations between EU states. Formally, both complementary

[137] Jaeger, 'Back to Square One? An Assessment of the Latest Proposals for a Patent and Court for the Internal Market and Possible Alternatives', 43 *International Review of Intellectual Property and Competition Law* (2012) 286, at 299–300; For a diverging analysis, emphasizing the similarities between the Unified Patent Court and the Benelux Court, see Note from the Benelux countries annexed to Council Document 13984/11 of 9 September 2011.

[138] Such a post-ratification challenge has taken place in Belgium. The claimant before the Belgian constitutional court had not brought forward arguments based on EU law but only raised questions of compatibility of the UPC Agreement with principles of Belgian constitutional law. The case has been dismissed by the constitutional court because the time limit for bringing an action against the ratification law had already lapsed. See Cour Constitutionnelle, Arrêt du 21 mai 2015, no 71/2015, available at https://lex.be/fr/jurisprudence/decision-judiciaire/cour-constitutionnelle-cour-d-arbitrage/2015-belgique-arret-jr_2015052113 (last visited 9 January 2017).

and partial agreements are not acts of the EU institutions, and hence not part of the EU legal order. However, the links with that EU legal order are often so manifold and narrow that it may be justified to call them, as suggested in the title of this chapter, *quasi-instruments* of EU law. The possibility thus offered to, and taken by, the Member State governments to 'exit' from the EU legal order and to advance their mutual cooperation by means of instruments of international law raises serious issues of democratic legitimacy and effectiveness. So far, the primacy of EU law over those partial and parallel agreements has been respected, and the Member State governments continue to consider the EU institutional framework as the main venue for their cooperation strategies, but one cannot exclude the possibility that some EU Member States might feel tempted to make more systematic use of a legal instrument that allows them to escape the strictures of the European Union's sometimes very cumbersome decision-making process.

7

EU Acts and Member State Acts in the Negotiation, Conclusion, and Implementation of International Agreements

Alan Dashwood

1. Introduction

This chapter is concerned with issues going to the nature of, and the powers and procedures for adopting, the legal acts that may be required where the conduct of the external relations of the European Union (EU) entails entering into international agreements. The focus of the chapter is on the variety of acts envisaged under the procedural code organizing the negotiation and conclusion of international agreements on behalf of the Union, and some aspects of the implementation of such agreements, which is now governed by Article 218 TFEU. However, as the title of the chapter would suggest, there are issues to be discussed with regard to acts of the Member States when they are exercising their sovereign powers as subjects of the international legal order jointly with the Union, for the purposes of a mixed agreement.

The procedural law governing EU external action might sound like a rather dry topic. However, decision-making in this field has become a focal point of the contest between the institutions of the Union, as they seek to establish a new equilibrium in the era of the Treaty of Lisbon. The result has been a very high volume of litigation and a rapidly developing case law, the significance of which, it is hoped, will be seen to extend beyond the interpretation and application of Article 218.

The chapter is in five substantive sections, rounded off by a conclusion. Section 2 deals with general issues, including a survey of the contents of Article 218 TFEU and an analysis of the meaning of 'agreements' under the Article. Section 3 covers decisions on the opening and conduct of negotiations. One of the points discussed is the greater flexibility introduced by the Treaty of Lisbon regarding the appointment of the Union's negotiator. Section 4, relating to decisions on the signature and conclusion of agreements, is the most substantial element of this chapter. Among the topics covered are the rules governing the choice of the legal bases for such decisions, including some cases where the application of the rules by the Court of Justice may seem controversial. An important issue is whether the Court will prove willing to

EU Acts and Member State Acts in the Negotiation, Conclusion and Implementation of International Agreements. First Edition. Alan Dashwood © Alan Dashwood 2018.Published 2018 by Oxford University Press.

countenance the combination of legal bases for the exercise of EU competence in the field of the common foreign and security policy (CFSP) with legal bases figuring in the Treaty on the Functioning of the European Union (TFEU). Also of constitutional moment is the enhanced role of the European Parliament in the post-Lisbon era. Section 5 concerns the establishment under Article 128(9) TFEU of positions to be taken on behalf of the Union in a body, set up by an agreement, which has power to adopt decisions having legal effects. There is a significant volume of recent case law in this field, and doubts are expressed in Section 5 over some of the Court's rulings. Section 6 on Article 218 and Member States' sovereign powers looks at issues of decision-making in the framework of a mixed agreement, notably the recent controversy as to whether it is acceptable for 'hybrid' acts to be adopted, involving the exercise of EU and Member State powers within the same legal act. Section 7 offers some concluding remarks.

2. Article 218: General Issues

A. Article 218 in the Constitutional Order of the Union

Article 218 TFEU contains the most complete procedural code governing the negotiation and conclusion of international agreements on behalf of the EU, as well as certain related matters, that have existed to date. It covers (though with some differentiation) both agreements in policy areas where competence is derived from legal bases in the TFEU and agreements for the purposes of the CFSP. As such, it tends to reinforce the view that the Treaty of Lisbon has created an integral Union structure, in place of the former 'Pillars'.[1]

The procedural code has been progressively elaborated through successive amendments to the Union's foundational Treaties; earlier versions were found in Article 228 EEC, Article 228 EC,[2] and Article 300 EC.[3] Prior to the Treaty of Lisbon, the procedure for negotiating and concluding agreements relating to the CFSP ('the Second Pillar') was laid down by (then) Article 24 TEU, which had been introduced into the Treaty on European Union by the Treaty of Amsterdam and was subsequently amended by the Treaty of Nice. Pursuant to (then) Article 38 TEU, the same procedure was applicable to agreements in the field of police and judicial cooperation in criminal matters ('the Third Pillar'). Episodes in the pre-history of Article 218 will be referred to later in this chapter, as part of the explanation of elements of the present text.

The special constitutional significance of Article 218 TFEU lies in the fact that international agreements provide one of the sources of the EU's positive law. A long

[1] The main basis for this view is Article 1, third para. TEU, which provides that 'the Union shall be founded on this Treaty and on the Treaty on the Functioning of the European Union' and that the two Treaties 'shall have the same legal value', and in the corresponding wording of Article 1(2) TFEU.

[2] Hereinafter 'the post-Maastricht code'.

[3] Hereinafter 'the post-Amsterdam code'. As noted later, there was a further minor amendment to the post-Amsterdam code by the Treaty of Nice.

line of authority, beginning with the *Haegeman* case in 1974,[4] has established that international agreements concluded in the name of the Union have the status, so far as concerns the Union, of acts of one of its institutions; that from their entry into force such agreements automatically form an integral part of the Union's internal legal order, with no need for any formal act of incorporation; and that they are capable, in appropriate circumstances of producing direct effects.[5] Indeed, their status is superior to that of the secondary law of the Union, though not to its primary law.[6] What is more, similar legal consequences attach to the acts of bodies established under such agreements, which are given power to amend or develop their provisions.[7]

The procedures laid down by Article 218 and by its predecessors have, accordingly, been designed to reflect, so far as practicable, the current balance between the political institutions of the EU that applies with regard to internal law-making.

B. Anatomy of Article 218 TFEU

Article 218 comprises no fewer than 11 paragraphs. The Treaty of Lisbon renumbered and radically amended the former Article 300 EC, inserting new paragraphs and reorganizing its structure. The Article begins with a new paragraph (1), which provides:

> Without prejudice to the specific provisions laid down in Article 207, agreements between the Union and third countries or international organisations shall be negotiated and concluded in accordance with the following procedure.

As will be seen, not all of the provisions of Article 218 are directly concerned with negotiating and concluding international agreements, though they all have some connection with the process.

The 'specific provisions' referred to in the opening phrase of paragraph (1) are found in paragraphs (3) and (4) of Article 207 TFEU, the legal basis for Union action in the field of the common commercial policy (CCP). Article 207(3) is a historical survival, harking back to the primordial EEC Treaty. In the drafting style of that Treaty, Article 113 EEC, then the legal basis for the CCP, included certain procedural provisions; its paragraph (3) related to the formal opening and the conduct of negotiations,[8] on which the meagre procedural code contained in Article 228 EEC

[4] Case 181/73, *Haegeman v. Belgium*, [1974] ECR 00449 (ECLI:EU:C:1974:41).

[5] See also Case 104/81, *Kupferberg*, [1982] ECR 03641 (ECLI:EU:C:1982:362); Case C-12/86, *Demirel*, [1987] ECR 03719 (ECLI:EU:C:1987:400); Case C-286/90, *Poulsen*, [1992] ECR I-6019 (ECLI:EU:C:1992:453).

[6] Case C-61/94, *Commission v. Germany* (IDA Agreement), [1996] ECR I-3989 (ECLI:EU:C:1996:313); Joined Cases C-402 and C-415/05P, *Kadi and Al Barakaat International Foundation v. Council and Commission*, [2008] ECR I-06351 (ECLI:EU:C:2008:461).

[7] Case C-192/89, *Sevince*, [1990] ECR I-03461 (ECLI:EU:C:1990:322).

[8] Article 113(3) EEC provided: 'Where agreements with third countries need to be negotiated, the Commission shall make recommendations to the Council, which shall authorise the Commission to open the necessary negotiations. The Commission shall conduct these negotiations in consultation with a special committee appointed by the Council to assist the Commission in this task and within the framework of such directives as the Council may issue to it.'

was silent. That paragraph was retained in Article 113 EC, even after the incorporation of corresponding provisions into Article 228 EC by the TEU (Maastricht); and it survives, with minor and arguably redundant additions,[9] in the TFEU. Article 207(4) prescribes unanimity (rather than the default rule of qualified majority voting (QMV))[10] for decisions by the Council with respect to the negotiation and conclusion of certain categories of CCP agreements,[11] and it is probably this that accounts for the inclusion of the 'without prejudice' clause in Article 218(1).

Paragraph (2) of Article 218 defines the role assigned to the Council under the procedure in these terms:

> The Council shall authorise the opening of negotiations, adopt negotiating directives, authorise the signing of agreements and conclude them.

Thus the 'EU acts' that fall to be adopted in different phases of the procedure are all acts of the Council (though other institutions have their allotted roles in the process of decision-making).

Article 218(3) and (4) govern the formal initiation of the procedure referred to in paragraph (1) and the conduct of negotiations.[12] As indicated earlier, elements relating to this stage of the procedure, which were missing from the original Article 228 EEC, were inserted into Article 228 EC by the TEU (Maastricht), taking Article 113(3) EEC as a model.[13]

Under Article 218(3), the power of initiative belongs, as it does normally in the legislative procedure,[14] to the Commission, except where the agreement envisaged relates 'exclusively or principally' to the CFSP, in which case it belongs to the High Representative of the Union for Foreign Affairs and Security Policy.[15] In both instances, the power is exercisable by way of a recommendation, rather than a proposal in the sense of Article 293(1) TFEU. Power to authorize the opening of negotiations and, depending on the subject of the agreement envisaged, to nominate the negotiator is conferred on the Council.[16]

[9] These make the Council and the Commission 'responsible for ensuring that the agreements negotiated are compatible with internal Union policies and rules' and impose on the Commission an express obligation to report regularly on the progress of the negotiations to the special committee appointed by the Council to assist it in its task, as well as to the European Parliament. Such requirements might be thought to flow from the mutual duty of sincere cooperation in Article 4 TEU.

[10] See Article 16(3) TEU and Articles 207(4) and 218(8), first subpara. TFEU.

[11] Agreements in the field of trade in services and the commercial aspects of intellectual property, as well as foreign direct investment, where such agreements include provisions that would require unanimity for the adoption of internal rules (Article 207(4), second subpara.); and agreements relating to certain politically sensitive service sectors (Article 207(4), third subpara.).

[12] The full texts of paras (3) and (4) are set out, and their provisions are analysed in detail, in Section 3 below.

[13] The Council had previously adopted the practice of applying the procedure of Article 113 EEC on the opening of negotiations, by analogy, to agreements outside the domain of the CCP.

[14] Article 17(2) TEU. [15] Hereinafter 'the High Representative'.

[16] The nature of the Council's act and whether it is reviewable is among the issues analysed in Section 3 below.

Paragraph (4) empowers the Council, if it so chooses (as normally it does), to address directives to the negotiator and to designate a special committee in consultation with which the negotiation must be conducted.

Paragraphs (5) and (6) of Article 218 provide, respectively, for the adoption by the Council, on a proposal by the negotiator, of a decision authorizing the signing of the agreement and, if necessary its provisional application before entry into force, and a decision concluding the agreement.[17] The procedures under the two paragraphs are, however, very different. On the one hand, decisions under paragraph (5) relating to signature and provisional application require no formal participation by the European Parliament.[18] On the other hand, except where an agreement relates exclusively to the CFSP, paragraph (6), second subparagraph, provides that, in the case of the five categories of agreements specified under its point (a), the Council decision concluding an agreement may only be adopted after obtaining the consent of the European Parliament; and, in other cases, after consulting the Parliament, as provided for by its point (b). The development of the Parliament's role at the stage of the conclusion of an international agreement is more fully considered in Section 4(D) below.

Article 218(7) enables the Council, when concluding an agreement, to authorize the negotiator (the Commission or the High Representative, as the case may be), to approve on the Union's behalf modifications to the agreement, where the latter provides for modifications to be adopted by a simplified procedure or by a body it has set up. The power appears to be invoked rather infrequently, though uncontroversially.[19]

Article 218(8) prescribes the Council's voting rule. This is said to be QMV throughout the procedure. However, in specified cases—where the agreement covers a field for which unanimity is required for the adoption of internal measures, as well as for association agreements, for accession agreements, and in case of the agreement on accession of the EU to the European Convention for the Protection of Human Rights and Fundamental Freedoms[20]—the Council is required to act by unanimity.[21]

Article 218(9) lays down a special procedure for two kinds of decision that may fall to be adopted by the Council within the framework of an international agreement that already exists: decisions suspending the application of the agreement; and decisions establishing the position to be put forward on the Union's behalf in a body

[17] The full texts of paras (5) and (6) are set out, and their provisions are analysed in detail, in Section 4 below.

[18] However, the obligation, pursuant to Article 218(10), that the European Parliament be 'immediately and fully informed' applies at this, as at all other stages, of the procedure: see Section 4 below.

[19] For a recent instance, see Decision 2011/265/EU of 16 September 2010 on the signing on behalf of the European Union and the provisional application of the Free Trade Agreement between the EU and its Member States, of the one part, and the Republic of Korea, of the other part, OJ 2011 L 127/1, recital (6) and Article 4.

[20] The Council's decision in this case must further be approved by the Member States in accordance with their respective constitutional requirements.

[21] Whether the unanimity rule prescribed by para. (8), second subpara., applies in relation to decisions adopted under para. (9), in the framework of an association agreement, is among the issues analysed in Section 4(E) and Section 5(B) below.

set up by the agreement, when that body is called upon to adopt acts having legal effects.[22] In the cases to which paragraph (9) applies, the Council acts on a proposal from the Commission or the High Representative, with no formal involvement of the European Parliament. The nature and scope of the Council decisions that may be taken under this special procedure are more fully considered in Section 5 below.

Article 218(10) provides: 'The European Parliament shall be immediately and fully informed at all stages of the procedure.' This provision has been the subject of a recent ruling by the Court of Justice, which establishes that failure strictly to observe the requirement of consultation of the Parliament 'at all stages' will provide grounds for the annulment of an eventual Council decision on the conclusion of the agreement in question.[23]

Finally, paragraph (11) of Article 218 establishes the jurisdiction under which an opinion of the Court of Justice, as to the compatibility with the Treaties of an agreement the Union is contemplating entering into, may be obtained by any Member State, the European Parliament, the Council, or the Commission.[24] That provision has remained substantially unchanged since it figured as the second subparagraph of Article 228(1) EEC, except for the addition of the Parliament to the list of institutions with the right to seek an opinion.

C. The Meaning of 'Agreements'

Key to the scope of the procedure laid down by Article 218 is the notion of 'agreements'. Since Opinion 1/75,[25] it has been clear that this term must be given a broad meaning. As the Court of Justice has explained, Article 218 and its predecessors use the term 'in a general sense to indicate any undertaking entered into by entities subject to international law which has binding force, whatever its formal designation'.[26] The procedure of Article 218, therefore, applies to the negotiation and conclusion in the Union's name of all contractual instruments intended to have binding force under international law, whether they be designated a treaty, a convention, a memorandum of understanding, an exchange of letters, or whatever else.[27]

The Court has also found expressly that, where negotiations take place within the framework of an international organization, what matters in determining the applicable provisions of the Treaties is the question whether the negotiations are

[22] The full text of para. (9) is set out, and its provisions are analysed in detail, in Section 5 below.

[23] Case C-658/11, *Parliament v. Council*, judgment of 24 June 2014 (ECLI:EU:C:2014:2025), which is more fully considered in Section 4(D), below. Hereinafter 'the *Mauritius Suspected Pirates* case'.

[24] In spite of its importance as a source of jurisprudence on the external relations law of the Union, Article 218(11) will not be subjected to detailed analysis in this chapter, since it does not entail the adoption of 'EU acts'.

[25] Opinion 1/75, *Opinion of the Court of 11 November 1975 given pursuant to Article 228 of the EEC Treaty*, [1975] ECR 01355 (ECLI:EU:C:1975:145).

[26] *Ibid.*, at 1360. See also Case C-327/91, *France v. Commission*, [1994] ECR I-03641 (ECLI:EU:C:1994:305), at para. 27; and, more recently, Opinion of AG Sharpston of 15 May 2014 in Joined Cases C-103/12 and C-165/12, *Parliament and Commission v. Council* (*Venezuelan Fishing Opportunities*) (ECLI:EU:C:2014:334), at para. 96.

[27] See P. Eeckhout, *External Relations of the European Union* (2nd edn, 2013), at 195. Opinion 1/75, for instance, concerned an OECD Understanding on a Local Cost Standard.

intended to lead to an 'undertaking entered into by entities subject to international law which has binding force'; if so, it is the provisions on the negotiation and conclusion of international agreements, now contained in Article 218 TFEU, that apply.[28]

Further light has recently been shed on the notion of an agreement for the purposes of Article 218 TFEU by Opinion 1/13.[29] Under the procedure laid down by Article 38 of the Hague Convention of 1980 on civil aspects of international child abduction, when a state accedes to the Convention, existing parties have to indicate their willingness to establish bilateral relations with it by depositing a declaration of acceptance. One of the issues going to the admissibility of the Commission's request for an Opinion in the case concerned the characterization of such declarations as a matter of EU law.[30] Could they be treated as a constituent part of an international agreement within the meaning of Article 218(1) TFEU, so as to fall within the scope of the jurisdiction conferred on the Court of Justice by Article 218(11)? The Court recalled that, under Article 2(1)(a) of the Vienna Convention on the Law of Treaties,[31] an international agreement may be embodied in a single instrument or in two or more related instruments; those instruments may thus constitute the expression of the 'convergence of intent' on the part of two or more subjects of international law, which they establish formally.[32] In this instance, Article 38 of the 1980 Hague Convention made provision for two related instruments: the instrument of accession and the declaration of acceptance of accession. Those separate instruments gave expression, overall, to the requisite 'convergence of intent' of the states concerned and thus amounted to an international agreement.[33]

A similar issue arose in the *Venezuelan Fishing Opportunities* case.[34] The disputed instrument in the case was a Council Decision approving a Declaration on the granting, subject to certain conditions, of fishing opportunities in EU waters (specifically, the Exclusive Economic Zone of French Guiana) to vessels flying the flag of Venezuela.[35] The dispute was about the choice of the substantive legal basis for the

[28] Opinion 1/78, *Opinion given pursuant to the second subparagraph of Article 228(1) of the EEC Treaty—International Agreement on Natural Rubber*, [1979] ECR 02871 (ECLI:EU:C:1979:224), at para. 51; Opinion 2/92, *Competence of the Community or one of its institutions to participate in the Third Revised Decision of the OECD on national treatment*, [1995] ECR I-00521 (ECLI:EU:C:1995:83), at para. 8. See the analysis of Article 218(9) in Section 5 below.

[29] Opinion 1/13, *Opinion pursuant to Article 218(11) TFEU*, 14 October 2014 (ECLI:EU:C:2014:2303).

[30] The practice had been for declarations of acceptance to be made by Member States individually. The substantive issue in the case was whether the 1980 Hague Convention related to an area of exclusive EU competence, since it partially overlapped with Council Regulation 2201/2003 of 27 November 2003 concerning jurisdiction and the recognition and enforcement of judgments in matrimonial matters and the matters of parental responsibility, repealing Council Regulation (EC) 1347/2000, OJ 2003 L 338/1. The Court of Justice agreed with the Commission that EU competence was exclusive in principle, although the Union was not itself party to the Convention.

[31] Vienna Convention on the Law of Treaties of 23 May 1969, 1155 UNTS 331.

[32] Opinion 1/13, *supra* note 29, at para. 37. [33] *Ibid.*, at para. 41.

[34] Joined Cases C-103/12 and C-165/12, *Parliament and Commission v. Council*, judgment of 26 November 2014 (ECLI:EU:C:2014:2400).

[35] See Decision 2012/19/EU of 16 December 2011 on the approval, on behalf of the European Union, of the Declaration on the granting of fishing opportunities in EU waters to fishing vessels flying the flag of the Bolivarian Republic of Venezuela in the exclusive economic zone off the coast of French

Decision.[36] For present purposes, however, the interesting feature of the case was the assumption, apparently unchallenged on either side of the argument, that the procedural legal basis was to be found in Article 218. It was, Advocate General Sharpston remarked with gentle irony, 'a little puzzling that the decision was apparently adopted in accordance with Article 218(6) TFEU without any of the institutions involved exactly knowing *why* and to *what* that procedure was applied'.[37] There were, the Advocate General suggested, two options for characterizing the disputed Declaration: it must either be a unilaterally binding instrument or it must have been intended to produce legal effects only when subsequently accepted by the third state in whose favour it was made, in which case it would constitute one side of an international agreement.

The latter option was chosen by the Court of Justice: the Declaration was to be regarded as an offer made by the EU to Venezuela, which accepted it by sending specific applications for fishing authorizations to the Union and by refraining, when doing so, from expressing any reservations regarding the conditions to which the offer was subject.[38] Whether that interpretation of the respective parties' intentions was factually accurate appears dubious; Advocate General Sharpston was unable to find any evidence that the Declaration was seen, on either the Venezuelan or the Union side, other than as a purely unilateral measure.[39] However, as a legal authority, the judgment confirms the lesson of Opinion 1/13—that EU law follows international law in allowing a binding agreement be formed, without any negotiations, 'through a unilateral instrument which expresses the intention to be bound by an offer already made or which is an offer that is subsequently accepted'.[40]

Because, in the circumstances of the *Venezuelan Fishing Opportunities* case as it understood them, the Court of Justice was satisfied that an agreement had been reached, it did not address the other, more intriguing, option mentioned by Advocate General Sharpston: that the Declaration might have been a unilateral instrument intended by the Council to bind the EU under international law. This raises the question whether, in the absence of express Treaty authorization, the Union is competent to undertake obligations towards third states and international organizations in this way.

In the Advocate General's view, the reference to 'agreements' in Article 218 TFEU (and its predecessors) could not be stretched to cover unilateral instruments. As she points out:

> However wide the definition of the term, it is clear that (in whatever context) an agreement presupposes the meeting of minds of at least two parties. It thus does not cover the circum-

Guiana, OJ 2012 L 6/8. As explained by Advocate General Sharpston in Opinion of AG Sharpston, *supra* note 26, at para. 1, the fish processing industry of French Guiana is dependent on landings by Venezuelan vessels.

[36] On the choice of legal bases for the conclusion of international agreements, see Section 3(C), below.

[37] Opinion of AG Sharpston, *supra* note 26, at para. 71.

[38] Joined Cases C-103/12 and C-165/12, *supra* note 34, at paras 68–71.

[39] Opinion of AG Sharpston, *supra* note 26, at paras 72–82.

[40] The language is that of AG Sharpston, *ibid.*, at para. 79.

stance where the EU expresses its intention to be bound by the terms of its declaration without the need for acceptance by the third State in whose favour that declaration is made. Nor does it apply to instruments whereby no binding commitment is entered into.[41]

That is surely incontestable. So also, it is submitted, is the conclusion reached by Advocate General Sharpston that the Union, nevertheless, possesses competence to bind itself internationally by a unilateral declaration adopted with that intention. As the Opinion indicates, this may be thought to follow from the reasoning that gave birth, in *AETR*[42] and the case law descended from it, to the doctrine of implied competence to enter into international agreements, which is now enshrined in Article 216(1) TFEU.[43] If competence for the Union to undertake international obligations in a given field of external action can arise by implication where the instrument used is consensual in character, because it is needed to secure the attainment of an objective for which internal legislative competence has been expressly conferred,[44] there is no good reason why this should not also be the case where the chosen means is a unilateral instrument. A trace of support for this view can be found in the language of the passage of Opinion 2/94 discussing the fact that the powers of the then Community to undertake international action 'are not necessarily the express consequence of specific provisions of the Treaty but may also be implied from them'. The Court says that 'in the field of international relations... it is settled case law that the competence of the Community to enter into international *commitments* may not only flow from express provisions of the Treaty but also be implied from those provisions'—without differentiating between the types of instrument by which such 'commitments' may be made.[45]

Could Article 218 TFEU serve as the procedural legal basis for adopting unilateral acts intended to give rise to international obligations for the Union? After considering other possibilities, including recourse to the creation of subsidiary powers pursuant to Article 352 TFEU or to the procedure for the adoption of internal measures under the relevant substantive legal bases, Advocate General Sharpston concluded that, on balance, 'applying Article 218 TFEU by analogy appears to be the most workable solution, even if that conclusion requires stretching and squeezing the text of the provision because not each and every part can apply to unilaterally binding declarations in the same way as an international agreement'.[46]

[41] *Ibid.*, at para. 96.

[42] Case C-22/70, *Commission v. Council*, [1971] ECR 00263 (ECLI:EU:C:1971:32).

[43] Opinion of AG Sharpston, *supra* note 26, at paras 97–101.

[44] The classic authorities are Joined Cases 3, 4, and 6/76, *Cornelis Kramer and Others*, [1976] ECR 01279 (ECLI:EU:C:1976:114), at paras 15–32; Opinion 1/76, *Laying-up Fund*, [1977] ECR 00741 (ECLI:EU:C:1977:63), at paras 3 and 4; Opinion 2/91, *Opinion delivered pursuant to the second subparagraph of Article 228(1) of the EEC Treaty*, [1993] ECR I-01061 (ECLI:EU:C:1993:106), at para. 7; Opinion 1/94, *Opinion pursuant to Article 228(6) of the EC Treaty*, [1994] ECR I-05267 (ECLI:EU:C:1994:384), at paras 72–105. Post-Lisbon, see Article 216(1) TFEU.

[45] Opinion 2/94, *Accession by the Community to the European Convention for the Protection of Human Rights and Fundamental Freedoms*, [1996] ECR 01759 (ECLI:EU:C:1996:140), at paras 25–26 (emphasis added).

[46] *Ibid.*, at para. 123.

Again, it is hard to disagree with the Opinion. Admittedly, several provisions of Article 218, notably paragraphs (2) to (4) on the formal initiation and conduct of negotiations, would have no useful purpose with regard to unilateral declarations;[47] however, the same is true of agreements concluded by the 'offer and acceptance method' that was approved in Opinion 1/13 and in *Venezuelan Fishing Opportunities* (hereinafter 'offer and acceptance agreements'). Moreover, the decision-making procedure laid down by paragraph (6) of the Article seems more appropriate for the adoption of such declarations than the alternatives would be: Article 352 TFEU, because this would require the Council to act by unanimity in all cases, whatever the subject matter of the declaration; and the respective procedures for adopting internal measures, because these entail a different series of interactions between the EU institutions, better adapted to the enactment of legislation. Also—and for the present author this is the decisive consideration—the special jurisdiction established by Article 218(11), to enable the compatibility of envisaged international agreements with the Treaties to be determined in advance of their conclusion by the Union, is every bit as necessary in cases where international commitments are accepted by way of a unilateral declaration.

3. Decisions on the Opening and Conduct of Negotiations

The provisions to be examined in detail under this heading are paragraphs (3) and (4) of Article 218 TFEU:

> 3. The Commission, or the High Representative of the Union for Foreign Affairs and Security Policy where the agreement envisaged relates exclusively or principally to the common foreign and security policy, shall submit recommendations to the Council, which shall adopt a decision authorising the opening of negotiations and, depending on the subject of the agreement envisaged, nominating the Union negotiator or the head of the Union's negotiating team.
> 4. The Council may address directives to the negotiator and designate a special committee in consultation with which the negotiations must be conducted.

A. The Initiation of the Procedure

The procedure laid down by Article 218 is set in motion by the Commission or by the High Representative, depending on the subject matter of the envisaged agreement. This formal step may have been preceded by informal 'conversations' between the potential Union negotiator and the third party or parties concerned. While such 'conversations' may be a necessary prelude to a complex negotiation, the judgement as to how far they should be taken calls for sensitivity on the EU side. It is liable to damage the Union's international standing if the Council is asked effectively to rubberstamp a negotiating *fait accompli* and refuses to do so.

[47] *Ibid.*, at para. 117.

The means prescribed for the exercise of the right of initiative is a recommendation. The significance of the reference to a recommendation rather than a proposal is found in Article 293(1) TFEU, which provides: 'Where, pursuant to the Treaties, the Council acts on a proposal from the Commission, it may amend that proposal only by acting unanimously...'[48] Regarding the authorization to open negotiations, there is no possibility of amendment: a simple 'yes' or 'no' from the Council is all that is required. However, if the recommendation includes draft negotiating directives, which it normally will do, these can be amended by the Council acting by QMV (unless the envisaged agreement falls into one of the categories in Article 218(8), second subparagraph, for which unanimity is prescribed). The non-application, in this context, of the rule in Article 293(1) seems justifiable to the present author. The rule is a focal element of the Council/Commission relationship in the legislative process, enabling the Commission, as the institution responsible for promoting the general interest of the Union,[49] to retain influence over the progress of its proposals at the critical stage when a compromise position is being negotiated between national representatives within the Council.[50] However, unlike draft legislation which could, if adopted without amendments, become a legally binding instrument, negotiating directives merely set objectives for, and the parameters of, a negotiating process that will eventually, if successful, result in the establishment of a concrete text, to be formally agreed by the different parties.

The Commission's right of initiative is displaced in favour of the High Representative where the agreement envisaged relates 'exclusively or principally' to the CFSP. The meaning of the phrase 'exclusively or principally' in Article 218(3) needs to be examined in conjunction with that of the reference in paragraph (6), second subparagraph of the Article to agreements that relate 'exclusively' to the CFSP, in the conclusion of which the European Parliament plays no formal part. The latter provision has been the subject of a recent ruling by the Court of Justice, in the light of a closely reasoned Opinion of Advocate General Bot, in the *Mauritius Suspected Pirates* case.[51] Discussion of this issue is, therefore, postponed to Section 4(D) below.

B. The Council's Decision

1. Nature of the Act

The act whereby the Council authorizes the opening of negotiations is normally adopted in the form of a decision with no specific addressee.[52] This seems right, because the act is not intended to bind only the negotiator but will have wider legal consequences, setting in motion a procedure that may lead to the creation of new EU law. Although prior to the Treaty of Lisbon such 'untargeted' decisions were not covered by the definition in Article 249, fourth paragraph EC, they have long been

[48] Some exceptions are provided for, but none of relevance here.

[49] Article 17(1) TEU.

[50] In the ordinary legislative procedure, that will be the first reading stage.

[51] See *supra* note 23.

[52] In German legal parlance, a *Beschluss*, as distinct from an *Entscheidung*.

recognized as capable of producing the legal effects intended by their author (provided that this was an institution with power to adopt binding acts), being commonly referred to as 'decisions *sui generis*'. Post-Lisbon, both targeted and untargeted decisions are covered by the definition in Article 288, fourth paragraph TFEU, which provides: 'A decision shall be binding in its entirety. A decision which specifies those to whom it is addressed shall be binding only on them.'

Article 218(3) should probably be interpreted as using the term 'decision' in the technical sense of Article 288;[53] though whether it does or not is immaterial, since the act is manifestly one intended to have binding legal consequences, by authorizing action that could not otherwise lawfully be taken on behalf of the Union.

It follows that such Council decisions must, in principle, be susceptible to review under Article 273 TFEU, and this has recently been confirmed by the judgment in Case C-114/12.[54] In those proceedings the Commission was seeking the annulment of a 'hybrid' decision of the Council and the Representatives of the Governments of the Member States meeting within the Council, which authorized the opening of negotiations regarding a prospective Council of Europe Convention on the protection of neighbouring rights of broadcasting organizations. The Commission based its case on several grounds,[55] including that the subject matter of the envisaged agreement would be liable to affect common EU rules and that, accordingly, Union competence to conclude the agreement was exclusive, under the *AETR* principle now enshrined in Article 3(2) TFEU.[56] The Court of Justice agreed with that argument, holding that the content of the agreement would fall within an area that was covered to a large extent by common EU rules[57] and, therefore, annulled the Decision. The significance of the case for present purposes is that a half-hearted attempt by certain Member States to challenge the admissibility of the action was brushed aside. The judgment recalls that 'an action for annulment must be available in the case of all measures adopted by the institutions, whatever their nature or form, which are intended to have legal effects'[58] and recognizes that the disputed Decision 'produces legal effects as regards relations between the European Union and its Member States and between the EU institutions'.[59] The Court's language is sufficiently general

[53] In contrast, the term 'directives' in Article 218(2) and(4), discussed later in this section, is evidently not used in the sense of Article 288, third paragraph.

[54] Case C-114/12, *Commission v. Council (Protection of Neighbouring Rights)*, judgment of 4 September 2014 (ECLI:EU:C:2014:2151). See also the Opinion of AG Sharpston of 3 April 2014 in this case (ECLI:EU:C:2014:224), at para. 54.

[55] The issue whether such 'hybrid' Decisions are legally permissible, which the Court did not address, though it was examined at some length by AG Sharpston, is considered in Section 6(A) below.

[56] Case C-22/70, *supra* note 42, at paras 6–32.

[57] Case C-114/12, *supra* note 54, at para. 102.

[58] *Ibid.*, at para. 39. The Court cites: Case C-22/70, *supra* note 42, at para. 42; Joined Cases C-181/91 and C-248/91, *Parliament v. Council and Commission*, [1993] ECR I-03685 (ECLI:EU:C:1993:271), at para. 13; Case C-27/04, *Commission v. Council*, [2004] ECR I-06649 (ECLI:EU:C:2004:436), at para. 44.

[59] Case C-114/12, *supra* note 54, at para. 40. The disputed Decision was explicitly addressed to the Commission: see Article 2. However, the Court evidently regarded its legal effects as being felt more widely.

to remove any doubt that Council decisions on the opening of negotiations are reviewable acts.

While the disputed Decision in *Protection of Neighbouring Rights* cited Article 218(3) and (4) as its procedural legal basis, it mentioned no substantive legal basis,[60] a fact on which the judgment makes no comment. It would not be appropriate for the specification of a substantive legal basis in such decisions to be a condition of their legality, since the correct choice cannot usually be made with certainty until the text representing the outcome of the negotiations has been finalized. However, in making arrangements for the conduct of the negotiations, the Council must at least have an idea as to whether the Union competence to be exercised at the stage of concluding the agreement is likely to be exclusive or non-exclusive.

2. *Nomination of the Negotiator*

According to Article 218(3), besides authorizing the opening of negotiations, the Council's decision has the additional function of, 'depending on the subject of the agreement envisaged, nominating the negotiator or the head of the Union's negotiating team'. How wide a discretion does this provision give the Council? The issue is controversial, because it is connected with the strong assertion by the Commission in the post-Lisbon era of its right to represent the Union internationally. The claim is based on the passage of Article 17(1) TEU that provides: 'With the exception of the common foreign and security policy, and other cases provided for in the Treaties, [the Commission] shall ensure the Union's external representation'. While it is probably correct that negotiating an international agreement can be regarded as a form of 'external representation',[61] the power conferred on the Commission is not unqualified. First and foremost, the power is limited to the representation of the Union as such. As noted elsewhere,[62] following their amendment by the Lisbon Treaty, the foundational Treaties of the Union remain, as they have been hitherto, silent on the topic of mixed agreements. Article 17(1) certainly cannot be interpreted as restricting the right of Member States to participate in the negotiation and conclusion of an agreement that extends to matters falling within their exclusive or non-exclusive competence;[63] nor their right to determine how they will be represented in the negotiating process—whether by the Commission, by the Presidency or individually. Secondly, the power conferred by Article 17(1) does not apply to the CFSP or to 'other cases provided for in the Treaties', a limitation of obvious relevance to Article 218(3).

In Article 300(1) EC and all earlier versions of this provision going back to Article 228 EEC, the Commission was specified as the negotiator of agreements on behalf of the Community. The new language of Article 218(3) seems to have been deliber-

[60] *Ibid.*, at para. 32. [61] Eeckhout, *supra* note 27, at 196.

[62] Dashwood, 'Mixity in the Era of the Treaty of Lisbon', in C. Hillion and P. Koutrakos (eds), *Mixed Agreements Revisited: The EU and its Member States in the World* (2010).

[63] This is an aspect of their essential state functions, which the Union is bound to respect: see Article 4(2) TEU.

ately chosen to give the Council a greater measure of flexibility in deciding how the Union should be represented for the purpose of a given agreement. If it had been intended that the Council be bound by the same rule as that governing the right of initiative, it would have been perfectly easy to have stated this textually. The phrase 'depending on the subject of the agreement' will, of course, normally direct the Council towards nominating the High Representative, where the agreement relates exclusively or principally to the CFSP, and otherwise the Commission. However, there may be cases that call for a more sophisticated approach. For instance, the CFSP element of an agreement may not be sufficient to constitute its 'principal' content, though still substantial, and incapable of being fairly regarded as 'incidental' to the other elements; so that, when the moment comes to conclude the agreement, it may well be considered appropriate to give it a CFSP legal basis, in addition to any relevant legal bases in the TFEU.[64] There would clearly be a strong case for the High Representative to be formally associated with the Commission in negotiating such an agreement. Together, they would represent 'the Union's negotiating team' and if the balance of subject matter were that indicated in the hypothesis, the Council should appoint the Commission as 'leader' of that team.

What of the situation where the agreement that is envisaged seems destined to be 'mixed' and the Member States are unwilling to entrust the Commission with sole responsibility for conducting the negotiations? There are many precedents, both pre- and post-Lisbon, for the adoption, often by way of Council Conclusions, of special negotiating arrangements designed to accommodate representation of the Member States alongside the Union.[65] For instance, it has been the practice for the Union and its Member States to be represented in the negotiation of multilateral environmental agreements by a 'Troika' comprising the Commission together with the current holder of the rotating Presidency and the incoming Presidency.[66] Could such an arrangement now be formalized by the adoption of a Council decision under Article 218(3), nominating the head of a 'Union negotiating team' that includes Member State representatives; and, if so, would it be open to the Council to nominate a 'head' that was not the Commission (or the High Representative), for example the current Presidency?

Guidance as to the correct answer to those questions may be found in the fact that there is no further mention of 'the head of the Union's negotiating team' anywhere in Article 218: it is the 'negotiator' to whom directives may be addressed pursuant to

[64] The issue whether it is permissible to combine TFEU and CFSP legal bases is considered in Section 4(C)(4) below.

[65] See Smyth, 'Mixity in Practice – A Member State Practitioner's Perspective', in C. Hillion and P. Koutrakos (eds), *supra* note 62, at 304–319.

[66] See Delreux, 'The Rotating Presidency and the EU's External Representation in Environmental Affairs: the Case of Climate Change and Biodiversity Negotiations', 8 *Journal of Contemporary European Research* (2002), at 210. This gives a full account of the background to, and the arrangements for, participation by the EU and its Member States in the 10th Conference of the Parties to the Convention on Biological Diversity in Nagoya in October 2010 and the 16th Conference of the Parties to the United Nations Framework Convention on Climate Change in Cancun in November/December 2010. See also, more generally, S. Woolcock, *European Union Economic Diplomacy: The Role of the EU in External Economic Relations* (2012).

paragraph (4) and who proposes authorization of the signature of the agreement and, if necessary, its provisional application pursuant to paragraph (5), and also the conclusion of the agreement pursuant to paragraph (6). This may be taken as an indication that, in appropriate circumstances, and depending on the balance between EU and Member State competences in respect of the agreement envisaged, the function of heading up 'the Union's negotiating team' may be separated from that of the officially designated Union negotiator. Such an interpretation of Article 218(3), allowing formal recognition to be given by the Council to flexible arrangements organizing 'the EU side' of a negotiation, would help reconcile political reality with the requirement of unity in the external representation of the Union.[67] The role of a designated leader, who was not the Union negotiator, would be limited to the conduct of the negotiations. In such a case, the Commission or the High Representative, as appropriate, would still have to be nominated as negotiator to ensure that the directives issued by the Council are respected in so far as the agreement envisaged relates to matters within the Union's competence and, eventually, to propose the signature and conclusion of the agreement on behalf of the EU.

It should be added that, if that interpretation of Article 218(3) is not accepted, there can be no impediment to continued recourse by the Council and the Member States to ad hoc procedural solutions under which the Presidency is authorized to negotiate the elements of an agreement falling within Member State competence, on the basis of a common position reached by consensus.

A final point on the choice of negotiator is that the flexibility that Article 218(3) appears to give the Council does not apply to the negotiation of CCP agreements. The wording of Article 207(3), second subparagraph makes clear that it is the Commission alone to which authorization to negotiate may be given. The retention of CCP particularism in this matter provides an additional indication that Article 218(3) was designed to introduce a more flexible rule regarding other kinds of agreement.

3. *The Negotiating Directives and the Consultative Committee*

It has rightly been pointed out that the term 'directives' in paragraphs (2) and (4) of Article 218 cannot be used in the technical sense of Article 288, third paragraph TFEU.[68] A 'directive' within the meaning of the latter provision is an instrument of indirect legislation, which can only be addressed to Member States.

A question that remained judicially unresolved until recently was whether negotiating directives issued by the Council are legally binding on the designated negotiator. It would have been surprising if they were not, since they are annexed to the authorization to open negotiations, which is binding, and condition such authorization. Where a

[67] The disputed Decision in the *Protection of Neighbouring Rights* case, *supra* note 54, does not appear to have been an instance of the exercise of such a power. This follows from the 'hybrid' character of the Decision. The Presidency was not appointed as 'team leader' but only as the negotiator of any elements of the agreement within the competence of Member States.

[68] Eeckhout, *supra* note 27, at 197, where it is pointed out, in n. 10, that in other language versions of the Treaty different terminology is used.

negotiator deviates from the directives it has received, a political sanction would be for the Council to rescind the authorization or, if a text has already been finalized, to refuse to conclude the agreement. However, that option may not always be available: for instance, where the deviation relates to a small element of a negotiating package, which there is strong political pressure for the Council to conclude as a whole; or where a minority of Member States perceives the likelihood of being outvoted in respect of an agreement that can be concluded by QMV.[69] In such cases, it is submitted, the fact that the negotiator has strayed beyond the directives set by the Council ought to constitute sufficient grounds for a ruling by the Court of Justice in proceedings brought under Article 218(11) that the agreement envisaged is, to that extent, incompatible with the Treaties; or, if a decision on the conclusion of the agreement has already been adopted, for its partial annulment in proceedings under Article 263 TFEU.

At all events, the matter appears to have been settled in Case C-425/13,[70] where the Commission sought the annulment of a Council Decision authorizing the opening of negotiations with a view to linking the EU's emissions trading system with the emissions trading system of Australia, on the ground that certain elements of the negotiating directives were incompatible with Article 218(2)–(4) TFEU and a number of other Treaty provisions.[71] The substantive issues in the case, going to the institutional balance under the procedure laid down by Article 218 TFEU, are considered later. The point of present concern is the rejection by the Court of Justice of the objection to the admissibility of the action that had been raised by the Council, based on its contention that in other institutional disputes the Commission had taken the position that negotiating directives were not binding. Citing its judgment in the *Protection of Neighbouring Rights* case as authority for the proposition that 'a decision adopted on the basis of Article 218(3) and (4) TFEU produces legal effects as regards relations between the European Union and its Member States and between the EU institutions',[72] the Court found that this applied to the contested Decision. In the present author's view, there is no merit in the argument put forward by the Commission that negotiating directives, while having legal effects sufficient

[69] The 'framework agreement' on bananas with certain Central American countries, which the Commission slipped into the WTO package of agreements without seeking the Council's approval, illustrates the first of these situations. However, Germany's eventual success in securing the (very) partial annulment of the Council Decision on the conclusion of the WTO package was based, not on the procedural ground that the Commission had acted outside the bounds of its negotiating mandate, but on the substantive ground that an element of the framework agreement was incompatible with the general principle of non-discrimination: see Case C-122/95, *Germany v. Council*, [1998] ECR I-00973 (ECLI:EU:C:1998:94). The saga of the framework agreement on bananas is well explained in Eeckhout, *supra* note 27, at 198.

[70] Case C-425/13, *Commission v. Council*, judgment of 16 July 2015 (ECLI:EU:C:2015:483). Hereinafter, '*Australian Emissions Trading*'.

[71] The other provisions relied on by the Commission were: Article 13(2) TEU (requirement that each institution 'act within the limits of the powers conferred on it in the Treaties, and in conformity with the procedures, conditions, and objectives set out in them', and that the institutions 'practice mutual sincere cooperation'); and Article 295 TFEU (requirement that the European Parliament, the Council and the Commission 'consult each other and by common agreement make arrangements for their cooperation . . .'. It also invoked 'the principle of institutional balance'.

[72] Case C-425/13, *supra* note 70, para. 28.

to render them reviewable, were nevertheless not binding upon the negotiator. The 'effects as regards relations between the European Union and its Member States and between the EU institutions', referred to by the Court, must surely include an obligation upon the Commission (or, as the case may be, the High Representative) to respect the limits imposed by the Council on the scope of the negotiations.

The Commission's substantive objection in the *Australian Emissions Trading* case was essentially that certain requirements laid down in the body of the contested Decision, as well as in Annex A thereto containing the negotiating directives, would unduly fetter its discretion as negotiator. The contested elements were broadly of two kinds.

There was, first, a set of quite detailed procedural arrangements governing the interaction, in the course of the negotiations, between the Commission, on the one hand, and the Council and the special committee designated by the Council pursuant to Article 218(4) TFEU, on the other. These covered matters such as: the organization of meetings of the special committee; the obligation of the Commission to report in writing to the Council on the outcome of the negotiations after each negotiating session and, in any event, at least quarterly; its obligation to inform the Council of the schedule anticipated and the issues to be negotiated and forward the relevant documents as early as possible, in order to allow the members of the special committee reasonable time to prepare themselves properly; and a further obligation for the Commission to inform the Council and consult the special committee on any major problem that might arise during the negotiations. All of the arrangements in question were found by the Court of Justice to be perfectly consistent with the consultative role assigned to the special committee by Article 218(4), with the other Treaty provisions cited by the Commission and with the principle of institutional balance.[73]

The second category of contested elements consisted of a stipulation that '[w]here appropriate, detailed negotiating positions of the Union shall be established within the special committee... or within the Council', and one permitting the special committee, before each negotiating session, to 'establish negotiating positions'. Those stipulations, the Court held, constituted provisions seeking to bind the negotiator, going beyond both the consultative function of the special committee and the Council's power to draw up negotiating directives.[74]

The ruling in the *Australian Emissions Trading* case is soundly based on the principled distinction between the strategic role of the Council and the tactical role of the Commission (or, as the case may be, the High Representative) in the negotiating process of Article 218 TFEU. The Council addresses negotiating directives to the Commission, reflecting its policy choices; and it is able, through the special committee (if it designates one) to guide the general course of the negotiations, ensuring that the directives are adhered to, or adjusted if this is called for. The conduct of the negotiations is the task of the Commission. If the Council or the special committee had power to lay down detailed negotiating positions, this would inhibit the Commission's ability to respond flexibly to the developing dialogue with the other party (or parties) to the negotiations. There is anecdotal evidence that the Commission

[73] *Ibid*, paras 59 to 84. [74] *Ibid*, paras 85 to 93.

has failed, in the past, to provide special committees punctually with the information they need in order to perform their consultative function effectively. That function has been reinforced by a balanced judgement that also protects the powers of the negotiator. Whether it has removed a source of interinstitutional tension liable to result in litigation, only time will tell.

As a purely practical matter, it will often be wise for negotiating directives to be framed in broad terms that enable the negotiator to respond flexibly to the positions taken by other parties to the negotiation as it develops. If the Council has concerns about the direction that the negotiation is taking, it can always require the negotiator to give an account of itself and, if necessary, issue new directives.

4. Decisions on Signature and Conclusion

The provisions to be examined in detail under this heading are paragraphs (5) and (6) of Article 218 TFEU:

> 5. The Council, on a proposal by the negotiator, shall adopt a decision authorising the signing of the agreement and, if necessary, its provisional application before entry into force.
> 6. The Council, on a proposal by the negotiator, shall adopt a decision concluding the agreement.
>
> Except where agreements relate exclusively to the common foreign and security policy, the Council shall adopt the decision concluding the agreement:
>
> (a) after obtaining the consent of the European Parliament in the following cases:
> (i) association agreements;
> (ii) agreement on Union accession to the European Convention for the Protection of Human Rights and Fundamental Freedoms;
> (iii) agreements establishing a specific institutional framework by organising cooperation procedures;
> (iv) agreements with important budgetary implications for the Union;
> (v) agreements covering fields to which either the ordinary legislative procedure applies, or the special legislative procedure where consent by the European Parliament is required.
>
> The European Parliament and the Council may, in an urgent situation, agree upon a time-limit for consent.
>
> (b) after consulting the European Parliament in other cases. The European Parliament shall deliver its opinion within a time-limit which the Council may set depending on the urgency of the matter. In the absence of an opinion within that time-limit, the Council may act.

A. Ways of Expressing Consent to Be Bound

The successful outcome of negotiations is customarily marked by the initialling of the text of the future agreement. Unless the parties agree otherwise,[75] this is not an

[75] See Article 12(2)(a) of the Vienna Convention, *supra* note 31.

act that has binding consequences in international law but simply identifies the text as the one to be taken forward in the conclusion process. It is treated as incidental to the task of the negotiator and, accordingly, receives no mention in Article 218.

Article 11 of the Vienna Convention identifies a variety of ways in which the parties to an international agreement may express their consent to be bound by it, namely: 'signature, exchange of instruments constituting a treaty, ratification, acceptance, approval or accession'.[76] The method to be applied in a given case will normally be specified in the agreement itself, or it may be inferred from the conduct of the parties.

Where an agreement is to be signed subject to conclusion, signature in itself merely gives rise to an obligation to refrain from acts that would defeat the agreement's object and purpose,[77] and the applicable EU procedure is that of Article 218(5). Authorization to sign the agreement is given by the Council, on a proposal by the negotiator, and by way of a decision within the meaning of Article 288, fourth paragraph TFEU. The European Parliament plays no formal role in the adoption of the decision.[78] The procedure is the same where it is considered necessary to decide on the provisional application of the agreement prior to its entry into force. This power was first introduced into the then Article 300(2) EC by the Treaty of Amsterdam.[79] It is especially useful in relation to mixed agreements, where the process of ratification by 28 Member States can be very lengthy,[80] enabling immediate effect to be given to parts of the agreement that can be concluded on the basis of EU competences.

The Council will then proceed to the conclusion of the agreement under the procedure laid down by Article 218(6). In the case of mixed agreements, the practice is to delay conclusion by the Union until ratifications by the Member States, in accordance with their respective constitutional requirements, have been completed. Under Article 218(6) the Council, once again, acts on a proposal by the negotiator; here, however, except where the agreement relates exclusively to the CFSP, it must first, depending on the subject matter of the agreement, have obtained the consent of the European Parliament or have consulted it.

In cases where the consent of the Union to be bound is to be expressed by signature alone, the Council's authorization to sign the agreement amounts to a decision on its conclusion. Here, therefore, the full procedure of Article 218(6), involving the consent or consultation of the European Parliament (except in the case of exclusively CFSP agreements) will apply. It is similar with regard to offer and acceptance agreements, like the ones in issue in Opinion 1/13 and *Venezuelan Fishing Opportunities.*

[76] Vienna Convention, *supra* note 31. Detailed provisions regarding each of these methods are set out in Articles 12–17.

[77] *Ibid.*, Article 18.

[78] As to the Parliament's right to be 'immediately and fully informed', see *supra* note 18.

[79] Prior to the Treaty of Amsterdam, the practice had been to conclude a free-standing interim agreement, where appropriate, relating to the parts of the agreement capable of being given provisional application. See the examples cited in I. MacLeod, I.D. Hendry, and S. Hyett, *The External Relations of the European Communities: A Manual of Law and Practice* (1996), at 285–286. This is still, of course, an available alternative.

[80] Eeckhout, *supra* note 27, at 201.

When adopting a unilateral instrument expressing the Union's intention to be bound by an offer already made, or one representing an offer by the Union that it intends subsequently to be accepted, the Council must comply with the formalities laid down by Article 218(6).[81] It is submitted that the same would apply, by analogy, in the case of the adoption of a unilateral declaration intended to create binding obligations under international law, assuming (as contended by Advocate General Sharpston in *Venezuelan Fishing Opportunities*) that EU law allows for such a possibility.

At one time, acts of the Council concluding international agreements were not infrequently adopted in the form of regulations.[82] Now the established practice is for the Council to adopt a decision in the sense of Article 288, fourth paragraph.

B. Is Signature and Conclusion a Council Monopoly?

The text of Article 218 is unequivocal on this issue. Paragraph (2) provides that '[t]he Council shall... authorise the signing of agreements and conclude them', while paragraphs (4) and (5) refer, without any saving of powers for other institutions, to the adoption by the Council, on a proposal by the negotiator, of decisions respectively authorizing the signature of, and concluding, the agreement.

Earlier versions of the procedural code prefaced the provision conferring the power of decision on the Council with the apparent saving clause: 'Subject to the powers vested in the Commission in this field....'[83] In Case C-327/91, *France v. Commission*,[84] the Court of Justice rejected a claim by the Commission, based partly on the wording of that clause, partly on an analogy with Article 101 of the EURATOM Treaty, and partly on alleged institutional practice, to be able to negotiate and conclude certain categories of international agreements—notably those of an 'administrative' character—independently of the Council. The judgment makes it very clear that the Commission enjoys no such autonomous treaty-making power, either on its own behalf or on that of the Union; and this has been confirmed at the level of primary EU law by the omission from Article 218 TFEU of the misleading clause. Thus the Commission has power to enter into international agreements on behalf of the Union only in the very limited situations where this is provided for in primary law, for example Article 7(1) of the Protocol on the Privileges and Immunities of the European Communities relating to recognition of the *laissez passer* that is issued to senior officials of the Union's institutions.

[81] As indeed the Council purported to do in *Venezuelan Fishing Opportunities*, *supra* note 26. It consulted the Parliament, which would have been sufficient, if Article 43(3), rather than Article 43(2), had been the correct legal basis for the disputed Decision.

[82] MacLeod, Hendry, and Hyett, *supra* note 79, at 80–81.

[83] See Article 228(1), first subpara. EEC; Article 228(2) EC; Article 300(2), first subpara. EC.

[84] Case C-327/91, *supra* note 26. The case concerned an agreement with the USA designed to enhance cooperation and coordination between that country and the (then) EEC in the application of their respective rules on competition.

The ruling in the *Competition Agreement* case has recently been confirmed in Case C-660/13.[85] The case concerned a Decision by the Commission authorizing two of its members to sign an Addendum to the Memorandum of Understanding (MOU) with Switzerland on that country's contribution to the EU budget, for which prior leave had not been obtained from the Council.[86] The infringement of Article 13(2) TEU by the Commission was alleged by the Council on two grounds: violation of the principle of distribution of powers, by usurping the function of deciding on the policy of the Union, which is a power of the Council pursuant to Article 16 TEU; and violation of the principle of sincere cooperation. It was accepted by both institutional parties and by the intervening Member States that the MOU, and hence the Addendum, were non-binding instruments. Nevertheless, the Court upheld the Council's contention that the Commission did not have power to authorize the signing of the Addendum without securing its prior approval. It rejected the argument that signature of such an instrument fell within the scope of the power of external representation conferred on the Commission by Article 17(1) TEU. The decision concerning the signing of a non-binding instrument like the Addendum was, the Court said, 'one of the measures by which the Union's policy is made and its external action planned for the purpose of the second sentence of Article 16 (1) and the third subparagraph of Article 16 (6) TEU'.[87] Accordingly, it annulled the Decision, while maintaining its effect to provide an opportunity for the adoption of a replacement measure, in order to avoid damaging negative consequences for the relationship between Switzerland and the Union.[88]

Finally on this issue, it is noted that power to enter into an international agreement, which is a prerogative of the Council, can clearly be distinguished from the presentation of written submissions on behalf of the Union to an international tribunal; this, as the Court of Justice has unsurprisingly held, is an aspect of the task of ensuring the external representation of the Union entrusted to the Commission by Article 17(1).[89]

[85] Case C-660/13, *Council v. Commission*, judgment of 28 July 2016 (ECLI:EU:C:2016:616).

[86] The purpose of the Addendum was to increase Switzerland's financial contribution, to match the increased size of the internal market resulting from the accession of Croatia to the EU.

[87] Case C-660/13, *supra* note 85, para. 40. The second sentence of Article 16(1) reads: '[The Council] shall carry out policy-making and coordinating functions as laid down in the Treaties.' The third subparagraph of Article 216(6) reads: 'The Foreign Affairs Council shall elaborate the Union's external action on the basis of strategic guidelines laid down by the European Council and ensure that the Union's action is consistent.'

[88] *Ibid.*, para. 53.

[89] See Case C-73/14, *Council v. Commission*, judgment of 6 October 2015 (ECLI:EU:C:2015:663). The present author is grateful to Professor Marise Cremona for having drawn his attention to this case. The Council sought the annulment of a Commission Decision of 29 November 2013 to submit a 'Written statement of the Commission on behalf of the European Union' for the purposes of a request for an advisory ruling by the International Tribunal for the Law of the Sea (ITLOS) on certain questions relating to illegal, unreported, and unregulated fishing. The Council's contention that, in so doing, the Commission had infringed the principle of the distribution of powers (and hence that of institutional balance) and the principle of sincere cooperation, both now enshrined in Article 13(2) TEU, was rejected by the Court of Justice.

C. Legal Basis of Decisions on Signature and Conclusion

Article 218 TFEU is a procedural legal basis. To comply with the principle of conferral, as defined by Article 5(2) TEU, a Council decision on the signature or conclusion of an international agreement must identify the provision that constitutes the substantive legal basis authorizing action by the Union in the policy area to which the agreement relates. The rules governing the choice of the appropriate substantive legal basis are the same as those that apply in respect of internal measures. They are a purely judicial creation and the terms in which they are expressed have evolved with the development of the case law. However, there is now what appears to be a standard formulation, which may conveniently be broken down into the four rules that are set out below using the Court's own words.[90]

1. Rule (i)

> [T]he choice of the legal basis for a European Union measure, including the measure adopted for the purpose of concluding an international agreement, must rest on objective factors amenable to judicial review, which include the aim and content of that measure.

Rule (i) lays down the guiding principle that the legal basis for the adoption of any EU measure, including a Council decision on the signature or conclusion of an international agreement, must be determined in the light of objective factors. The Court of Justice used to preface its formulation of the Rule by emphasizing that the choice of legal basis 'may not depend simply on an institution's conviction as to the objective pursued . . . '.[91] Evidently, it no longer feels the need to labour this point.

The factors mentioned in Rule (i) are the aim and content of the measure, and these are the subject of the remaining three Rules, although the Court's language implies that other factors may also be relevant. The latter would, presumably, include the respective scope of the provisions of EU law competing for consideration as possible legal bases.

Any assessment of the aim and content of a decision on signing or concluding an international agreement will depend crucially on those of the agreement itself; and it may aid understanding of the latter to place it in the context of another international instrument that it implements. Thus in Opinion 2/00, the fact that the Cartagena Protocol on Biosafety had been drawn up pursuant to a decision of the Conference of the Parties to the Convention on Biological Diversity, indisputably an instrument of environmental protection, was treated by the Court as relevant

[90] Opinion 2/00, *Opinion pursuant to Article 300 EC*, [2001] ECR I-09713 (ECLI:EU:C:2001:664), at paras 22–23; Case C-281/01, *Commission v. Council*, [2002] ECR I-12049 (ECLI:EU:C:2002:761), at paras 33–35; Case C-130/10, *Parliament v. Council*, judgment of 19 July 2012 (ECLI:EU:C:2012:472), at paras 42–45. The formulation of the rules is that found in Case C-377/12, *Commission v. Council*, judgment of 11 June 2014 (ECLI:EU:C:2014:1903), at para. 34.

[91] Case C-300/89, *Parliament v. Council*, [1991] ECR I-02867 (ECLI:EU:C:1991:244), at para. 10.

to the choice of legal basis for the Council Decision authorizing signature of the Protocol.[92]

2. *Rules (ii) and (iii)*

Rule (ii) and Rule (iii) need to be considered together, since the latter constitutes an exception to the former.

According to Rule (ii):

> If examination of a European Union measure reveals that it pursues a twofold purpose or that it has a twofold component and if one of those is identifiable as the main or predominant purpose or component, whereas the other is merely incidental, the measure must be founded on a single legal basis, namely that required by the main or predominant purpose or component.

According to Rule (iii):

> By way of exception, if it is established that the measure pursues several objectives which are inseparably linked without one being secondary or indirect in relation to the other, the measure must be founded on the various corresponding legal bases.

Rule (ii) establishes 'the main or predominant purpose or component' of an EU measure as the general test for determining its legal basis.[93] This is sometimes referred to as the 'centre of gravity' test. In the case of a Council decision authorizing signature or conclusion of an international agreement, the test may be expressed in this way: what, having regard to the aims expressed in the respective preambles to the decision and the agreement, and to their respective content (as well as to any other relevant factors), is the decision essentially about? If a clear answer can be given, the Rule stipulates that the legal basis applicable to the area of external action in question, and it alone, must be cited in the decision. That is so even if, as will often be the case, the agreement is likely to have an incidental effect on other fields of EU competence.

Rule (iii) comes into play when it is at least arguable that no particular objective or component of a measure is so predominant that citation of a single legal basis will be enough to satisfy the principle of conferral, making it necessary either to specify dual or multiple legal bases, or to exclude certain elements from the package. The Court of Justice never fails to mention the exceptional character of this Rule, an indication that the conditions for relying on it will be hard to satisfy. A first condition is that the objectives (or components) in question be 'inseparably linked'. This surely cannot mean that they must be so inextricably linked as to be incapable of being pursued separately;[94] pragmatism would suggest it will suffice for them to be necessary

92 Opinion 2/00, *supra* note 90, at para. 28.

93 Commonly referred to as the 'centre of gravity' test.

94 This is how the Court of Justice understands the principle of so-called Opinion 1/76 exclusivity, which applies in the rare situations (such as those of Opinion 1/76) where a Treaty objective can only be attained if the Union's internal and external competences are both exercised together: see Opinion 1/76, *supra* note 44; Opinion 1/94, *supra* note 44, at paras 85–86.

constituents of a bargain that is being stitched together, otherwise the Union would find itself at a severe disadvantage in international negotiations. A second condition is that the objectives or components in question be sufficiently distinct from each other to call for the exercise of Union competences conferred by different Treaty provisions. This will not be the case, where one of them is 'secondary', which presumably means that it is incidental or ancillary to another element of the agreement;[95] or where an element is 'indirect', presumably meaning that it does not represent the immediate object of the agreement but one that is ulterior or remote.[96]

Rules (ii) and (iii) are now familiar and, in themselves, uncontroversial; although over the years their practical application to the signature or conclusion of international agreements has given rise to a considerable number of interinstitutional disputes, and is still doing so. Two recent cases illustrate different ways in which such disputes may arise and be resolved (if not, perhaps, wholly satisfactorily).

One kind of dispute is where the parties are in agreement that the decision in question is one with a predominant purpose or component calling for a single legal basis, but disagree as to what this should be. Here the task for the Court of Justice is to decide which of the competing legal bases is the correct one; though it may find that the measure pursues the objectives identified on both sides of the argument simultaneously, in which case a dual legal basis may be called for.[97]

The dispute in the *Conditional Access Services* case[98] was of this type. This is one of a long line of cases where the issue has been whether an agreement falls within the scope of the CCP, and hence of Article 207 TFEU (or one of its predecessors), or whether it belongs to some other sphere of the Union's external action, to which a different legal basis applies.[99] Often underlying such disputes is the Commission's preference for Article 207, because Union competence for the CCP is exclusive, and Member States', and hence the Council's, preference for a legal basis that confers non-exclusive competence, which may open the way to concluding a mixed agreement.[100] Prior to the Lisbon Treaty the European Parliament used often to be the Council's ally in these disputes, because Articles 113 EEC and 133 EC gave it no formal role in decision-making on the CCP; now, however, the ordinary legislative procedure is prescribed for the adoption of framework CCP measures, enabling the Parliament to claim that its consent must be obtained before a decision on the con-

[95] Thus, where trade-related measures are just one of several means provided for by a multilateral agreement designed to strengthen environmental protection, there is no need for Article 207 TFEU to be cited in addition to the legal basis for action on the environment, Article 192 TFEU: see Opinion 2/00, *supra* note 90. On the other hand, Article 207 may have to be added, where aspects of trade regulation are central to the protective mechanism established by the agreement in question: see Case C-94/03, *Commission v. Council*, [2006] ECR I-00001 (ECLI:EU:C:2006:2) and C-178/03, *Commission v. Parliament and Council*, [2006] ECR I-00107 (ECLI:EU:C:2006:4).

[96] See Case C-281/01, *supra* note 90, where (then) Article 133 EC was found to be a sufficient legal basis for an agreement on the use of a logo indicating that office equipment was energy efficient, since this would have a 'direct and immediate' impact on trade in the equipment, whereas any positive environmental effect would be 'indirect and distant'.

[97] As it did in Case C-94/03, *supra* note 95.

[98] Case C-137/12, *Commission v. Council*, judgment of 22 October 2013 (ECLI:EU:C:2013:675).

[99] *Ex abundantia*, see the authorities cited in *supra* notes 92 and 93.

[100] Except in the cases of supervening exclusivity provided for by Article 3(2) TFEU.

clusion of a CCP agreement is adopted. In Case 137/12 the Parliament supported the Commission.[101]

The *Conditional Access Services* case concerned the choice of legal basis for the Council Decision authorizing the signature by the Union of the European Convention on the protection of services based on, or consisting of, conditional access; such services include, for example, pay television. An EU harmonization Directive, which was adopted in 1998 on the internal market legal basis that has become Article 114 TFEU, covers much of the same ground as the Convention.[102] The main thrust of both instruments is to combat the manufacture of so-called 'illicit devices' that could be used to circumvent the encryption technology protecting the delivery of conditional access services. Regarding the Council's Decision as a CCP measure, the Commission had proposed Article 207 TFEU as the sole substantive legal basis; whereas the Council, taking the view that the Decision fell rather to be regarded as an internal market measure, had substituted Article 114 TFEU.

The Court of Justice found that the primary object of the Decision on signing the Convention was not to improve the functioning of the internal market but to extend legal protection of the services in question beyond the territory of the EU, and thereby to promote international trade in those services; and that Article 207 TFEU was, accordingly, the appropriate basis for its adoption. The Council had argued that conclusion of the Convention would prevent the export of illicit devices to the EU from non-member European countries, thus helping to ensure the proper functioning of the internal market. However, the Court said, a ban on the export of such devices to the EU concerned the defence of the Union's global interests and fell by its very nature within the ambit of the CCP.

That reasoning, which treats the case as one for the straightforward application of Rule (ii), appears rather less convincing on closer examination. There are two provisions of the Convention, Articles 6 and 8, relating respectively to seizure and confiscation measures and to international cooperation, that have no counterpart in the EU's Directive 98/84. The Court seemed willing to accept that those provisions could be seen as improving the conditions for the functioning of the internal market, but it dismissed this objective as purely incidental to the main one of facilitating trade. Suppose, however, that there had been no Directive 98/84; in that scenario conclusion of the Convention would have operated a far-reaching harmonization of Member States' legislation on the protection of conditional access services. Moreover, being party to the Convention prevents the Union from amending the Directive in the future, unless the amendment can be agreed with the other parties. It is not obvious that an international agreement capable of having such a notable impact on regulation in the internal market should be negotiated and concluded under the Union's exclusive competence for the CCP. At least, it may be asked, should not an agreement with the dual objective of harmonizing a given body of internal rules,

[101] Cf. Case C-411/06, *Commission v. Parliament and Council*, [2009] ECR I-07585 (ECLI:EU:C:2009:518).

[102] Directive 98/84 of the European Parliament and of the Council of 20 November 1998 on the legal protection of services based on, or consisting of, conditional access, OJ 1998 L 320/54.

while helping to liberalize international trade, have a dual legal basis? Such a solution does not appear to have been entertained by the parties on either side of the argument or by the Court itself.

A different kind of dispute is where one of the parties contends that, even though the decision in question may comprise a number of elements, one of them is predominant and the others are secondary or indirect; whereas the other party contends that certain of the elements covered by the decision are sufficiently distinct from the one that is allegedly predominant to require specific legal bases. Here the Court has to decide whether the conditions of Rule (iii) are fulfilled, so as to displace Rule (ii) and allow recourse to a dual or multiple legal basis.

The *Philippines PCA* case[103] provides an example of such a dispute. It illustrates the interplay between Rule (ii) and Rule (iii) in a situation where the EU competence representing the allegedly predominant element of the agreement in question was that for development cooperation. The disputed act was a Council Decision authorizing signature of a framework agreement on partnership and cooperation with the Philippines.[104] The substantive legal bases the Commission had proposed for the Decision were those relating to the CCP (Article 207 TFEU) and to development cooperation (Article 209 TFEU). To these the Council had added three further legal bases, relating respectively to the re-admission of nationals of the parties (Article 79(3) TFEU), transport (Articles 91 and 100 TFEU), and the environment (Article 191(4) TFEU). The Court of Justice accepted the Commission's contention that the additional legal bases could not be justified as necessary for the pursuit of objectives distinct from those of development cooperation, and proceeded to annul the Decision in so far as they had been added to it.

The question whether an agreement covering a range of matters for which specific legal bases exist in the Treaty could be concluded as a single development cooperation 'package' on the basis of the provision corresponding to present Article 209 TFEU received an answer from the Court of Justice in Case C-268/94, *Portugal v. Council*.[105] The fact that a development cooperation agreement contained clauses concerning various specific matters, the Court said, could not alter the characterization of the agreement; this must be determined 'having regard to its essential object and not in terms of individual clauses, provided that those clauses do not impose such extensive obligations concerning the specific matters referred to that those obligations in fact constitute objectives distinct from those of development cooperation'.[106] When examining the provisions of the PCA with India relating to the 'specific matters' at issue in the case (which included drug abuse control, then a 'Third Pillar' competence) the Court found that, taken as a whole, they were 'limited to determining the areas for cooperation and to specifying certain of its aspects, but

[103] Case C-377/12, *supra* note 90.

[104] 'The PCA with the Philippines' or, where the context permits, 'the PCA'.

[105] Case C-268/94, *Portugal v. Council*, [1996] ECR I-06177 (ECLI:EU:C:1996:461); Case C-91/05, *Commission v. Council*, [2008] ECR I-03651 (ECLI:EU:C:2008:288). The case concerned the Partnership and Development Agreement between the EC and India ('the PDA with India').

[106] Case C-268/94, *supra* note 105, at para. 39, cited in the judgment in Case C-377/12, *supra* note 90, at para. 39.

contained nothing that prescribed in concrete terms the manner in which cooperation in each specific area envisaged was to be implemented'.[107] Following a more detailed examination of the relevant provisions, the Court held that there was no reason to stipulate additional legal bases.

In his Opinion in the *Phillipines PCA* case Advocate General Mengozzi expressed the view that the criteria enunciated in *Portugal v. Council* were merely a specific application of the general rules governing the choice of legal bases for EU acts;[108] adding, however, that the breadth of the definition of development cooperation in EU law may make it more than usually difficult to establish that certain objectives are distinct from those of the cooperation in question, while still being inseparably linked to it.[109] Without adverting specifically to this passage of the Opinion, the Court seems to have accepted the identity between the different sets of criteria, since language from Rule (ii) features in the formulation of the issues the judgment identifies as the core of the dispute, namely whether the provisions of the PCA with the Philippines relating to the three disputed matters also contribute to the pursuit of the objectives of development cooperation; and, if they do, 'whether those provisions do not nevertheless contain obligations so extensive that they constitute distinct objectives that are *neither secondary nor indirect in relation to the objectives of development cooperation*'.[110] For the purposes of the present discussion, it will be sufficient to limit consideration of the Court's analysis of those issues to the case for the addition of a legal basis relating to the re-admission of nationals of the parties, since that was the matter on which the position of the Council seemed strongest.

As to the first issue, indications that the relevant provisions of the PCA with the Philippines—those of its Article 26—contribute to the objectives of development cooperation were found by the Court of Justice[111] in various references to the linkage between migration and development contained in the so-called 'European Consensus' on development,[112] as well as in Regulation 1905/2006, which is the financing instrument for development cooperation.[113] It is further noted in the judgment[114] that Article 26 has the heading, 'Cooperation on Migration and Development' and provides that migration concerns are to be included in the national strategies for economic and social development of countries of origin, transit, and destination of migrants (Article 26(1), *in fine*) and that such cooperation will focus in particular on migration and development issues (Article 26(2)(h)).

[107] Case C-377/12, *supra* note 90, at para. 40, adapting para. 45 of the judgment in Case C-268/94, *supra* note 105.

[108] Opinion of AG Mengozzi, Case C-377/12, *Commission v. Council*, (ECLI:EU:C:2014:29), at para. 25.

[109] *Ibid.*, at para. 29.

[110] Case C-377/12, *supra* note 90, at para. 48 (emphasis added).

[111] *Ibid.*, paras 49 and 50.

[112] Joint Statement by the Council and the Representatives of the Governments of the Member States meeting within the Council, the European Parliament and the European Commission on European Development Policy: The European Consensus, OJ 2006 C 46/1.

[113] Regulation 1905/2006 of the European Parliament and of the Council of 18 December 2006 establishing a financing instrument for development cooperation, OJ 2006 L 378/41.

[114] Case C-377/12, *supra* note 90, at para. 52.

As to the second issue, the Court of Justice acknowledged that, unlike the provisions of the PCA relating to transport and the environment, those contained in Article 26(3) impose specific obligations.[115] The Philippines, on the one hand, and Member States, on the other, undertake to re-admit their nationals who do not fulfil, or no longer fulfil, the conditions of entry or residence on the territory of the other party, upon the request of that other and without undue delay, once the nationality of the persons concerned has been established and the requirements of due process fulfilled; and they agree to provide their nationals with the necessary documentation. They also accept, pursuant to Article 26(4), an obligation to conclude as soon as possible an agreement governing admission and re-admission (including as regards nationals of other countries and stateless persons, though that is not mentioned in the judgment). However, in spite of all this, the Court concludes that the provisions in question do not pass the test of imposing obligations that are sufficiently 'extensive' to constitute objectives distinct from those of development cooperation—apparently because they are not as detailed and concrete as those that will eventually be laid down by the envisaged re-admission agreement.

Again, the Court's reasoning seems less than compelling, not least because the judgment fails to address the fact that the provisions of Article 26(3) and (4), in the words of Advocate General Mengozzi 'depart from the PCA's first concern—steady progress in development in the Philippines—to fulfil one of the European Union's own objectives and to serve its interests: the commitment by the contracting third country to take back its own nationals who are illegally resident in European Union territory'.[116] The vision promoted in those paragraphs is said by the Advocate General to be 'rather a defensive one which places European Union interests first'; the idea being 'to protect the Union and its Member States from the deficiencies of the contracting third State with regard to the protection of migratory flows'.[117] In spite of the fact that a corresponding re-admission obligation is imposed on EU Member States, Advocate General Mengozzi is surely correct as to the aim of those provisions. As he points out, '[i]t is public knowledge that the flow of migrants from the Philippines to the European Union is much greater than the movement of Union citizens in the opposite direction'.[118]

Can provisions having such an aim and content be regarded as contributing to the objectives of development cooperation? The Advocate General's answer is that they can, because 'there would not be such a commitment without the overall cooperation put in place by the PCA, the focus of which is on the contracting third country's development'.[119] In other words, the fact that the development cooperation objectives provide leverage enabling the Union to further its own objective of securing more effective arrangements to deal with illegal immigration and over-staying, is seen as rendering the latter ancillary to the former.

[115] *Ibid.*, at para. 57.
[116] Opinion of AG Mengozzi, Case C-377/12, *supra* note 108, at para. 70.
[117] *Ibid.*, at para. 71. [118] *Ibid.*, at para. 69. [119] *Ibid.*, at para. 72.

However, a different analysis is possible and, in the respectful submission of the present author, more plausible. The re-admission clause does not represent one of the areas of the cooperation envisaged by the PCA as a contribution to the sustainable development of the Philippines; it is neither a means of furthering nor an incidental effect of, but rather the *quid pro quo* for, such cooperation. It is designed, as Advocate General Mengozzi clearly explained, to serve the purposes of the EU's immigration policy. The relationship between the re-admission clause and the development cooperation objectives of the PCA is, therefore, that of an element of the bargain *inseparably linked* to those objectives, but neither secondary nor indirect in relation to them. Accordingly, it is submitted, there were solid grounds for the addition of Article 79(3) TFEU as one of the legal bases of the disputed Decision.

A final comment on the case concerns the triggering of the mechanism of Protocol 21, which applies for the benefit of Ireland and the United Kingdom, and that of Protocol 22, which applies for the benefit of Denmark, whenever any of the legal bases in Title V of Part Three of the TFEU is resorted to, including Article 79(3). Where the act in question is a decision on the signature or conclusion of an international agreement, the effect, in broad terms, will be to allow the three Member States concerned to decide for themselves whether they wish to be bound by the agreement as part of the EU or as separate contracting parties, or not to be bound at all.[120] It is important to be clear that the existence of Protocols 21 and 22 can never provide a reason for not choosing a legal basis contained in Title V, where the aim and content of the measure in question indicates that this would be the right choice to make. Advocate General Mengozzi had occasion to recall this point in the *Philippines PCA* Case, emphasizing the primacy of substance over procedure,[121] since the Commission had cited the 'unwarranted legal effects' of the Protocols as a consideration militating against recourse to Article 79(3).[122] What is more, although the Advocate General reached the conclusion that Article 79(3) had wrongly been cited in the disputed Decision, he went out of his way to emphasize that it would be the correct legal basis for any future re-admission agreement with the Philippines, at which stage 'the full effectiveness of Protocols Nos 21 and 22 will be ensured, together with the rights of the Member States concerned'.[123]

[120] Established practice is for the legal situation to be explained in the preamble to the decision and to the agreement; as indeed was done in the case of the disputed Decision and the PCA with the Philippines.

[121] He noted that 'according to settled case law, it is not procedures that define the legal basis of a measure but the legal basis of a measure that determines the procedures to be followed in adopting that measure', in Opinion of AG Mengozzi, Case C-377/12, *supra* note 108, at para. 57. See also the Opinion of AG Bot of 10 September 2013 in Case C-43/12, *Commission v. Parliament and Council*, [2014] (ECLI:EU:C:2013:534), at para. 14.

[122] The Commission's argument is summarized at para. 22 of the judgment in Case C-377/12, *supra* note 90.

[123] Opinion of AG Mengozzi, Case C-377/12, *supra* note 108, paras 74–77.

3. Rule (iv)

However, no dual legal basis is possible where the procedures required by each legal basis are incompatible with each other.

Rule (iv) is formulated as an exception to Rule (iii). At first sight, it seems liable to impose unattractive choices on the EU institutions: between hiving off elements of a measure that should properly be regarded as inseparable from its other elements; or adopting the measure under a legal basis that does not fully reflect the competences that are being exercised. Fortunately, the Court of Justice has adopted a flexible approach to the practical application of the Rule; unfortunately, this is not reflected in the formulation that is constantly reiterated in the case law.

The Rule was first applied by the Court in Case C-300/89,[124] where the dispute was about the legal basis for a Council Directive on the harmonization of programmes for combating pollution caused by titanium dioxide waste.[125] The choice was between Article 100a EEC, then the legal basis for internal market measures, favoured by the Commission, and Article 130s, then the legal basis for environmental measures, favoured by the Council. The Court was satisfied, in the light of the aim and content of the Directive, that it displayed the features of both kinds of measure. However, it was held that the normally orthodox solution of combining the two legal bases was unavailable, because the adoption procedure prescribed by Article 100a was the cooperation procedure,[126] whereas that prescribed by Article 130s required the Council to act by unanimity after consulting the European Parliament. As the Court explained, the elements of the cooperation procedure designed to enhance the role of the Parliament in the legislative process of the then Community depended on its ability to effect or to influence a shift in the voting rule of the Council from QMV to unanimity.[127] That mechanism would be undermined if, pursuant to Article 130s, the Council were required, in any event, to act unanimously. Since a dual legal basis was excluded, the Court opted for Article 100a EEC, on the ground that a measure adopted under that Article could effectively pursue the objective of protecting the environment at the same time as that of eliminating distortions of competition within the internal market. This was because environmental protection was required to be 'a component of the Community's other policies',[128] and because the Commission was required, in its proposals for internal market measures, to take as a base a high level of protection in matters of environmental protection (among other things).[129]

[124] Case C-300/89, *supra* note 91.

[125] Council Directive 89/428/EEC of 21 June 1989 on procedures for harmonizing the programmes for the reduction and eventual elimination of pollution caused by waste from the titanium dioxide industry, OJ 1989 L 201/56.

[126] The cooperation procedure was introduced by the Single European Act. It was the forerunner of codecision, first introduced by the TEU (Maastricht), which has become the ordinary legislative procedure.

[127] By rejecting the Council's common position or by persuading the Commission to incorporate amendments into its re-examined proposal: see Case C-300/89, *supra* note 91, paras 19 and 20.

[128] Article 130r(2) EC. See now Article 11 TFEU.

[129] Article 100a(3) EC. See now Article 114(3).

In spite of the uncompromising terms of Rule (iv), the present author has been unable to identify a single instance since the *Titanium Dioxide Waste* case in which the application of the Rule has resulted in the non-citation of a legal basis that would otherwise have met the conditions of Rule (iii).

In some cases, having referred to Rule (iv), and indicated that it considers the legal bases in question to be mutually exclusive, the Court of Justice has gone on to decide that one (or more) of them is either incidental or inappropriate, so the incompatibility of the prescribed decision-making procedures has not become an issue.[130] In other cases, the Court has found a dual legal basis to be acceptable, even though the provisions relied upon prescribe different procedures, because these are regarded as compatible. For example, in judgments relating, respectively, to the conclusion and the implementation within the then EC of the Rotterdam Convention on the Prior Informed Consent Procedure for Certain Hazardous Chemicals and Pesticides in International Trade,[131] the Court, of its own motion, approved the combination of the CCP legal basis (then Article 133 EC), which gave the European Parliament no formal role, with the legal basis for action on the environment (then Article 175(1) EC), under which codecision was the prescribed procedure. The judgments note that the dual legal basis would not affect the Council's voting rule, which was QMV in both cases, and that the prerogatives of the European Parliament would not be encroached upon, because there was no impediment to the adoption of the implementing measure by codecision.

More significantly, the Court has held that former Article 308 EC, under which the Council acted by unanimity (as it still does under Article 352 TFEU) could be combined with a legal basis under which the Council acted by QMV, in cases where it was considered necessary to supplement the competence conferred by the latter, in order to attain an objective of the (then) Community. Thus in *Kadi (No. 1)*[132] a dual legal basis comprising Article 308 and Article 301 EC (under which the Council acted by QMV on a proposal from the Commission) was found acceptable as a means of extending, to asset-freezing measures against individuals not controlling any particular country or territory, the Union's competence for the imposition of economic sanctions. Similarly, in *International Fund for Ireland*[133] Article 308 EC was used to extend the competence conferred by former Article 159 EC, a provision prescribing the codecision procedure, in order to allow a contribution to be made to the Fund that would cover elements falling outside the scope of the (then) Community's competence for economic and social cohesion. The Court saw no objection to complying with both the codecision procedure and the requirement that the Council act by unanimity.[134]

130 See Joined Cases 164/97 and 165/97, *Parliament v. Council*, [1999] ECR I-01139 (ECLI:EU:C:1999:99); Case C-338/01, *Commission v. Council*, [2004] ECR I-04829 (ECLI:EU:C:2004:253); Case C-130/10, *supra* note 90; Case C-377/12, *supra* note 90, discussed earlier.

131 Case C-94/03, *supra* note 95 and C-178/03, *supra* note 95.

132 Joined Cases C-402 and C-415/05P, *supra* note 6, at paras 235–236.

133 Case C-166/07, *Parliament v. Council*, [2009] ECR I-07135 (ECLI:EU:C:2009:499).

134 *Ibid.*, at para. 69.

The lesson to be drawn from the case law, it seems, is that Rule (iv) will only defeat Rule (iii) in exceptional circumstances like those of the *Titanium Dioxide Waste* case, where elements of the procedure applicable under one of the provisions in question would, to borrow the Court's language, 'divest [the other] procedure of its very substance'.[135] For the reasons explained earlier, such would have been the effect on the cooperation procedure of combining (then) Article 100a EC with a provision prescribing the unanimity rule, like (then) Article 130s. However, as the Court of Justice found in *International Fund for Ireland*, a requirement that the Council act by unanimity is perfectly compatible with codecision (now the ordinary legislative procedure).[136]

So far as concerns the conclusion of international agreements, it is difficult to think of any combination of legal bases in the TFEU that would produce what might be termed a '*Titanium Dioxide Waste* effect'. For instance, if an agreement includes internal market elements together with elements relating to direct and indirect taxation, a legal basis consisting of Articles 113, 114, and 115 TFEU would require the Council to act by unanimity, after obtaining the consent of the European Parliament. This, it is submitted, would effectively be on all fours with the dual legal basis in *International Fund for Ireland*, which the Court considered unproblematic.

4. *Joint TFEU/CFSP Legal Bases*

What, then, of the possibility of combining TFEU and CFSP legal bases (so-called 'TFEU/CFSP mixity'; formerly 'cross-Pillar mixity')? The Court of Justice seemed to set its face against this in Case C-130/10, which concerned the choice between Article 75 TFEU and Article 215(2) TFEU as the legal basis for the adoption of a regulation amending earlier legislation imposing an asset freeze on persons associated with Al-Qaeda and the Taliban.[137] By way of a 'preliminary observation' the Court ruled out the possibility of combining the two legal bases, pointing out that the ordinary legislative procedure was prescribed for the adoption of measures under Article 75, whereas Article 215(2) involved only informing the European Parliament; moreover, recourse to the latter provision required a previous decision in the domain of the CFSP, and '[a]s a general rule, adoption of such a decision calls for unanimous voting in the Council acting alone'.[138]

This is not the place to consider whether the dynamics of decision-making under the ordinary legislative procedure of the TFEU are reconcilable with those of decision-making for the purposes of the CFSP. The same issues do not arise under Article 218 TFEU, because the interaction between the Parliament and the Council in the

[135] Case C-300/89, *supra* note 91, at para. 18.

[136] Indeed, when codecision was first introduced by the TEU (Maastricht), the Council was required to act by unanimity, at all stages of the procedure, for the adoption of incentive measures in the field of culture (then Article128(5), first indent) and that for the adoption of the multiannual framework programme for research (then Article 130i(1)).

[137] See Case C-130/10, *supra* note 90.

[138] *Ibid.*, at paras 46 and 47.

course of successive readings, which characterizes the ordinary legislative procedure, is lacking here. It is submitted that there would be nothing resembling a '*Titanium Dioxide Waste* effect' if, say, a partnership and cooperation agreement included elements (such as a police mission) belonging to the sphere of the CFSP. It has been suggested earlier in this chapter that, in such a case, the agreement could be negotiated by a 'Union team' comprising the Commission and the High Representative;[139] and it could be concluded by the Council acting unanimously, after obtaining the consent of the Parliament. The drafting of Article 218(3) and (6) appears to militate in favour of such a possibility. It hardly seems likely that those provisions, which explicitly contemplate the negotiation and conclusion of agreements containing both CFSP and TFEU elements, were intended to apply only in cases where one of those elements was predominant and the other incidental or indirect in relation to it, so as to exclude the application of Rule (iii).

For the moment, judicial authority on the point is limited to *obiter dicta* of Advocate General Bot in the *Mauritius Suspected Pirates* case. The dispute in the case concerned an agreement between the EU and Mauritius on the conditions for the transfer to Mauritius of suspected pirates and associated seized property from the EU-led naval force in the Indian Ocean. The main issues in dispute, regarding participation by the European Parliament in the process of negotiating and concluding the agreement, are discussed in the next section. For present purposes, it is sufficient to note that Advocate General Bot seems to have taken for granted that a joint or multiple legal basis including both CFSP and TFEU elements would have been legally possible;[140] and he refers in a footnote,[141] with evident approval, to a recent Council Decision on the accession of the EU to the Treaty of Amity and Cooperation in Southeast Asia,[142] which had as its legal bases Articles 37 and 31(1) TEU, together with Articles 209 and 212 TFEU and Article 218(6)(a) and Article 218(8) second subparagraph TFEU. There is no indication in the judgment as to whether or not the Court agreed with the Advocate General.[143]

D. The Role of the European Parliament in the Conclusion of Agreements

Article 218(6) TFEU represents the latest stage in the progressive involvement of the European Parliament in the formal procedure for concluding international agreements, which goes back to the primordial EEC Treaty. Issues that have arisen as a result of the changes brought about by the Lisbon Treaty will provide the main focus of the present discussion.

[139] See the discussion of Article 218(3) TFEU.

[140] Opinion of AG Bot, Case C-658/11, *supra* note 23, (ECLI:EU:C:2014:41), at para. 33.

[141] *Ibid.*, at n. 7.

[142] Council Decision 2012/308/CFSP of 26 April 2012, OJ 2012 L 154/1.

[143] Case C-263/14, OJ 2014 L 108/1, which was brought by the European Parliament against the Council on 28 May 2014, raises similar issues to Case C-658/11 and may provide an opportunity for clarifying the matter of TFEU/CFSP mixity.

1. *The Meaning of 'Exclusively' in Article 218(6), Second Subparagraph*

The introductory phrase of the second subparagraph of Article 218(6) TFEU creates a sole exception to the requirement that a Council decision on the conclusion of an international agreement may be adopted only after obtaining the consent of the European Parliament in the five cases stipulated in the subparagraph, and after consulting it in other cases; that is to say, 'where agreements relate *exclusively* to the [CFSP]'.[144] There were two possible interpretations of the word 'exclusively' in that provision: either that the agreement in question contains no elements whatsoever that relate to other policy areas but is entirely concerned with the CFSP; or that, applying the centre of gravity test in Rule (ii), as explained earlier, the CFSP represents 'the main or predominant purpose or component' of the agreement, so that a CFSP legal basis for the Council's decision is necessary and sufficient. In other words, even though the agreement does contain other elements, these are secondary or incidental and, accordingly, do not require legal bases additional to the CFSP one.

The issue has been settled in favour of the second of those two interpretations by the *Mauritius Suspected Pirates* case.[145] The European Parliament, which unsurprisingly embraced the first interpretation, had argued that the Council had been wrong to treat the agreement as one relating exclusively to the CFSP, and therefore covered by the derogation in Article 218(6), first subparagraph, because some of its provisions relating to the treatment of suspects and to the provision of technical assistance in dealing with them impinged upon the Union's competences for police and judicial cooperation in criminal matters and for development cooperation; though the Court understood the Parliament to have conceded that such elements of the agreement were incidental to those falling within the CFSP and that the contested Council Decision on the conclusion of the Agreement had therefore properly been founded exclusively on Article 37 TEU.[146]

Adopting the reasoning of Advocate General Bot, the Court held that 'Article 218(6) establishes symmetry between the procedure for adopting EU measures internally and the procedure for adopting international agreements in order to guarantee that the Parliament and the Council enjoy the same powers in relation to a given field, in compliance with the institutional balance provided for by the Treaties'.[147] It was, the Court said, to ensure the preservation of that symmetry that the rule 'that it is the substantive legal basis of a measure that determines the procedures to be followed in adopting that measure'[148] applies not only to the adoption of internal acts but also to the conclusion of international agreements.[149] Anchoring the procedural legal basis to the substantive legal basis also contributes to legal certainty, by enabling the applicable procedure to be determined on the basis of objective criteria amenable to judicial review.[150]

[144] Emphasis added. [145] Case C-658/11, *supra* note 23.

[146] *Ibid.*, at para. 45. It does not appear that AG Bot took the same view, since he analysed the choice of legal basis in detail, reaching the conclusion that Article 37 TEU, on its own had been correctly chosen.

[147] *Ibid.*, at para. 56. [148] Case C-130/10, *supra* note 90, was cited as authority for this rule.

[149] Case C-658/11, *supra* note 23, at para. 57.

[150] *Ibid.*, at para. 60.

The Parliament had argued, not unreasonably, that the term 'exclusively' must have the same meaning in paragraph (6) of Article 218 TFEU as in paragraph (3) of the same Article, in which the phrase 'exclusively or principally' seems intended to distinguish the case of an envisaged agreement relating solely to the CFSP from that of an agreement concerned mainly with the CFSP but also with certain other matters. The argument was brushed aside by the Court on the ground that the two provisions serve different purposes: while paragraph (3) is about specifying the authority empowered to submit recommendations to the Council in the context of the procedure for negotiating an agreement, paragraph (6) relates to the Council's decision on its eventual conclusion. The point is well taken: at the stage before negotiations have even started, it is possible only to reach an approximate view as to where the centre of gravity of the envisaged agreement will be found, whereas at the conclusion stage the established rules on the choice of the legal basis for an EU act must be applied strictly. However, the inconsistent use of a term within the same Treaty article is clearly unfortunate.

2. *The European Parliament's Right under Article 218(10) TFEU to Be Kept Informed*

Another issue settled by the judgment in the *Mauritius Suspected Pirates* case was the nature and scope of the European Parliament's right under Article 218(10), newly conferred by the Treaty of Lisbon, to 'be immediately and fully informed at all stages of the procedure'. The Court found from the file submitted to it, that 'after having announced the opening of negotiations to the Parliament, the Council did not inform it of the adoption of the contested decision and the signing of that agreement until three months later and 17 days after their publication in the *Official Journal*'.[151] Harking back to its judgment in the famous *Isoglucose* case of 1980,[152] the Court of Justice characterized the rule in Article 218(10) as 'an expression of the democratic principle on which the Union is founded'.[153] The exclusion of the Parliament from the procedure for the negotiation and conclusion of agreements relating solely to the CFSP did not mean that it had no right of scrutiny over that EU policy; on the contrary, the information requirement had been laid down by Article 218(10) precisely for that purpose. The Court accordingly found that the Council's failure to keep the Parliament 'immediately and fully informed at all stages of the procedure…, including that preceding the conclusion of the agreement' amounted to the infringement of an essential procedural requirement, and it went on to annul the disputed decision.[154]

The case established that the right of the European Parliament to information pursuant to Article 218(10) has, as its corollary, an imperative obligation for the institutions involved in the procedure for the negotiation and conclusion of international agreements, including those relating exclusively to the CFSP.

[151] *Ibid.*, at para. 77.
[152] Case C-138/79, *Roquette v. Council*, [1980] ECR 03333 (ECLI:EU:C:1980:249).
[153] Case 658/11, *supra* note 23, at para. 81.
[154] *Ibid.*, at paras 86–87.

3. Agreements that Require the Consent of the European Parliament for their Conclusion

The procedure for concluding international agreements has marched roughly in step with that of the Union's legislative procedures. Article 228, first paragraph, EEC provided for agreements to be concluded by the Council 'after consulting the Assembly where required by the Treaty', consultation being the highest level of involvement of the then Assembly in the law-making process of the Community as originally established.[155] There have subsequently been two major amendments of the rules defining the participation of the European Parliament[156] in the conclusion of international agreements, by the TEU (Maastricht) and by the Treaty of Lisbon.

The TEU (Maastricht) established that the Parliament must be consulted by the Council prior to the conclusion of international agreements other than ones relating to the CCP (where no formal participation by the Parliament was required); while four categories of agreement were identified, which were only to be concluded after the assent of the Parliament had been obtained.[157] These were: agreements establishing the especially intimate relationship with a third country or countries or an international organization, which is known as 'association';[158] other agreements establishing a specific institutional framework by organizing cooperation procedures;[159] agreements having important budgetary implications for the Community;[160] and agreements entailing the amendment of a measure adopted under the new legislative procedure introduced by the TEU and known conventionally as 'codecision',[161] which has evolved into the ordinary legislative procedure. The reform was, however, double-edged. While the requirement of assent by the Parliament to the conclusion of agreements in the four prescribed categories was an important enhancement of its powers, the text of Article 228(3) (and subsequently of Article 300(3) EC) stated explicitly that the cases in which the Parliament's participation was limited to a simple right to be consulted included those 'where the agreement covers a field for which the [codecision procedure] or the [cooperation procedure] is required for the

[155] For a critical analysis of the procedure applicable during this period, see R. Bieber, 'The Democratic Control of European Foreign Policy', 1 *European Journal of International Law* 148, 158–164.

[156] The change of name was first formally recognized in the Single European Act, which came into force on 1 July 1987.

[157] In addition, the assent of the Parliament was made a condition for the conclusion of accession agreements.

[158] The legal basis for the conclusion of an agreement establishing an association is now Article 217 TFEU. In Case C-12/86, *supra* note 5, [1987] ECR 3719, at para. 9, the Court of Justice described such agreements as 'creating special, privileged links with a non-member country which must, at least to a certain extent, take part in the Community system'.

[159] This obscurely phrased provision, which nevertheless still survives in Article 218(6)(a)(iii), presumably refers to decision-making bodies created under an international agreement, of the kind referred to in Article 218(9).

[160] In Case C-189/97, *Parliament v. Council*, [1999] ECR I-04741 (ECLI:EU:C:1999:366), which concerned the sum payable under a fisheries agreement with Mauretania, the Court of Justice held that the appropriate test was to consider that sum as a proportion of the total budget appropriations for the (then) Community's external operations.

[161] The formal designation was 'the procedure referred to in Article 189b'.

adoption of internal rules'. Part of the reason for amending Article 228 was, therefore, to make clear that the greater role given to the Parliament under the new decision-making procedures introduced, for internal legislative purposes, by the Single European Act (SEA) and subsequently by the TEU were not intended to be applicable in the field of the Community's external action.[162] The overall effect of the reform by the TEU of the procedure for the conclusion of international agreements was to make consultation of the Parliament the rule, and the requirement to obtain its assent the exception, though an important one.

The effect of the reform by the Treaty of Lisbon has been to reverse that balance. Of the five instances identified by Article 218(6)(a) where the consent of the European Parliament must be obtained, those under points (i), (iii), and (iv) remain substantially unaltered;[163] while point (ii) refers to the 'one-off' case of the conclusion of the agreement on Union accession to the European Convention for the Protection of Human Rights and Fundamental Freedoms. The main change is the replacement of the rule that the assent of the Parliament was needed where an agreement would entail the amendment of an existing measure adopted by codecision, with the rule in Article 218(6)(a)(v) that the Council must obtain the consent of the Parliament before concluding agreements covering fields to which the ordinary legislative procedure applies (or the special legislative procedure where the Parliament's consent is required). The crucial factor is, therefore, no longer the need for an existing measure to be amended; it suffices that the ordinary legislative procedure be stipulated for the exercise of the competence in question by means of an internal act. The impact of this change has been all the greater, owing to the extended applicability of the ordinary legislative procedure under the post-Lisbon dispensation. Thus it can be said that, pursuant to Article 218(6) TFEU, the requirement of consent by the Parliament to the conclusion of an international agreement has become the rule, and the requirement of consultation the exception.

That view is reinforced by another change, namely that the Parliament is no longer excluded from formal involvement in the conclusion of CCP agreements, which had been the case from the time of the primordial EEC Treaty. Indeed, the Treaty of Lisbon seems to have gone to the opposite extreme, by requiring the consent of the Parliament for all CCP agreements. This may be thought to follow from the fact that post-Lisbon the CCP has become a 'field' to which the ordinary legislative procedure applies. It is true that Article 207(2) TFEU provides for the ordinary legislative procedure to be used only for adopting, by means of regulations, 'the measures defining the *framework* for implementing the [CCP]';[164] however, there is

[162] The cooperation procedure was introduced by the SEA, mainly for the adoption of internal market measures. It was finally abolished by the Treaty of Lisbon. The procedure made it easier for the European Parliament to exert influence over the outcome of decision-making, through mechanisms under which the Council, if it wished to override the will of the Parliament, could be forced to act by unanimity, even where the voting rule prescribed by the substantive legal basis of the act in question was QMV. For a fuller description of this procedure, see D. Wyatt and A. Dashwood, *European Union Law* (3rd edn, 1993), at 40–41.

[163] Cf. the first three instances referred to in previous Article 300(3), second subpara. EC.

[164] Emphasis added.

no procedure prescribed for other types of CCP measure.[165] While, pursuant to Article 291(2) TFEU, a CCP framework measure may confer implementing powers on the Commission or 'in duly justified specific cases' on the Council,[166] it is not clear that Article 218 would allow such powers to be exercised by way of an international agreement concluded under a procedure other than that prescribed by paragraph (6)(a)(v). But can it really have been intended that the consent of the Parliament be required for concluding even the most banal and technical of trade agreements?

E. The Council's Voting Rule

Article 218(8) provides:

> The Council shall act by a qualified majority throughout the procedure.
>
> However, it shall act unanimously when the agreement covers a field for which unanimity is required for the adoption of a Union act as well as for association agreements and the agreements referred to in Article 212 with the States which are candidates for accession. The Council shall also act unanimously for the agreement on accession of the Union to the European Convention for the Protection of Human Rights and Fundamental Freedoms; the decision concluding this agreement shall enter into force after it has been approved by the Member States in accordance with their respective constitutional requirements.

The general rule is, therefore, that the Council acts by QMV, except with regard to the agreements identified in the second subparagraph of Article 218(8), where it must act by unanimity.

A natural reading of paragraph (8) would be that its second subparagraph represents an exception to the QMV rule 'throughout the procedure' laid down by Article 218. In other words, regarding the categories of agreements referred to in the second subparagraph, the Council is required to act by unanimity, whatever the point in the procedure at which it may be called upon to take a decision. Doubt, however, has been cast on that proposition by a recent judgment of the Court of Justice, where QMV was held to be the appropriate voting rule for a decision adopted by the Council under Article 218(9) within the framework of an association agreement.[167]

[165] Cf. Article 43 TFEU, the legal basis for CAP measures. Para. (2) of the Article prescribes the use of the ordinary legislative procedure (combined with consultation of the Economic and Social Committee) to establish the common organization of agricultural markets 'and the other provisions necessary for the pursuit of the objectives of the common agricultural policy and the common fisheries policy'; while para. (3) of the Article lays down a simpler procedure (the Council acting on a proposal from the Commission) for 'measures on fixing prices, levies, aid and quantitative limitations and on the fixing and allocation of fishing opportunities'.

[166] For instance, Council Regulation 1225/2009 of 30 November 2009 on protection against dumped imports from countries not members of the European Community, OJ 2009 L 343/51. See the special procedure in Article 9 for the imposition of definitive antidumping duties. Regulation 1225/2009 was adopted under the EC Treaty but its successor will evidently be a framework agreement within the meaning of Article 207(2) TFEU.

[167] Case C-81/13, *United Kingdom v. Council*, judgment of 18 December 2014 (ECLI:EU:C:2014:2449).

The Court's reasoning will be examined more fully in the context of the discussion of Council decisions under Article 218(9) in Section 5. It is uncertain whether the Court intended the analysis to apply only in respect of decisions under Article 218 that are taken by the Council downstream of the conclusion of an agreement, or also in respect of decisions that it takes upstream, under paragraphs (3) or (5).[168] All that can be said with certainty is that the unanimity rule applies to any Council decision that actually concludes an agreement falling into one of the categories mentioned in Article 218(8), second subparagraph.

5. Decisions under Article 218(9) TFEU

Article 218(9) TFEU provides:

> The Council, on a proposal from the Commission or the High Representative of the Union for Foreign Affairs and Security Policy, shall adopt a decision suspending application of an agreement and establishing the positions to be adopted on the Union's behalf in a body set up by an agreement, when that body is called upon to adopt acts having legal effects, with the exception of acts supplementing or amending the institutional framework of the agreement.

As noted earlier,[169] Article 218(9) lays down a simplified procedure for decision-making by the Council in two rather different situations: where, for some reason, it is thought appropriate to suspend the application of an international agreement;[170] and where it is necessary to establish the position to be taken on behalf of the Union in a body set up by an international agreement, which is called upon to adopt an act having legal effects.[171]

An equivalent provision was first inserted into the EC Treaty, as the second subparagraph of then Article 300(2) EC, by the Treaty of Amsterdam.[172] The drafting history of Article 218(9) is discussed in the following sections, with more particular reference to decisions on EU positions.

[168] Former Article 300(1) EC provided, in its second subparagraph: 'In exercising the powers conferred upon it by this paragraph, the Council shall act by a qualified majority, except in cases where the first subparagraph of paragraph 2 provides that the Council shall act by unanimity.' As we shall see, pursuant to Article 300(2), first subparagraph EC, the cases in which the unanimity rule applied were 'when the agreement covers a field for which unanimity is required for the adoption of internal rules and for the agreements referred to in Article 310'. Article 310 EC was the legal basis for association agreements (now Article 217 TFEU).

[169] See Section 2(B).

[170] This will be referred to, for convenience, as 'the first limb of Article 218(9)'. The Council decisions in question will be referred to as 'decisions on suspension'.

[171] This will be referred to, for convenience, as 'the second limb of Article 218(9)'. Bodies endowed by an international agreement with power to adopt acts having legal effects will be referred to as 'decision-making bodies' or 'DMBs'. Council decisions establishing a position to be taken on the Union's behalf in such a body will be referred to as 'decisions on positions to be taken within DMBs'.

[172] On the background, see A. Dashwood, 'External Relations Provisions of the Amsterdam Treaty', 35 *Common Market Law Review* (1998) 1019, at 1025–1027.

A. The First Limb of Article 218(9)—Decisions on Suspension

Decisions on the suspension of agreements with international partners of the EU form part of the armoury of soft power available to the Union for the pursuit of its foreign policy objectives, to which the imposition of restrictive measures under Article 215 TFEU also belongs. The close connection with the CFSP may be part of the explanation for the exclusion of the European Parliament from the procedure;[173] though justification for the application of a simplified procedure can also be found in the fact that decisions on suspension may need to be taken urgently in order to have maximum political impact.

A typical instance of recourse by the Union to suspension would be as a sanction for the violation of the fundamental rights of its own people by the third country that is party to the agreement concerned.[174] Since the 1990s, it has been standard practice for agreements between the Union and one or more third countries, other than sectoral trade agreements, to include a clause stating that respect for human rights and democracy constitutes 'an essential element' of their relationship. This allows any serious violation of human rights to be considered a 'material breach' for the purposes of Article 60 of the Vienna Convention on the Law of Treaties.

The introduction, by the Treaty of Amsterdam, of the simplified procedure now contained in Article 218(9), and the developing practice with respect to so-called 'human rights clauses' (or 'political clauses'), seems to have resolved the issues that once led to disputes about the suspension of agreements.[175] The discussion in this Section will, therefore, be focused mainly on the second limb of Article 218(9), the application of which has been the subject of recent case law.

B. The Second Limb of Article 218(9)—Decisions on Positions to Be Taken within DMBs

1. *Drafting History*

In the late 1980s it was recognized by the Court of Justice that acts adopted by a decision-making body (DMB) set up under an agreement to which the then EEC was party would produce consequences within the internal legal order of the Community similar to those of provisions contained in the agreement itself.[176] Such acts, therefore, amounted to a way of making new Community law; and this raised

[173] Eeckhout, *supra* note 27, at 209.

[174] See, among many examples, Council Decision 2011/523/EU of 2 September 2011 partially suspending the application of the Cooperation Agreement between the European Economic Community and the Syrian Arab Republic, OJ 2011 L 228/19; amended by Council Decision 2012/123/CFSP of 27 February 2012, OJ 2012 L 54/18.

[175] E.g. Case C-162/96, *Racke v. Hauptzollamt Mainz*, [1998] ECR I-03655 (ECLI:EU:C:1998:293). See Eeckhout, *supra* note 27, at 209.

[176] Case C-192/89, *supra* note 7; Case C-237/91, *Kus v. Landeshauptstadt Wiesbaden*, [1992] ECR I-06781 (ECLI:EU:C:1992:527); Case C-355/93, *Eroglu v. Land Baden-Württemberg*, [1994] ECR I-05113 (ECLI:EU:C:1994:369).

a question as to the appropriate procedure for authorizing in advance the position to be taken on the Community's behalf within the DMB.

While there was no provision in the EEC Treaty corresponding to Article 218(9) TFEU, the Treaty did contain an Article 116, which provided:

> From the end of the transitional period onwards, Member States shall, in respect of all matters of particular interest to the common market, proceed within the framework of international organisations of an economic character only by common action. To this end, the Commission shall submit to the Council, which shall act by a qualified majority, proposals concerning the scope and implementation of such common action ...[177]

As noted by Advocate General Cruz Villalón in his Opinion in the *OIV* case,[178] despite the location of Article 116 in the Treaty chapter on Commercial Policy, the obligation imposed upon Member States to proceed only by way of common action was interpreted by the Court of Justice as applying irrespective of the particular objectives of a given international organization, so long as these were economic in character.[179] Clearly, however, the Article was precluded by its express terms from being used in the case of action to be taken within the framework of an international organization by the Community itself. It was, the Court of Justice explained in Opinion 1/78, 'conceived with a view to evolving common action by the Member States in international organisations of which the Community is not part; in such a situation the only appropriate means is concerted, joint action by the Member States as members of the said organisations'.[180] Where a decision by an international organization would have binding force for the Community under international law, it was the provisions on the procedure for the conclusion of agreements, then contained in Article 228 EEC, that should be used.[181] At all events, Article 116 EEC was deleted from the Treaty by the TEU (Maastricht). The reason for this, Advocate General Cruz Villalón suggests, was that the Member States regarded the Article as encroaching too far upon their sovereignty. In particular, it enabled the Council to act by QMV in all cases, including on matters which, for internal purposes, would require unanimity; and possibly even on matters falling within Member States' exclusive competence.[182]

[177] As cited by AG Cruz Villalón in Case C-399/12, *Germany v. Council (OIV)*, [2014] (ECLI: EU:C:2014:289), at para. 40.. The paragraph omitted from the citation referred to arrangements that applied during the transitional period.

[178] Opinion of AG Cruz Villalón, Case C-399/12, *supra* note 177, at para. 41. The dispute in the case is fully considered later in the chapter.

[179] See Case C-22/70, *supra* note 42, at para. 76, where Article 116 was invoked in the field of transport; Joined Cases 3, 4, and 6/76, *supra* note 44, paras 42–43 and 44–45 where the Article was invoked in the field of transport.

[180] Opinion 1/78, *Opinion given pursuant to the second subparagraph of Article 228(1) of the EEC Treaty—International Agreement on Natural Rubber*, [1979] ECR 02871 (ECLI:EU:C:1979:224), para. 50. Cited by AG Cruz Villalón at para. 41 of his Opinion in the *OIV* case, *supra* note 178.

[181] *Ibid.*, at para. 51. See also Opinion 2/92, *supra* note 28, at para. 8; Opinion of AG Cruz Villalón, Case C-399/12, *supra* note 177, at para. 44.

[182] Opinion of AG Cruz Villalón, Case C-399/12, *supra* note 177, at paras 41–42 and n. 38.

Thus, prior to the Treaty of Amsterdam, the legally watertight solution for authorizing the EU position to be taken within a DMB would have been to use the full procedure for concluding international agreements (or perhaps that for adopting internal legislation) pursuant to the relevant legal basis. However, procedures that would have entailed a role for the European Parliament (as by then had come to be the case, except for the conclusion of CCP agreements) were evidently considered impracticable; the inevitable delay would have been liable to impede the Union's effective participation in DMBs, where positions may need to be taken frequently and expeditiously. Learned authors with direct experience of the Council's practice at the time have noted that EU positions continued to be established in coordination and expressed within the relevant DMB under arrangements agreed between the Council and the Commission;[183] while in some cases a simplified decision-making procedure would be provided for in the Council act concluding the agreement in question.[184] Alternatively, special procedures were sometimes laid down by internal implementing legislation, as was done in the case of the EEA Agreement.[185] While such ad hoc solutions may have been satisfactory in themselves, it was never certain that the political pressures surrounding the conclusion of an agreement would permit the adoption of an appropriate procedure.

Hence the importance of the inclusion in the Treaty of Amsterdam of a provision introducing the standard simplified procedure now enshrined in Article 218(9) TFEU. In the original version of the provision, its second limb applied only where the DMB in question was operating within the framework of an association agreement. This rather puzzling limitation has been explained by Advocate General Cruz Villalón on the ground that association councils would, by definition, be DMBs established under an agreement to which the EU would have been an original party.[186] The limitation was removed by the Treaty of Nice, which extended the simplified procedure to decisions on the adoption of positions within DMBs set up by international agreements of all kinds.

The pre-Lisbon version of the simplified procedure was located in the second subparagraph of Article 300(2) EC. This provided, in pertinent part:

> By way of derogation from the rules laid down in paragraph 3, *the same procedures* shall apply...for the purpose of establishing the positions to be adopted on behalf of the Community in a body set up by an agreement, when that body is called upon to adopt decisions having legal effect, with the exception of acts supplementing or amending the institutional framework of the agreement.[187]

[183] MacLeod, Hendry, and Hyett, *supra* note 79, at 175–176.

[184] *Ibid.* They cite as examples: Article 3 of Regulation 3955/92 concerning the conclusion of an Agreement establishing an International Scientific and Technology Centre, OJ 1992 L 409/1; and Article 2 of Council Decision 93/743 on the conclusion of a Europe Agreement with Poland, OJ 1993 L 348/1.

[185] Council Regulation 2894/94 of 28 November 1994 concerning arrangements for implementing the Agreement on the European Economic Area, OJ 1994 L 305/6.

[186] Opinion of AG Cruz Villalón, Case C-399/12, *supra* note 177, at para. 50.

[187] Emphasis added.

Paragraph 3 of Article 300 EC laid down rules on participation by the European Parliament in the conclusion of international agreements, while 'the same procedures' referred to in the second subparagraph of paragraph (2) were those prescribed by the first subparagraph for the conclusion of international agreements. The location and the drafting of the second subparagraph made clear that decisions were to be adopted by a procedure simplified by comparison with that applicable to the conclusion of agreements in one respect only; namely, the derogation from the rules of paragraph (3) defining the role of the European Parliament (subject to an exception in the case of acts supplementing or amending the institutional framework itself).

2. *The Post-Lisbon Procedure*

As a result of the reorganization by the Lisbon Treaty of the procedural code formerly contained in Article 300 EC, Article 218(9) TFEU has become a separate paragraph placed after the provisions relating to the Council's voting rule, which are now found in paragraph (8). Its text has also been amended, as compared with that of the second subparagraph of Article 300 EC, by the deletion of the opening phrase referring to paragraph (3) of that Article, as well as of the reference to 'the same procedures'.

Those have been described by Advocate General Cruz Villalón as 'editorial changes', which 'did not, however, come with any fundamental changes of substance';[188] and he went on to state that 'the editorial changes did not alter the status of the provision at issue as a *lex specialis*, as is clear from the fact that it continued to form part of the rules on the procedure for the conclusion of agreements (Article 218 TFEU)'.[189] The Advocate General reached that conclusion in the light of a detailed analysis of the drafting history of Article 218(9). The case law on the choice between the procedural legal bases provided for by, respectively, former Article 116 and former Article 228 EEC,[190] he suggested, lent weight to the view 'that the adoption of decisions within international organisations is equivalent to the conclusion of agreements'.[191] The simplified procedure now laid down by Article 218(9) thus constituted a *lex specialis*, by comparison with the full procedure that would otherwise be applicable,[192] for the purposes of this 'special form of concluding an agreement under the Treaty'.[193]

It would follow from that analysis that the procedure for the adoption of decisions on positions to be taken within DMBs must be understood to have remained unchanged. In particular, the Council's voting rule should be the same as for the conclusion of agreements; that is to say, normally QMV but unanimity in the cases provided for by the second paragraph of Article 218(8). As previously, the simplified procedure is excluded in the case of acts supplementing or amending the institutional framework of the agreement in question.

188 See his Opinion in Case C-399/12, *supra* note 177, at para. 52. 189 *Ibid.*

190 Opinion 1/78 and Opinion 2/92, *supra* note 28, at para. 8.

191 Opinion of AG Cruz Villalón, Case C-399/12, *supra* note 177, at para. 44.

192 *Ibid.*, at para. 50. 193 *Ibid.*, at para. 74.

However, the Court of Justice, following the lead given by Advocate General Kokott,[194] appears to take a different view. The *EU/Turkey* case[195] concerned the choice of the substantive legal basis for a Council Decision[196] on a position to be put forward on the Union's behalf in the Association Council set up by the Ankara Agreement between the Union and Turkey,[197] which concerned the rules on the coordination of social security systems applicable to migrant workers.[198] Considering that the chosen legal basis (Article 48 TFEU) was inadequate, the Court held that Article 217 TFEU, the legal basis for the conclusion of association agreements, must be added, but that this would not have the effect of altering the procedure for the adoption of the disputed Decision from QMV, as prescribed by the first subparagraph of Article 218(8), to unanimity, as prescribed by its second subparagraph. Referring with approval to the Opinion of Advocate General Kokott, the Court explained its position as follows:

> ... since the contested decision does not relate to the *conclusion* of an association agreement or is not aimed at supplementing or amending the institutional framework of such an agreement, but is aimed solely at ensuring its *implementation*, it is, in accordance with the combined measures of the first paragraph of Article 218 (8) TFEU and Article 218 (9) TFEU, by a qualified majority and without the approval of the European Parliament, that the Council should have, in any event, adopted the contested decision...[199]

That reasoning, it is respectfully submitted, is flawed in several important respects.[200]

First, like Advocate General Kokott, the Court of Justice ignores the drafting history of the procedure laid down by Article 218(9), which shows that it was conceived as a variant of the procedure for the conclusion of agreements. That conception was reflected in the structure of Article 300(2) EC, where the Council's voting rule was the same under both subparagraphs. Indeed, the Court appeared to acknowledge this in its *CITES* judgment, where the need to determine the applicable voting rule for the Council is mentioned among the reasons militating in favour of the requirement that a decision on the position to be taken within a DMB indicate the legal basis on which it was adopted.[201] For the voting rule under Article 218(9) to have been amended by the Treaty of Lisbon, limiting it to QMV as provided for

[194] See her Opinions in Case C-431/11, *United Kingdom v. Council*, judgment of 26 September 2013 (ECLI:EU:C:2013:589), Opinion (ECLI:EU:C:2013:187), at para. 61, and Case C-81/13, *supra* note 167, Opinion (ECLI:EU:C:2014:2114), paras 97 and 123.

[195] Case C-81/13, *supra* note 167.

[196] Council Decision 2012/776/EU of 6 December 2012, OJ 2012 L 340/19. Where the context permits, 'the disputed Decision'.

[197] Agreement establishing an Association between the European Economic Community and Turkey, concluded by Council Decision 64/732/EEC of 23 December 1963 ('the Ankara Agreement'), OJ 1964, p. 3687/64. For the English text of the Ankara Agreement, see OJ 1973 C 113.

[198] The *EU/Turkey* case is more fully considered in Section 5(B)(5), below, in connection with the choice of legal basis for decisions on positions within DMBs.

[199] Case C-81/13, *supra* note 167, at para. 66 (emphasis added).

[200] The present author was counsel for the United Kingdom in this case. The views expressed here are his own and should not be attributed to those by whom he was instructed.

[201] Case C-370/07, *Commission v. Council*, [2009] ECR I-08917 (ECLI:EU:C:2009:590). See Section 5(B)(5) below.

by the first subparagraph of Article 218(8), would, to borrow language from Advocate General Cruz Villalón, amount to a fundamental change of substance. It is submitted that the authors of the Lisbon Treaty cannot be assumed to have intended to make so important a change, in the absence of evidence to this effect in the *travaux préparatoires*—which, to the best of the present author's knowledge, is lacking. At all events, there is nothing in the judgment to indicate that the Court was aware of such evidence, or even recognized the need for it.

Secondly, the notion of a procedure designed to ensure the implementation, as distinct from the conclusion, of an association agreement, and consisting of 'the combined measures of the first paragraph of Article 218 (8) TFEU and Article 218 (9) TFEU', has no textual basis.[202] As suggested earlier, a natural reading of Article 218(8) would be that both the general rule of QMV in the first subparagraph, and the unanimity rule in the exceptional cases provided for in the second subparagraph, apply 'throughout the procedure', that is, to all the different kinds of procedural decisions envisaged by the Article including those downstream as well as upstream of conclusion. There is no hint in the drafting of the second subparagraph of Article 218(8) that it only concerns the conclusion of agreements. The language of the subparagraph ('when the agreement covers a field for which unanimity is required for the adoption of a Union act as well as for association agreements . . .') is apt to apply to decisions taken for the purposes of Article 218(9). Had the intention been otherwise, an express reference to, for example, 'the *conclusion* of association agreements' might have been expected, especially since this would have represented a change in the law.

For Advocate General Kokott, it seems, the textual basis for recourse to QMV as the voting rule for Council decisions under Article 218(9) was the default rule in Article 16(3) TEU, which applies 'where the Treaties do not provide otherwise'.[203] It is true that no specific reference to a voting rule is found in Article 218(9); however, that is readily explicable by the fact that Article 218(8) applies to decisions under Article 218(9), as it does to all Council decisions taken 'throughout the procedure'. Evidently, the Court was not persuaded by that part of the Advocate General's argument since, as we have seen, the judgment refers, not to Article 16(3) TEU, but to 'the combined measures of the first paragraph of Article 218 (8) TFEU and Article 218 (9) TFEU'.

Finally, it is respectfully submitted, the reasoning in the *EU/Turkey* judgment fails to pay sufficient regard to the very wide discretion that some DMBs may enjoy, especially those set up under association agreements of an evolutive character, such as the Ankara Agreement. While the measure at issue in the *EU/Turkey* case was relatively modest in scope, being confined to the sphere of social security coordination,[204] the objectives of the Agreement are far more ambitious. In particular, Article 36 of

[202] The objection is not to describing decisions under Article 218(9) as 'implementing' measures but to the idea that this makes any difference to the procedure for their adoption.

[203] See *supra* note 196. This must, presumably, be the significance of the elliptical reference to Article 16(3) TEU in the two relevant paragraphs of the cited Opinions.

[204] See the discussion in Section 5(B)(4) below.

the Additional Protocol to the Agreement[205] provides that freedom of movement for workers between Turkey and the EU is to 'be secured by progressive stages', with power for the Association Council to 'decide on the rules necessary to that end'. On the Court's understanding of the procedure applicable under Article 218(9) TFEU, the decision establishing a position in favour of granting full rights of free movement for workers between the EU and Turkey could be adopted by QMV; and basing this decision on Article 217 TFEU would not make any difference.

3. *Must the DMB Have Been Set Up by an Agreement to Which the EU is Party?*

Whether a decision on a position within a DMB can be adopted on the basis of Article 218(9) TFEU, if the EU is not itself a party to the agreement by which the body in question was set up, was one of the issues before the Court of Justice in the *OIV* case.[206]

The remit of the International Organisation of Vine and Wine[207] includes contributing to the international harmonization of existing practices and standards, and the preparation of new standards, in order to improve conditions for producing and marketing vine and wine products.[208] There are 21 EU Member States that belong to the OIV but the Union itself is not a member.[209] The OIV acts by way of recommendations of its General Assembly. These are not legally binding, though the Organisation is responsible for monitoring their implementation in liaison with its members.

The dispute in the *OIV* case concerned a Council Decision adopted on the basis of Article 218(9) TFEU, which established the position Member States belonging to the OIV should adopt jointly, in respect of certain proposed recommendations on the agenda of a forthcoming meeting of the Organisation's General Assembly.[210] The previous practice had been for the Member States that were OIV members to coordinate, on their own initiative, the positions to be taken at such meetings. The validity of the disputed Decision was challenged in proceedings brought by Germany, with the support of seven other Member States. Part of Germany's case was that the Council ought not to have adopted the Decision on the basis of Article 218(9), owing to the fact that the EU was not a party to the OIV Agreement.

[205] Additional Protocol and Financial Protocol to the EEC-Turkey Association Agreement [1972] OJ 1972 L 293/4. For the English text, see OJ 1973 C 113.

[206] Case C-399/12, *Germany v. Council (OIV)*, judgment of 7 October 2014 (ECLI:EU:C:2014:2258).

[207] Hereinafter 'the OIV' or, where the context permits, 'the Organisation'.

[208] Agreement Establishing the International Organisation of Vine and Wine, Article 2.

[209] This in spite of the fact that membership by an 'international intergovernmental organisation' is provided for by Article 8 of the OIV Agreement.

[210] Council Decision of 18 June 2012 establishing the position to be adopted on behalf of the European Union with regard to certain resolutions to be adopted within the framework of the International Organisation of Vine and Wines (OIV); where the context permits, 'the disputed Decision'. It seems the Decision was never published in the *Official Journal*. In n. 13 of his Opinion in Case C-399/12, *supra* note 177, Advocate General Cruz Villalón cites Council document 11436/12.

Advocate General Cruz Villalón upheld that objection, in the light of the wording, context, and purpose of the second limb of Article 218(9). A central plank of his analysis was the drafting history of the provision, as a *lex specialis* designed to simplify the procedure for concluding international agreements, in a situation where the full procedure would otherwise have been applicable.[211] The learned Advocate General explained:

> ... a *lex specialis* simplifying the procedure for the conclusion of agreements cannot be applied to agreements to which the European Union's procedure for concluding agreements is not applicable anyway. As the procedure for the conclusion of agreements applies to European Union agreements, the procedure laid down in Article 218 (9) can also apply only to European Union agreements.[212]

The Court of Justice reached the opposite conclusion, giving two main reasons for doing so.

First, Article 218(9) refers to a body set up by 'an agreement' but does not specify that the EU must be a party to that agreement. Nor can such a requirement be inferred from the reference to positions being adopted 'on the Union's behalf'.[213] There was, therefore, nothing in the wording of the provision to prevent the EU from adopting a decision on a position to be taken on its behalf within a DMB set up by an agreement to which it is not a party.[214]

Secondly, the case concerned matters relating to the Common Agricultural Policy (CAP), and more specifically the common organization of the wine markets, 'an area which is regulated for the most part by the EU legislature in the exercise of its competence under Article 43 TFEU'.[215] The Court went on:

> Where an area of law falls within a competence of the European Union, such as the one mentioned in the previous paragraph, the fact that the European Union did not take part in the international agreement in question does not prevent it from exercising that competence by establishing, through its institutions, a position to be adopted on its behalf in the body set up by that agreement, in particular through the Member States which are party to that agreement acting jointly in its interest.[216]

The quoted passage evokes a settled principle going back as far as the *AETR* case,[217] that, where the Union is unable for some reason to exercise an exclusive competence directly in the international sphere, the Member States may be authorized to act jointly in its interests.[218] That being so, it may seem puzzling that recourse to Article 218(9) in the circumstances should have been questioned at all.

Also puzzling is the response of the Court of Justice to the contextual argument put forward by Germany, that all the other provisions of Article 218 could apply

[211] See Section 5(B)(2) above.

[212] Opinion of AG Cruz Villalón, Case C-399/12, *supra* note 177, at para. 75.

[213] Case C-399/12, *supra* note 206, at para. 49.

[214] *Ibid.*, at para. 50.

[215] *Ibid.*, at para. 51.

[216] *Ibid.*, at para. 52.

[217] Case C-22/70, *supra* note 42, at paras 69–91.

[218] See, e.g. the cases cited in para. 52 of the judgment: 'see judgment in *Commission v. Greece*, C-45/07, EU:C:2009:81, paragraphs 30 and 31; see also, to that effect, Opinion 2/91, EU:C:1993:106, paragraph 5'.

only in relation to agreements between the EU and third countries or international organizations, so the same must be true of the second limb of Article 218(9). Instead of reiterating its point that establishing a position to be taken on the Union's behalf within a DMB is a different matter from negotiating and concluding an international agreement, the Court could simply have recalled that the possibility of authorizing the Member States to step in if the Union is unable to act externally on its own account, applies equally to the negotiation, signing, and conclusion of agreements. If, as seems to be accepted in the post-Lisbon era, Article 218(6) may serve as the procedural legal basis for authorizing the Member States to conclude an agreement on behalf of the Union,[219] surely when it comes to adopting a decision on the position to be taken within a DMB, Article 218(9) should apply *a fortiori*?

The puzzle may be explained by uncertainty as to whether the Union's competence with respect to the matters covered by the OIV recommendations to which the disputed Decision related was, in fact, exclusive. This seems to be implicit in the judgment,[220] but is not spelled out, and Germany took the view that the competence was non-exclusive. If the ruling in the *OIV* judgment meant that an obligation may be imposed on Member States to act within a DMB set up by an agreement to which the Union is not a party, on the basis of a common position adopted by QMV, even in respect of matters for which the Union does not enjoy exclusive competence, it would not be an exaggeration to regard this as a partial reinstatement of the old Article 116 EEC. However, it seems unlikely that such a radical departure from the clearly expressed will of the makers of the Maastricht Treaty could have been intended.

4. *The Meaning of 'Acts Having Legal Effects'*

The meaning of the phrase 'acts having legal effects' in Article 218(9) TFEU was another issue considered by the Court of Justice in the *OIV* case.[221] Germany had argued that the procedure provided for by Article 218(9) is only available where the decision to be adopted by the DMB in question will be binding in international law upon the parties to the agreement, which OIV recommendations are not.

That argument was also rejected by the Court of Justice as grounds for the annulment of the disputed Decision. The Court recalled the OIV's responsibility for monitoring the implementation of its recommendations, in liaison with members;[222] and it further noted that OIV recommendations have been explicitly incorporated into various provisions of the internal EU legislation governing the wine sector.[223] The recommendations under consideration in the case related to matters covered by those provisions and they were, accordingly, found to be 'capable of decisively influencing the content of the legislation adopted by the EU legislation in the area of the

[219] See, e.g. Council Decision 2014/165/EU of 3 March 2014 authorizing Member States to ratify, in the interests of the European Union, the Arms Trade Treaty, OJ 2014 L 89/44.

[220] See Case C-399/12, *supra* note 206, paras 51 and 64.

[221] *Ibid.*

[222] *Ibid.*, at para. 60.

[223] *Ibid.*, at paras 61 and 62.

common organisation of the wine markets'.[224] It followed that 'such recommendations, in particular by reason of their incorporation into EU law..., have legal effects in that area for the purposes of Article 218 (9) TFEU and that the European Union, while not a party to the OIV Agreement, is entitled to establish a position to be adopted on its behalf with regard to those recommendations, in view of their direct impact on the European Union's acquis in that area'.[225]

The lesson to be drawn from this part of the *OIV* judgment is that the 'legal effect' requirement in Article 218(9) relates, not to whatever effect the relevant decision by the DMB may have in international law, but to its consequences for the legal order of the EU, even if these result from choices previously made by the Union legislator. That interpretation appears consistent with the objective of ensuring that decisions adopted by a DMB that effectively create new EU law must have been properly authorized in advance.[226]

In a different context, the Court of Justice has held that recommendations adopted by a DMB have an effect within the internal legal order of the EU, and are thus within the scope of the Court's jurisdiction under Article 267 TFEU, by virtue of the fact that, without being bound by them, national courts may nevertheless be required to take them into account.[227] It remains to be seen whether that would be sufficient, in the absence of legislation of the kind that applied in the *OIV* case, to justify recourse to Article 218(9). In the view of the present author, a case could plausibly be made for such recourse.

5. *Legal Basis of Decisions on Positions within DMBs*

At one time, it was not the regular practice of the Council to specify the substantive and procedural legal bases of decisions adopted under Article 300(2), second subparagraph EC, the forerunner of Article 218.[228] Now, however, there is clear judicial authority that failure to do so provides grounds for the annulment of the decision in question.

The leading case concerned a decision establishing the position to be expressed by the Member States acting jointly in the interest of the EC at a meeting of the Conference of the Parties to the Convention on International Trade in Endangered Species of Wild Flora and Fauna, known as 'CITES'.[229] The Commission had proposed a dual substantive legal basis for the decision, namely Articles 175(1) and 133 EC, which were then the legal bases for, respectively, action on the environment and on the CCP.[230] As the judgment notes, the Council could not agree on the choice of

[224] *Ibid.*, at para. 63. [225] *Ibid.*, at para. 64.

[226] See the earlier discussion of the drafting history of Article 218(9).

[227] Case C-188/91, *Deutsche Shell v. Hauptzollamt Hamburg/Harburg*, [1993] ECR I-00363 (ECLI:EU:C:1993:24), at paras 17 and 18.

[228] Nor, indeed, were such decisions regularly published. They would simply be entered in the Council's minutes.

[229] Case C-370/07, *supra* note 201. The EU is not a party to CITES; however, in contrast to the *OIV* case, no objection was raised to the use of the procedure provided for by then Article 300(2), second subpara. EC.

[230] Now, respectively, Article 192(1) and Article 207 TFEU.

a dual legal basis, several Member States preferring to rely upon Article 175 alone.[231] The absence of consensus led to the adoption of the Decision with no legal basis specified. The Court of Justice rejected the submissions of the Council and the United Kingdom that this amounted to a purely formal defect and proceeded to annul the decision.

The need for decisions on positions within DMBs to indicate their legal bases was explained by the Court of Justice in *CITES* as a corollary of the fact that, since they produce binding legal effects for the EU institutions and the Member States, such decisions must be reasoned.[232] The indication of the legal basis was also said to be necessary in order to ensure compliance with the principle of conferral, now enshrined in Article 5(1) and (2) TEU,[233] as well as to preserve the prerogatives of the EU institutions,[234] and to determine the division of powers between the Union and the Member States in the matter in question.[235]

The rules determining the choice of the substantive legal basis for decisions on positions within a DMB are the familiar ones discussed earlier.[236] In some cases it may be clear that the legal basis should be the same as that used for the conclusion of the agreement setting up the DMB in question, but this will not always be the case. Association agreements, in particular, usually comprise a 'package' of elements for which specific legal bases exist under the Treaties; while the agreement creating an association between the EU and a given third country must itself be concluded under Article 217 TFEU, the practice of the institutions has been for any measure subsequently adopted for the purposes of the association to have as its substantive legal basis the provision(s) conferring competence on the Union in the matter(s) to which it relates. For instance, if the measure concerns trade, the legal basis will be Article 207 TFEU; if the protection of the environment, then it will be Article 192 TFEU. Justification for this practice can, it is submitted, be found in the principle of conferral. Because, as the Court of Justice has said, an association agreement creates 'special, privileged links with a third country which must, at least to a certain extent take part in the [Union] system',[237] it is necessary to be clear as to which of the range of competences available to the Union is being exercised on a particular occasion.

That correctly determining the appropriate legal basis in such cases may not always be a straightforward matter, is illustrated by a group of 12 Decisions under Article 218(9) TFEU, taken by the Council in the years 2010 to 2012, which concerned the rules on the coordination of social security systems applicable under the

[231] Case C-370/07, *supra* note 201, at para. 58.
[232] *Ibid.*, paras 38–45.
[233] *Ibid.*, paras 46 and 47.
[234] *Ibid.*, at para. 48. The relevance of this consideration is less obvious, since the European Parliament plays no part in the adoption of decisions under Article 218(1). Intriguingly, in view of the position it took in Case C-81/13, *supra* note 167, the Court refers to the different voting rules prescribed by (then) Article 300(2) EC as an instance where the choice of substantive legal basis may be significant.
[235] *Ibid.*, at para. 49.
[236] See Section 4(C), above.
[237] Case C-12/86, *supra* note 5.

association agreements between the EU and the third countries concerned.[238] The common purpose of these decisions was the updating of the rules in the light of amendments to the EU's internal system of social security coordination, notably through the replacement of the long-standing Regulation 1408/71[239] by Regulation 883/74.[240] The rules apply for the benefit both of workers from the associated third countries legally resident within the Union, and of EU workers legally resident in those countries.

Nine of the Decisions (those establishing the Union's position on social security coordination under the association agreements with, respectively, Morocco,[241] Tunisia,[242] Algeria,[243] Israel,[244] the Former Yugoslav Republic of Macedonia (FYROM),[245] Croatia,[246] Albania,[247] Montenegro,[248] and San Marino[249]) had as their substantive legal basis Article 79(2)(b) TFEU (collectively 'the nine Decisions'). This is the provision authorizing the adoption of measures on 'the definition of the rights of third-country nationals residing legally in a Member State, including the conditions governing freedom of movement and of residence in other Member States'.[250] The other three Decisions (collectively, 'the three disputed Decisions') (those establishing the Union's position on social security coordination under the EEA Agreement,[251] the EU/Swiss Free Movement Agreement,[252] and the Ankara Agreement[253]) had as their substantive legal basis Article 48 TFEU. This provision, found in the Chapter of the TEU on the free movement of workers, relates to the coordination of social security systems within the EU's internal market. Because it considered Article 79(2)(b) to have been the appropriate legal basis for all 12 Decisions,

[238] One of them was the Decision that was the subject of the proceedings in *EU/Turkey* case, considered above in relation to the issue of the Council's voting rule under Article 218(9).

[239] Council Regulation 1408/71 of 14 June 1971 on the application of social security systems to employed persons, to self-employed persons and to members of their family moving within the Community, OJ 1971 L 149/2.

[240] Regulation 883/2004 of the European Parliament and of the Council of 29 April 2004 on the coordination of social security systems, OJ 2004 L 166/1.

[241] Council Decision 2010/697/EU, OJ 2010 L 306/1.

[242] Council Decision 2010/698/EU, OJ 2010 L 306/8.

[243] Council Decision 2010/699/EU, OJ 2010 L 306/14.

[244] Council Decision 2010/700/EU, OJ 2010 L 306/21.

[245] Council Decision 2010/701/EU, OJ 2010 L 306/28.

[246] Council Decision 2010/702/EU, OJ 2010 L 306/35.

[247] Council Decision 2012/773/EU, OJ 2012 L 304/1.

[248] Council Decision 2012/774/EU, OJ 2012 L 340/7.

[249] Council Decision 2012/775/EU, OJ 2012 L 340/13.

[250] Article 79(1) provides for the development of a common immigration policy aimed at ensuring, among other things, 'fair treatment of third country nationals residing legally in Member States'. Para. (2)(a) of the Article is concerned with the conditions of entry and residence and para. (2)(b) with the treatment of persons who are legally resident.

[251] Council Decision 2011/407/EU, OJ 2011 L 182/12. The parties to the EEA Agreement which are not Member States of the EU are here referred to as 'the EFTA countries'.

[252] Council Decision 2011/863/EU, OJ 2011 L 341/1. The full title of the EU/Swiss Free Movement Agreement is 'Agreement between the European Community and its Member States of the one part, and the Swiss Confederation, on the other, on the free movement of persons', OJ 2002 L 114/6.

[253] Council Decision 2012/776/EU, OJ 2012 L 340/19.

the United Kingdom brought proceedings seeking the annulment of the three Decisions that were based on Article 48, with Ireland intervening in its support.[254] A particular interest of those Member States in the legal basis issue was to preserve their opt-in right, pursuant to Protocol 21 to the Treaties, in respect of measures adopted under Title V of Part Three of the TFEU, to which Article 79 belongs.[255]

Against the Council's choice of Article 48 TFEU, it could be argued that this is a provision ancillary to the fundamental principle of freedom of movement within the internal market for workers and self-employed persons who are nationals of EU Member States, and not available for the adoption of measures on the treatment of third-country nationals;[256] whereas the three disputed Decisions, amending the rules on the coordination of social security systems in relations between the EU and the associated third countries concerned, might be thought to fall, like the other nine Decisions, within the express terms of Article 79(2)(b), since they define certain rights of nationals of those countries who are lawfully resident in Member States. There was a question as to whether an additional legal basis might be needed, to cover the corresponding situation of EU citizens lawfully resident in an associated third country. However, any new burdens in respect of such EU migrants would fall mainly upon the host third country; given the accessory character, from the Union's point of view, of this aspect of the changes to the rules on social security coordination, Article 79(2)(b) could serve as the legal basis of each of the disputed Decisions, regarded as a whole. Such was evidently the view taken by the Council regarding the nine Decisions that have Article 79(2)(b) as their sole substantive legal basis, in spite of the fact that they similarly cover the treatment of EU citizens working in the various third countries concerned.

Article 48 TFEU was found, nevertheless, to be the appropriate substantive legal basis for the Decisions at issue in the *EEA* case and the *EU/Swiss* case. It appeared to be the view of the Court of Justice that the EFTA countries and Switzerland have been assimilated, through the operation of their respective association agreements with the Union, to the position of EU Member States in the matter of the free movement of persons. As the Court put it in the *EU/Swiss* case, citing its judgment in the *EEA* case: 'Article 48 TFEU can constitute an appropriate legal basis for the adoption of a decision such as that at issue where, as is the case with the Swiss Confederation, the third State has already been *equated*, on the basis of Article 217 TFEU, with a Member State of the European Union'.[257] Effectively, therefore, the disputed Decisions in those cases were to be regarded as internal market measures. Article 79(2)(b), on the other hand, was given short shrift by the Court, as a legal basis forming part of the machinery for the development of a common EU immigration

[254] Case C-431/11, *supra* note 194; Case C-656/11, *United Kingdom v. Council*, judgment of 27 February 2014 (ECLI:EU:C:2014:97); Case C-81/13, *supra* note 167. The disclaimer, in *supra* note 202, regarding Case C-81/13 applies also to Case C-431/11 and Case C-656/11.

[255] Area of Freedom, Security and Justice.

[256] Opinion 1/94, *supra* note 44, provides clear authority for the proposition that internal market provisions cannot serve as legal bases for measures to facilitate freedom of movement between the EU and third countries. See, in particular, para. 81.

[257] Case C-656/11, *supra* note 254, at para. 65 (emphasis added).

policy, and hence not equal to the far-reaching objectives of the association agreements in question.[258]

In the *EU/Turkey* case the Court of Justice noted that the Ankara Agreement was 'characterised by the desire of the contracting parties to secure by progressive stages freedom of movement for workers between them';[259] and it found Article 79(2)(b), once again, to be an unsuitable legal basis for a measure which 'constitutes a further stage in progressively securing freedom of movement for workers between the European Union and Turkey and in developing the links created by their association agreement'.[260] At the same time, the Court acknowledged that recourse to Article 48 TFEU as a sole substantive legal basis was possible only 'in the sphere of the internal policies and actions of the European Union *or of the external actions relating to third countries which can be placed on the same footing as a Member State of the European Union*'; and this was not the case with Turkey.[261] The right course was, therefore, to combine Article 217 with Article 48 as the legal basis of the disputed Decision, 'since it has been adopted in the framework of an association agreement and is aimed at the adoption of measures coordinating social security systems'.[262]

The solution of incorporating Article 217 TFEU into the legal basis of the disputed Decision ought, arguably, to have recommended itself to the Court of Justice in the *EEA* and *EU/Swiss* cases, no less than in the *EU/Turkey* case. There is an unbridgeable gap between association with, and membership of, the EU. Only through the legal magic of association can a third country qualify, to the extent defined by the agreement in question, for treatment equivalent to that of a Member State. In each of the three cases, it was the effect of Article 217 TFEU that brought the disputed Decision within the scope of Article 48, while excluding it from the scope of Article 79(2)(b).

It must, however, be remembered that the Court of Justice held in the *EU/Turkey* case that adding Article 217 to the legal basis of the disputed Decision did not entail any change to the Council's voting rule, which would remain QMV. There is an evident tension between the need, which the Court recognized as compelling, to reinforce the legal basis by incorporating Article 217, and the fact that this would have no effect whatsoever on the procedure for the adoption of the Decision. Unless and until the Court changes its mind on the relationship between paragraphs (8) and (9) of Article 218 (or the Treaty is amended), it seems that the choice of legal basis for a decision establishing the position to be taken within a DMB will be of rather less practical significance than the judgment in *CITES* would suggest.[263]

[258] Case C-431/11, *supra* note 194, at para. 63. It did not even receive a mention in the findings of the Court in Case C-656/11, *supra* note 254.

[259] Case C-81/13, *supra* note 167, at para. 43, citing Article 12 of the Ankara Agreement and Article 36 of the Additional Protocol.

[260] *Ibid.*, at paras 44–46 (emphasis added).

[261] *Ibid.*, at para. 59.

[262] *Ibid.*, at para. 63.

[263] The choice of legal basis may still be of significance in determining whether the Union's competence is exclusive or non-exclusive, or whether it is subject to an opt-in or -out in favour of one or more Member States.

6. Article 218 TFEU and Member States' Sovereign Powers

A mixed agreement is the product of the joint exercise of Union and Member State competences. The mixed character of an agreement may, therefore, call for acts to be adopted by the participating Member States[264] under their sovereign external powers at each of the various decision-making stages of the procedural code laid down by Article 218 TFEU: authorization of the opening of negotiations and the appointment of a negotiator; signature and provisional application of the agreement; conclusion of the agreement; should the occasion arise, suspension of the agreement; and the adoption of decisions on positions to be taken within DMBs. It is for the Member States to determine how they will exercise their sovereign powers for these purposes; though the chosen means must be such as 'to ensure close cooperation between the Member States and the [Union] institutions, both in the process of negotiation and conclusion and in the fulfilment of the commitments entered into', an obligation which 'flows from the requirement of unity in the external representation of the Union'.[265]

Intergovernmental acts of the Member States can be given binding force under international law, if they are adopted with that intention, as international agreements in simplified form. Such is the character of decisions of the representatives of the governments of the Member States meeting within the Council, which have been used, from the early days of the EEC, for a great variety of purposes, and with the approval of the Court of Justice.[266] They provide a convenient method of organizing the collective exercise of Member State powers on a formal basis. As international agreements, decisions of Representatives can be adopted only by common accord (distinguished from unanimity in the sense of Article 238(4) TFEU, since there is no room for abstention) and they are not susceptible to review by the Court.

In current practice, when a mixed agreement is envisaged, it is usual for the Council decision authorizing the opening of negotiations and appointing an EU negotiator to be matched by a parallel decision of Representatives relating to matters falling within Member States' competence. The precise arrangements provided for by such a decision will be determined by the wishes of the Member States. The Commission may be authorized to negotiate on their behalf; though such a solution, it has been said, is more likely to be considered acceptable in the case of bilateral agreements covering areas of exclusive or shared EU competence, than where

[264] An agreement may be concluded by the EU and only some of the Member States, usually because its subject matter relates to a particular geographical area, and is not, therefore, of interest to all of them: see MacLeod, Hendry, and Hyett, *supra* note 79, at 144–145. An example would be the Barcelona Convention on the Protection of the Mediterranean Sea against Pollution of 1976, to which the EU and Croatia, Cyprus, France, Greece, Italy, Malta, Slovenia, and Spain are parties. The non-participating Member States will, of course, be bound, pursuant to Article 216(2) TFEU, by the agreement in question, in so far as the Union is bound by it.

[265] Ruling 1/78, [1978] ECR 02151 (ECLI:EU:C:1978:202), at paras 34–36; Opinion 2/91, *supra* note 44, at para. 36; Opinion 1/94, *supra* note 44, at para. 108.

[266] Joined Cases C-181/91 and C-248/91, *supra* note 58; Case C-316/91, *Parliament v. Council*, [1994] ECR I-00625 (ECLI:EU:C:1994:76).

national competence is exclusive, or in the case of multilateral agreements.[267] Alternatively, Member States may reserve to themselves the right to participate in the negotiations directly, or authorize the Presidency to act on their behalf on the basis of an agreed position, if one can be arrived at, and in close cooperation with the Commission.[268] The possibility of setting up more complex negotiating arrangements, particularly in view of the explicit recognition in the post-Lisbon version of Article 218(3) that an EU 'negotiating team' may have its 'head' nominated by the Council, has been canvassed earlier.[269]

A decision of Representatives may be used to authorize the signature of a mixed agreement on behalf of the Member States, and also its provisional application, to the extent that this is permissible under the applicable national law.[270] Conclusion is a different matter: each Member State will have to ratify the agreement in accordance with its national constitutional requirements. This may take a very considerable time now that there are 28 Member States, and represents probably the most serious disadvantage of conducting the Union's external relations by way of mixed agreements. The practice has long been for the conclusion of a mixed agreement to be delayed until all Member State ratifications have been completed, hence the importance of the power to give provisional application to an agreement (if only to the parts of it concluded under EU competences).

Post-conclusion, there may be a call for a decision of Representatives, matching an EU decision under Article 218(9), where it is proposed to suspend a mixed agreement, or where a decision is called for on a position to be taken within a DMB set up by the agreement.[271] That will only be the case, however, if the action to be taken for either purpose affects the part of the agreement concluded under Member State competence.

A practice has been developing of adopting so-called 'hybrid' acts at the different procedural stages referred to earlier. These are decisions of the Council and of the Representatives of the governments of the Member States meeting within the Council, which purport to embody the will of the Union and of the Member States, expressed jointly through the simultaneous exercise of their respective powers. The hybrid character of the decision in question was one of the grounds of alleged illegality relied upon by the Commission in the *Protection of Neighbouring Rights* case;[272] and this ground was upheld by Advocate General Sharpston,[273] though the case was

[267] Smyth, *supra* note 65, at 305. [268] *Ibid.* [269] See Section 3(B)(2).

[270] See Article 3 of Decision 2011/708/EU, which was the subject of the proceedings in Case C-28/12, *Commission v. Council*, considered later. It is unclear to the present author why the Decision refers to the provisional application of the Agreement in question by the Member states but not to its signature.

[271] As to the latter, see the parallel decisions that were the subject of the Opinion of AG Kokott in Case C-13/07, *Commission v. Council* (ECLI:EU:C:2009:190). The Commission withdrew its application, after the dispute in the case was rendered obsolete by the entry into force of the Treaty of Lisbon, so there is no judgment of the Court.

[272] See Section 3(A), above.

[273] Case C-114/12, *supra* note 54. The relevant passage of the Advocate General's Opinion begins at para. 170.

decided by the Court of Justice on a different ground.[274] The Court has now had a further opportunity to consider the practice in the *ATA* case.[275] This concerned a hybrid decision on the signing and provisional application of a pair of agreements relating to the accession of Iceland and Norway to a mixed agreement, the Air Transport Agreement between the United States and the EU and its Member States.[276] Following the recommendation of Advocate General Mengozzi,[277] the Court concluded that the disputed Decision was incompatible with Article 218(2), (5), and (8) TFEU and therefore also with Article 13(2) TEU.[278] Two reasons are briefly given in the judgment for reaching that conclusion.

The first is that the Decision merged two different acts, without it being possible to discern which act reflected the will of the Council and which that of the Member States.[279] 'It follows', the Court says, 'that the Member States participated in the adoption of the act relating to the signing of the agreements at issue on behalf of the European Union and their provisional application by it although, under Article 218 (5) TFEU, such an act must be adopted by the Council alone'; while 'the Council was involved, as an EU institution, in the adoption of the act concerning the provisional application of those agreements by the Member States although such an act falls within the scope of, first of all, the internal law of each of those States and, then, of international law'.[280]

The present author is uncertain whether the Court was making a point of principle—that hybridity somehow offends inexorable EU legal logic—or a point about the unsatisfactory drafting of the disputed Decision. Would it have made a difference, had the text of the Decision indicated clearly that the citation of Article 100(2), in conjunction with Article 218(5) and the first subparagraph of Article 218(8), as legal bases, concerned only the exercise of EU competence, not that of the Member States; and had the text included language demarcating, if only in broad terms, the matters in respect of which EU and Member State competences were, respectively, being exercised? Such language can be found, for instance, in the Decision at issue in the *Protection of Neighbouring Rights* case, where recital (1) authorized the Commission to participate in the negotiations for the prospective Convention 'as regards matters falling within the Union's competence and in respect of which the Union has adopted rules', while recital (2) referred to Member States' participating on their own behalf 'only in so far as matters that arise in the course of the negotiations fall within their competence'. As a practical matter, it is submitted, careful drafting could have made the demarcation of the exercise of competences

274 Namely the exclusivity of EU competence.

275 Case C-28/12, *Commission v. Council*, judgment of 28 April 2015 (ECLI:EU:C:2015:282).

276 Decision 2011/708/EU, OJ 2011 L283/1. Where the context permits, 'the disputed Decision'.

277 Case C-28/12, *Commission v. Council*, Opinion of AG Mengozzi, delivered on 29 January 2015 (ECLI:EU:C:2015:43). The Advocate General's reasoning reflects that of AG Sharpston in the *Protection of Neighbouring Rights* case, *supra* note 54.

278 Case C-28/12, *supra* note 275, at para. 53.

279 *Ibid.*, at para. 49.

280 *Ibid.*, at para. 50.

within the disputed Decision every bit as clear as it would have been, if separate parallel decisions had been adopted.[281]

The second reason the judgment gives for the illegality of the disputed Decision concerns its adoption by a procedure 'which involved without distinction elements falling within the decision-making process specific to the Council and elements of an intergovernmental nature'.[282] The act concerning the provisional application of the Agreements at issue by the Member States entailed the consensus of their Representatives, and hence the latter's 'unanimous agreement'; whereas Article 218(8) TFEU provides that the Council must act on behalf of the EU by QMV. This meant that the two different acts could not validly be adopted under 'a single procedure', as they had been.[283]

The argument is not entirely convincing. The Court purports to apply, by analogy, its case law on the choice of legal basis for an EU act, and more particularly Rule (iv), discussed under Section 4(C)(3), above, according to which 'no dual legal basis is possible where the procedures required by each legal basis are incompatible with each other'. As there explained, despite constant reiteration of the Rule, usually in cases where it is not determinative of the final outcome,[284] the Court's approach to its application has been reasonably flexible. Thus in *Kadi (No. 1)*[285] and in *International Fund for Ireland*[286] the Court found no objection to the combination of a legal basis prescribing unanimity with one prescribing QMV—the very issue identified in para. 52 of the *ATA* judgment as ruling out recourse to a hybrid decision. It is submitted that the 'single procedure' under which the disputed Decision was adopted did not entail what has been described as a '*Titanium Dioxide Waste* effect',[287] such as to undermine the mechanism of Article 218(8). The Council acted on a proposal from the Commission and by consensus, which is greater than a qualified majority.[288] It is certainly true, as Advocate General Mengozzi pointed out, citing Advocate General Sharpston in the *Protection of Neighbouring Rights* case,[289] that 'a decision to which no one is opposed is *not necessarily the same* as a decision on which a qualified majority can agree, in so far as the content of a decision that can command a qualified majority might need to be watered down in order to be approved unanimously or without any opposition'.[290] However, as the italicized phrase seems to concede, there may be situations in which the existence of a qualified majority may not be sufficient to enable the Council to act. That is so in the context of the negotiation and conclusion of a mixed agreement, where it is impractical and

[281] Indeed, a drafting solution was contemplated by AG Mengozzi as possibly acceptable: see para. 90 of his Opinion, *supra* note 277.

[282] *Ibid.*, at para. 51. [283] *Ibid.*, at para. 52.

[284] Because one (or more) of the envisaged legal bases is found to be incidental or inappropriate. Case C-338/01, *supra* note 130, which was the only authority cited on this point in the *ATA* judgment, was one such case.

[285] Joined Cases C-402 and C-415/05P, *supra* note 6.

[286] See Case C-166/07, *supra* note 133. [287] See Section 4(C)(3), above.

[288] A point made by the Council and the Member States that intervened in its support: see Opinion of AG Mengozzi, *supra* note 277, at para. 33.

[289] Opinion of AG Sharpston, *supra* note 54, at para. 189.

[290] Opinion of AG Mengozzi, *supra* note 277, at para. 81 (emphasis added).

indeed illogical to expect even EU decisions to be taken otherwise than by consensus. Whether this be expressed through the medium of a single decision or parallel decisions, makes no difference.

Moreover, the present author finds it a pity that the Court should have so easily dismissed the Council's argument that the adoption of a hybrid act is a reflection of the duty of close cooperation, on which such importance is normally placed. In the light of the analysis in this section, it appears, with respect, a considerable exaggeration to describe recourse to hybridity as the Council's 'setting itself free from compliance with the procedural rules and voting arrangements laid down in Article 218 TFEU'.[291]

Be that as it may, it would probably be wise for the Council and the Member States in the future to eschew the adoption of hybrid decisions, for all their convenience, and to employ parallel decisions when acting jointly for the purposes of a mixed agreement.

7. Concluding Remarks

It is still comparatively early days in the application of the amended procedural code, which is now contained in Article 218 TFEU. However, the case law resulting from the volume of litigation that was remarked upon in the Introduction has already provided answers to a number of questions, while making it easier to identify issues that may prove troublesome in the future. The aim of this concluding section is to highlight points that seem now to be reasonably settled and to identify areas of continuing uncertainty or where, it is hoped, the Court of Justice may clarify or modify positions it has taken. Finally, an indication will be given as to where, in the present author's view, the institutional balance under the Article is currently resting.

The breadth of the notion of an agreement in EU law, and hence under Article 218, has been confirmed by Opinion 1/13 and the *Venezuelan Fishing Opportunities* case, where it was recognized that agreements may be concluded through the offer and acceptance method, without the need, or indeed the possibility, of any negotiation between the parties. The latter case, moreover, saw Advocate General Sharpston put forward the intriguing idea that the Union may have implied competence to undertake international obligations by way of a binding unilateral declaration. That appears to be reconcilable with the principle of conferred powers, by applying the logic of the line of authorities on implied competence to enter into international agreements, which descends from *AETR* and Opinion 1/76, as the learned Advocate General suggested.

There has also been confirmation (unsurprisingly) that acts adopted by the Council at each decision-making stage of the Article 218 procedural code are susceptible to review by the Court of Justice. Hence also the necessity of identifying the substantive legal basis of decisions, as the Court held in the *CITES* case with respect

[291] Case C-28/12, *supra* note 270, at para. 55.

to the establishment of positions to be taken within DMBs. However, this is not necessarily to be expected at the stage of authorizing the opening of negotiations, when the precise content of the contemplated agreement has yet to be determined; though whether the envisaged subject matter falls within an area of exclusive or non-exclusive Union competence may well be the source of disputes, as it was in the *Protection of Neighbouring Rights* case.

Following the judgment in the *Mauritius Transfer of Suspected Pirates* case, the effect of two important provisions, that help to define the prerogatives of the European Parliament under Article 218, is now clear. One of these is the second subparagraph of paragraph (6), which excludes the Parliament from the formal process of concluding agreements relating 'exclusively' to the CFSP. The provision has been interpreted as not meaning that the agreement in question must be entirely concerned with the CFSP; it suffices that, applying the 'centre of gravity test', the decision on the conclusion of the agreement needs only a CFSP legal basis, because any elements of the agreement that relate to other policy areas are secondary or incidental. The other provision is paragraph (11) of the Article requiring that the Parliament 'be immediately and fully informed at all stages of the procedure'. This has been interpreted as imposing a strict obligation, and that failure to comply with this provides grounds for the annulment of a relevant Council decision.

In applying the rules on the choice of the substantive legal bases for decisions under Article 218, recent cases have confirmed (again, unsurprisingly) that these are the same as when internal legislation is being adopted. The predilection of the Court of Justice for the centre of gravity test of Rule (ii), and its reluctance to countenance dual or multiple legal bases pursuant to Rule (iii), even in the face of strong arguments militating in favour of such a solution, is illustrated by the *Philippines PCA* case.

The principal area of continuing uncertainty is the initial stage of the procedure under Article 218, where the Treaty of Lisbon has increased the flexibility of the rules governing the designation by the Council of the Union negotiator. The extent of such flexibility remains unclear, however: in particular, whether it is open to the Council to nominate a 'head of the Union's negotiating team' other than the Commission or the High Representative; and, if so, whether a formally designated EU negotiator would still be needed, to take charge at the stage when a proposal has to be made for the signature and conclusion of the agreement. However, clarification has been provided on another issue, namely the relationship between the Council's power to lay down negotiating directives, the consultative role of the special committee, when one is designated by the Council, and Commission's role as negotiator.[292] It seems that there may still be scope for potential conflict between the Council and the Commission at this stage of the procedure.

Returning to the subject of the choice of legal bases, a further source of continuing uncertainty is the contrast between the fierce reiteration by the Court of Justice of Rule (iv), which precludes recourse to a dual legal basis 'where the procedures

[292] See Case C-425/13, *supra* note 70.

required by each legal basis are incompatible with each other', and its rather more flexible practice. It has been pointed out, earlier, that the Court appears willing to accept (as it did, e.g. in *International Fund for Ireland*) that combining a legal basis which prescribes the ordinary legislative procedure with one requiring the Council to act by unanimity will not 'denature' the former procedure; and the hope has been expressed that a similar approach will be adopted in the case of decisions under Article 218: for instance, allowing Article 114 TFEU (internal market) to be combined with Article 113 TFEU (tax harmonization). For the moment, however, this remains nothing more than a hope.

It is still more uncertain whether the Court of Justice will recognize the possibility of combining a CFSP legal basis with one or more TFEU legal bases. As argued earlier, there are strong reasons why it should do so, not least the drafting of Article 218(3) and (6), which contemplates the negotiation and conclusion of agreements containing both CFSP and TFEU elements. It would be an oddly perverse dogmatism that excluded, for reasons of procedural purity, the possibility of 'all-Union agreements' involving the joint exercise of CFSP and TFEU competences, in cases where old-fashioned EU/Member State mixity was the only alternative. Unfortunately, however, procedural purity seemed to be the choice of both the Court of Justice and Advocate General Mengozzi in the recent *ATA* case. Though this was on the different issue of hybridity, we have seen that the Court invoked Rule (iv) as one of its reasons for deciding that the disputed Decision must be annulled.

On a narrower, though constitutionally significant point, it was noted earlier that the *OIV* judgment might give the impression that Article 218(9) can be used by the Council to impose upon Member States an obligation to act on the basis of a common position, within a DMB set up by an agreement to which the EU is not a party, even in respect of matters for which the Union's competence is non-exclusive. If the judgment did mean that, it would amount to a partial restoration of Article 116 EEC, which was abolished by the TEU (Maastricht), and would therefore entail an infringement of the principle of conferral. It is hoped that the Court of Justice will find an opportunity to correct this impression.

Another matter of serious concern is the position the Court of Justice has taken on the voting rule for Council decisions under Article 218(9)—and possibly other provisions of the Article not relating to the 'conclusion' of agreements. In the *EU/Turkey* case, it will be recalled, the Court held that the addition of Article 217 to the legal basis of the disputed Decision would not cause the general rule of QMV prescribed by the first subparagraph of Article 218(8) to be displaced by unanimity, pursuant to the second subparagraph. To the present author, Member States' vital interests, in the sensitive areas of EU competence to which the second subparagraph of Article 218(8) relates, including association, appear no less deserving of the protection afforded by the unanimity rule when a decision is taken under Article 218(9), than when an agreement is concluded. This was recognized in the drafting of Article 300(2) EC, which has become Article 218(8) and (9) TFEU, and it is hardly conceivable that the Member States, when they ratified the Treaty of Lisbon, can have intended to forego such protection. It is hoped the Court will revise its position when the implications of this have been more fully considered. If not, the cure may have to be sought in a Treaty amendment.

Turning finally to the question of the institutional balance under Article 218, there can be no question that this has tipped significantly in favour of the European Parliament, thanks not only to the much wider range of circumstances in which its consent to the conclusion of an agreement is now required, but also to the reinforcement of its right to be kept informed at every stage of the procedure, as a result of the ruling in the *Mauritius Transfer of Suspected Pirates* case. The interpretation given by the Court of Justice in the same case to the reference to agreements relating 'exclusively' to the CFSP, in Article 218(2), second subparagraph does not affect that judgment: the effect of the interpretation, the Court itself noted, was simply to equate the Parliament's position in respect of international agreements with a sole CFSP legal basis to that applicable to the adoption of internal acts. As for the relationship between the Council and the Commission, it was pointed out earlier that this seems most likely to be affected at the initial stage of the procedure. It remains to be seen how the recognition by Article 17(1) TEU of the Commission's function of ensuring the external representation of the Union will balance out against the wider discretion the Council has been given by Article 218(3) in choosing a Union negotiator.

So, a great deal has been illuminated in a surprisingly short space of time; and, given the institutions' current appetite for litigation on such matters, there will evidently be opportunities for continuing uncertainties to be illuminated and—it is respectfully hoped—for some second thoughts on the part of the Court of Justice.

Index

Tuori, K 74, 100

The manufacturer's authorised representative in the EU for product safety is Oxford University Press España S.A. of El Parque Empresarial San Fernando de Henares, Avenida de Castilla, 2 - 28830 Madrid (www.oup.es/en or product.safety@oup.com). OUP España S.A. also acts as importer into Spain of products made by the manufacturer.
Printed and bound by CPI Group (UK) Ltd, Croydon, CR0 4YY
14/09/2026
02216305-0007